THE HINDU LAW OF MARRIAGE AND STRIDHANA

THE HINDU LAW OF MARRIAGE AND STRIDHANA

(Being the Tagore Law Lectures for 1878)

By

GOOROODASS BANERJEE, M.A., D.L.

GYAN

Published by

GYAN

Gyan Publishing House
5, Ansari Road
Daryaganj, New Delhi-110002
Phone: 011-47034999, 9811692060
E-mail: books@gyanbooks.com

Distribution Network
gyanbooks.com
India, USA, Canada, UK, Australia, France

ISBN : 978-81-212-6681-9 (PB)
First Published, 1879

2nd Impression 2022

Printed at: Gyan Press, Delhi.

THE HINDU LAW OF MARRIAGE AND STRIDHANA
Author: GOOROODASS BANERJEE

Tagore Law Lectures—1878.

THE HINDU LAW

OF

MARRIAGE AND STRIDHAN

BY

(GOOROODASS) BANERJEE, M.A., D.L.,

TAGORE LAW PROFESSOR.

1879.

TABLE OF CONTENTS.

LECTURE IV.

Legal Consequences of Marriage.

LECTURE V.

Dissolution of Marriage—Widowhood.

Page.

LECTURE VIII.

Rights of a Woman over her Stridhan.

LECTURE IX.

Succession to Stridhan according to the Benares School.

Page.

LECTURE X.

SUCCESSION TO STRIDHAN ACCORDING TO THE MAHARASHTRA, DRAVIDA, AND MITHILA SCHOOLS.

LECTURE XI.

SUCCESSION TO STRIDHAN ACCORDING TO THE BENGAL SCHOOL.

LECTURE XII.

SUCCESSION TO WOMAN'S PROPERTY OTHER THAN HER STRIDHAN.

TABLE OF CASES CITED.

ERRATA.

Page 29, line 10, *for* "adversity" *read* "diversity."

„ 190, line 10, *insert* "him" *after* "follow."

„ 219, line 11, *omit* the comma *after* "authorities."

THE HINDU LAW

OF

MARRIAGE AND STRIDHAN.

LECTURE I.

INTRODUCTORY REMARKS.

Remarks on Hindu law generally—What is Hindu law—Rules of civil conduct not distinguished from religious ordinances—The *Dharma Sastra* and its three divisions—Nature of the authority on which Hindu law was originally based—The nature of the *Smritis*—Constitution of Hindu courts—Growth of Hindu law—Different schools of Hindu law—Sources of the Hindu law—Original authorities—Custom—Judicial decisions—Who are governed by the Hindu law—How far Hindu law applies to persons other than Hindu—The institution of Marriage—Primitive notions regarding the relation of the sexes—Origin of the institution of marriage—Different forms of the conjugal relation—Polyandry—Polygamy—Monogamy—Marriage by capture—Marriage in Hindu law a sacrament—Different forms of marriage in Hindu society—Scantiness of case-law on the subject of marriage—*Stridhan*—Plan of the present course.

Remarks on Hindu law generally.

THE subject of the present course of lectures being the Hindu law of Marriage and *Stridhan*, a few words touching the nature of Hindu law generally may not be deemed here quite out of place.

The questions that arise for consideration under this head are :—What is Hindu law? What are the sources of that law? Who are governed by it?

What is Hindu law.

While many would deem it idle to discuss the first of the above questions, there are some among scholars and lawyers who are disposed to think that it is impossible to refrain from asking, "Has such a thing as '*Hindu law*' at any

LECTURE I.

time existed in the world? or is it that '*Hindu law*' is a mere phantom of the brain imagined by Sanskritists without law, and lawyers without Sanskrit?"[1]

The fact is, that though the Hindus have, from time immemorial, been governed by laws, their law, until the accession of the British rule, was not law in the sense in which the term is used by English jurists.

Rules of civil conduct not distinguished from religious ordinances.

In the first place, the distinction drawn by modern jurists between municipal or positive law and moral law, is not observed in Hindu jurisprudence. The whole body of rules regulating the life of a Hindu, in relation to civil conduct as well as to the performance of religious ceremonies, is included under the general name of *Dharma Sastra*, or religious ordinances; and though in some *Smritis*, as in the Institutes of Yajnavalkya, the *Dharma Sastra* is divided into three sections, relating, respectively, to *Achara*, or ritual, *Vyavahara*, or jurisprudence, and *Prayaschitta*, or expiation, no such clear division is to be found in the Code of Manu, the highest authority on the subject. Nor does the division between *Vyavahara* and *Achara* coincide with that between law and religion. Thus, the law relating to marriage—an important branch of every system of jurisprudence—is contained, not in the chapter on *Vyavahara*, but in the part treating of *Achara*. Indeed, the distinction between law and religion is so completely overlooked, that Manu, in more instances than one, provides purely religious sanctions to enforce obedience to rules relating to civil rights. Thus, when laying down the law of inheritance, he ordains that they who divide among

The *Dharma Sastra* and its three divisions.

[1] See A View of the Hindu Law as administered by the High Court of Judicature at Madras, by Nelson, p. 2.

themselves certain articles belonging to the women of the family, or neglect to maintain certain persons excluded from inheritance, fall deep into sin.[1]

It is true that, in a later work, the Dayabhaga, the distinction between moral and legal injunctions is once introduced;[2] but Jimutavahana, in another place in the very same chapter, admits as legally binding a certain rule which threatens violation with no other penalty than consignment to a region of torments in the next world.[3]

Nature of the authority on which Hindu law was originally based.

In the second place, the notion that every law is a command of the sovereign, so fully developed in the analysis of Austin, was never associated with the Hindu's idea of law. The Hindu regards his laws as commands, not of any political sovereign, but of the Supreme Ruler of the Universe[4]—commands which every political sovereign is most imperatively enjoined to obey.[5] As obedience to the law implied only obedience to the divine will, it never wounded the pride of the most absolute despot; and the thought never entered the mind of a Hindu king that he could, if he chose, alter or abrogate any of the existing laws. The highest possible ambition of every Hindu ruler was to govern according to primeval law; and the most perfect type of administrative ability, which the imagination of the Hindu poet could conceive, was the power to lead the subjects, without the least deviation, in the beaten track marked out by Manu.[6] When the government of the country passed to the hands of the Mahomedans, the new rulers, from indolence or avarice, were satisfied with imposing the Jezia, and they refrained from interfering with

[1] Ch. IX, 200—202.
[2] Ch. II, 28—30.
[3] *Ibid*, 23, 24.
[4] See Manu, I, 58.
[5] See *Ibid*, VIII, 8.
[6] Raghuvansa, I, 17.

LECTURE I. the civil laws of the Hindus. The Mahomedan government, like most other Asiatic governments, was, as Sir H. Maine observes,[1] a tax-taking and not a law-making government; and thus, notwithstanding the mighty political revolution which it effected in India, the Hindu's idea of law, and the rules which regulated his domestic life, remained unchanged.

The nature of the *Smritis.*

We must not suppose that any of the so-called codes, such as those ascribed to Manu and Yajnavalkya, though they embody many of the prevailing practices of the times, ever represented the entire body of laws actually obtaining in the Hindu community, or was meant to be enforced as the positive law of that community. The researches of modern scholars have shown that most of these codes or *Smritis*, in their present form, are metrical redactions of certain older compilations called *Sutras*, and that the older *Smritis* and the originals of the rest are not codes, but simply manuals for the instruction of the students of the *Charanas* or schools.[2] Moreover, the importance assigned to custom in the *Smritis*[3] amply proves that, besides the rules laid down in those writings, there has always been a large body of customary laws in full force among the Hindus.

Constitution of Hindu courts.

The peculiar constitution of the machinery for the administration of justice in former times, also helped to make Hindu law a law of conscience and right feeling, free from the interference of temporal power. Of the several grades of courts, the tribunal of first instance and

[1] Early History of Institutions, p. 384.

[2] West and Bühler's Digest of Hindu Law, Introd., pp. xx—xxvi.

[3] See Manu, I, 108; VIII, 3; Yajnavalkya, I, 7; Brihaspati, cited in Colebrooke's Digest, Bk. I, Ch. II, 78.

two successive courts of appeal were courts of arbitration and not constituted courts of law; so that litigation very often came to a close before coming to the king or his chief judge.[1]

Growth of Hindu law.

The influence of these peculiarities in the nature of Hindu law on the gradual development of that law, has been most remarkable. While on the one hand, the belief in its emanation from the Deity made it in theory absolutely unalterable by any temporal power, on the other hand, the very absence of temporal sanctions in the majority of cases, and the feebleness of its connection with temporal authority, rendered it practically a system most readily adaptable to the varying wants of society. Now, the changes which have taken place in the course of time, both in the internal structure and the external surroundings of Hindu society, must have continually presented motives for deviating from the rules laid down in the primeval code—motives which could be but insufficiently counteracted by the spiritual sanctions by which most of those rules were enforced. This led to innovation; and what was excused as necessary or desirable innovation in one generation, came to be revered as custom in the next; and thus have been brought about, slowly but steadily, those numerous and important changes in the Hindu law, which may be seen at a glance by comparing the prevailing practices of the Hindus with those enjoined or reprobated in the Institutes of Manu or any other ancient sage. Instances might be multiplied in which practices prohibited by Manu have become

[1] Macnaghten's Hindu Law, pp. 223, 224 (Translation of the Mitakshara); 1 Strange, pp. 321—323.

LECTURE I.

prevalent, whilst others allowable in his time have become not only obsolete, but actually repugnant to the feelings of the people.[1]

Different Schools of Hindu law.

To this mode of development of the Hindu law by the displacement of old and obsolete rules by growing usages, the interpretation of texts by commentators has served as an important auxiliary. Each commentator, under the guise of interpretation, often moulded the ancient texts according to his own views of justice or expediency. And as the authority of each commentator was received in some places, and rejected in others, there arose what have been styled the different schools of Hindu law. They are five in number, *viz.*, the Benares, Mithila, Bengal, Dravida, and Maharashtra schools.[2]

I ought in this place to notice an objection raised by some eminent scholars and lawyers[3] against the assumption of the existence of different schools of Hindu law. The term 'School' was, I believe, first used by Colebrooke with reference to the diversity of doctrine prevailing in different parts of India on points of law.[4] Some critics then took exception to the appropriateness of the term, but Colebrooke himself answered his critics,[5] and the expression 'Schools of law' has since become current in Anglo-Indian law literature. The present objection relates not to the propriety of the

[1] See, for instance, Manu, IV, 15, 80; X, 117; and the General Note to Manu in Sir W. Jones's translation.

[2] 1 Strange's Hindu Law, pp. 315—319.

[3] Burnell and Nelson. See A View of the Hindu Law, &c., by the latter, pp. 20, 21.

[4] 1 Strange, p. 315.

[5] 1 Strange, p. 319.

name, but to the reality of the thing named. Now it is not denied that different commentaries on Hindu law are followed in different parts of India, and that they differ from one another in point of doctrine in some respects; but these differences are not admitted to be numerous, and it is urged that the idea of schools of law is foreign to Hindu lawyers. Whether the diversity of doctrine in different parts of India is so considerable as to justify the use of the phraseology in question, I need not here pause to consider, as I shall have ample occasion hereafter to point out the nature and extent of such diversity, in connection with the law on the subject of *stridhan*. For the present, it will be sufficient to say that two well-known writers on Hindu law, Srikrishna Tarkalankar and Mitramisra, evidently recognize the existence of different schools of law when they speak of the doctrine of the Mithila lawyers, the doctrine of the Eastern lawyers, and that of the Southern lawyers.[1] The expression schools of law is not, therefore, altogether foreign to Hindu law; and as it represents a real distinction, it may conveniently be retained. LECTURE I.

There is one other point in connection with the schools of Hindu law which deserves notice, namely, the determination of their geographical limits. Baboo Prasanna Kumar Tagore has annexed to his translation of the Vivada Chintamani a map of ancient Mithila, but it is not easy to say that the Mithila school does not extend beyond the boundaries of ancient Mithila. Mr. Morley observes, that it would be almost impossible to define with accuracy the limits of these several schools, though he has roughly

---

[1] Dayakrama Sangraha, Ch. VII; Viramitrodoya, 2 W. & B., 101.

LECTURE I. indicated these limits to some extent.[1] The question, whether any particular locality falls within the limits of a particular school, will, in every case, have to be determined by evidence showing what authorities are mainly followed in that locality.

It will be seen from the foregoing observations that the Hindu law is a body of rules intimately mixed up with religion, and it was originally administered for the most part by private tribunals. The system was highly elastic, and had been gradually growing by the assimilation of new usages and the modification of ancient text-law under the guise of interpretation, when its spontaneous growth was suddenly arrested by the administration of the country passing to the hands of the English, and a degree of rigidity was given to it which it never before possessed.

Sources of the Hindu law.

I now come to consider the sources of the Hindu law. These, according to Manu[2] and Yajnavalkya,[3] are the *Sruti* or the *Veda,* the *Smriti* or the codes of law, and approved usage. A more practical division of the sources of the Hindu law at the present day would be that into the following three classes—the original authorities consisting of the texts and the commentaries, custom, and judicial decisions.

Original authorities.

The original authorities on Hindu law are the *Srutis,* the *Smritis,* and the commentaries. Every Hindu appeals to the *Veda* as the ultimate source of his law and religion, though it may be said, without the slightest exaggeration, that his actual practices at the present day differ from those enjoined in the *Vedas* as widely as the language he now speaks differs from the language of those sacred

[1] Morley's Digest, Introdn., pp. clxxxix—cxcii.
[2] II, 12. [3] I, 7.

writings. The fact, moreover, that legal rules are given in the *Vedas* only incidentally and occasionally,[1] must have made reference to them on questions of law extremely inconvenient. Thus the *Smritis* or the institutes of the sages, which are professed to be based on the *Vedas*, gradually became the sole exponents of the Vedic authority; and though by a rule of interpretation,[2] if the *Sruti* and the *Smriti* differ on any point, the former is to prevail, such differences were seldom, if ever, discovered; and in course of time, the institutes came to be regarded as infallible guides, rendering further reference to any higher source unnecessary. But if the veneration in which the *Vedas* are held at the present day is only theoretical, the deference shown to the *Smritis* is almost equally so. Numerous instances may be given in which practices reprobated by the sages have become common, while others allowed by them have become actually prohibited. Thus, to give one instance out of many, in the Institutes of Manu there is a clear prohibition against intermarriage with the daughter of a maternal uncle,[3] while marriage with a girl of an inferior caste is allowed;[4] and yet, at the present day, the former practice is common in Southern India,[5] while the latter is regarded as prohibited.[6] However strange it may seem that the Hindu should profess to allow a body of rules, and yet observe practices widely at variance with them, and howsoever he may be charged with inconsistency for this difference between his creed and his conduct, the fact

[1] 1 West and Bühler's Digest of Hindu Law, Introdn., p. xxxvii.

[2] See the text of Vyasa cited in Vidyasagar's Widow Marriage, 4th ed., p. 14.

[3] III, 5.

[4] III, 12, 13.

[5] 2 Strange, pp. 164, 165.

[6] General Note to Sir W. Jones's translation of Manu.

LECTURE I. of this difference should never be ignored by the Courts; and they ought never to impose upon the Hindu people any rule of law, simply because it finds a place in the Institutes of Manu or Yajnavalkya, without ascertaining whether it is living law or dead letter. This has been very clearly recognized by the highest judicial authority. The Judicial Committee observe:—"The duty, therefore, of an European Judge, who is under the obligation to administer Hindoo Law, is not so much to inquire whether a disputed doctrine is fairly deducible from the earliest authorities, as to ascertain whether it has been received by the particular School which governs the district with which he has to deal, and has there been sanctioned by usage. For, under the Hindoo system of law, clear proof of usage will outweigh the written text of the law."[1]

It is the commentaries, therefore, that form the most important branch of the original authorities on Hindu law. If these commentaries had been sufficiently precise and exhaustive on all important points of law, the administration of Hindu law by the Anglo-Indian Courts would have been far more satisfactory than it is. Whilst every one must admire the wise and just policy of the British Government in not interfering with the civil law of the Hindus, the untiring perseverance of English scholars in making the sources of that law accessible to English judges, and the scrupulous care of those judges in administering that law as correctly as possible, no intelligent observer can help being dissatisfied with the uncertainty and incorrectness which often mark this branch of Indian

[1] The Collector of Madura v. Muttu Ramlinga Satthupathy, 10 W. R. (P. C.), 21.

case-law. The difficulty lies in the nature of the subject. LECTURE I. The commentaries on Hindu law are more like speculative disquisitions on points of law than practical treatises for the guidance of judges. They treat of some questions at great and unnecessary length, while they leave others almost untouched. The judges of the native Courts, who were mostly arbitrators with considerable local knowledge, used to supply these deficiencies in the written law, either from their knowledge of local usage or from their knowledge of law derived from tradition; but such knowledge is not always within the reach of foreign judges. Perhaps the only commentary which bears the character of a practical treatise on law in the eye of an English lawyer is the Dayakrama Sangraha of Srikrishna Tarkalankar.

Custom.

Custom is another important source of law, and Hindu sages have repeatedly declared the authority and binding force of custom. I have already referred to Manu and Yajnavalkya to show that approved usage is a source of law. Manu further ordains that "immemorial custom is transcendent law, approved in the scared scripture, and in the codes of divine legislators,"[1] and he directs kings to observe "*rules drawn from local usages*"[2] in the decision of cases. So a text of the Vamana Purana, quoted by Vachaspati and Raghunandana, declares:" "A man should not neglect the approved customs of districts, the equitable rules of his family, or the particular laws of his race. In whatever country whatever usage has passed through successive generations, let not a man there disregard it; such

---

[1] I, 108. [2] VIII, 3.

LECTURE I. usage is law in that country."[1] And there is the well known saying in the Mahabharat,—"Reasoning is not reliable; the *Vedas* differ from one another; and there is no sage whose doctrine can be safely accepted;—the true rule of law is not easy to be known;—the ways of venerable persons are, therefore, the best to follow."[2] Nor is this respect for custom a mere theoretical doctrine of Hindu law. Though in Upper India and the Gangetic provinces, which have been the seat of Aryan influence from very early times, customs in derogation of the Brahmanical law are not very numerous, yet, in places outside of those provinces, as Assam and Orissa, and throughout Southern India, where the Aryan settlers seem to have migrated at a later epoch, the preponderance of the aboriginal element in the population has brought into existence numerous usages directly at variance with that law, which govern the conduct of men in the most important affairs of life. Accordingly, the Privy Council have laid down the rule that, in Hindu law, "clear proof of usage will outweigh the written text of the law;"[3] and in some of the later enactments of the Legislature, such as the Punjab Laws Act and the Madras Civil Courts' Act,[4] it is provided that in cases in which the Hindu law has been modified by custom, such custom, and not the Hindu law, shall form the rule of decision.

But then there arises the question, how to ascertain these usages. If they are to be ascertained by the judges

---

[1] Colebrooke's Digest, Bk I, Ch. III, 98, 99.

[2] Vana Parva, Ch. 312.

[3] The Collector of Madura *v.* Muttu Ramlinga Satthupathy, 10 W. R. (P. C.), 21.

[4] Act IV of 1872, s. 5; Act III of 1873, s. 16.

from the examination of private individuals, then, as the Government of Bombay in a Minute recorded in 1823 pointed out, "the looseness of tradition must lead to contrary opinions," and there would also be "the chance of corruption, faction, favor, and other sources of partiality among the witnesses."[1] To obviate this difficulty, under the direction of the Local Government, Steele prepared his admirable compilation of the Law and Custom of Hindoo Castes in the Bombay Presidency. Similar compilations for the other Presidencies are certainly a desideratum. It is true that customs which have once been judicially recognized can be ascertained from the records of the Courts; but we must not suppose that these are all the customs that ought to have binding force. The Madras High Court has, it is true, laid down a contrary doctrine, *viz.*, that "no custom how long soever continued, which has never been judicially recognized, can be permitted to prevail against distinct authority;"[2] but this ruling is opposed to the dictum of the Judicial Committee already quoted; and with all deference to the learned judges who laid it down, it is, I think, equally opposed to reason. For its effect would be to uphold those customs only which by a mere accident have received judicial recognition already; while other customs equally good and vaild in other respects, would be ignored altogether, merely because they have not been questioned hitherto, and have not, therefore, had any opportunity of receiving judicial recognition yet.

In order that a custom may have the force of law, it is necessary that it should fulfil certain conditions. It must

[1] Steele's Law and Custom of Hindoo Castes, Pref., p. iv.

[2] Narasammal v. Balaramacharlu, 1 Mad., 424.

LECTURE I. be of long standing, so as to show that it has by common consent been submitted to as the established governing rule of the particular family, class, or district of country.[1] Upon the question how old a custom in this country must be shown to be in order that it may have legal force, the following observations of Sir Charles Grey, C. J., may be usefully consulted: "Although in this country we cannot go back to that period which constitutes legal memory in England, *viz.*, the reign of Richard I, yet still there must be some limitation without which a custom ought not to be held good. In regard to Calcutta, I should say that the Act of Parliament in 1773, which established the Supreme Court, is the period to which we must go back to find the existence of a vaild custom, and that, after that date, there can be no subsequent valid custom, nor any change made in the general laws of the Hindus, unless it be by some Regulation by the Governor-General in Council, which has been registered in this Court. In regard to the mofussil, we ought to go back to 1793; prior to that there was no registry of the Regulations, and the relics of them are extremely loose and uncertain."[2] A custom must also be certain, invariable, and continuous.[3]

Judicial decisions.

I now come to the third and the most important branch of the sources of Hindu law—judicial decisions. Though the Hindu does not yield to the English lawyer in his

---

[1] Sivananaanja Perumal Sethurayar *v.* Muttu Ramalinga Sethurayar, 3 Mad., 77.

[2] Clarke's Rep., 113, 114; Shama Charan's Vyavastha Darpana, p. 314, note.

[3] Rajah Rajkishen Singh *v.* Ramjoy Surma Mozoomdar and others, 19 W. R., 12; Ramalakshmi Ammal *v.* Sivanantha Perumal Sethurayar, 14 Moo. I. A., 570.

respect for precedent, yet, owing perhaps to the fact that the decisions of Hindu courts were never recorded in writing, case-law never formed a part of the juridical system of the Hindus. But since the establishment of the Anglo-Indian Courts, judicial decisions have not only become a source of the Hindu law, but have been the chief agency by which changes have been effected in that law. Except in a few rare instances, the British Indian Legislature has, in pursuance of the policy of religious toleration, abstained from interfering with the Hindu law. Nor has any new commentator been able to modify the law by engrafting his own views on it; for, with the establishment of the British rule in India, the doctrine has been established that the power of effecting changes in the existing law is vested exclusively in the Legislature. So that, for nearly a century, the progress that Hindu law has made has been due entirely to the action of the Courts. One distinctive feature of this progress is the development of the distinction between legal and moral injunctions, and the separation of the religious element in the law from the civil.

Some of the decisions on Hindu law, though professing to be founded on the written law, have, either from an imperfect understanding of that law, or from a designed non-compliance with its purely religious injunctions, deviated completely from the original rule; and the question arises, how far they are entitled to be followed in preference to the original authorities. While, on the one hand, lawyers who set a high value on the uniformity and consistency of the law, maintain that these decisions ought to be followed; on the other hand, scholars who have critically studied the subject, and who place an equally high

LECTURE I. value on the correctness of the law, protest against the perpetuation of error. No doubt, there are arguments in favor of both sides. Where a decision at variance with the original authorities stands alone and has not been followed, there will be no inconvenience in departing from it when the error is discovered. But where a decision, though erroneous, has been followed as a precedent in a series of cases, the solution of the question involves some difficulty. For, though it is wrong to perpetuate an error, it would hardly be right to rectify the error by unsettling the law and overruling a precedent which might have long been the basis of men's expectations and conduct. Where there has been a uniform current of decisions, notwithstanding that they may be erroneous, the reasons for following them will, on the whole, be found to preponderate, unless the error appears to be so clear as to lead to a fair presumption that the rule laid down in the decisions could not have been uniformly accepted as settled law by the profession or the public. But the question is one of degree. What is meant by a uniform current of decisions, and how clear the error involved must be in order to justify departure from established precedents, are questions for the determination of which no hard and fast rule can be laid down.

Who are governed by the Hindu law.

I pass on to the consideration of the third question—Who are governed by the Hindu law?—a question of much practical importance, and not altogether free from difficulty. The readiest answer which one would be tempted to return to the question is, that the Hindus are the people who are governed by the Hindu law; and this, no doubt, is in accordance with the provision of the Charters of the several

High Courts and the different Civil Courts' Acts,[1] which declare that in cases relating to marriage, succession, and a few other matters, the Hindu law shall apply to Hindus. But the question then arises, who are the Hindus? The name 'Hindu' is not very definite in its signification. In the Anglo-India law-language of the last century, the word '*Gentoo*' (a word of curious derivation and supposed to be connected with *gentoo*, or rather *jantu*, an animal, and *gentile*, a pagan) occurs as a frequent substitute for it; and Halhed, the translator of the Digest of Hindu Law known as the Code of Gentoo Laws, tells us that that word was used as a name for those who professed the Brahmanical religion.[2] The word 'Hindu' is of foreign origin,[3] and is derived from the word 'Indus' or 'Sindhu'; and it was used by the Mahomedans to designate the people living to the east of that river. Etymologically, therefore, the word means an inhabitant of India, and applies to a Buddhist as much as to a Vaishnava. But this evidently is not its meaning in the enactments above referred to. There are indications in the law[4] from which it is clear that 'Hindu' in legal phraseology originally meant a *bonâ fide* follower of the Brahmanical religion, or, as the Privy Council in the case of *Abraham* v. *Abraham*[5] expressed it, a Hindu not by birth merely but by religion also. And considering that it is in pursuance of the policy of religious toleration that the Leg-

---

[1] Act VI of 1871, s. 24; Act IV of 1872, s. 5; Act III of 1873, s. 16.

[2] Code of Gentoo Laws, Pref., p. xxii.

[3] In the Merutantra, quoted in the Sabdakalpadruma, the word 'Hindu' is sought to be derived from two Sanskrit words *Hina* (low), and *Dosayati* (condemns); so that a Hindu would mean one who condemns the low; but this *Tantra* bears evident traces of recent fabrication, and the derivation it gives, however flattering to the national pride of the Hindus, must be given up as incorrect.

[4] See Ben. Reg. VII of 1832, s. 9.

[5] 1 W. R. (P. C.), 1.

LECTURE I. islature has abstained from enacting territorial laws applicable to all India, and has allowed particular races to be governed by their own laws, one would expect this to be the sense in which the term is used in above-mentioned Acts. But it would hardly be right at the present day to limit the application of the term to *bonâ fide* followers of the Brahmanical faith. To say nothing of those, and they are not a few, whose observance of Hinduism is mere matter of outward form and social convenience, there are classes of persons, such as the Brahmos, who do not observe even that outward form. Such persons cannot be called Hindus in the above sense of the term; and yet it would be going too far to hold that they are not Hindus within the meaning, for instance, of section 331 of Act X of 1865, and that succession to their property should be regulated by the Indian Succession Act, and not by the Hindu law. To include such persons within the category of Hindus, we must extend the meaning of the term, and take it to signify not only Hindus by religion, but also their descendants who have not openly abjured the Hindu religion.

It remains, however, to ascertain who are Hindus by religion. For our present purpose, we may divide the population of India into three sections,—*first*, the descendants of the aboriginal tribes who have more or less avoided complete conversion to the Brahmanical religion; *second*, the descendants of the early Aryan settlers and of such aboriginal races as have been completely absorbed in the Aryan community; and, *third*, modern settlers of various religious persuasions, such as Mahomedans, Christians, and Parsis. As the third class can never be confounded with the Hindus, we may leave it out of consideration. The second division, which comprises the Hindus properly so called, has never been completely homogeneous in religion, and it has thrown off various sects at different times. But as this heterogeneous body and its numerous offshoots admit more or less the authority of the *Vedas*, and conform to a few other fundamental tenets of the Brahmanical faith, the highly tolerant character of that faith admits them all as being within the pale of orthodoxy, and so they may all be regarded as Hindus. There are only three Indian sects of importance—the Buddhists, the Jainas, and the Sikhs—who have entirely repudiated Brahminism, and who ought to be excluded from the category of Hindus; and judging from the language of certain enactments[1] in which those three sects are mentioned as classes co-ordinate with the Hindus, it would follow that the Legislature intends such exclusion. But I may observe that, in the absence of evidence of any separate law or usage governing these sects, the Hindu law has been held to apply to them.[2] The first section comprises a considerable portion of the population of the Madras Presidency and Central India, and the hill tribes of various other parts of India. Their customs and their religion differ widely from those of the Hindus properly so called. They have no codes of law, but in some instances they have adopted much that is Hindu in their customs and religion, and some of these tribes, such as the Koch and others, have been described by Dalton as the hinduised aborigines of India.[3] These semi-Hindu races have been sometimes regarded as Hindus, and, therefore, subject to

---

[1] Act XVII of 1875, s. 4; Act XXI of 1870.

[2] Lalla Mohabeer Pershad *v.* Massamut Kundun Koowar, 8 W. R., 116; Lopes *v.* Lopes, 5 Bom., O. C. J., 185; Bhagvandas Tejmal *v.* Rajmal, 10 Bom., 258, 259. See also Sheo Singh Rai *v.* Dakho, I. L. R., 1 All., 688.

[3] Descriptive Ethnology of Bengal, pp. 2, 89, &c.

LECTURE I. the Hindu law. But this is an error which proceeded from our ignorance of the customs and religion of these races. As more is now known of them than before, better provision is now made for the administration of justice to them. Thus we find in the Civil Courts Acts and Local Laws Acts, that, in addition to Hindu law, custom, which is the chief source of their law, is expressly declared to be the rule of decision in certain cases.

How far Hindu law applies to persons other than Hindus.

Though the Hindu law, being only the personal law of the Hindus, can have no binding force on any one who renounces the Hindu religion, yet, he may, if he chooses, "abide by the old law, notwithstanding he has renounced the old religion." This doctrine was laid down by the Privy Council in the case of *Abraham* v. *Abraham*.[1] Lord Kingsdown, in delivering the judgment of the Judicial Committee in that case, observed:—"The profession of Christianity releases the convert from the trammels of the Hindoo law, but it does not of necessity involve any change of the rights or relations of the convert in matters with which Christianity has no concern, such as his rights and interests in, and his powers over, property. The convert, though not bound as to such matters either by the Hindoo law or by any positive law, may, by his course of conduct after his conversion, have shown by what law he intended to be governed as to these matters. He may have done so either by attaching himself to a class which, as to these matters, has adopted and acted upon some particular law, or by having himself observed some family usage or custom, and nothing can surely be more just than that the rights and interests in his property, and his powers

[1] 1 W. R. (P. C.), 1.

over it, should be governed by the law which he has adopted or the rules he has observed." LECTURE I.

It is to be observed that this liberty of renouncing or abiding by the Hindu law, extends only to matters not provided for by legislation.[1]

The institution of Marriage.

I shall now make a few general observations on the institution of Marriage. Marriage, as you all know, means union between man and woman for certain social, and sometimes religious, purposes. Considering the great variety of forms which this relation has assumed in different ages and countries, it would not be easy to give a more precise general definition of it.

Primitive notions regarding the relation of the sexes.

The next point for enquiry is, what is the origin of this institution. The strong moral sentiment with which it is associated in the minds of men in civilized society, and the firm conviction they have of its necessity for the preservation and well-being of the race, have led most people to think that marriage is a natural relation, and must have existed from the infancy of mankind; and deviations from their own ideal of this natural relation, as well as the observance of formalities which seem unnecessary to the creation of such relation, are either regarded as puzzling anomalies, or explained away as abnormal practices—the result of human caprice. Thus the polyandry of Thibet is viewed as a shocking practice, and the mock fight attending the celebration of marriage among the Khonds of Orissa[2] is regarded as a foolish and unmeaning custom. And yet we have convincing evidence that they are survivals of old practices which were once common and regarded as natural. The truth is, that to understand social

[1] Joseph Vathiar of Nazareth, 7 Mad., 121.

[2] M'Lennan's Primitive Marriage, 2nd ed., pp. 20, 21.

LECTURE I. institutions properly, you must know, not only what they are, but also what they have been. They do not stand isolated from the past, and are often unintelligible without a knowledge of the past. The chief sources of such knowledge are the study of the laws and legends of ancient societies, which always bear traces of a very remote past, and the observation of the present condition of savage people, which represents a past stage of social progress. It is true that this second source of knowledge has been sometimes characterized as "the slippery testimony concerning savages which is gathered from travellers' tales;"[1] but as such evidence has not been shown to be untrustworthy, it is acted upon by those who have devoted their best attention to it.[2] From such evidence, Sir John Lubbock has shown that marriage as we understand it, was unknown to primitive man, and that the earlier notions about it were very different from those prevailing in advanced society. "Marriage," says he, "and the relationship of a child to its father and mother, seem to us so natural and obvious, that we are apt to look on them as aboriginal and general to the human race. This, however, is very far from being the case. The lowest races have no institution of marriage; true love is almost unknown among them; and marriage, in its lowest phases, is by no means a matter of affection and companionship."[3] And in another place he observes: "Bachofen, M'Lennan, and Morgan, the most recent authors who have studied this subject, all agree that the primitive condition of man, socially, was one in which marriage did not exist, or, as we may perhaps for convenience call it,

---

[1] Maine's Village Communities, p. 17.

[2] See Spencer's Sociology, pp. 713, 714.

[3] Origin of Civilisation, 3rd ed., p. 67.

of communal marriage, where all the men and women in a small community were regarded as equally married to one another."[1] The legend of Swetketu, preserved in the Mahabharat,[2] that rich record of Indian traditions, also points to the same conclusion.

What is termed communal marriage in the above extract, is really no marriage at all, but is only another name for promiscuous intercourse.

Origin of the institution of marriage.

How the institution of marriage was evolved out of promiscuity, and why it assumed so many different forms, are questions which can hardly be discussed within the limits of the present lecture. I must content myself with barely indicating the nature of the genesis of this institution, and refer you for further information on the subject to works on Sociology.[3]

Though the sexual relation among savages is of the most loose and indefinite character, it would be erroneous to suppose that unqualified promiscuity could ever have prevailed. The savage has his crude notions of individual ownership as regards his weapons, implements, and dress, and it is not likely that he would be altogether without such notion as regards women. Thus, in the midst of prevailing promiscuity, there would be formed unions of some degree of permanence which would be maintained by force if necessary.

Again, indefinite sexual relation is less favorable to the welfare of the offspring and the parents than any definite form of that relation. For, in promiscuity the paternal relation of the child being unknown from its uncertainty,

[1] Origin of Civilisation, 3rd ed., p. 91.

[2] Adiparva, Ch. 122.

[3] See Spencer's Sociology, Part III, Chs. III—VIII.

LECTURE I. it has to depend for its subsistence solely on maternal care Thus the rearing of children is imperfectly provided for. At the same time it entails excessive labor on the women, and thereby brings on early decline. And the men, deprived of domestic assistance of every sort, must close their later years comparatively sooner.

Hence, by the law of the survival of the fittest in the struggle for existence, groups having definite sexual relations would evolve out of groups with prevailing promiscuity. I cannot describe this process of evolution better than in the words of Herbert Spencer:[1]

"Out of this lowest state, however, there tend to arise higher states. In two ways do groups thus loose in their sexual relations evolve into groups having sexual relations of more definite kinds.

"If, as we have concluded, prevailing promiscuity was from the first accompanied by unions having some duration — if, as we may infer, the progeny of such unions were more likely to be reared and more likely to be vigorous than the rest,—then the average result must have been multiplication and predominance of individuals derived from such unions. And, bearing in mind that among these there would be inherited natures leaning towards such unions more than other natures leaned, we must infer that there would, from generation to generation, be an increasing tendency to such unions along certain lines of descent. Where they favored race-maintenance, survival of the fittest would further the establishment of them. I say advisedly—where they favored race-maintenance; because it is conceivable that in very barren habitats they might not do this. Sexual relations condu-

[1] Sociology, § 295.

cive to the rearing of many children would be of no advantage: the food would not suffice. It may be, too, that in very inclement habitats more careful nurture would be useless; since where the hardships to be borne in adult life were extreme, the raising of children that could not bear them would not help to preserve the society—nay, by wasting food and effort, might prove detrimental. The ability of a child to survive with no care beyond that which its mother can give, may in some circumstances be a test of fitness for the life to be led. But save in such extreme cases, the favorable effects on offspring must tend to establish in a social group, persistent relations of the sexes.

"The struggle for existence between societies conduces to the same effect. Subject to the foregoing limitation, whatever increases the power of a tribe, either in numbers or in vigour, gives it an advantage in war; so that other things equal, societies characterized by sexual relations that are the least irregular, will be the most likely to conquer. I say other things equal, because co-operating causes interfere. Success in battle does not depend wholly on relative numbers or relative strengths. There come into play courage, endurance, swiftness, agility, skill in the use of weapons. Though otherwise inferior, a tribe may conquer by the quickness of its members in tracking enemies, by cunning in ambush, etc. Moreover, if among a number of adjacent tribes there are no great differences in degrees of promiscuity, conflicts among them cannot tend to establish higher sexual relations. Hence only an occasional effect can be produced; and we may anticipate that which the facts indicate—a slow and very irregular diminution. In some cases, too, profusion of food and favorable climate may render less important the advantage which the offspring of regular sexual relations have over those of irregular ones. And this may be the reason why in a place like Tahiti, where life is so easily maintained and children so easily reared, great sexual irregularity was found to co-exist with large population and considerable social advance.

"As, however, under ordinary conditions the rearing of more numerous and stronger offspring must have been favored by more regular sexual relations, there must, on the average, have been a tendency for the societies most characterized by promiscuity to disappear before those less characterized by it."

Thus, marriage is first a practice, then that practice grows into a custom, and finally the custom passes into law.

Different forms of the conjugal relation.

The essential difference between promiscuity and marriage is the exclusiveness of the latter relation; and different forms of marriage result from the different degrees of this exclusiveness. These last are determined by the number of parties to the relation, and the duration of it. As depending upon the number of parties to the relation, the different possible forms of marriage are as follows:—

I. The union between a certain number of males and a certain number of females, which is the form of marriage commonly prevailing amongst the Nairs of Malabar. This is but little removed from promiscuity.

II. The union between one woman and several men, related or unrelated. This form of marriage is called polyandry, and prevails in Thibet and Ceylon, where the husbands are generally related, being most commonly brothers. I need hardly tell you that the marriage of Draupadi with the Pandavas, which forms the subject of so much discussion in the Mahabharat, is an instance of this kind. LECTURE I.

III. The union between one man and several women, known as polygamy, or polygyny, which is found to exist amongst the Hindus, the Mahomedans, and several other nations.

IV. The union of one man with one woman, which is called monogamy, and which prevails in Christian countries. This is the most exclusive form of the conjugal relation.

As depending upon the duration of the union, the different forms of marriage are:—

I. Marriage for a definite term or terminable at the option of the parties, which is one of the forms that prevails, under certain restrictions, amongst the Mahomedans.

II. Marriage for the joint lives of the parties, which is the form prevailing amongst Christians.

III. Marriage for the life of the wife leading to perpetual widowhood in the event of her surviving the husband, which is the form that prevails amongst the Hindus.

IV. Marriage in which the union is life-long for the husband as well as for the wife, a form which is not found to exist any where practically, but which is regarded by Positivism as the most perfect form.

Polyandry.

In polyandry the paternity of offspring is uncertain, as polyandry is promiscuity; but this uncertainty is reduced within limits, and when, as is commonly the case, the husbands are brothers, such uncertainty does not altogether deprive the children of paternal care. For, though not sure of being the sons or daughters of any particular member of the household, they are at least his nephews or nieces. In unfavourable climates, where food is scarce, this form of marriage conduces to the preservation of the

LECTURE I. race by checking over-population and consequent starvation and misery. Fraternal polyandry has its parallel in other archaic institutions, such as that of joint property.

Polygamy. It is, however, inferior to polygamy, ethically as well as socially; for in the latter, the paternity of the offspring being known as certainly as their maternal relation, they equally share the fostering care of both parents, and repay it to both in the shape of filial tenderness in their old age; while collateral relationship being known and traceable both in the maternal and the paternal line, the family tie is extended and strengthened; so that, on the whole, the result is beneficial alike to the young, the adult, and the old.

Monogamy. In monogamy, these beneficial effects become still greater by reason of the greater strength of the marriage tie, and the amelioration of the condition of women. During the earlier or militant stage of social progress, when there is greater mortality among men, polygamy may be necessary, and may even prove beneficial as a better means of maintaining the population than monogamy. But as society settles into a peaceful condition, and the numerical inequality between males and females becomes less and less, monogamy becomes a social necessity. And hence, even in countries where polygamy is legal, its extent is practically small.

Marriage by capture. There is one peculiarity in connection with primitive marriage, which, from its almost universal prevalence and the effect it has had upon ancient law, deserves some notice in this place. I mean marriage by capture. It is singular that the most tender of all relations, the source of all that is sweet and charming in our domestic life, should have originated in force and violence. But such is the fact, and the evidence in its support is considered by competent judges to be overwhelming.[1] It existed amongst the Jews, the Spartans, and the Romans, and is found to prevail amongst numerous savage tribes.[2] In our own ancient code, marriage by capture called the Rakshasa marriage,[3] is recognized as one of the eight forms of marriage, though in consequence of the advance that Hindu society had made in Manu's time, it is regarded as an inferior form. Concerning the origin of the practice, great adversity of opinion prevails. Mr. M'Lennan thinks that it originated from female infanticide, leading to scarcity of women within the tribe, which must have compelled its members to obtain wives by capture from neighbouring tribes.[4] According to Sir John Lubbock, this view is erroneous, and the practice really owes its origin to the fact that forcible possession would be the only mode by which individual marriage,—that is the appropriation of a woman by a single man,—could arise out of communal marriage.[5] But Spencer has shown that the practice must have originated from a number of concomitant causes, such as the hostile relation of primitive neighbouring groups, resistance from female coyness, and opposition of parents against the taking away of daughters.[6] Whatever be the origin of the practice, its necessity ceases as society advances, and changes its character from the militant to the peaceful; but the sentiments of honor

[1] Lubbock's Origin of Civilisation, p. 99.
[2] M'Lennan's Primitive Marriage, Ch. IV.
[3] Manu, III, 33.
[4] M'Lennan's Primitive Marriage, 2nd ed., p. 111.
[5] Origin of Civilisation, pp. 95, 97.
[6] Sociology, pp. 649-655.

LECTURE I.

already associated with it still survive and produce a leaning in favour of its feigned observance; and thus what was at first a stern reality, becomes transformed into a harmless ceremony. This accounts for the extensive prevalence of the form of capture as a marriage ceremony in archaic law; and the practice among the Khonds already alluded to is only an instance of this.

The prohibition against marriage between members of the same stock, which is another peculiarity of primitive law, and which is still in force with us,[1] has been generally considered to be connected with the practice of marriage by capture, though, as to the precise nature of this connection, opinion is not altogether unanimous.[2]

Marriage in Hindu law a sacrament.

The importance of the institution of marriage is too well recognized to require any comment. It is the source of every domestic comfort from infancy to old age; it is necessary for the preservation and the well-being of our species; it awakens and developes the best feelings of our nature; it is the source of important legal rights and obligations; and in its higher forms, it has tended to raise the weaker half of the human race from a state of humiliating servitude. To the Hindu, the importance of marriage is heightened by the sanctions of religion. "By no people," says Sir T. Strange, "is greater importance attached to marriage than by the Hindoos."[3] In Hindu law it is regarded as one of the ten *sanskars*, or sacraments[4] necessary for regeneration of men of the twice-born classes,

---

[1] Manu, III, 5.
[2] M'Lennan's Primitive Marriage, pp. 84—93.
[3] Elements of Hindu Law, Vol. I, p. 35.
[4] Coleb. Dig., Bk. V, 134, note.

and the only sacrament for women[1] and *Sudras.*[2] It being a settled doctrine of the Hindu religion that one must have a son to save him from a place of torment called *put,*[3] marriage, as the primary means to that end, becomes a religious necessity. This necessity, as regards the Brahman, is further pointed out in another way. "A Brahman," says the *Veda,* "immediately on being born, is produced a debtor in three obligations: to the holy saints, for the practice of religious duties; to the gods, for the performance of sacrifice; to his forefathers, for offspring."[4] Accordingly, Manu ordains that, "after he has read the *Vedas* in the form prescribed by law, has legally begotten a son, and has performed sacrifices to the best of his power, he has paid his three debts, and may then apply his heart to eternal bliss; but if a Brahman have not read the *Veda,* if he have not begotten a son, and if he have not performed sacrifices, yet shall aim at final beatitude, he shall sink to a place of degradation."[5]

The earlier rules of Hindu law, having reference to Hindu society in that stage of its progress when the Aryans had recently settled in a healthy and fertile country, and when rapid multiplication of the race was an important object, no doubt, regard marriage chiefly as a source of progeny. But you must not imagine that the higher or spiritual aspect of marriage has been altogether overlooked. The Vaidik texts that are recited on the completion of the seventh step by the bride,[6] clearly show that the Hindus, even in those early days, had learned to regard marriage as a true companionship of the purest character, a union

[1] Manu, II, 67. [2] Coleb. Dig., Bk. V, 122. [3] Manu, IX, 138.
[4] Cited in the Dattaka Mimansa, Sec. I, 5. [5] VI, 36, 37.
[6] See Asiatic Researches, Vol. VII, pp. 303—305; and Lecture III, *infra.*

LECTURE I. of pure hearts, for the cultivation of the best feelings of our nature.

Different forms of marriage in Hindu society.

India has sometimes been regarded as an epitome of the world in respect to the variety of its climate, flora, and fauna, and I may add that it may equally well be regarded as such in respect to variety in its forms of marriage. In the Hindu law, strictly and properly so called, there are no less than eight different forms of marriage, differing from one another in no slight degree, being in fact typical of different stages of social progress; and in consequence of the varying rates at which society has advanced in different parts of India, the customary and statutory forms of marriage prevailing amongst the Hindus and the semi-Hindu races, mostly of non-Aryan origin, are of the most varied description.[1] So that Indian life presents almost every possible form of the conjugal relation, from the grossest polyandry verging on promiscuity, to the purest and the most rational form of monogamy.[2]

It is this last circumstance that attaches peculiar value to the Hindu law of marriage. While, like every other branch of living law, it has an interest for the practical lawyer, and like every other branch of archaic jurisprudence, an interest for the jurist, it is a rare collection of varied materials for the student of sociology.

Scantiness of case-law on the subject of marriage.

From the above remarks you may infer that the Hindu law of marriage is a complicated subject, and so to some extent it really is; but it is free from one source of complication which often perplexes the student of law. It has not to be disentangled out of a mass of unconnected

---

[1] See Nelson's View of the Hindu Law, &c., pp. 144, 145.

[2] See Act III of 1872.

precedents. "It is remarkable," observes Morley, "that there have been no cases relating to the Hindu law of husband and wife reported in the Presidencies of Bengal and Madras: the reader will perceive that, with one exception (a case in the Supreme Court at Calcutta), all the *placita* refer to cases decided in the Adawlut Courts of Bombay."[1] Though, since the above was written, there has been some addition to the case-law on the subject, yet that addition is but small. The Bombay cases alluded to are cases relating to certain customary forms of marriage. LECTURE I.

One cause of this scantiness of case-law is, I believe, the sacramental character of marriage in Hindu law. Owing to this, the Hindus are so careful to observe the rules concerning marriage, and to avoid error, unless it be on the safe side, and so strong is their disinclination to question the validity of marriage in any case, that disputes concerning this topic seldom arise for judicial determination.

Stridhan. It remains now only to say a few words by way of introduction to the law of *Stridhan*. The word *stridhan* is derived from *stri*, woman, and *dhan*, property, and means literally woman's property. While declaring the perpetual tutelage of women,[2] and their general incapacity to hold property,[3] the Hindu law concedes to them the privilege of holding property of certain descriptions with absolute power of disposal. It appears also to have regarded their interests in prescribing the order of succession to woman's property, as may be seen from the very prominent position therein assigned to the daughter, who in many cases inherits her mother's property to the exclu-

[1] 1 Dig., p. 287 note. [2] Manu, IX, 3. [3] Manu, VIII, 416.

LECTURE I. sion of male issue. The law of *stridhan* stands, therefore, in favorable contrast with the general spirit of the Hindu law, which in other respects is, no doubt, not very equitable towards women; and when it is remembered that in no ancient or mediæval system of law, except the Mahomedan and the later Roman, have so large concessions been made in favor of the proprietary rights of women, the Hindus may find some reason for just complacency in this chapter of their law.

Concerning the nature of *stridhan* and the order of succession to it, great diversity of doctrine prevails in the different schools. In tracing this diversity to its source, you will be furnished with ample illustration of the manner in which the interpretation of texts by commentators has served as an agency for the gradual development of the Hindu law.

Plan of the present course.

I shall conclude this Lecture with a rough outline of the plan I intend to follow.

As the law of *stridhan* depends in some of its provisions on the law of marriage, the consideration of marriage will precede that of *stridhan*.

The Hindu law of marriage divides itself into two branches, one being the Hindu law of marriage strictly and properly so called,—that is the law as found in the institutes and commentaries; and the other, the law relating to certain forms of marriage which are legalized by custom or by statute law, and which prevail among the Hindus in the widest sense of the term, as including Hindus strictly so called, as well as those who are popularly known by that name. I shall treat of each of these branches separately, and begin with the former, which will be discussed under the following four heads, to which the points for consideration on the subject may be reduced, *viz.*:— LECTURE I.

I.—Parties to marriage.

II.—Modes of contracting marriage.

III.—Incidents of marriage, that is, rights and duties arising out of it.

IV.—Dissolution of marriage.

Having finished the law of marriage, I shall take up the law of *stridhan*. In this subject the questions for consideration are three—

First—What constitutes *stridhan*?

Second—What are the rights of a woman over her *stridhan*?

Third—What is the order of succession to *stridhan*?

These questions will be considered in the order indicated above.

LECTURE II.

PARTIES TO MARRIAGE.

Questions for consideration—Who are incompetent to marry—Minors—Idiots and lunatics—The deaf and dumb, and persons incurably diseased—Impotent persons—One having a wife living—Polygamy—One whose elder brother is unmarried—Who are unfit to be taken in marriage—Females how far viewed as parties to marriage—Minors—Marriageable age for a female—Guardianship in marriage—Betrothed girl—One whose husband is living—Widows—Girls with visible or other minor defects—One whose elder sister is unmarried—Woman of the same *gotra*—Girls related within the prohibited degrees—Prohibited degrees in different systems compared—Daughter of one's spiritual guide or pupil—Girl bearing one's mother's name—Girl older in age—Girl belonging to a different caste—Daughters of illegitimate persons—Effect of disqualification on marriage already completed.

Questions for consideration.

I shall begin with the law relating to parties to marriage. The rule is, that *primâ facie* all persons are to be deemed qualified for every purpose, unless it is shown that the law has disqualified any of them for any purpose. We have, therefore, to enquire what persons are, by the Hindu law, disqualified from becoming parties to marriage. This disqualification is either absolute or relative, according as it renders a party altogether incompetent to marry, or only incompetent to marry a particular person. Thus a woman whose husband is living is, as you will see, absolutely incompetent to marry, while a woman who is related to a man within certain prohibited degrees is disqualified only as regards marriage with that particular man, and may marry any other man to whom she is not so related. If, in accordance with the view that is taken of marriage in the Hindu law, we regard man as the active party, or the party who *marries*, and woman as merely the passive party, or the party who *is taken in marriage*, the two questions,—Who are incompetent to marry? and Who are unfit to be taken in marriage?—will embrace the whole scope of the enquiry into absolute and relative disqualifications; for the answer to the former will include all absolute disqualifications in the male, while the answer to the latter will include all absolute disqualifications in the female, as well as all relative disqualifications in both.

Who are incompetent to marry.

I shall consider first the question, Who are incompetent to marry? Here you will bear in mind that marriage is regarded in Hindu law not only as a civil contract, but also as a sacrament, being one of the ten regenerating ceremonies[1] necessary for men of the twice-born classes, and the only one necessary for Sudras;[2] and that in consequence of this religious necessity, the grounds of disqualification for marriage are fewer in the Hindu law than in any other polished system of law. I shall notice the cases of persons who are generally considered incompetent to marry, and point out their position in the Hindu law.

Minors.

Persons below a certain age are in most other systems of law considered incompetent to marry; but that age is not the same in all, nor is it the same as the age of majority for other purposes. Thus in the Roman law, males below the age of fourteen years are declared incompetent to marry,[3] but the age of majority for other purposes is twenty-five years.[4] By the Code Napoleon, a man under eighteen cannot marry without a dispensation from Gov-

---

[1] They are *Garbhadhana*, *Jatakarma*, *Namkarana*, *Niskramana*, *Annaprasana*, *Chudakarana*, *Upanayana*, *Savitri*, *Samavartana*, and Marriage. *See* Coleb. Dig., Bk. V, 134 note.

[2] *Ibid*, V, 122.

[3] Inst. of Justinian, Lib. I, Tit. X and XXII.

[4] Inst., Lib. I, Tit. XXIII.

LECTURE II. ernment,[1] while the ordinary age of majority is twenty-one.[2] Under the English law, while the ordinary age of majority is twenty-one, the age of consent to matrimony is fourteen in males and twelve in females; but if a boy under fourteen actually go through the form of marriage, such marriage is not absolutely void, but voidable only.[3] But in the Hindu law, want of age, though a disqualification for other purposes,[4] does not render a person incompetent to marry, and there is no age fixed as the age of consent to marriage. Though our ancient sages fully perceived that the cares of matrimony are incompatible with the life of a professed student; and accordingly a twice-born man is directed by Manu not to marry until the completion of his period of studentship;[5] yet that period is indefinite, as it commences with *Upanayan*, or investiture with the sacred thread, and may, as the same sage ordains, last for thirty-six years or for half that time, or for a quarter of it, or until he perfectly understands the *Vedas*.[6] At the present day this period of studentship is, as you are aware, entirely nominal, being reduced to a few hours or at the most, days; and the ceremony of *Samavartan*, or return from the house of the preceptor, is performed sometimes on the very day of the *Upanyan*, and sometimes only a few days later. But as investiture with the sacred thread, which takes place for the Brahman, Kshatriya, and Vaisya, ordinarily at the ages of eight, eleven, and twelve years,[7] must precede marriage, practically, the limits of the marriageable age for

[1] Arts. 144, 145.
[2] Art. 488.
[3] Stephen's Commentaries, Bk. III, Ch. II.
[4] Coleb. Dig., Bk. II, Ch. IV, 15, 57, 58; Manu, VIII, 163.
[5] Manu, III, 4.
[6] Manu, III, 1; see also IX, 94.
[7] Manu, II, 36.

these classes are eight, eleven, and twelve years respectively; and for the Sudra, there is no limit at all. LECTURE II.

But though a boy may marry at an early age, when his own consent is hardly worth anything, the consent of his father or other guardian is necessary so long as he is a minor.[1] The texts of Hindu law speak of guardianship in marriage only with reference to female minors,[2] but in a case given in Macnaghten's Precedents of Hindu Law,[3] one of these texts was held applicable to the case of a male; and that text, which is evidently the text of Yajnavalkya (I, 63), cited in Colebrooke's Digest (Bk. V, 135), provides that the father, the paternal grandfather, the brother, a *sakulya* or kinsman on the paternal side, and the mother, are the guardians in succession. The want of a guardian's consent would not, however, invalidate a marriage otherwise legally contracted.[4]

The marriage of a Hindu minor is not only allowable, but has been held to be a legitimate cause of expense in regard to which his guardian has power to bind him.[5]

Marriage being one of the matters not affected by the provisions of the Indian Majority Act (IX of 1875), for the purposes of marriage, a Hindu attains majority on completing his fifteenth year.[6]

Aiding and abetting the marriage of a minor under the Court of Wards in the Madras Presidency, without the

---

[1] Nundlal Bhugwandas *v.* Tapeedas and another, cited in 1 Morl., 287; Steele's Law and Custom of Hindoo Castes, p. 26.

[2] Coleb. Dig., Bk. V, 135; Narada, XII, 20—22

[3] Ch. VII, Case II.

[4] Modhoosoodun Mookerjee *v.* Jadub Chunder Banerjee, 3 W. R., 194; Baee Rulyat and others *v.* Jeychund Kewul, 3 Morl., 181; Steele, 30.

[5] Juggessur Sircar *v.* Nilambur Biswas, 3 W. R., 217.

[6] Coleb. Dig., Bk. I, Ch. V, 188; Bk. II, Ch. IV, 15.

LECTURE II. leave of the Collector, is made punishable under section 9 of Act XXI of 1855.

Idiots and lunatics.

Persons of unsound mind,—that is, idiots and lunatics,—though disqualified for civil purposes generally,[1] have not been declared incompetent to marry. On the contrary, there are indications in the law from which it would appear that they are considered to be competent to marry. Thus Manu, after declaring the exclusion of these and other disqualified persons from inheritance, ordains:[2]

"If the eunuch and the rest should at any time desire to marry, *and if the wife of the eunuch should raise up a son to him by a man legally appointed, that son and* the issue of such as have children, shall be capable of inheriting." And Jimuta Vahana, in his chapter on exclusion from inheritance, makes the following comments on the above passage:—"It must not be objected, how can they contract marriages, since the eunuch not being male, is incapable of procreation, and the dumb man and the rest [or those born deaf or blind], are degraded for want of initiation and investiture, because they are unapt for [the preparatory] study? The eunuch may obtain issue from his wife by means of another man; and a person unfit for investiture with the sacerdotal string is not degraded from his tribe for want of that initiation, any more than a Sudra."[3] And the leading authorities of all the other schools, the Mitakshara,[4] the Vivada Chintamani,[5] the Vyavahara Mayukha,[6] and the Smriti Chandrika,[7] agree with the Dayabhaga in

[1] Coleb. Dig., Bk. II, Ch. V, 57, 58.

[2] IX, 203.

[3] Ch. V, 18.

[4] Ch. II, Sec. X, 9—11.

[5] Prossonno Coomar Tagore's translation, p. 244.

[6] Ch. IV, Sec. XI, 11.

[7] Ch. V, 32.

treating the issue of such persons as legitimate and as competent to inherit. It was accordingly held in an early case,[1] that the marriage of a lunatic was valid, and the same view of the law is quoted as correct in West and Bühler's Digest of Hindu Law (p. 288). LECTURE II.

But, on the other hand, it should be noticed that the idiot and the lunatic being, where the loss of reason is complete, incompetent to accept the gift of the bride, which is a necessary part of the ceremony of marriage,[2] it is not easy to understand how their marriage in such cases can be regarded as marriage at all. And I may add here that Hindu law permits the wife to neglect a mad husband.[3]

It needs hardly to be pointed out that such marriages are exceedingly improper. The answer of the Pandits in the case above mentioned declares the marriage of a lunatic immoral. To say nothing of the objections based upon reason, the authorities on the Hindu law itself clearly discountenance such marriages. Thus Manu declares[4]—"But it is better that the damsel, though marriageable, should stay at home till her death than that he (the father) should ever give her in marriage to a bridegroom void of excellent qualities." Marriages of idiots and other naturally disqualified persons must obviously be of rare occurrence, and the rule which declares them valid and legal can be justified only on the ground that the opposite rule would be hard against the unfortunate offspring, and would deprive the unhappy wife of her legitimate conjugal status without giving her any compensating advantage.

---

[1] Dabychurn Mitter and others *v.* Radachurn Mitter, 2 Morl., 99.

[2] See Lecture III. [3] See Manu, IX, 79. [4] IX, 89.

F

LECTURE II.

The deaf and dumb, and persons incurably diseased.

The cases of persons who are deaf and dumb, or are affected with loathsome and incurable maladies, are analogous to those of idiots and lunatics, in this respect that their incapacity to participate in the necessary rites[1] does not render their marriage void.[2] But I may add that such persons have been held[3] not to be entitled to enforce restitution of conjugal rights.

Impotent persons.

Impotency, which is generally considered as a disqualification for marriage, is not viewed in that light in the Hindu law, as will appear from the passages of Manu and the Dayabhaga already quoted. This is because impotency did dot formerly render marriage absolutely fruitless, as the impotent could appoint kinsmen to beget issue on their wives. This vicarious mode of fulfilling one of the primary objects of matrimony, being, however, interdicted[4] in the *Kali* or present age, it is doubtful whether impotency ought not now to be regarded as a disqualifying cause, especially as Parasara, the sage whose institutes are held to be peculiarly authoritative in the present age,[5] in his celebrated text[6] in favor of the remarriage of widows, allows a woman to take a second husband if the first is impotent. Among the inferior classes, impotence is a ground of disqualification for marriage.[7] Among the higher classes, happily, the point has never been raised; but some authorities hold that impotence in their case would not nullify marriage.[8]

One having a wife living—Polygamy.

The marriage of a person having a wife living is prohibited in Christian countries; but Hindu law permits poly-

---

[1] Manu, XI, 36. [2] Steele, p. 30.

[3] Bai Premkuvar *v.* Bhika Kallianji, 5 Bom., A. C. J., 209.

[4] See General Note to Manu.

[5] Parasara quoted in Vidyasagar's Marriage of Hindu Widows, p. 4.

[6] Quoted in the same, p. 7.

[7] Steele, p. 167. [8] *Ibid.*

gamy, though it does not approve the practice. It is true that polygamy is expressly allowed only under certain circumstances;[1] but considering the nature of some of these circumstances, and considering that a wife who speaks unkindly is allowed to be superseded without delay, it would follow that polygamy is not illegal in any case. Macnaghten,[2] Strange,[3] and Shamacharan[4] consider polygamy prohibited except for allowable reasons; and Pandit Iswarchandra Vidyasagar has cited the following passage of Manu,[5]—

"For the first marriage of the twice-born classes, a woman of the same class is recommended; but for such as are impelled by inclination to marry again, women in the direct order of the classes are to be preferred:

"A Sudra woman only must be the wife of a Sudra; she and a Vaisya, of a Vaisya; they two and a Cshatriya, of a Cshatriya: those three and a Brahmani, of a Brahman,"— as authority for the position that one cannot have more than one wife of equal caste with him at the same time, except for certain allowable reasons; in other words, that polygamy such as now prevails is prohibited by the *sastras*. But his interpretation of the above text has called forth much hostile criticism and an elaborate rejoinder. It is not my object here to take part in this learned controversy as to what is the correct exposition of the above passage; but I cannot help observing that the text quoted above refers not to the number of wives that a man can have, but to the castes in which he can marry;[6] and I think I can safely affirm that the prohibition against polygamy, such as is inferred from this and other texts, is merely directory and not imperative.[7]

---

[1] Manu, IX, 77, 80, 81.
[2] Principles of Hindu Law, 58.
[3] Hindu Law, Vol. I, 52.
[4] Vyavastha Darpana, 672.
[5] III, 12 and 13.
[6] See Dyabhaga, Ch. IX, 2—6.
[7] See Verasvami Chetti *v.* Appasvami Chetti, 1 Mad., 375.

LECTURE II. The practice has always prevailed among the Hindus, and it reached its climax in Bengal as an incident of *kulinism.* This last-named institution has exercised its pernicious influence upon marriage for several centuries, but happily it is now fast becoming obsolete, and will soon become purely matter of history.[1]

It was established by Ballal Sen with a view to honor the deserving amongst the Brahmans in his kingdom; but there is one radical error in the system which has rendered it an unmixed evil. The distinction is made hereditary, so that though possessing no other merit, the descendant of a *kulin* would rank as such, provided that no female in his family has been married to any but a *kulin:* while persons of the inferior class called *vansaja,* though they can never become *kulins,* are considered highly honored if they can marry their daughters to *kulins.* Hence, sometimes from fear of degradation, and sometimes from a desire to elevate their position, people were led to select *kulin* husbands for their daughters. Thus, while the *kulins* generally obtained a plurality of wives, the *vansajas* necessarily found it difficult to obtain wives, and were driven to the reprehensible practice of buying girls for marriage.

One whose elder brother is unmarried.

One whose elder brother is unmarried is considered in Hindu law incompetent to marry;[2] but the elder brother must be one by the same mother.[3] He who violates this rule is called a *parivettri,* and his offence is styled *parivedana.* This offence, however, is not committed where the elder brother is living in a foreign country, or is impotent, or degraded, or under any such bodily or mental infirmity as

---

[1] For an account of *Kulinism,* see Vidyasagar's first Tract on Polygamy, pp. 15—28.

[2] Manu, III, 171, 172.

[3] Dattaka Mimansa, Sec. VI, 54.

would render his marriage improper.[1] The above rule owes its origin to the influence of the joint family system. It is really no impediment to marriage, but rather operates as an inducement to it. For the marriage of every man thus becomes not only a necessity by itself, but a condition necessary for the marriage of his younger brothers. The rule, it appears, was never treated as anything more than a moral injunction; and now with the disintegration of the joint family, and the consequent change of ideas and feelings, its force is becoming less and less.

Who are unfit to be taken in marriage.

I now come to the second question, Who are unfit to be taken in marriage? Marriage is more imperatively necessary for a female than for a male. It is the only sacrament for women.[2] Manu declares,—"Reprehensible is the father who gives not his daughter in marriage at the proper time;"[3] and other sages also declare the same thing.[4] As a consequence of this necessity for marriage, hardly any maiden is deemed absolutely disqualified for matrimony; and the nuptials of daughters form a charge on their father's property,[5] and a legal necessity for alienation by the widow.[6]

Females how far viewed as parties to marriage.

I have said above that a woman is not regarded in Hindu law as an active party in marriage. In fact, she is hardly regarded as a party at all. Marriage is viewed as a gift of the bride by her father or other guardian to the bridegroom: the bride, therefore, is regarded more as the subject of the gift than as a party to the transaction. Sometimes, as in

---

[1] See the text of the Chhandoga Parisistha cited in the Udvahatattwa, Raghunandan's Institutes, Serampore Ed., Vol. II, p. 66.

[2] Manu, II, 67.

[3] Manu, IX, 4.

[4] Coleb. Dig., Bk. IV, 15—17; Udvahatattwa, Raghunandan's Institutes, Vol. II, pp. 68, 69.

[5] Mitakshara, Ch. I, Sec. VII, 5; Dayabhaga, Ch. III, Sec. II, 34—39.

[6] Dayabhaga, Ch. XI, Sec. I, 66; Preaj Narain v. Ajodhyapurshad, 7 Sel. Rep., 513.

LECTURE II. *swayamvara*, or the selection of a husband by the damsel herself, which was a privilege accorded by kings to their favorite daughters, or in the case where the guardian neglects to dispose of a girl in marriage, a female may become a party to the matrimonial contract.[1] But these are exceptional cases.

The early age at which a girl is enjoined to be married, makes her unfit to act as a party to the nuptial contract, and throws upon her guardian the sole responsibility of negotiating a proper match for her.

Minors.

Minors are not only eligible for marriage, but are the fittest to be taken in marriage.

Marriageable age for a female.

Regarding the marriageable age of a female, the higher limit is definitely fixed. Manu, Brishaspati, Vasistha, Paithinasi, Kasyapa, and Vyasa all strictly enjoin that a girl must be given in marriage before puberty.[2] As for the text of Manu, which says that 'it is better that the damsel though marriageable should stay at home till her death, than that he (the father) should ever give her in marriage to a bridegroom void of excellent qualities,'[3] Raghunandana explains it as being a prohibition against a bad match.[4] Practically, fear of the conventional shame that attaches to a family in which a girl attains puberty before marriage, makes every father anxious to dispose of his daughter in marriage as early as possible. The lower limit of age is not exactly defined. Ordinarily, the lowest age for marriage is eight years, but Manu allows a girl to be married even before the proper age, if a proper union is secured.[5]

---

[1] Yajnavalkya, I, 64; Coleb. Dig., Bk. IV, 18.

[2] Coleb. Dig., Bk. IV, Ch. I, 14—17; Udvahatattwa, Raghunandan's Institutes, Vol. II, pp. 68, 69.

[3] IX, 89.

[4] Udvahatattwa, Inst., Vol. II, p. 69.

[5] Manu, IX, 88, and note by Kulluka.

I ought here to add that the marriage of a woman after she has attained puberty, though declared sinful, is not absolutely void, though some degree of blame is always attached to it. LECTURE II.

Guardianship in marriage.

The necessity for early marriage and the future irrevocability of the union make guardianship in marriage a matter of immense practical importance, and it forms a topic of discussion in the writings of the sages and the commentators. The order in which the right to guardianship in marriage vests in the different relations of a girl, is given somewhat differently by different sages. Yajnavalkya, whose text is adopted in the Mitakshara, and is followed in all the schools except the Gauriya, declares,—"The father, paternal grandfather, brother, kinsman (*sakulya*), and mother, being of sound mind, are the persons to give away a damsel—the latter respectively on failure of the preceding."[1]

Raghunandana, the leading authority of the Bengal school on the subject of marriage, has, by a comparison of the above text of Yajnavalkya with the texts of two other sages, Vishnu and Narada, deduced the order of guardianship, which is the law in Bengal, and which may be stated thus:

The father, paternal grandfather, brother, *sakulya*, maternal grandfather, maternal uncle, and mother, if of sound mind, are entitled in succession to give a girl in marriage.[2]

These two rules call for some remarks. In the first place, you may ask why it is that while all the schools equally acknowledge the authority of the sages, Bengal should follow one rule, and the other schools another, and how the

[1] Yajnavalkya, I, 63: see also 2 Strange, 28.

[2] Udvahatattwa, Institutes, Vol. II, p. 70.

LECTURE II. second rule is deduced. As this is the first instance in which these questions arise, I shall pause for a moment to answer them. The Mitakshara, though referring to other sages now and then for the purpose of illustration, is in the main a running commentary on Yajnavalkya, and accordingly in the present instance adopts the text of that sage as it finds it. Raghunandana, on the other hand, was a compiler of Hindu law, and as such, he was not bound to follow exclusively the text of Yajnavalkya, especially when he found that it assigned no place to the maternal relations who, for reasons not necessary to be here dwelt upon, had already acquired importance in the school to which he belonged.[1] Accordingly he compares the text of Yajnavalkya with those of two other sages, Vishnu and Narada, which run thus :[2]—

"A father, paternal grandfather, brother, *sakulya*, maternal grandfather, and mother are the givers of a damsel in marriage; in default of the first, the next in order, if in the natural state of mind, is entitled to perform the ceremony of gift."—Vishnu.

"The father himself will give the daughter (in marriage), or her brother by the father's consent, the maternal grandfather, the maternal uncle, the *sakulya*, and relations in the maternal line, the mother in default of all (these), provided she be of sound understanding, otherwise the kinsmen of her father will give the daughter in marriage."—Narada.

And he adopts as the basis of his rule, the text of Vishnu, with this qualification only, that the maternal uncle is to have a place before the mother, as laid down in Narada's text. So much for the treatment of texts by commentators.

---

[1] Compare the position of these relations in the order of succession in the Dayabhaga (Ch. XI, Sec. VI) with that in the Mitakshara (Ch. II, Sec. VI.)

[2] Udvahatattwa, Institutes, Vol. II, p. 70; and Shama Charan's Vyavastha Darpana, p. 651.

In the second place, you will observe that the order of guardianship in each of the foregoing rules differs from the order of guardianship for other purposes, and assigns a very inferior position to the mother, though, next to the father, she is the natural guardian of a girl in ordinary cases.[1] One reason for this seems to be the fact that in marriage, the guardian, or, as he is styled, the giver of the bride, has to perform certain religious ceremonies which the mother, being a female, is the least competent to perform. Perhaps a second reason for this is the fact that as marriage affects the social position of a family, the male relations of a girl are considered better qualified than her mother to provide a suitable match for her;[2] and the dependence of women is a third reason for the same. Accordingly, in *Ex parte Jankiprasad Agarwala*,[3] the Supreme Court of Calcutta held that the brother was the person entitled to give a girl in marriage in preference to the mother. But in a recent case[4] the above text of Yajnavalkya has received a construction which, to some extent, reconciles it with the natural rights of the mother. In that case, the plaintiff, a divided brother of the defendant's deceased husband, claimed an exclusive right to give in betrothal the infant daughter of his deceased brother, and to have a sum of money paid to him by the defendant for the expenses of the marriage. The High Court of Madras, in deciding against the plaintiff, appellant, observed:—

LECTURE II.

"Upon reason and principle, therefore, and the applica-

[1] Coleb. Dig., Bk. V, 453, commentary.

[2] There is a common saying that "the bride cares for the beauty, her mother for the wealth, and her father, for the learning, of the bridegroom; her kinsmen care for his high lineage; and neighbours care only for the marriage feast." See Mallinath's note to Kumara Sambhava, V, 72.

[3] Boulnois' Rep. (Part II), 114; Vyavastha Darpana, 655.

[4] S. Namasevayam Pillay *v.* Annammai Ummal, 4 Mad, 339.

LECTURE II. tion of the existing law in regard to the independent position of the defendant, both as guardian and proprietor of the estate derived from her husband, we come to the conclusion that the law does not warrant a declaration of the absolute right set up by the plaintiff. We are of opinion that the duty was enjoined on the husband's kinsmen in order to ensure the making of a suitable provision for the betrothal of daughters before reaching the age of puberty, just as it is declared to be their duty in the case of sons, to provide for the several ceremonies required to perfect the regeneration of a twice-born man. It appears to be so treated by *Jagannatha* in the *Digest*, Sections 303 and 113, and that they were left to perform it like all other 'auspicious' family ceremonies in harmony, if possible, with the mother and other members of the family. If on a choice being made of a person in every way suitable to be affianced, a mother, without sufficient cause, improperly refused to accept him, and obstructed the betrothal, a suit to compel her to allow the ceremony to take place, and if she was chargeable, to provide means for its celebration, would probably be successful. But no Court, we think, would be justified in granting such relief if the mother's refusal and resistance were because of serious objections to the person chosen, or for other good and sufficient cause, nor, we think, would the betrothal of a daughter with an unobjectionable person of the mother's selection be restrained at the suit of the brother, or other kinsman, of the father, who had been consulted by the mother and had without any sufficient cause objected to the betrothal. It would seem from the express provision made by the law for the choice of a husband by the girl herself in case of neglect on the part of her relatives of their duty to betroth her for three years from the time she became marriageable (*Manu*, Ch. IX, Sl. 90, 91; 1 *Strange's Hindu Law*, 36), that the duty does not amount to an enforceable legal obligation, and the effect of restraining the betrothal in such a case would probably be to aid in thwarting betrothal before puberty, the very purpose for which the duty was enjoined."

The above decision, you will observe, also lays down the important rule that a guardian in marriage, having selected a fit and unobjectionable match, can by a suit compel the guardian of a girl's person to allow the marriage to take place, and can also compel the party chargeable to pay the expenses of the same.

I may here tell you that the Hindu law relating to guardianship in marriage and the restraint on the freedom of choice on the part of the bride, resembles very much the Attick law on the subject. Speaking of that law, Sir W. Jones observes:[1] "All unnecessary restraints upon love, which contributes so largely to relieve the anxieties of a laborious life, and upon marriage, which conduces so eminently to the peace and good order of society, are odious in the highest degree; yet at Athens, whence arts, laws, humanity, learning, and religion are said to have sprung, a girl could not be legally united with the object of her affection without the consent of her *controller*, who was either her father or her grandsire, her brother or her guardian."

It has been held in the case of *Maharanee Ram Bunsee Koonwaree* v. *Maharanee Soobh Koonwaree*,[2] that the word "mother" in the above texts does not include a stepmother. It has also been held in the same case that

---

[1] Collected Works of Sir W. Jones, Vol. IV, p. 211.

[2] 7 W. R., 321.

LECTURE II. where, as in the instance of the *sakulyas*, the order of guardianship is not definitely laid down, the Court has the discretion to select a proper person as guardian; and in the exercise of this discretion, the Court held that the paternal grandmother of a girl was preferable to her stepmother as her guardian in marriage.

Though the father is undoubtedly entitled to dispose of his daughter in marriage in preference to all others, yet, under certain circumstances, he may lose this preferential right. Thus, when he neglects to exercise it in proper time, and allows the daughter to remain for a long time unprovided with a husband, he forfeits the right altogether.[1] So it has been held that a *kulin* Brahman, who has many wives, and visits the mother of his daughter after long intervals of absence, during which she continues under the guardianship of her mother, is not such a natural guardian of that daughter as her mother.[2] This ruling is certainly not favourable to the prospects of *kulinism*, and is perhaps not in accordance with the strict letter of the Hindu law; but it undoubtedly accords with the spirit of that law.

A guardian may delegate his authority to another, and the delegated guardian will have the right to dispose of the ward in marriage. Such delegation may be presumed from the conduct of the parties.[3]

Where there is no one authorized to give a girl in marriage, or where her guardians neglect to do so, she is allowed to choose her own husband; but in the latter case, she must wait for three years after attaining the marriage-

---

[1] The King *v.* Kistnama Naick, 2 Strange's Notes of Cases, 89; 1 Norton's Leading Cases on Hindu Law, 1.

[2] Modhoosoodun Mookerjee *v.* Jadub Chunder Banerjee, 3 W. R., 194.

[3] Golamee Gopee Ghose *v.* Juggessur Ghose, 3 W. R., 193.

able age, that is the eighth year.[1] Speaking of this latter case, Strange observes: "Though the law be so, it may be a question whether, according to modern practice, the right do not, in this case, continue to attach to the substitutes for the father instead of vesting in the girl."[2] LECTURE II.

Though the consent of the guardian is declared necessary with a view to secure a proper marriage, it has been held that the absence of such consent "would not invalidate a marriage otherwise legally contracted and performed with all the necessary ceremonies."[3]

This rule, however, seems to be too broad in its terms, and to require some qualification. No doubt, it does not protect forced or fraudulent marriages, for they are not marriages *legally contracted;* but force and fraud are not the only grounds of objection. Apart from these, it is easy to conceive a case where a neighbour, or a distant relative, may, through mere recklessness, unite an infant girl in matrimony without the consent of her guardian, who may be her father; and in such cases it would be gross injustice not only to the father, but also to the girl, to allow the union to last, when the father might have secured an incomparably better match for his daughter. With every regard for the indissoluble character of marriage, it would be more correct therefore to say that though the want of the guardian's consent would not necessarily invalidate a marriage otherwise legally valid, the guardian may, for any sufficient reason affecting the propriety of such marriage, obtain a declaration that it is void. This view of the law is to some extent supported by the decision of

[1] Coleb. Dig., Bk. IV, 18; Manu, IX, 88, 90, 91.

[2] 1 Strange, 36.

[3] Modhoosoodun Mookerjee v. Jadub Chunder Banerjee, 3 W. R., 194: see also Steele, p. 30.

LECTURE II. the High Court in the case of *Anjona Dossee* v. *Proladh Chunder Ghose*,[1] in which it has been held that the Courts have jurisdiction to declare a marriage void, if procured by fraud or force, and celebrated without the consent of the necessary parties. And the rule of the Hindu law is clear on the point. It is the gift of the bride (by which must be understood a gift with the consent of the legal guardian, express or implied), and not the mere ceremony of marriage, that forms the basis of the rights of the husband over the wife. For Manu declares,—"The recitation of holy texts, and the sacrifice ordained by the lord of creatures, are used in marriages for the sake of procuring good fortune to brides, but the first gift (of the bride) is the primary cause of marital dominion."[2]

Betrothed girl. Regarding the fitness of girls already betrothed to others to be taken in marriage, there is some difference of opinion.[3] Betrothment, however, is only a promise to give in marriage, and, as will be shown to you in the next Lecture, it is not irrevocable. It is allowed by Yajnavalkya[4] to be broken if a worthier bridegroom is found; and so it has been held that specific performance of such a promise is not enforceable by a suit.[5] A girl betrothed to one person is not, therefore, unfit to be taken in marriage by another,[6] though some degree of blame is generally attached to such marriage.

---

[1] 14 W. R., 403.

[2] V, 152; I have here departed a little from Sir W. Jones's translation, as there seems to be a slight inaccuracy in it.

[3] See Shama Charan's Vyavastha Darpana, pp. 645, 646.

[4] I, 65. See Mitakshara, Ch. II, Sec. XI, 27.

[5] Umedkika *v.* Nagindas Narotamdas, 7 Bom. O. C. J., 122; see also In the matter of Gunput Narain Singh, I. L. R., 1 Calc., 74.

[6] See the opinion of the Pandit in Lakhi Priya *v.* Bhairab Chandra Chaudhuri, 5 Sel. Rep., 374.

A woman whose husband is living is absolutely prohibited to be married again. Hindu law does not permit polyandry, and the practice exists only as a custom amongst particular tribes in certain localities. The only instance of polyandry among the Hindus is that of the mythical Draupadi; but it has been the cause of much discussion in the Mahabharat,[1] and is regarded as an exceptional case. Not only is it prohibited in the institutes of the sages,[2] but there is direct authority in the Vedas against such practice.[3] The marriage of a woman whose husband is living is not only illegal, but is an offence punishable under section 494 of the Indian Penal Code.

LECTURE II.

One whose husband is living.

The marriage of widows, though permitted by Parasara[4] and Narada,[5] has never been the practice among Hindus. It is reprobated by Manu, who says,—"A widow who, from a wish to bear children, slights her deceased husband by marrying again, brings disgrace on herself here below, and shall be excluded from the seat of her lord;"[6] and it is prohibited for the *Kali* or the present age in the Puranas and other sacred writings.[7] Accordingly it has always been held to be prohibited by the Hindu law.[8] This rule of Hindu law has, however, been abrogated by Act XV of 1856; and a Hindu widow is now eligible for marriage under the provisions of that Act.

Widows.

Manu directs every twice-born man to avoid marrying a girl belonging to any of the ten following families,

Girls with visible or other minor defects.

[1] Adiparva, Ch. XVI, 9, 22—27.

[2] See Manu, VIII, 226; IX, 46, 47. 71.

[3] Aitareya Brahmana, quoted in Vidyasagar's second Tract on Vahuvibaha, p. 106; Taittiriya Sanhita, quoted in *ibid*, p. 199.

[4] Parasara, Ch. IV, quoted in Vidyasagar's Marriage of Hindu Widows, p. 7.

[5] XII, 97.

[6] V. 161.

[7] See General Note to Manu, I, V, & VI.

[8] 1 Strange, 37, 241.

LECTURE II. namely:—"The family which has omitted prescribed acts of religion; that which has produced no male children; that in which the Veda has not been read; that which has thick hair on the body; and those which have been subject to hæmorrhoids, to phthisis, to dyspepsia, to epilepsy, to leprosy, and to elephantiasis;"[1] and also a girl that is immoderatively talkative or sickly, or has visible defects, such as too much hair on the skin; as well as one with the name of a constellation or of a river or other name raising an image of terror; and likewise one who has no brother, or whose father is not well known.[2] Now these rules are evidently not meant to imply any legal prohibition. If it were so, half the female population of India would be excluded from matrimony. But we are not left to decide for ourselves whether these rules are imperative or merely directory. The inconvenience of observing them as imperative prohibitions must have been perceived long before our time. They were originally meant to be mere rules of caution and advice, and found a place in the Institutes as it is a mixed treatise on law, ritual and hygiene; and so long as their real nature was known from tradition, they exacted their due share of obedience and caused no difficulty; and when time had raised their sanctity, and it became necessary to invent reasons for excusing their non-observance, reasons were readily found. Thus, Kulluka Bhatta, in his commentary on these texts, remarks that they are prohibitions the violation of which would be improper, but would not invalidate the wifehood of the girls therein enumerated; and his reason seems to be this, that wifehood or the matrimonial relation being a spiritual or abstract entity, cannot be affected by the violation of a rule having for its

---

[1] III, 6, 7.

[2] III, 8, 9, 11.

reason the existence of defects that are perceptible by the senses; and Raghunandan in his Udvahatattwa[1] adopts the same view.

The foregoing rules, therefore, are of no value to the practical lawyer. For the scholar, they may possess some interest, as being evidence of the wisdom of the Hindus.[2] But to the student of Hindu law they are of the highest value, as they serve to illustrate the nature of that law, and the manner of its elaboration by commentators in their attempt to reconcile practice with precept.

One whose elder sister is unmarried.

A girl whose elder sister remains unmarried is declared not eligible for marriage.[3] This rule is not peculiar to the Hindu law, but is to be found in other archaic systems such as the Jewish.[4] A girl married contrary to this rule is called *agre didhisu*, and her elder sister *didhisu*. This rule is analogous to the corresponding rule in the case of males, and the remarks made there would apply here, *mutatis mutandis*, with this difference, that considering the express declaration of commentators on the subject, it is doubtful whether the violation of the rule in this case would not invalidate the marriage. In practice, however, such marriages are of extremely rare occurrence.

We have been hitherto considering that part of our question which refers to the absolute unfitness of girls to be taken in marriage. We now come to the other part of it, which refers to relative disqualifications,—that is, disqualifications which render a girl unfit to be taken in marriage by some particular person or class of persons only.

[1] Institutes of Raghunandan, Vol. II, pp. 82, 83.

[2] It may not be without interest to the curious to compare Manu's rules relating to hairiness of the skin with the remarks of Darwin in his Descent of Man, pp. 600, 601.

[3] Udvahatattwa, Inst., Vol. II, p. 68; Vyavastha Darpana, 669, 670.

[4] Genesis, XXIX, 26.

LECTURE II.

A woman belonging to the same *gotra*, or primitive stock, is prohibited to be taken in marriage by a man of any of the three twice-born classes.[1]

Woman of the same *gotra*.

To understand this rule properly, you must know what *gotra* is. It comes from *go* (a cow), and meant originally an enclosure for kine. Max Müller points out the connection between its etymological and secondary meanings thus: "In ancient times, when most wars were carried on, not to maintain the balance of power of Asia or Europe, but to take possession of good pasture, or to appropriate large herds of cattle, the hurdles grew naturally into the walls of fortresses, the hedges became strongholds; Anglo-Saxon *tun*, a close (German *Zaun*) became a town; and those who lived behind the same walls were called a *gotra*, a family, a tribe, a race."[2] *Gotra*, as used in the above rule, means a family descended from one of the several patriarchs, who are, according to some, twenty-four, and according to others, forty-two in number;[3] so that, taking the higher estimate, there are forty-two *gotras* in all. Now, since a woman by her marriage passes from her father's *gotra* to that of her husband,[4] therefore, in order that two persons may be of the same *gotra*, each of them must be descended from the common patriarch through an uninterrupted line of males. As these patriarchs, or founders of *gotras*, were Brahmans, the Kshatriyas and Vaisyas (except, perhaps, those who are descended from Brahman fathers and mothers of their own classes, and who are held by some to belong to the same classes respectively as their mothers[5]), can have no *gotra* of

[1] Manu, III, 5. One is also prohibited to marry a girl of a *gotra* having the same *pravaras*, or principal sages, as his own; see Udvahatattwa.

[2] Chips from a German Workshop, Vol. II, p. 28.

[3] Sabdakalpadruma, art. *Gotra*.

[4] Udvahatattwa, Inst., Vol. II, 72.

[5] Dattaka Mimansa, Sec. II, 84; but see Manu, X, 6—10.

their own. But they having adopted the *gotras* of the spiritual guides or family priests of their remote progenitors,[1] Manu applies the foregoing rule to all the three twice-born classes alike. LECTURE II.

The case of the Sudras, however, is different. In early days, when it was thought improper to officiate at the religious ceremonies of the Sudras,[2] the Sudras could have had no family priests, and consequently, they did not belong to any *gotra*. And though in course of time Brahmans have been induced to become family priests of that class, and the Sudras have in some places, as in Bengal, got themselves affiliated to different *gotras*, yet that is not considered sufficient to make the above prohibition applicable to them.[3]

The above rule is imperative in its nature, and a marriage celebrated in violation of it is null and void.[4] "He who inadvertently marries a girl sprung from the same original stock with himself, must support her as a mother." So says Bandhayana.[5] And in the Udvahatattwa, several other texts are quoted to the same effect.

The reason for the prohibition of marriage in the same primitive stock has been the subject of much speculation and controversy. M'Lennan[6] traces the origin of the rule to the primeval practice of marriage by capture, which he thinks led to exogamy, or marriage out of the tribe, as the only allowable form of marriage. Other writers who have examined the subject do not agree with him. But it would be out of place here to enlarge upon this subject.

Girls related within the prohibited degrees.

Girls related to a man within certain degrees of relation-

---

[1] Dattaka Mimansa, Sec. II, 76. [2] Manu, IV, 80.

[3] See Udvahatattwa, Raghunandan's Institutes, Vol. II, 62; Coleb. Dig., Bk. V, 340, commentary.

[4] Steele, p. 166. [5] Coleb. Dig., Bk. V, 340.

[6] Primitive Marriage, pp. 84—86.

LECTURE II. ship, commonly called the prohibited degrees, are not to be taken in marriage by him.

Marriage between near blood relations is so universally repugnant to our feelings, that every system of law has its rule of prohibited degrees. The prohibition is also extended by analogy more or less to relations by affinity, fosterage, and adoption. I shall first of all give you the rules regarding prohibited degrees in the Hindu law, and then compare them with those of other systems.

These rules are chiefly based upon the following texts:—

I. "She who is not descended from his paternal or maternal ancestors within the sixth degree (*sapinda*), and who is not known by his family name to be of the same primitive stock with his father or mother, is eligible by a twice-born man for nuptials and holy union."—Manu, III, 5.

Sapinda is the word in the original which has been rendered as '*descended from ancestors within the sixth degree*'—that is, from persons in the ascending line within the *seventh degree* from the intending husband. This rendering is in accordance with the text of Manu (V, 60), which says that the *sapinda* relationship ceases with the seventh person.

II. "Having finished his studentship, let a man espouse a girl endowed with good qualities, one who was never married before, who is possessed of beauty, is not a *sapinda*, and is younger in age."—Yajnavalkya, I, 52.

As it is of importance that you should clearly understand the import of the word *sapinda*, I shall here subjoin the very full explanation of it given by Vijnaneswar in his commentary on the above text:[1]

"(He should marry a girl) who is non-Sapinda (with himself). She is called his Sapinda who has (particles of)

---

[1] Mitakshara (Sans.) Acharadhyaya, leaf 6 *et seq.*

the body (of some ancestor, &c.,) in common (with him). Non-Sapinda means not his Sapinda. Such a one (he should marry). Sapinda-relationship arises between two people through their being connected by particles of one body. Thus, the son stands in Sapinda-relationship to his father, because of particles of his father's body having entered (his). In like (manner stands the grandson in Sapinda-relationship) to his paternal grandfather and the rest, because through his father, particles of his (grandfather's) body have entered into (his own). Just so is (the son a Sapinda-relation) of his mother, because particles of his mother's body have entered (into his). Likewise (the grandson stands in Sapinda-relationship) to his maternal grandfather and the rest through his mother. So also (is the nephew) a Sapinda-relation of his maternal aunts and uncles, and the rest, because particles of the same body (the paternal grandfather) have entered into (his and theirs); likewise (does he stand in Sapinda-relationship) with paternal uncles and aunts, and the rest. So also the wife and the husband (are Sapinda-relations to each other), because they together beget one body (the son). In like manner, brothers' wives also are (Sapinda-relations to each other), because they produce one body (the son), with those (severally) who have sprung from one body (*i. e.*, because they bring forth sons by their union with the offspring of one person, and thus their husbands' father is the common bond which connects them). Therefore, one ought to know that, wherever the word Sapinda is used, there exists (between the persons to whom it is applied), a connection with one body, either immediately or by descent."

. . . . .

LECTURE II. "In the explanation of the word 'asapindam' (non-Sapinda, verse 52), it has been said that Sapinda-relation arises from the circumstance that particles of one body have entered into (the bodies of the persons thus related), either immediately or through (transmission by) descent. But inasmuch as (this definition) would be too wide, since such a relationship exists in the eternal circle of births, in some manner or other, between all men, therefore, the author (Yajnavalkya) says, v. 53:—'After the fifth ancestor on the mother's, and after the seventh on the father's side.' On the mother's side, in the mother's line, after the fifth; on the father's side, in the father's line, after the seventh (ancestor), the Sapinda-relationship ceases; these latter two words must be understood; and, therefore, the word Sapinda, which on account of its (etymological) import '(connected by having in common) particles (of one body)' would apply to all men, is restricted in its signification, just as the word pankaja (which etymologically means 'growing in the mud,' and therefore, would apply to all plants growing in the mud, designates the lotus only), and the like; and thus the six ascendants beginning with the father, and the six descendants beginning with the son, and one's self (counted) as the seventh (in each case), are Sapinda-relations. In case of a division of the line also, one ought to count up to the seventh (ancestor), including him with whom the division of the line begins (*e. g.*, two collaterals A and B are Sapindas, if the common ancestor is not further removed from either of them than six degrees), and thus must the counting of the (Sapinda-relationship) be made in every case."[1]

[1] The above translation is taken from West and Bühler's Digest, Part I, pp. 141—143.

I ought to add here that the word *sapinda* has, in other places, a meaning different from what is given above. Thus in the chapter on inheritance in the Code of Manu (IX, 186, 187) a *sapinda* means one who is related within the third degree: the *sapinda* relation being there based not on connection through one common body, but on connection through common oblation.[1]

III. "One must not marry a girl of the same *gotra* or *pravaras*, or as far as the fifth in degree from the mother and seventh from the father."—Vishnu Sutra, cited in the Udvahatattwa.

IV. "Girls descended from the father's or mother's *bandhus* are not to be taken in marriage as far as the seventh and fifth respectively, as well as those of the same *gotra* or of equal *pravaras*."—Narada, cited in the Udvahatattwa.

The word *bandhu*, which occurs in the above text, has been defined in a text quoted anonymously in the Udvahatattwa, which runs thus:—

"The sons of his father's paternal aunt, the sons of his father's maternal aunt, and the sons of his father's maternal uncle, must be considered his father's *bandhus*. The sons of his mother's maternal aunt, the sons of his mother's paternal aunt, and the sons of his mother's maternal uncle, must be reckoned his mother's *bandhus*."[2]

From these texts and a few others, commentators have deduced the following rules:—

Rule I.—(a.)—The female descendants as far as the seventh degree, from the father and his six ancestors, namely, the paternal grandfather, &c.,

---

[1] See Dattaka Chandrika, Sec. IV, 7—9; Dattaka Mimansa, Sec. VI, 32.

[2] See Mitakshara, Ch. II, Sec. VI, 1.

LECTURE II. *(b.)*—The female descendants as far as the seventh degree, from the father's *bandhus* and their six ancestors, through whom those females are related,

(c.)—The female descendants as far as the fifth degree, from the maternal grandfather and his four ancestors, namely, the maternal great grandfather, &c., and

(d.)—The female descendants as far as the fifth degree, from the mother's *bandhus* and their four ancestors, through whom those females are related,

are not to be taken in marriage.[1]

Rule II.—A stepmother's brother's daughter and his daughter's daughter are not to be taken in marriage.[2]

Clauses *(a)* and *(c)* in Rule I are clear enough; but clauses *(b)* and *(d)* may require a word of explanation. Take clause *(b)*. Then, as defined above, the father's maternal aunt's son is one of the father's *bandhus;* and the rule excludes his female descendants within the seventh degree. It also excludes the female descendants (within the same degree) of each of his six ancestors in a certain line,—namely, that in which those female descendants are connected by blood with the intending husband. This line must, therefore, be the *bandhu's* maternal line, for his paternal line is not connected by blood with the bridegroom; and the six ancestors in question would be the *bandhu's* mother, his maternal grandfather, maternal great grandfather, &c., and not the *bandhu's* mother, his mother's mother, &c.; for though these females are connected by blood with the bridegroom, a line of female ancestors is not regarded as a line in the Hindu law. The same is to be

---

[1] Udvahatattwa, Raghunandan's Institutes, Vol. II, p. 65.
[2] *Ibid*, p. 66.

understood in the case of any other *bandhu*, whether of the father or of the mother. LECTURE II.

Clauses (*b*) and (*d*) may be illustrated by the following diagram,—where A is the bridegroom; M and F with the several suffixes denote males and females respectively, M_1 and F_1 being the father and the mother of A; and B_1, B_2, B_3, denote the three *bandhus* of the father, and B′, B″, B‴, the three *bandhus* of the mother. The girls prohibited under clauses (*b*) and (*d*) would be the female descendants (within the seventh degree) of B_1, B_2, B_3, and of each of their six ancestors that are represented in the scheme; and the female descendants (within the fifth degree) of B′, B″, B‴, and of each of their four ancestors that are represented there.

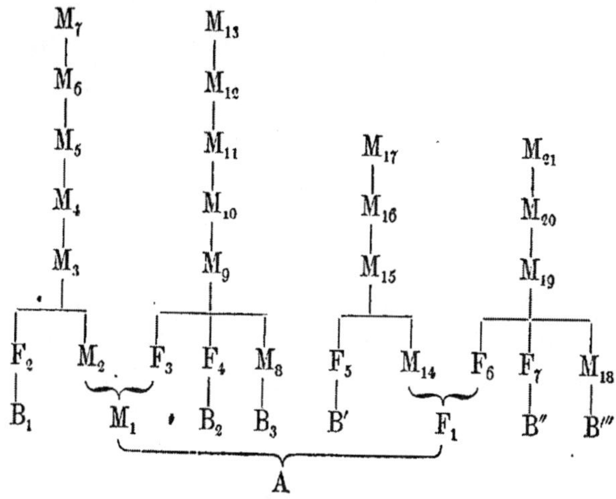

It will be seen from the above, that in Rule I, the exclusion of collateral relations from eligibility for marriage is carried rather too far, and intermarriage is prohibited between relations who may be practically regarded as

LECTURE II. strangers. Consequently, that rule has been qualified by the following exceptions :—

Exception I.—A girl who is removed by three *gotras* from the bridegroom is not unmarriageable, though related within the seven or five degrees as above described.[1]

The three *gotras* in the case of the descendants of a *bandhu* are always to be counted from his (*bandhu's*) own *gotra*. So also, in the case of the descendants of the ancestors of a *bandhu*, who is the father's or the mother's maternal uncle's son, they are to be counted from the *bandhu's* own *gotra*. But in the case of the descendants of the ancestors of each of the other *bandhus*, the three *gotras* are to be counted from his (*bandhu's*) maternal grandfather's *gotra*.

This exception is based upon a text of Brihat Manu, and another of the Matsya Purana, cited in the Udvahatattwa.[2] To understand it, you must bear in mind that marriage effects change of *gotra* in a female by transferring her from her father's *gotra* to that of her husband. The exception may be illustrated by the following example :— Suppose the paternal great grandfather of the bridegroom to be of the *Sandilya gotra ;* his daughter (by transfer by marriage) to be of the *Kasyapa gotra ;* her daughter, of the *Vatsya gotra ;* and this daughter's daughter to be of the *Bharadwaja gotra :* the maiden daughter of this last, being of the *Bharadwaja gotra*, and being beyond three *gotras*, *viz*, the *Sandilya*, *Kasyapa*, and *Vatsya*, is eligible for marriage, though within the prohibited degrees in Rule I (*a*).

Exception II.—When a fit match is not otherwise procurable, the Kshatriyas in all the forms of marriage, and the other classes in the *Asura* and other inferior forms of marriage, may marry within the above degrees, provided that

---

[1] Raghunandana's Inst., Vol. II, p. 64.

[2] *Ibid.*

they do not marry within the fifth degree on the father's side, and the third degree on the mother's. LECTURE II.

This exception is based on the authority of Sulpani, but Raghunandana differs from him. It is, however, supported by a text of Paithinasi and another of Sakatayana, and is generally considered to be a valid exception.[1]

Besides these two, various other exceptions have been introduced, and they are all regarded as valid if sanctioned by custom, according to the doctrine of the *Chaturvingsati*, or the twenty-four sages.[2] Thus, in the South of India, intermarriage with the daughter of a maternal uncle is not only allowed, but is considered desirable.[3]

In the case of a person whose filial relation has been changed by adoption, as well as in the case of his descendants, while the above rules about prohibited degrees continue in full force with reference to their relations by consanguinity, the same rules apply with regard to relations in the families of the adoptive parents in the same way as if the adopted son were their legitimate son.[4] There may, however, be some difficulty in fixing the maternal line by adoption. If the adopting father has only one wife, she is considered the adoptive mother; if he has more wives than one, but joins with one of them only in the ceremony of adoption, or if only one of them takes the child with his permission, then, too, she is considered as the mother by adoption. But where the adopter has several wives, and does not join with any one of them in the act

---

[1] Shama Charan's Vyavastha Darpana, pp. 663, 664.

[2] *Ibid*, p. 664.

[3] 2 Strange's Hindu Law, p. 165.

[4] Dattaka Chandrika, Sec. IV, 7—9.

LECTURE II. of adoption, it is not settled which of them is to become the adoptive mother, though some maintain that they all equally become his mothers, and that, consequently, he must have as many maternal lines as there are mothers.[1]

The rules as to prohibited degrees, subject of course to the exceptions noticed above, are absolutely imperative in their nature, and would nullify any marriage contracted in contravention of them.[2]

Prohibited degrees in different systems compared.

The prohibited degrees in the case of collaterals extend much further in the above rules than they do in other systems, such as the Jewish,[3] the Roman,[4] the English,[5] the French,[6] and the Mahomedan.[7] In none of these does the prohibition of marriage between collaterals extend further than to marriages between brother and sister, uncle and niece, aunt and nephew, and great-aunt and grand-nephew.

In the direct line, marriage is prohibited between ascendants and descendants, in all these systems. This prohibition, as you have seen, is not to be found in so many words in the Hindu law. But the above rules of Hindu law embody such prohibitions to an extent which is sufficient for all practical purposes. For one of the rules given above prohibits marriage with any female descendant within the seventh degree from the father; and this must be

---

[1] Colebrooke's Digest, Bk. V, 273, commentary, Vol. II, p. 394 (Madras edition); Shama Charan's Vyavastha Darpana, p. 890; see also Dattaka Mimansa, Sec. VI, 50—53.

[2] Udvahatattwa, Institutes of Raghunandana, Vol. II, p. 82; Kulluka Bhatta's commentary on Manu, Ch. III, 5 and 11.

[3] Leviticus, XVIII and XX.

[4] Inst. Lib. I, Tit. X, 2—5.

[5] Stephen's Commentaries, Bk. III, Ch. II.

[6] Code Napoleon, arts. 162, 163.

[7] Hedaya, Bk. II, Ch. I.

practically a sufficient prohibition in all cases as regards females in the descending line. As for females in the ascending line, widow marriage being prohibited, no further prohibition was necessary. And though widow marriage has been now legalized, the prohibition of marriage with *sapindas* would be practically sufficient for such cases. LECTURE II.

The prohibition by reason of affinity, which exists in other systems, has no place in Hindu law. But the prohibition of marriage with *sapindas* to some extent supplies its place, and so did the prohibition of widow marriage. The Hindu law, however, does not prohibit marriage with the wife's sister, or even with her niece, or her aunt. The prohibition on the ground of adoption resembles, to some extent, the corresponding provision in the Roman law,[1] and the prohibition by reason of fosterage in the Mahomedan law.[2]

The reason why marriage between cousins-german, though allowed in so many other systems, is so repugnant to the feelings of a Bengali, is to be found in the peculiar mode of naming those relations in our language. That mode is what is termed the classificatory mode, as distinguished from another mode, which is called the descriptive mode, and which obtains in most other civilized countries.[3] According to the former system of nomenclature as it exists in our language, relations are *classified* into groups of equal degrees in the ascending and descending lines, and general names are givin to these groups. Thus, all male relations in the same degree with a man himself are con-

---

[1] Inst., Lib. I, Tit. X, 1—5.

[2] Hedaya, Bk. II, Ch. I.

[3] See Lubbock's Origin of Civilisation, p. 153 *et seq.*

LECTURE II. sidered as belonging to the brother's class, and are styled brothers (being called brothers through the uncle or the aunt, or other relation as the case may be); and all female relations in the same degree are styled sisters. And hence marriage between cousins-german sounds in a Bengali's ear as repugnant as that between brother and sister. This will not, however, account for the extensive rule of prohibited degrees in the collateral line, for the nomenclature of relations in the Sanskrit is not one in the classificatory mode. To find out the true reason for the rule in Hindu law, let us first of all ascertain the reason for the rule of prohibited degrees in general.

It is thought by some that the rule is based upon physical grounds, and that it is meant to prevent that physical degeneracy of the race which marriages between near relations would lead to. That may be true. But there is a still stronger reason for the rule: it is intended to prevent moral degeneracy and consequent social evils which would otherwise result. These have been so forcibly pointed out by Bentham,[1] that I feel tempted to quote his words: "If there were not an insurmountable barrier between near relatives called to live together in the greatest intimacy, this contact, continual opportunities, friendship itself, and its innocent caresses, might kindle fatal passions. The family—that retreat where repose ought to be found in the bosom of order, and where the movements of the soul, agitated by the scenes of the world, ought to grow calm—would itself become a prey to all the inquietudes of rivalry, and to all the furies of passion. Suspicions would banish

[1] Principles of the Civil Code, Part III, Ch. V, Sec. I.

confidence—the tenderest sentiments of the heart would be quenched—eternal enmities or vengeance, of which the bare idea is fearful, would take their place. The belief in the chastity of young girls, that powerful attraction to marriage, would have no foundation to rest upon; and the most dangerous snares would be spread for youth in the very asylum where it could least escape them." Now you will at once see the bearing of these remarks upon the state of Hindu society at the time when the rules in question were framed. The Hindus in those days lived in joint families and under the same roof for generations together; and their remote collaterals (of course, on the paternal side only) were brought into contact in the same way as brothers and sisters in modern society. The prohibition of marriage between remote collaterals was not, therefore, as unnecessary as it may now seem to be. The rule when once established for the paternal side, was extended to the maternal side by analogy.

Daughter of one's spiritual guide or pupil.

A man is prohibited to marry the daughter of his spiritual preceptor or pupil in the Vedas. A text of the Matsya Sukta, cited in the Udvahatattwa, says: "The marriage with a girl of equal *pravaras*, or with a daughter of a pupil, or of the *guru* who instructs in the Vedas, is prohibited." A Hindu's repugnance towards such marriage is strikingly illustrated by the story of Devajani in the Adiparva of the Mahabharata. The reason for this rule is to be found in the nature of the relation between pupil and preceptor in the early days of Hinduism. In those days, the student of the Vedas had to live for a series of years in the house of the preceptor; and to prevent all chance of illicit intimacy with the preceptor's daughters, connection with them was de-

LECTURE II. clared incestuous. The *Acharya* (teacher), moreover, was regarded in the same light as a father.[1] But Vaidik education has become nominal now, and is completed by the student learning to repeat the *Gayatri;* and though at the *Upanayana*, an *Acharya* is appointed for the neophyte for form's sake, one seldom remembers afterwards who his *Acharya* was. As the place of the Vaidik preceptor is now in most cases supplied by the *Guru*, who imparts the mystic *Tantric mantra*, some think that, by parity of reason, the above prohibition ought to extend to the case of the *Tantric Guru* as well.[2] But, considering all the circumstances, it is very doubtful whether at the present day a Court of Justice would in any case consider the rule as anything more than a mere moral injunction.

Girl bearing one's mother's name.

A man is likewise prohibited to marry a girl who bears the same name as his mother. This rule is so imperative that if one inadvertently marries in violation of it, he is required to forsake the wife entirely and to perform penance. Considering, however, the fact that if the objection on the score of name is discovered after betrothal, Hindu law allows the marriage to take place on the birde's name being changed,[3] it is doubtful whether, after marriage has taken place, a Court of Justice would regard this rule as more imperative than most other rules of the same class.

Girl older in age.

Yajnavalkya[4] directs that a man should marry a damsel younger than himself. The exercise of marital authority, and the implicit obedience that is held to be due to it, appear to a Hindu so incompatible with seniority in

[1] Manu, II, 171.

[2] See Shama Charan's Vyavastha Darpana, p. 665, note.

[3] Udvahatattwa.

[4] I, 52.

the wife, that in practice this rule is never departed from ;[1] and the early age at which Hindu females are required to be married, renders the occasions for such deviation extremely rare. But the rule seems to be only directory in its nature, and it can hardly be expected that its violation would nullify a marriage already celebrated. LECTURE II.

Girl belonging to a different caste.

A girl belonging to a different caste is prohibited to be taken in marriage in the present *(Kali)* age. Formerly, intermarriage between persons of different castes, though not approved, was permitted according to the following text of Manu :[2]—

"For the first marriage of the twice-born classes, a woman of the same class is recommended; but for such as are impelled by inclination to marry again, women in the direct order of the classes are to be preferred."

"A Sudra woman only must be the wife of a Sudra; she and a Vaisya, of a Vaisya; they two and a Kshatriya, of a Kshatriya; those three and a Brahmani, of a Brahman."

But though a woman of any caste was allowed to be married to a man of a higher caste, her marriage with one of a lower class was greatly discountenanced, and the children of such marriage were called low-born.[3]

Upon the authority of certain texts of the Puranas, intermarriage between different castes is now absolutely prohibited,[4] and the practical question now in such cases is, what constitutes a difference of caste sufficient to prevent intermarriage.

Caste, in the days of the Vedas, was an ethnological distinction. There were then two great castes, the Aryas, or the

[1] See Steele, 161. [2] IV, 12 and 13. [3] Manu, X, 41.
[4] See Udvahatattwa, Institutes of Raghunandan, Vol. II, p. 62; Steele, p. 26; 1 Strange, 40; General Note to Manu.

LECTURE II. fair-complexioned new settlers, and the Dasyus, sometimes called the Sudras, or the dark-complexioned aborigines. *Varna,* literally colour, was then a strictly appropriate word for caste. Gradually, as the Aryas, according to their occupations, divided themselves into the three classes of priests, warriors, and traders or agriculturists, there arose the fourfold division into Brahmans, Kshatriyas, Vaisyas, and Sudras.[1] By intermarriage among these castes, which was then allowable, there arose a number of mixed classes, which have been treated of in the tenth chapter of Manu; and further, by a division of the Sudras according to their occupations, there arose a number of sub-castes, such as the Karmakars (blacksmiths), the Tantis (weavers), the Kumars (potters), &c. Whether some of the castes, such as the Kayasthas and others, are really Sudras or not, whether the Vaidyas are a mixed class or are genuine Vaisyas, and whether the Kshatriya class still exists,[2] are questions which are sometimes keenly contested at the present day.

Such being the nature and origin of caste, it has been sometimes held that the prohibition of intermarriage applies only with reference to the four primary castes, and is inapplicable to the sub-divisions of the Sudra caste. Thus, in the case of *Pandaiya Telaver* v. *Puli Telaver,*[3] Sir Colley Scotland, C.J., observed: "It is not, however, to be understood that supposing the late zemindar and the second plaintiff had been of different castes, the marriage would in my opinion have been invalid. The general law applicable to all the

---

[1] See Max Müller's Chips from a German Workshop, Vol. II, p. 323 *et seq.*

[2] Regarding the existence of the true Kshatriya caste at the present day, see Chuoturya Run Murdun Syn *v.* Sahub Purluhad Syn, 7 Moo. I. A., 18; 4 W. R., P. C., 132.

[3] 1 Mad., 478.

classes or tribes does not seem opposed to marriage between individuals of different sects or divisions of the same class or tribe, and even as regards the marriage between individuals of a different class or tribe, the law appears to be no more than directory. Although it recommends and inculcates a marriage with a woman of equal class as a preferable description, yet the marriage of a man with a woman of a lower class or tribe than himself, appears not to be an invalid marriage, rendering the issue illegitimate. *Manu*, Ch. III, cl. 12 *et seq.*; *Mitakshara*, Ch. I, Sec. 11, cl. 2, and note; 1 *Strange's H. L.*, p. 40. According to this view of the law, there being no proof of special custom or usage, the marriage would be valid, even though the parties had been of different sects or caste divisions of the fourth or Sudra class." And Mr. Justice Holloway in his judgment in the same case remarked: "Moreover, it is not invalid if it took place, because of the difference of class. The opinion of the pandits is, as usual, vague and unsatisfactory. As the twice-born man is instructed to marry a wife of the same class with himself, the reasonable inference is that, upon one not twice-born, the precept is not binding.

"Further, I am clearly of opinion that the classes spoken of are the four classes recognized by Manu, and not the infinite sub-divisions of these classes introduced in the progress of time. I think, therefore, that being a Sudra, the woman was of the same class in the sense of the authority quoted."

On appeal, the Privy Council, though not concurring in all that has been said in the judgment of the High Court, made the following observations:[1]—

"Then, if there was a marriage in fact, was there a mar-

[1] 3 B. L. R., 3, 4; 12 W. R., P. C., 41.

LECTURE II. riage in law? When once you get to this, *viz.*, that there was a marriage in fact, there would be a presumption in favor of there being a marriage in law. The zemindar, according to the usages of his country and nation, on parting with his first wife, would be naturally desirous of marrying again and having male issue.

"It would be a most unlikely thing for a person of his race to go through the ceremony of marriage, if it was known that that marriage was a marriage which was invalid in law. Then upon what is it that the invalidity of the marriage in law depends? It depends upon this, and upon nothing else, *viz.*, that all the parties being, as is clear from the evidence, of the Sudra caste, it is said that because it is shown by a decree that the father of the mother of the present plaintiff and respondent was illegitimate, therefore the child of that father could not contract a valid marriage, and was in substance of no caste at all. The only foundation for this is the opinions of the Pundits; those opinions are not satisfactory; no decision or authority is brought forward supporting any such proposition. The opinions are matter of reasoning; and where they refer to authority, it is to authority which applies to persons of two different but higher castes, not to the Sudra caste at all, and still less to what may be called different classes or divisions of one and the same Sudra caste.

"Their Lordships are not aware that there is any authority. There has been none quoted, and it does not appear that there is any authority supporting any such proposition as that which is contended for by the Pundits; and though their Lordships do not agree in everything that has been stated in the Court of Appeal, they are satisfied that in the Sudra caste illegitimate children may inherit, and have a right to maintenance; and that in this very instance the illegitimate father of the mother of the plaintiff, as well as his daughter, were treated as members of the family; and on the whole, seeing that these parties are both of the Sudra caste, and that the utmost that has been alleged really is, that the zemindar was of one part of the Sudra caste, and the lady to whom he was married was of another part, or of a sub-caste, their Lordships hold the marriage to have been valid; to hold the contrary would, in fact, be introducing a new rule, and a rule which ought not to be countenanced."

Here it should be borne in mind that this was a case in the Madras Presidency, where, especially among the classes to which the parties to the suit belonged, caste distinctions are not so rigidly observed as in other parts of India; and that the Privy Council viewed the question in this case as a mixed one of law and fact, with especial reference to the particular facts of the case. But in Bengal, at least, the practice is very different. Here, except where custom has sanctioned otherwise, absolute equality of caste in the parties is necessary for marriage, and no prohibitory rule in marriage is more strictly observed than this;[1] and the weight of judicial authority seems to be in conformity with practice. Thus, in a case in which a *Dome* Brahman had married a girl of the *Haree* caste, the High Court of Bengal held that "local custom is the only authority by which such marriage can be sanctioned, the general Hindu law being against it."[2] And in a recent case,[3] where the legality of a marriage between a man of the *Kaivarta* and a woman of the *Tantee* caste was one of the points for decision, Mr.

[1] Shama Charn's Vyavastha Darpana, p. 1038.

[2] Melaram Nudial v. Thanooram Bamun, 9 W. R., 552.

[3] Narain Dhara v. Rakhal Gain, I. L. R., 1 Calc., 1; 23 W. R., 334.

LECTURE II. Justice Romesh Chunder Mitter held that, as the parties were of different castes, a valid marriage between them was impossible, unless sanctioned by any peculiar custom governing them; and though Mr. Justice Markby expressed a doubt on the point, he concurred in remanding the case to the first Court to try whether by any usage or custom there could be any valid marriage between the parties in question.

According to the opinion of some of the Bombay Sastris, as we learn from Steele,[1] "Should the husband prove of lower caste, provided Gurbhadhan has not been performed, the girl is to perform Prayuschit, and be remarried; and this is the only case in which a woman can be married a second time. ... But if Gurbhadhan has been performed, the wife must remain with her low-caste husband. Should the wife prove of lower caste, the husband must perform Prayuschit, and she may be repudiated with maintenance."

Daughters of illegitimate persons.

In the Madras case above referred to, the principal question raised was, whether the daughter of an illegitimate person, being an outcast,—that is of no caste,—could be taken in marriage by a man of any caste among the Sudras. The question was answered in the affirmative, on this, among other grounds, that illegitimacy by itself is no disqualification for caste; and the Privy Council, as you have seen from the portion of the judgment already quoted, concurred in this answer.

At the present day, when caste is become so elastic, and loss of caste so rare, the general question, whether an outcast is eligible for marriage at all, and if so, in what caste, is not of much practical importance. The only case of some real difficulty is that of a person who is born of parents

---

[1] Law and Custom of Hindoo Castes, pp. 29, 30.

belonging to two different castes. But even in these cases, which, however, are by no means common, the child, if recognized by relatives and others as belonging to the caste of either parent, is married in that caste, though the family that connects itself by such alliance becomes lowered in social estimation. And it may perhaps be laid down as a general rule, that so far as the prohibition of intermarriage between different castes is concerned, a marriage would be valid or void according as the parties to it are or are not in point of fact recognized as belonging to the same caste, irrespective of the propriety of such recognition. LECTURE II.

Besides the relative disqualifications enumerated above, there are several others based on astrological considerations, which are avoided in order to render marriage auspicious and happy.[1] They do not affect the legality of a marriage, though they may excuse the non-performance of an executory contract of marriage.

Effect of disqualification on marriage already completed.

To sum up then the substance of this Lecture, most of the rules about disqualifications for marriage are in the nature of directions for regulating choice in matrimony, which it would certainly be improper to disregard, and which would be duly considered by the Courts in deciding suits relating to executory contracts of marriage, whether they are suits for specific performance, or for compensation, or the like. But excepting the disqualifications arising from difference of caste, identity of *gotra*, and relationship within the prohibited degrees, no other disqualification would, it seems, be held by a Court of Justice to be sufficient to invalidate a marriage already completed and otherwise valid.

---

[1] See Steele, pp. 24, 25.

LECTURE III.

FORMS OF MARRIAGE AND FORMALITIES REQUISITE FOR A VALID MARRIAGE.

Different forms of marriage in Hindu law—*Brahma*—*Daiva*—*Arsha*—*Prajapatya*—*Asura*—*Gandharba*—*Rakshasa*—*Paisacha*—Mode of contracting marriage—Betrothment—Its legal effects—Specific performance of contract of betrothal—Agreements in restraint of marriage—Marriage brokerage contracts—Ceremonies attending marriage—Necessity of their observance—Time for celebration of marriage—Consummation—Questions of validity of marriage how far cognizable in the Courts.

Different forms of marriage in Hindu law.

In this Lecture I shall describe the different forms of marriage in Hindu law and the formalities necessary for the same.

Owing to the large extent over which Hindu society is spread, and the dissimilar elements of which it is composed, different forms of marriage have always been prevalent among the Hindus. Apart from those legalized by custom, the Hindu law recognizes eight distinct forms. They are described in the institutes of the sages, and are called the *Brahma*, *Daiva*, *Arsha*, *Prajapatya* or *Kaya*, *Asura*, *Gandharba*, *Rakshasa*, and *Paisacha*.[1] I shall give a short description of each.

Brahma.

The *Brahma* form is thus described by Manu:—

"The gift of a daughter, clothed and decked, to a man learned in the Veda, whom her father voluntarily invites and respectfully receives, is the nuptial rite called Brahma."[2] (III, 27.)

According to Manu and Yajnavalkya, the son born of a

[1] See Manu, III, 21—41; Yajnavalkya. I, 58—61; Narada, XII, 39—44.

[2] The above version differs slightly from the translation of Sir W. Jones, but agrees with the text and the gloss of Kulluka.

Brahmi, or wife by such marriage, redeems from sin ten ancestors, ten descendants, and himself. LECTURE III.

It is called the *Brahma* form, because it is the form peculiarly fit for Brahmans; and it is the only form now "practised by good men."[1] Though originally intended for Brahmans only, the *Brahma* form has now been held to be legal even among Sudras.[2] It must not be confounded with a modern form of marriage, which also is called *Brahma* marriage, and is the form adopted by some members of the sect called the Brahmos. It is the best form of marriage in Hindu law, and, no doubt, indicates an advanced stage of social progress. This form of marriage disagrees with the enlightened modern notions on the subject only in this, that the bride here is the subject of gift instead of being one of the contracting parties. No doubt, the best form of marriage is that in which the bride makes a voluntary gift of herself to the bridegroom. But next to that must be the form in which the father, unmoved by any other consideration but the fitness of the bridegroom, voluntarily invites him to receive the hand of his daughter in marriage.

Daiva.

The *Daiva* marriage is thus described :—

"The rite which sages call *Daiva*, is the gift of a daughter whom his father has decked in gay attire when the sacrifice is already begun, to the officiating priest, who performs that act of religion." (Manu, III, 28.)

Jagannath, following Sulpani's commentary on Yajnavalkya, describes the *Daiva* form as that in which the damsel is given to the family priest attending a sacrifice at the time when the sacrificial fee should be given.[3]

---

[1] Coleb. Dig., Bk. V, 499, commentary.

[2] Sivarama Casia Pillay *v.* Bagavan Pillay, Mad. S. R. for 1859, p. 44, cited in Norton's Leading Cases on Hindu Law, Part I, p. 5.

[3] Coleb. Dig., Bk. V, 499, commentary.

LECTURE III. The male issue of such marriage is said to redeem from sin seven ascendants and seven descendants. It is the second form in order of merit, and marks that stage of Hindu society in which the performance of great sacrifices was most common. This form also was peculiar to the Brahmans, but it is now obsolete.

It is called the *Daiva* as being the ceremony of the Devas, or gods. What that means is not very clear; but we learn from the gloss of Kulluka, that the names *Brahma*, *Daiva*, &c., are given to the forms 'to intimate praise or blame;' and as the form under notice is a praiseworthy one, it is called the form proper for the gods.

Arsha. The third form according to Manu, namely, the *Arsha*, is thus described by him:

"When the father gives his daughter away after having received from the bridegroom one pair of kine, or two pairs, for uses prescribed by law, that marriage is termed *Arsha*." (III, 29.)

The cattle here constitute the price for the bride, and the taking of this price renders this form, though the third in order of enumeration, inferior to the next or the fourth form, as you will presently see; and, accordingly, the number of persons redeemed by the male offspring of such marriage is only six, while the corresponding number in the next form is twelve. It means the ceremony of the Rishis, and is, perhaps, indicative of the pastoral state of Hindu society, when free gift of daughters in marriage was not common, and cattle formed the pecuniary consideration for the gift. It was in reality the same form as the *Asura*, to be described presently, and was less objectionable, only because the sale of the bride was apparently less noticeable. This form also was peculiar to the Brahmans, and is now obsolete.

The fourth form called the *Prajapatya* is, according to Manu, that in which the father gives away his daughter with due honor, saying distinctly—"May both of you perform together your civil and religious duties." (III, 30.) LECTURE III

Prajapatya.

This is, however, not very easily distinguishable from the *Brahma* form, and to find out the distinction, we must look to the description given by Yajnavalkya. According to him, when the father gives his daughter to a *suitor* saying, "perform all duties together," the marriage is called *Kaya* or *Prajapatya.*[1] It is the fact of the bridegroom being a *suitor,* an applicant for the bride's hand, that distinguishes this form from the *Brahma,* and makes it inferior to the latter, in which the bridegroom is voluntarily invited by the father to accept the bride. Marriage being according to Hindu notions a gift, loses a portion of its merit if the gift is not voluntary, but has to be applied for. It is called the *Kaya* or *Prajapatya,* as being the ceremony of the *Kas* or *Prajapatis,* that is, lords of created beings or progenitors of mankind.[2] This form also was peculiar to the Brahmans. It is obsolete in name only, as in point of fact, in the *Brahma* form as it now obtains, the bridegroom is at least as often a suitor as an invited guest. This and the three preceding are regarded as the four approved forms of marriage.

Asura.

The fifth form, *Asura,* is that in which "the bridegroom, having given as much wealth as he can afford to the father and paternal kinsmen and to the damsel herself, takes her voluntarily as his bride." (Manu, III, 31.)

Being an avowed sale of the bride for a pecuniary consideration, it is no doubt a base form of marriage; and though according to some it is permitted to the mercan-

---

[1] Yajnavalkya I, 60; Coleb. Dig., Bk. V, 499.

[2] Manu, I, 34.

LECTURE III. tile and servile classes,[1] the two lowest in Hindu society, Manu prohibits it altogether.[2] "But even a man of the servile class," says he, "ought not to receive a gratuity when he gives his daughter in marriage, since a father who takes a fee on that occasion, tacitly sells his daughter,"[3] and the same prohibition is repeated in other places.[4] It is called the *Asura* form, as being the ceremony of the *Asuras*, or the aboriginal non-Aryan tribes of India. It marks a very low state of society. But the practice of taking a fee for giving one's daughter in marriage seems at one time to have been very common. The fee was called the Bride-Price, and part of it, says Sir H. Maine, "went to the bride's father as compensation for the patriarchal or family authority which was transferred to the husband."[5] "A woman," observes Herbert Spencer, "is of value not only as a wife, but also as a daughter; and all through, from the lowest to the highest stages of social progress, we find a tacit or avowed claim to her services by her father. It is so even with the degraded Fuegians; an equivalent in the shape of service rendered has to be given for her by the youth, "such as helping to make a canoe." It is so with numerous more advanced savages all over the world: there is either the like giving of stipulated work, or the giving of a price. And we have evidence that it was originally so among ourselves: in an action for seduction, the deprivation of a daughter's services is the injury alleged."[6] Though not considered unobjectionable, the *Asura* form still prevails largely, especially among the lower castes.[7] According to Sir T. Strange, it is questionable whether in Southern India,

---

[1] Manu, III, 24. [2] III, 25. [3] IX, 98. [4] III, 51.
[5] Early History of Institutions, 324. [6] Sociology, p. 655.
[7] Norton's Leading Cases, Part I, p. 5.

any other form than the *Asura* be now observed.[1] In Bengal it is practised even among Brahmans, by those who stand low in the scale of *kulinism*, in consequence of the difficulty in which that pernicious institution has placed them in regard to marriage. The form is equally prevalent in the Western Presidency. There, "the lower castes," says Steele, "often receive money on the marriage of their females called Hoonda, which is the characteristic of the fifth (Usoor) variety, and it is suspected that Brahmans occasionally, in the present avaricious generation, incur sin on this account."[2] And in a recent case[3] before the Bombay High Court, Mr. Justice West makes the antecedent probability in favor of its prevalence one of the grounds for finding that a certain marriage among the caste called the Bhandaris was of this form. It may not be deemed unprofitable here to quote the following passage from the judgment of that learned Judge: "The different forms of marriage recognised by the Hindu law are probably to be traced historically to the customs of different tribes which afterwards coalesced to form a single community. The very name of the *Asura* form indicates it as one derived from the aboriginal inhabitants of this country, or those occupying it before the Aryan invasion. This would of itself cause the ceremony to be looked on with a degree of loathing by the sages of the strict Brahmanical school, however circumstances might compel them to tolerate it for those amongst whom it was an established custom. Manu (III, 51) denounces any father who knows the law and who receives a gratuity, however small, for giving his daughter in marriage; but the custom seems never to have

[1] 1 Strange, 43. [2] Law and Custom of Hindoo Castes, p. 159.

[3] Vijiarangam *et al.* v. Lukshuman *et al.*, 8 Bom., O. C. J., 244.

LECTURE III. died out amongst the lower castes, if indeed it has not, to some extent, obtained among the Brahmans also." In the same case it was held that the giving and receiving of money for the bride is the distinctive mark of the *Asura* marriage. But the giving of *palu*, or present of money, to the bride herself, which has been regarded as 'nothing else than a kind of rudimentary marriage settlement,' does not render the marriage an *Asura* one.[1]

Gandharba. "The reciprocal connection of a youth and a damsel with mutual desire is the marriage denominated *Gandharba*, contracted for the purpose of amorous embraces and proceeding from sensual inclination."[2] This is Manu's description of the sixth form of marriage. Though regarded as one of the four base forms of marriage,[3] in consequence of its proceeding from sensual inclination, it was formerly permitted to the military class, and is even now occasionally in practice in certain places, especially among Rajahs and Chiefs.[4] Marriages in this form, which depend merely upon the agreement of the contracting parties, resemble to some extent what are called Gretna Green marriages,—that is, runaway marriages by persons governed by the English law, at Gretna Green and elsewhere in Scotland, to evade the provisions of that law against ill-advised and clandestine marriages.

Rakshasa. "The seizure of a maiden by force from her house while she weeps and calls for assistance, after her kinsmen and friends have been slain in battle or wounded, and their houses broken open, is the marriage styled *Rakshasa*."[5]

---

[1] See Manu, III, 54; Jaikisondas Gopaldas *v.* Harkisondas Hullochandas, I. L. R., 2 Bomb., 15.

[2] Manu, III, 32.

[3] *Ibid*, III, 41.

[4] See Chuckrodhuj Thakoor *v.* Beer Chunder Joobraj, 1 W. R., 194.

[5] Manu, III, 33.

This is no doubt an extremely reprehensible form of marriage, and the very description of it is sufficient to show that it could never have prevailed in any polished society. It seems to have found a place in the institutes of the sages, either as a relic of a barbarous age preserved by tradition, though condemned by the prevailing sentiment of their time, or as an existing practice among the lawless tribes by which Hindu society was surrounded, and which occasionally claimed to come within the pale of that society by reason of unity of religion. But whether as a traditionary relic or as a contemporaneous practice in the days of Manu, it illustrates the value of ancient law as a record of the past; and the evidence furnished by that record in the present instance has been used to advantage by competent judges in ascertaining the nature of primitive marriage.[1] At the present day, when the hand of law is stronger than ever, marriage by force is not only condemned but punished.[2] **Lecture III.**

The last form of marriage, the *Pasiacha,* is thus described by Manu: *Paisacha.*

"When the lover secretly embraces the damsel, either sleeping or flushed with strong liquor, or disordered in her intellect, that sinful marriage called *Paisacha* is the eighth, and the basest." (III, 34.)

It is condemned in unqualified terms in the institutes of the sages, and is prohibited for all the classes; and it seems to have been enumerated as a form of marriage, only out of regard for the honor of the unfortunate damsel. It is a matter of some surprise, therefore, that such a high authority as Macnaghten[3] should have regarded this as an instance in which fraud is legalized by the Hindu law.

---

[1] See M'Lennan's Primitive Marriage, p. 63 *et seq.*

[2] See Indian Penal Code, s. 366.

[3] Principles of Hindu Law (3rd ed.), p. 60 note.

LECTURE III.

Of the four approved forms of marriage, the *Brahma* is the only one that now prevails, and all persons, even Sudras, are at the present day held competent to marry in that form. Of the four base forms, the *Asura* is the one that is now prevalent, and is in fact the most common form of marriage; and *Gandharba* marriages also sometimes take place.

Mode of contracting marriage.

I shall now proceed to consider the mode of contracting marriage. This consists of two parts,—the betrothment and the nuptial ceremony.

Betrothment.

The betrothment generally precedes marriage, but is not a necessary part of the nuptial rite. As betrothal in the Hindu law is sometimes mistaken for marriage, I shall describe it a little more fully. Betrothment is a promise to give a girl in marriage. It is called *vagdan*, or gift by word, as distinguished from gift by actual delivery of the bride; and its form is that of a promise by the father or other guardian of the bride in favour of the bridegroom, to give him the bride in marriage.[1] After betrothal, and separated from it by a variable interval, there comes the marriage ceremony, which will be described presently. After this, the bride, if an infant, is generally allowed, at the option of the husband however, to remain in her father's house for some time; and her first visit to her husband's house with the intention of staying there is called the *dwiragamana;* but this is no religious ceremony, and the time for it is determined by the choice of the husband or his guardian. On the first appearance of the menses, a religious ceremony is performed, which is called the *garbhadhana*, or ceremony to purify conception, which is quite

---

[1] See Sanskaratattwa, Institutes of Raghunandan, Vol. I, p. 506.

distinct from the ceremony of marriage,[1] but which is popularly named the *second marriage*. It might be perhaps from this misleading name of the ceremony that precedes consummation of marriage that English writers on the subject have been sometimes led to suppose, that all that precedes it, including the nuptial rite itself, constitutes betrothal only. Thus Sir T. Strange says: "The betrothment, once effected, by the bride and bridegroom walking seven steps hand in hand during a particular recital, the contract is perfected upon their arriving at the seventh step; and may be enforced by the husband on completion of the time."[2] But this walking of seven steps, as you will presently see, is the ceremony that completes marriage, and it forms no part of the contract of betrothal. LECTURE III.

Regarding the legal effects of betrothment, there is some difference of opinion. Some hold that betrothment, even in its strict and correct sense, constitutes marriage,[3] and it has been accordingly sometimes contended that it is irrevocable, and that a suit would lie to compel specific performance of a contract of betrothal.[4] There seems to be some authority in the Hindu law for such a contention. Thus a text of Manu declaring that "the damsel indeed whose *husband* shall die after troth verbally plighted, but before consummation, his brother shall take in marriage, &c.,"[5] shows that after betrothment the bridegroom is considered as the hus- Its legal effects.

[1] See Coleb. Dig., Bk. V, 134, note; 7 Asiatic Researches, p. 310; Remarks of Ellis, 2 Strange, 32.

[2] 1 Elements of Hindu Law, p. 37. Grady, following Strange, has fallen into the same error; see his Treatise on the Hindoo Law of Inheritance, p. 7.

[3] See Shama Charan's Vyavastha Darpana, pp. 645, 646.

[4] See Umed Kika v. Nagindas Narotamdas, 7 Bom., O. C. J., 122.

[5] IX, 69. There are other texts of Manu to the same effect, see IX, 71; V, 152.

LECTURE III. band of the bride. So again, a girl betrothed to one person, but subsequently married to another, is regarded by some sages as a twice-married girl;[1] and Raghunandan, in the Suddhitattwa,[2] holds that, on the death of a damsel verbally betrothed, the families, both of her father and her husband, contract impurity for three days. There are also cases decided by the Sudder Dewani Adalut at Bombay, which seem to support this view.[3] But the more correct view is that which regards betrothment as a revocable promise of marriage not constituting actual marriage, though such revocation would be improper if without a just cause; and this is the view which is in conformity with actual practice,[4] and has received judicial sanction.[5] It is amply supported by texts,[6] of which the following may be cited as instances:—

"The nuptial texts are a certain rule in regard to wedlock; and the bridal contract is known by the learned to be complete and irrevocable on the seventh step of the married pair hand in hand, after those texts have been pronounced."—(Manu, VIII, 227.)

"If her husband die after a damsel has been given to him with water poured on his hands, and troth verbally plighted, but before she has been contracted to him by holy texts, that virgin belongs to her father alone."—(Vasistha.)[7]

"Previous to the union of man and wife, the betrothal takes place; the betrothal and the marriage ceremony together constitute lawful wedlock."—(Narada, XII, 2.)

"Once is a damsel given in marriage: he who detains her

---

1 Coleb. Dig., Bk. IV, 165. 2 Institutes of Raghunandan, Vol. II, 147.

3 1 Morl. Dig., 288, pl. 5, 7.

4 Shama Charan's Vyavastha Darpana, p. 646; Steele, 24, 160.

5 In the matter of Gunput Narain Singh, I. L. R., 1 Calc., 74.

6 See Coleb. Dig., Bk. IV, 174–181. 7 Coleb. Dig., Bk. IV, 174.

shall incur the punishment of a thief; but if a worthier bridegroom offer, he may take the damsel, though given away."—(Yajnavalkya, I, 65.)[1]

This last text is cited in the Mitakshara[2] as authority for the position that one does not incur any penalty for retraction of a promise of betrothal if there be just cause; and the case of retraction of such promise without sufficient cause is thus provided for in that treatise: "One who has verbally given a damsel in marriage, but retracts the gift, must be fined by the king in proportion to the amount of property or the magnitude of the offence, and according to the rank of the parties, their qualities and other circumstances. This is applicable if there be no sufficient motive for retracting the engagement."[3]

According to Raghunandan,[4] marital dominion over a damsel results not from *vagdan*, but from the actual gift of the bride in marriage.

Specific performance of contract of betrothal.

The question whether specific performance of a contract of betrothal can be enforced by a suit has been sometimes raised. Sir T. Strange was of opinion that it could be so enforced. In some of the earlier cases,[5] it may at first sight appear as if specific performance of the promise of betrothal had been decreed. When examined, however, they amount merely to this, that the Court directed the betrothal or promise of marriage to be carried into effect, and decreed that if it was not carried into effect within a certain limited

---

[1] Coleb. Dig., Bk. IV, 176.

[2] Ch. II, Sec. XI, 27.

[3] Ch. II, Sec. XI, 27.

[4] Udvahatattwa (Inst., Vol. II, 72).

[5] Khooshal and others *v.* Bhugwan Motee, 1 Borr., 138; Atmaram Kesoor *v.* Sheolal Mulookchund, 1 Borr., 358; Kaseeram Joeetaram *v.* Bhugwan Poorshotum, 2 Borr., 432; Deochund Natha *v.* Juvehur Behchur, 2 Borr., 528; Mt. Ruliyat *v.* Madhowjee Panachund, 2 Borr., 680:—all cited in 1 Morley, 287, 288. See also Chingleroyalo *v.* Venertaroyalo, 2 Strange, 38; and also *ibid*, 35.

LECTURE III. period, the defendant should pay a certain sum by way of damages. But in a later case,[1] the Bombay High Court held, chiefly upon the authority of the passage of the Mitakshara quoted above, that betrothal not being complete marriage, specific performance of it could not be enforced; and this decision was followed by the High Court of Bengal in the case of *Gunput Narain Singh.*[2] The point has now been settled by the Legislature, and it has been provided by the Specific Relief Act (Act I of 1877), sec. 21, clause *b*, as explained by the illustrations to that clause, that a contract of betrothal cannot be specifically enforced.

But though specific performance cannot be enforced, the party injured by the breach of a contract of betrothal is entitled to recover compensation for any pecuniary damages that might have been sustained, and also for any injury to character or prospects in life which may naturally arise in the usual course of things from such breach.[3]

Agreements in restraint of marriage.

I may here notice an important rule governing executory contracts of marriage. Every agreement in restraint of the marriage of any person other than a minor is void. This is the form in which the rule is laid down in the Indian Contract Act (Act IX of 1872).[4] What is meant by an agreement in restraint of marriage may be best illustrated by an example. In the well-known case of *Lowe* v. *Peers*,[5] the defendant had promised not to marry any person besides the plaintiff, and agreed to pay her a certain sum in the event of his marrying any other person. On an action being brought against him

---

[1] Umed Kika *v.* Nagindas Narotamdas, 7 Bom., O. C. J., 122.

[2] I. L. R., 1 Calc., 74. See also Shaikh Bhugun *v.* Shaikh Rumjan, 24 W. R., 380.

[3] Act IX of 1872, sec. 73; Addison on Contracts (5th ed.), p. 743; Shaikh Bhugun *v.* Shaikh Rumjan, 24 W. R., 380.

[4] Sec. 26.

[5] 4 Burr., 2232.

for breach of his covenant, it was held that the promise was void as being in restraint of marriage. "It is not a covenant," it was observed, "to marry the plaintiff, but not to marry any one else: and yet she was under no obligation to marry him. So that it restrained him from marrying at all in case she had chosen not to permit him to marry her." The essential difference between an agreement in restraint of marriage and a contract of betrothal lies in this, that in the latter each party being restrained from marrying any one except the other, the restraint virtually operates in furtherance of the marriage of both.

Marriage brokerage contracts, or contracts for the payment of money, or the conveyance of property, or the doing of any other act on condition of the procurement of a particular marriage, are void, on the ground that it is immoral to allow marriage to be made the subject of mercenary speculation; and, under the English law, a bond by the husband to the wife's father to induce the latter to consent to the marriage, has been held to be in the nature of a marriage brokerage contract.[1] Therefore, though the Hindu law may allow marriage in the *Asura* form, it is very doubtful whether, after the marriage is completed, the father or other guardian of the bride would be entitled to recover from the bridegroom the nuptial fee agreed upon. Marriage brokerage contracts.

In the Presidency of Bombay, we learn from Steele,[2] persons negotiating marriage, if successful, often receive from 100 to 1,000 rupees according to the difficulty of the case and the circumstances of the parties; and in Bengal, as you are aware, the *Ghataks* make large gains by negotiating marriage. But it may well be doubted how far their claims for remuneration would be enforced by Courts

---

[1] Addison on Contracts, p. 741. [2] Law & Custom of Hindoo Castes, p. 334.

LECTURE III. of Justice. But where a person had paid a sum of money to another in consideration of a promise made by the latter to give the former his sister in marriage, and the contract had been broken and the girl married to a third party, it was held that a suit would lie to recover the money paid.[1]

Ceremonies attending marriage.

I now come to the ceremonies attending the celebration of marriage. In all the forms of marriage, ceremonies of some sort are necessary. Macnaghten is of opinion that the *gandharba* is the only one of the eight modes in which no forms are necessary. He thinks that the *phul veha*, or flower marriage in Cuttack (contracted by the exchange of flower garlands between the bridegroom and the bride), is a form of *gandharba* marriage; and as the *gandharba* marriage is declared to be peculiar to the military class, he asks the question, "may not the indulgence have originated in principles similar to those by which, according both to the civil and the English law, soldiers are permitted to make nuncupative wills, and to dispose of their property without those forms which the law requires in other cases?"[2] But the correctness of this opinion of Macnaghten appears to have been questioned by the High Court of Bengal in the case of *Chuckrodhuj Thakoor* v. *Beer Chunder Joobraj*,[3] and it is contrary to the opinion of Jagannath, which is based upon the following text of Devala:— "Nuptial rites are ordained in the marriage styled *gandharba* and the rest; to this contract the nuptial fire must be made witness by the men of the three classes;"[4] and it seems that the only formality which may be dispensed with in the *gandharba* marriage is the formal gift of the bride

---

[1] Juggessur Chuckerbutty *v.* Panchcowree Chuckerbutty, 14 W. R., 151.

[2] Principles of Hindu Law, 3rd ed., p. 61 note.

[3] 1 W. R., 194.

[4] Coleb. Dig., Bk. V, 500.

by her guardian, she being in this instance considered self-given.[1] LECTURE III.

At the present day, whether marriage is celebrated strictly according to the *Brahma* form, or whether a nuptial gratuity is taken by the bride's family, the same rites are observed in all cases. These rites, however, differ in their details according to local or family usage. The most common forms of these ceremonies are given in the compendia of Kalesi, Bhavadeva, and Pasupati, and also in the Sanskartattwa of Raghunandan.[2] The ceremonies have also been described by Colebrooke in his Essay on the Religious Ceremonies of the Hindus.[3] They are upwards of three thousand years old, and contain much that is curious and interesting. It may not therefore be deemed altogether unprofitable to subjoin a brief account of these ceremonies here.

On the forenoon of the day of gift, the *nandimukh* or *vriddhi sraddha* is performed by the bride's father or other kinsman. It is the ordinary *parvana sraddha*, and is performed on this as on other sacramental occasions, under the name of *vriddhi sraddha*, with a view to render the sacrament auspicious by the blessing of departed progenitors. It is a part of that system of ancestor-worship which seems to be one of the most common forms of primitive worship,[4] and which still survives in full force in Hinduism. On the same forenoon, the ceremonious bathing of the bride takes place. The *mantras* for this occasion partake of the simplicity of the times when they were first framed; but their

[1] See Vyavastha Darpana, p 650; see also Sri Gajapaty Hari Krishna Devi Garu *v.* Sri Gajapaty Radhika Patta Maha Devi Garu, 2 Mad., 374.

[2] Institutes of Raghunandan, Vol. I, p. 506 *et seq.*

[3] Asiatic Researches, Vol. VII, p. 288.

[4] See Spencer's Sociology, Part I, Ch. XX.

LECTURE III. recital at the present day would be thought indecorous, and so they are omitted in practice.

In the evening the bridegroom comes in procession to the bride's house, and is there received with every mark of hospitality. Anciently, it was the custom of the Hindus to slay a cow for the reception of any honored guest, and hence a guest was called *goghna*, or cow-killer.[1] Accordingly a cow was usually set apart for the wedding feast, but the life of the animal used to be spared on this joyous occasion at the intercession of the guest himself. Though the slaughter of kine has long since been prohibited,[2] and is now most repugnant to Hindu notions, the practice of tying a cow and then letting it loose is still occasionally observed at the nuptial ceremony.

On the arrival of the bridegroom, the first ceremony that takes place is called the *sampradan*, or gift. It consists in offering the bridegroom *padya*, or water for washing the feet, *arghya*, or water mixed with flowers, *durva* grass, rice, and sandal paste, for washing the head, a stool or cushion to sit upon, and *madhuparka*, or a mixture of honey, curds and clarified butter, each giving and taking being accompanied with a set formula, and the recitation of certain prayers; after which, along with other presents, the bride, whose right hand is joined with that of the bridegroom (these hands being tied with *kusa*), is formally given to the bridegroom by her father or other guardian in marriage, and is formally accepted by the bridegroom, who then recites the following text called the Hymn to Love: "Who gave her? To whom did he give her? Love gave her. To love he gave her. Love was the giver. Love was the taker. Love has pervaded the ocean. With love I ac-

[1] See the Uttaracharita, Act IV.

[2] General Note to Manu, IV.

cept her. Love! may this be thine." The giver next presents a piece of gold as *dakshina,* or gratuity, to complete the gift of the bride to the bridegroom; and the skirts of the mantles of the affianced pair are then tied together, to indicate their union. The bridegroom then recites a text for the release of the cow, and she is accordingly let loose. Crude as the notions of our ancestors must have been on many subjects in the Vedic times, the hymn to Love shows that their ideas on the subject of matrimony were perhaps as refined as the most enlightened views of the present day. Parental love, to secure the future happiness of the daughter, gives her to a fit bridegroom, and conjugal love accepts her. There is nothing sordid or sensual in this notion of marriage.

The next ceremony is the *panigrahana,* or the acceptance of the bride's hand. This takes place sometimes on the wedding night, and sometimes on the day following. This part of the ceremony commences with the kindling of the nuptial fire. Various oblations to it are then made, including the *mahavyahriti homa,* or the oblation in honor of the earth, sky, and heaven. In the course of these oblations, various texts are recited, of which I may notice the following, which is recited by the bridegroom: "May thou never admit sorrow to thy breast. May thou prosper in thy husband's house, blest with his survival and viewing cheerful children." The bride next treads upon a stone, while the bridegroom recites this text: "Ascend this stone: be firm like this stone. Distress my foe; and be not subservient to my enemies." The bride is then made to walk seven steps. This is the most material of all the nuptial rites, as, according to the sages,[1] marriage be-

---

[1] Manu, VIII, 227.

LECTURE III. comes complete and irrevocable on the completion of the seventh step. These steps typify deliberation, and the taking of the final step implies that the bride deliberately enters matrimonial life. The husband then addresses the wife thus: "Having completed seven steps be my companion. May I become thy associate. May none interrupt thy association with me. May such as are disposed to promote our happiness, confirm thy association with me." Water is next poured on the hands of the married pair, while the following prayer is recited: "May waters and all the gods cleanse our hearts: may air do so; may the Creator do so; may the divine instructress unite our hearts." The husband then joins his hands with the wife's, and recites certain prayers, concluding thus: "Give thy heart to my religious duties. May thy mind follow mine. Be thou consentient to my speech. May Brihaspati unite thee unto me."

The last ceremony in marriage is called the *uttara-vivaha*. It consists of two parts, one, in which the bridegroom shows the bride the pole-star, the emblem of stability, and exhorts her to be stable in her husband's family; and the other, in which the husband takes a part of a meal, and the wife takes the remainder. This latter ceremony resembles the Roman *confarreatio*.[1] The bride is then conducted in solemn procession to her husband's abode, and there various texts are recited, such as these: "May there be cheerfulness here. May thine own kindred be kind here. May there be pleasure here. Sport thou here. May there be kindness here with me, &c." Conjugal love, therefore, and not marital despotism, is what the wife is taught to expect in her husband's abode.

---

[1] Mackenzie's Roman Law (4th ed.), p. 101.

The ceremonies performed after *Sampradan* are popularly known under the name of *Kusandika*.[1]

The account given above is in accordance with the form prescribed for those who use the Samaveda. For those who follow the other Vedas, the forms are slightly different, especially in the order of the ceremonies that follow the *Sampradan*.

In the case of the Sudras who are incompetent to perform the *homa* or oblation to fire in person,[2] the *homa* is performed vicariously through the instrumentality of a Brahman. This is in accordance with the opinion of Raghunandan, who says that a Sudra also has the right to the performance of the *homa* through a Brahman, in marriage, and so forth;[3] and the Vyavahara Mayukha,[4] and the Nirnaya Sindhu,[5] take the same view.

Necessity of their observance.

The foregoing are the ceremonies usually observed at Hindu weddings. The important question here arises, how far they are necessary to constitute a valid marriage. So far as the question depends upon the original authorities on Hindu law, it is not at all difficult to answer it in the affirm-

---

[1] Mr. Wheeler, after describing the marriage of Rama and Sita, in a note observes: "It is impossible to avoid noticing the striking resemblance between the ancient marriage ceremony as it was performed by our Aryan forefathers in their private dwellings, and the more modern rite as it is performed in Christian churches. In Protestant countries, the fire on the altar has been rejected as Jewish; it belongs rather to the old Aryan fire-worship. Again the use of holy-water has been abandoned, although it is nothing more than an old rite of purification. But in all essential particulars the ceremony is the same. The bridegroom and the bride are still placed before the altar, and the father of the bride gives away his daughter; whilst the bridegroom takes her hand in his, and pledges his troth in the presence of the altar, although the fire is wanting."—*History of India*, Vol. III, p. 42 note.

[2] Manu, X, 126.

[3] Udvahatattwa, Institutes of Raghunandan, Vol. II, p. 76.

[4] Ch. IV, Sec. V, 12—14.

[5] Ch. III, Sec. I.

LECTURE III. ative. "The nuptial texts," says Manu,[1] "are a certain rule in regard to wedlock; and the bridal contract is known by the learned to be complete and irrevocable on the seventh step of the married pair, hand in hand after those texts have been pronounced." So says Yama: "Neither by water poured on her hands, nor by verbal promise, is a man acknowledged as husband of a damsel; the marital contract is complete after the ceremony of joining hands on the seventh step of the married pair."[2] And to the same effect are the words of Vasistha: "If her husband die after a damsel has been given to him with water poured on his hands, and troth verbally plighted, but before she has been contracted to him by holy texts, that virgin belongs to her father alone."[3] So likewise Narada ordains that the essential characteristic of wifehood consists in the marriage benediction.[4] Nor are the above texts mere obsolete dicta of the sages. They have been followed by commentator after commentator, and their age has only added to their force. Medhatithi, one of the earlier commentators of Manu, holds that "the non-material quality of being an adopted son, like the quality of wifehood, is the result of the performance of *homa*."[5] So Kulluka, in his gloss on the above text of Manu, says, that wifehood is not constituted without the *saptapadi* and the nuptial texts; and Raghunandan[6] and Jagannath[7] also take the same view. And in fact the very word *patni*, lawful wife, from its etymology, implies a connection with religious rites.[8] It is true that

---

[1] VIII, 227.
[2] Coleb. Dig., Bk. IV, 175.
[3] Coleb. Dig., Bk. IV, 174.
[4] XII, 3.
[5] See Nirnaya Sindhu, Ch. III, Sec. I.
[6] Udvahatattwa.
[7] Coleb. Dig., Bk. IV, 169, Commentary.
[8] Panini, IV, i, 33; Mitak., Ch. II, Sec. I, 5.

there are some texts which apparently support the opposite view. Thus Manu says:

"The recitation of holy texts and the sacrifices ordained by the Lord of creatures, are used in marriages for the sake of procuring good fortune to brides; but the first gift is the primary cause and the origin of marital dominion." (V, 152.)

"The gift of daughters in marriage by the sacerdotal class is most approved, when they previously have poured water into the hands of the bridegroom; but the ceremonies of the other classes may be performed according to their several fancies." (III, 35.)

But the former of these two texts has reference to the origin of the husband's rights over the wife, which is therein declared to be 'the first gift;' and as Kulluk Bhatta observes, it is not meant to contradict the text in the eighth chapter[1] quoted above, which declares that the quality of wifehood is not produced without the nuptial texts and the *saptapadi*. In other words, the meaning is that a damsel given by her guardian and accepted by a man without the observance of nuptial rites, becomes subject to the rights and control of that man as her husband, without acquiring the rights and status of a wife. As for the other text, it refers to the form of the gift only, and not to the nuptial rites that follow it.

Among foreign writers who have examined the subject, Colebrooke, the highest authority, is of opinion that "the marriage is complete and irrevocable so soon as she (the bride) has taken the seventh step; and not sooner."[2] Macnaghten when he says that "the *gandharba* marriage is the

---

[1] VIII, 227.   [2] Asiatic Researches, Vol. VII, p. 303.

LECTURE III. only one of the eight modes for the legalizing of which no forms are necessary,"[1] indirectly gives his opinion that formalities are necessary in the other forms. And even Sir T. Strange, though he says that the essence of the rite consists in the consent of the parties,[2] admits that the bridal contract is perfected upon the completion of the seventh step.[3]

The necessity of marrying girls at an early age, and the consequent interference of guardians in the nuptial contract, coupled with the sacramental nature of marriage, prevent irregular and informal marriages, and render the observance of forms as strict as possible. There being, therefore, no difference between the written law and the actual practice of the Hindus on this point, one need not feel much hesitation in saying that the observance of ceremonies is necessary to constitute a valid marriage. Nor can it be said that the rules enjoining the observance of ceremonies in marriage are not strict rules of law, but are mere moral injunctions—are rules that are not imperative in their nature but are directory only. This is a distinction which English judges and lawyers constantly draw with a view to simplify the Hindu law by separating its religious from its civil element, and thus to reduce it to harmony with more advanced notions; and in doing so they are not perhaps always wrong, nor do they necessarily depart from the judge's duty of administering the Hindu law as it is; for Hindu lawyers themselves have shown the way, by getting rid of inconvenient or obsolete rules upon this principle of interpretation. The principle is in general a very sound and wholesome one. But its application to the case of marriage is not only not warranted by the language of the

[1] Principles of Hindu Law, p. 61.

[2] 1 Elements of Hindu Law, 44. [3] *Ibid*, 37.

rules, but is likely to be attended with the most mischievous consequences. Happily the question as to the validity of informal marriages among Hindus has been seldom raised. In an early case,[1] it is true that the *pandits* gave their opinion that marriage is constituted by the persons saying "I marry," &c., &c., and agreeing to marry; but that opinion is not supported by any authority, and, moreover, the parties in that case were Sikhs, not Hindus. When the question is raised, judges ought carefully to guard against readily applying the above principle to it. As Fitz James Stephen in his speech on the Native Marriage Bill observed: "Scotch law goes far when it enables a man and woman to marry each other by a few words exchanged in the course of a casual conversation; but Anglo-Indian law would go infinitely further if it held that two people could in that manner convert their children into man and wife."[2]

No doubt, the essence of the contract of marriage, like that of every other contract, consists in the intention of the parties expressed in some clear way, and the observance of form is only evidence of their intention. But considering the fact that Hindu marriages are, for the most part, contracted, not by the parties themselves, but by their guardians, and considering the absolute indissolubility of marriage in Hindu law, one must ponder long and cautiously before coming to the conclusion that the forms and ceremonies which constitute, in that law, the only safeguards against undue influence and want of due deliberation, can be rightly dispensed with. I may add that, in almost every

---

[1] *Doe dem* Juggomohun Mullick and others *v.* Saumcoomar Bebee and others, 2 Morl., 43.

[2] Supplement to the *Gazette of India*, January 27th, 1872, p. 77.

*

LECTURE III. polished system of law, some definite form, either civil or religious, is prescribed as necessary to be observed in contracting marriage.

The two primary objects to be secured by formalities in marriage are the prevention of hasty and inconsiderate marriages, and the removal of doubts as to the nature of the relation that is created. In order to secure the former object, in the absence of more rational modes, long established ceremonious forms cannot well be dispensed with. As has been well observed, "ceremonies which strike the imagination serve to impress upon the mind the force and dignity of the contract;" while their observance secures publicity to some extent, and affords some time for deliberation. As for the latter object, as was observed by Lord Brougham in *Warrender* v. *Warrender*: "The laws of each nation lay down the forms and solemnities, a compliance with which shall be deemed the only criterion of the intention to enter into the contract."[1] Hindu law has its prescribed forms, and if we hold the observance of these to be optional, it would lead to loose forms of marriage, utterly subversive of morality, and there would be the greatest difficulty in distinguishing between concubinage and marriage.[2]

It might be urged that the nuptial rites in the Hindu law are so cumbrous and minute, that an exact observance of their details is by no means easy; and that if those ceremonies are held necessary, real and *bonâ fide* marriages would stand in danger of being rendered invalid in conse-

[1] 2 Clark and Finnelly, 531.

[2] The celebrated case of Dalrymple *v.* Dalrymple (2 Haggard's Consistory Reports, 54) furnishes a striking illustration of the difficulties pointed out above.

quence of trivial defects of form. But there is no reason for this apprehension. All that is required is a substantial compliance with the forms, to show that the parties intend to contract marriage. There is a broad distinction between an intentional omission to observe the ceremonies, and a defective observance of the same by reason of accidental error or inadvertence; and it is only the former that is required to be avoided. LECTURE III.

Here an important practical question arises, which ought not to be left altogether unnoticed. The Brahmos, who form a considerable section of the Hindu community in its widest sense, intentionally and out of religious scruples, omit to observe the Hindu ceremonies of marriage, and celebrate their nuptials in a peculiar form, which is called the *Brahma* form, but which I shall call the *Brahmic*, to distinguish it from the Hindu form of that name; and the question is, are these *Brahmic* marriages valid in law? This question has been discussed in the Legislative Council and in popular assemblies; and even in domestic circles it excites deep interest in many, as it concerns the welfare of their children and children's children. The question has a double aspect. As regards the Progressive Brahmos who profess not to come within the pale of Hinduism at all,[1] it would have to be answered without reference to the provisions of the Hindu law, and upon principles of justice, equity, and good conscience, which constitute the only law for such cases. But in the case of the Adi or Conservative Brahmos who claim to be Hindus, the Hindu law cannot altogether be left out of view in answering the question. The former case not being governed by the Hindu law, presents no conflict with that law, and so it is not necessary to dwell upon it here at

[1] See Supplement to the *Gazette of India* for January 1872, p. 67.

LECTURE III. length. It will come for our consideration in a future Lecture, and at present I would only remark that there is nothing in justice, equity, and good conscience, which should necessarily invalidate a form of marriage, merely because it is new, and differs from the old and ordinary form, when such new form is recognized by a considerable body of persons. In the latter case, I venture to affirm, though with some hesitation, for the point is not considered altogether free from doubt,[1] that the *Brahmic* marriages are valid. But you must bear in mind that their validity rests upon peculiar and exceptional grounds. It is very doubtful whether custom, which has the force of law in Hindu jurisprudence, can be invoked in favor of such marriages. For custom, to have the force of law, must be ancient, while the nuptial form in question is quite of recent origin. But though custom in the ordinary sense may not sanction these marriages, still we ought to hold that they are valid. To hold otherwise would be to hold that Hindu law incapacitates a Hindu for marriage, if he has religious scruples to comply with some of its prescribed forms. This would not only be unreasonable in itself, but would be contrary to the generally tolerant character of Hinduism, which allows, within limits of course, great latitude of principle in matters of doctrine and worship. The *Brahmic* form of marriage being one that is recognized by a considerable body of persons, there can be no objection on the ground of difficulty in distinguishing marriage from inferior forms of union between man and woman. The position of the *Brahmic* marriages in relation to the Hindu law is similar to that of Jew and Quaker marriages in relation to the English law.

[1] The opinion of Mr. Cowie (Advocate-General) was against the validity of the Brahmic marriages. See Supplement to the *Gazette of India*, January 27, 1872, p. 69.

The question, as I have already said, is an important one, and within the limits that I must here propose to myself, you cannot expect anything like an adequate treatment of it. You will find the question discussed at great length in FitzJames Stephen's elaborate speech on the Native Marriage Bill.[1] The point will again occupy our attention in a future Lecture,[2] when we come to consider the customary forms of marriage among the Hindus.

In connection with the observance of formalities in marriage, as well as other matters affecting its validity, there is an important rule of evidence which you should bear in mind, namely, that if a marriage in fact is established, there would be a presumption in favor of there being a marriage in law.[3]

Time for celebration of marriage.

The time for celebration of marriage has to be fixed in accordance with various astrological and other considerations.[4] These do not affect the validity of marriage, and so I need not take any further notice of them. There is only one question connected with time which seems to have a legal aspect,—namely, whether marriage solemnized during the impurity (*asauch*) of either party owing to the birth or death of a kinsman is valid. In the case of *Ramalinga Pillai* v. *Sadasiva Pillai*,[5] it was contended that adoption during impurity was invalid, but the point was not decided, as it was found as a fact that the adoption had taken place after the period of impurity had expired. There is no reported case with reference to marriage, but in practice marriage never takes place during impurity. The reason for this is, that one under impurity cannot take part in the

---

[1] Supplement to the *Gazette of India*, Jan. 27, 1872. [2] See Lecture VI.

[3] See Inderun Valungypooly Taver *v.* Ramaswamy Pandia Talaver, 12 W. R. (P. C.), 41.

[4] See Udvahtattwa, Raghunandan's Institutes, Vol. II, p. 69; Steele, pp. 27, 164.

[5] 1 W. R. (P. C.), 25.

LECTURE III. religious ceremonies in marriage.[1] But the prohibition of marriage during impurity would hardly be regarded as anything more than a mere moral injunction.

Consummation. The usual ceremonies being observed, marriage becomes complete and irrevocable, and consummation is not necessary to render it valid. There is no distinction in the Hindu law between consummation and non-consummation.[2]

Questions of validity of marriage how far cognizable in the Courts. It was at one time doubted whether questions of the validity or invalidity of Hindu marriages not involving questions of right to property, could be tried in the Courts of this country. In the case of *Anjona Dossee* v. *Proladh Chunder Ghose*,[3] Mr. Justice Glover, following an earlier case,[4] held that such questions could not be tried by the Civil Courts; but on appeal, this decision was reversed.[5] The facts of that case were shortly these: Anjona Dossee, as the mother and guardian of her minor daughter Kuppoora (an infant of about five years of age), sued the defendant Proladh Chunder Ghose, alleging that he (defendant) had forcibly carried off Kuppoora Dossee without her consent to the house of a third party, and there had gone through a marriage ceremony with her. The suit was brought to declare that marriage invalid. The Officiating Chief Justice Norman, in delivering the judgment on appeal, observed:—

"Suits relating to marriage deal with that which in the eye of the law must be treated as a civil contract, and with civil rights arising out of that contract. Suits for relief against contracts procured by force or fraud are ordinarily cognizable by Civil Courts.

"In a suit declaring the invalidity of a marriage, the Court could grant consequential relief. It might restrain the per-

[1] See Udvahatattwa, Inst., Vol. II, p. 76. [2] 2 Str., 33. [3] 14 W. R., 132.
[4] amsurn Mitter *v.* Rakhal Doss, 11 W. R., 412. [5] 14 W. R., 403.

son alleging himself to have the rights of a husband from enforcing any claim to the custody or possession of the person of the woman founded on the supposed marriage. LECTURE III.

"If such relief could be granted, it is not easy to see why a declaratory decree under section 15 might not be made. Such a declaration may be of the greatest importance to a girl circumstanced as the infant plaintiff is. If the marriage is in fact no marriage, unless she can obtain a declaration from a Court of Justice that the marriage is null and void, unless she can obtain the protection which such Court can give her, she may be obliged to live with the defendant in a state of concubinage, or at least she will be prevented from marrying any one else. The rights which a decree in this suit may protect, with which the defendant may be restrained from interfering,—the preservation of the personal purity of the infant plaintiff and her right and power to contract a valid marriage,—are amongst the highest rights which a human being can possess; and it would be a matter deeply to be lamented if the Court had no power to protect and defend them.

"We have, however, no doubt of the existence of that power. We think that a suit such as the present, which is a suit of a civil nature, may be entertained in the Civil Courts of this country under the provisions of section 1, Act VIII of 1859, and that view seems to me to be sanctioned by the opinion of the Lords of the Privy Council in the case we have referred to.

"We think that the Court must have jurisdiction in such suit to declare the marriage void, if procured by fraud or force, and celebrated without the consent of the necessary parties or without the formalities necessary to render it a binding marriage according to Hindu Law."

LECTURE IV.

LEGAL CONSEQUENCES OF MARRIAGE.

Scope of the present Lecture—Nature of the marriage contract—Nature of the marriage contract in the Hindu law—Rights of the husband and the wife over the person of each other—Custody of an infant wife—Restraint of wife's liberty—Correction of her person—Remedy of the husband against infringement of marital rights—Restitution of conjugal rights—Cases in which restitution of conjugal rights is not allowed—Effect of change of religion on the claim for restitution of conjugal rights—Act XXI of 1866—Adultery—Effects of marriage on personal capacity—Remarriage—Supersession—Present on supersession—Remarriage of a convert to Christianity relapsing to Hinduism—Man and wife one person in Hindu law only for religious purposes—Wife may contract—She may sue and be sued—She is not exempt from arrest in execution of civil process—Husband and wife competent witnesses for or against each other—Effects of marriage on the property of the husband and of the wife—Wife entitled to a share on partition—Wife entitled to maintenance—From whom—Maintenance when allowed to a wife living apart—Maintenance when forfeited—Rate of maintenance—Arrears of maintenance—Recovery of maintenance under the Code of Criminal Procedure—Maintenance of concubines—Husband and wife how far bound by each other's contracts—Bombay Act VII of 1866—Husband or wife entitled to compensation under Act XIII of 1855—Effects of marriage on offspring—Legitimacy—Effect of marriage in a different caste on legitimacy—Presumption of legitimacy—Bastard's right to inherit—Maintenance of children—Right to give or take a son in adoption—Paternal power under the Hindu law—Maintenance of parents—Rules for women whose husbands are away—Appointment of a wife to raise up offspring.

Scope of the present Lecture.

HAVING considered between what parties and in what mode the matrimonial union can be formed, I now come to the consideration of the legal consequences of that union.

From the very nature of the conjugal relation, each party acquires certain rights over the person of the other; and in most systems of law, the property of each also becomes subject, more or less, to the rights of the other. In some countries, again, marriage attaches to one of the parties, the wife, important personal privileges and disqualifications. Besides these results which affect the parties immediately concerned, the conjugal relation is the source of other important legal consequences. It confers on the issue of the union the status of legitimacy, and thus forms the foundation of the rights of inheritance, lineal and collateral; and it is the basis of the legal, as distinguished from the natural, relation of parent and child. Without aiming at strict logical precision, these several consequences of marriage may be conveniently arranged under the following four heads: *first*, those relating to the persons of the parties; *second*, those relating to their personal capacity; *third*, those relating to their property; and *fourth*, those relating to their offspring. This division will be kept in view in discussing the topics of the present Lecture.

Nature of the marriage contract.

Here it ought to be observed that the legal consequences of marriage depend in almost every civilized country, not upon the will of the parties to it, but upon the law which governs them. Parties may choose not to marry; but if they marry at all, they must do so, not upon their own terms, but on terms fixed by the law under which they live. If they once contract the tie, they cannot afterwards break it, even if they both agree, unless the law allows it. For this reason, it has been sometimes doubted whether marriage is, properly speaking, a contract. "It is rather," says Story, "to be deemed an institution of society, founded upon the consent and contract of the parties; and in this view it has some peculiarities in its nature, character, operation, and extent of obligation, different from what belong to ordinary contracts."[1] No doubt it is not a contract in the sense in which any other agreement, such as betrothal, is a contract. In one sense, however, marriage is a true contract; for the

[1] Conflict of Laws, § 108 note.

LECTURE IV. parties when they marry, in fact enter into an agreement to perform certain duties towards each other for the rest of their lives: it is a contract to be followed by a whole life of specific performance. "But," as a distinguished Scottish judge[1] observes, "it differs from other contracts in this, that the rights, obligations or duties arising from it are not left entirely to be regulated by the agreements of parties, but are, to a certain extent, matters of municipal regulation, over which the parties have no control by any declaration of their will." The object of this interference of law with the freedom of parties in their mutual dealings, is to guard against the consequences of individual caprice and want of foresight, in a transaction which is of the most serious importance not only to themselves, but to society in general. How far it is justifiable is another question, which it would be foreign to my present purpose to discuss. It will be sufficient here to observe that such interference marks to some extent a backward state of social progress. It was more extensive in ancient society than it is now, and it shows that the law has not full confidence in the judgment of the people in matters touching their own interests. There has, however, been a steady advance towards reducing this interference of the law as regards marriage. Thus, in England, though by the common law the wife loses all her rights of holding property independently of her husband during coverture, yet this rule has been allowed to be evaded by means of marriage settlements,[2] and now important exceptions to it have been created by the Married Woman's Property Act, 33 and 34 Vict., c. 93. So, as

[1] Lord Robertson in Fergusson on Marriage and Divorce, 397, quoted in Story's Conflict of Laws, § 109.

[2] See Stephen's Commentaries, Bk. III, Ch. II.

regards divorce, though the law regards marriage as generally indissoluble, and disfavours separation, arrangements for separation have long been allowed.[1] The Code Napoleon, while it enacts that "married persons cannot derogate from the rights resulting from the power of the husband over the persons of his wife and his children," nor from the prohibitory regulations of the Code, at the same time declares that "the law does not regulate the conjugal association as respects property, except in default of special agreements which the married parties may make as they shall judge convenient, provided they are not contrary to good morals."[2] Before the Revolution, the law of France regarded marriage as indissoluble; but the Code Napoleon allows divorce and separation of persons;[3] and though divorce was for a time abolished, it has been again allowed.[4]

Nature of the marriage contract in the Hindu law.

The Hindu law on this subject still retains its archaic character. Marriage in that law is not merely a contract but also a sacrament; and the rights and duties of the married parties are determined solely by the law, and are incapable of being varied by their agreement. As Manu emphatically declares, "neither by sale, nor desertion, can a wife be released from her husband."[5] Following the spirit of this rule, the High Court of Bengal, in the case of *Seetaram* v. *Mussamut Aheeree Heeranee,* said: "It is contrary to the policy of the law to allow persons by a contract between themselves to avoid a marriage on the happening of any event they may think fit to fix upon."[6] The event in that case was the husband's not continuing to live in the wife's village.

---

[1] See Stephen's Commentaries, Bk. III, Ch. II.

[2] Arts. 1387, 1388.

[3] Arts. 229—233, 306—311.

[4] Mackenzie's Roman Law, 4th ed., pp. 125, 126.

[5] IX, 46.

[6] 20 W. R., 49.

LECTURE IV.

The duties of man and wife form one of the eighteen titles of law according to Manu[1] and other sages.[2] As a text of the Smriti[3] declares litigation between man and wife to be illegal, Jagannatha opens his disquisition on this title of law with the question, "Is it not impossible that there should be such a title of judicial procedure as the Duties of Man and Wife, since litigation is forbidden in a controversy between man and wife, by a text of civil law cited in the Mitakshara?"[4] He notices several answers, of which the substance is, that such litigation is never laudable, and that it ought to be discouraged, though it must be sometimes allowed from the necessity of the case.

I now proceed to notice the legal consequences of marriage under the Hindu law, and first those relating to the persons of the parties.

Rights of the husband and the wife over the person of each other.

It follows from the very nature of the matrimonial relation that the husband and the wife must each be entitled to the society of the other. It is one of the express conditions in the nuptial vow of the Hindus that each party is to become the associate of the other.[5] Accordingly Manu declares, "Let mutual fidelity continue till death." "Let a man and woman united by marriage, constantly beware, lest at any time disunited they violate their mutual fidelity."[6] And the sages denounce the desertion or neglect of either party by the other without just cause as an act punishable in this world and in the next.[7] While the wife is directed to revere the husband as a god,[8] the husband is likewise

---

[1] VIII, 7.
[2] Narada, Pt. I, Ch. I, 19.
[3] Colebrooke's Digest, Bk. III, Ch. I, 10.
[4] *Ibid*, Bk. IV, Ch. I, Sec. I.
[5] See Asiatic Researches, Vol. VII, p. 303.
[6] IX, 101, 102.
[7] Colebrooke's Digest, Bk. IV, 57—61, 63, 72.
[8] Manu, V, 154.

required to honor a virtuous wife.[1] Nor is conjugal association limited to temporal purposes alone: religious rites are ordained in the Vedas to be performed by the husband in company with the wife.[2] So sacred and peculiarly favored is the association between man and wife in the eye of law, that our Penal Code, while punishing the harbouring of offenders generally, does not regard it an offence when the harbouring is by the husband or wife of the offender.[3]

So far the duties of the husband and the wife with respect to each other's person are reciprocal. But perfect equality of rights in the married couple has never yet been allowed by any system of law. Without denying the position maintained by some of the most advanced thinkers of our age, that conjugal society in equality is the best form of that society, it must be admitted that such equality is practically allowable only for persons of a high degree of culture; and that in the majority of cases, some form of domestic government is necessary to prevent disorder and discord, which would otherwise inevitably arise from the conflict of opposing wills, both equally supreme, in persons bound to live together. And if there must be inequality, it is not difficult to see that it must be in favor of man. "In his hands," to use the language of Bentham, "the power maintains itself. Give the authority to the woman, and every moment a revolt would break out on the part of her husband."[4] This inequality was originally very great, but the tendency of society has been to reduce it as far as possible. The Hindu law in respect of this inequality partakes to some extent no doubt, of the character of other archaic systems; but on the

---

[1] Manu, III, 55.

[2] Manu, IX, 96.

[3] Sec. 212.

[4] Theory of Legislation, p. 230.

LECTURE IV. whole, as you will see in the end, it is far more equitable towards the female sex than most of those systems.

As a rule, in the Hindu law, the state of women is one of perpetual tutelage. "Their fathers," says Manu, "protect them in childhood; their husbands protect them in youth; their sons protect them in age: a woman is never fit for independence."[1] Youth in this text is explained by Kulluka to mean coverture. The same rule is laid down by other sages, and adopted by authoritative commentators, such as Vijnaneswar and Sulpani.[2] Accordingly, after marriage, a woman, whether a major or a minor, comes under the protection and guardianship of her husband.[3] If the husband is himself, by reason of minority or the like, under the authority of another, the wife comes under the control of that other. This is perhaps what is indicated by the fact that by marriage a woman's *gotra*, or connection by birth with her primitive stock, is by a fiction of law supposed to be changed, and she is regarded as affiliated to the *gotra* of her husband.[4] It is a change of no consequence now, but seems to have meant at one time the transfer of a woman from the patriarchal authority of one family to that of another. This incident of marriage had its counterpart in the Roman law, by which the wife came under the *manus* or authority of her husband by being supposed to become his daughter.[5]

Custody of an infant wife.

The custody of an infant wife belongs, as a rule, not to her parents but to her husband. In the case of *Kateeram Dokanee* v. *Mussamut Gendhenee and others*,[6] Mr. Justice Markby observed: "The marriage of an infant being under

---

[1] IX, 3. [2] Colebrooke's Digest, Bk. IV, 4, 6.

[3] Macnaghten's Principles of Hindu Law, 104.

[4] See Udvahatattwa, Inst., Vol. II, p. 72.

[5] See Maine's Ancient Law, p. 155; Sandars' Justinian, p. 112.

[6] 23 W. R., 178.

the Hindoo law a legal and complete marriage, the husband, in my opinion, has the same right as in other cases to demand that his wife shall reside in the same house with himself. I do not think that any Court can deprive the husband of this right except upon some tangible and definite grounds, which show that, under the special circumstances of the case, the wife is absolved from this duty, and her parents or guardians from the duty of surrendering her to her husband; and we cannot, in my opinion, say, without contravening the Hindoo law, that infancy of a wife constitutes such a ground, though it might, I think, be right in the case of a very young girl to require the husband to show that she would be placed by him under the immediate care of some female member of his family." Where, however, a well-established custom exists 'for a child-wife to remain away from her husband, and not to come to live with him in his house until a certain event has occurred,' such custom has been recognized by the Courts.[1]

By the Acts relating to the guardianship of minors (Act XL of 1858, section 27, and Act XX of 1864, section 31) it is provided that nothing in those Acts shall authorize the appointment of a guardian of the person of a female whose husband is not a minor.

When the husband is himself a minor, his guardian would, as a rule, be also the guardian of the wife. This would follow from the rule that after the husband's death, his nearest kinsman is the guardian of the widow in preference to her father or any of her paternal relations.[2] But

---

[1] Suntosh Ram Doss v. Gera Pattuck, 23 W. R., 22; see also Steele, pp. 29, 165.

[2] Colebrooke's Digest, Bk. IV, 13; Macnaghten's Precedents of Hindu Law, Ch. VII, Cases i and iii.

 in exceptional cases, the Courts, as representing the sovereign who is the universal guardian in Hindu law,[1] may allow an infant wife during the minority of her husband to remain under the guardianship of her parents in preference to that of her husband's relations.

Restraint of wife's liberty.

Under the Hindu law, as indeed under most other systems, the liberty of the wife is liable to be considerably restrained by the husband. The duty of attendance on her husband, which is so strongly inculcated,[2] obliges her to follow him wherever he chooses to reside. And it is a general principle of law that the domicile of the wife follows that of her husband.[3] She is also bound to refrain from going to any place where her husband forbids her to go. Manu says: "Drinking spirituous liquor, associating with evil persons, absence from her husband, rambling abroad, unseasonable sleep, and dwelling in the house of another, are six faults which bring infamy on a married woman."[4] Being accustomed to seclusion almost from infancy, Hindu women seldom feel this restraint on their liberty with any degree of keenness. Nor would a Hindu husband be punishable under the Penal Code (section 339) for enforcing this restraint, as the person restrained in this case has no right to go wherever she chooses.

A man may deprive a disloyal wife of all her enjoyments and comforts, and make her live on bare subsistence.[5] The husband is enjoined to restrain the wife in various ways, to preserve her from vice; but after all, says Manu: "By

[1] Manu, VIII, 27, 28; Colebrooke's Digest, Bk. V, 450—453; 1 Strange, 71.

[2] Colebrooke's Digest, Bk. IV, 91, 92.

[3] Story's Conflict of Laws, § 46; Act X of 1865, ss. 15, 16.

[4] IX, 13.

[5] Colebrooke's Digest, Bk. IV, 81—83.

confinement at home, even under affectionate and observant guardians, they are not secure; but those women are truly secure who are guarded by their own inclinations."[1] LECTURE IV.

Correction of her person.

A wife, according to Manu, may be corrected when she commits faults, 'with a rope or small shoot of a cane; but on the backpart only of the body, and not on a noble part by any means;' and the rule is qualified by the provision that he who strikes her otherwise than by this rule incurs the guilt of a thief.[2] Barbarous as this rule is, it is not peculiar to the Hindu law. There was such a rule in the Civil law. And even in a system regarded as more polished, a similar rule was at one time well recognized; and we read in Stephen's Commentaries on the Laws of England, that though this power of correction began to be doubted in the reign of Charles II, "yet the lower rank of people, who were always fond of the old common law, still claim and exert their antient privilege: and the Courts of law will still permit a husband to restrain his wife of her liberty, in case of any gross misbehaviour."[3] But the rule in the Hindu law is seldom carried into execution, and the weight of Manu's authority is in this instance almost balanced by a text of high authority, which says: "Strike not even with a blossom a wife guilty of a hundred faults."[4] And later Hinduism, though justly meriting the reproach of being the cause of many social evils, has in this instance helped to raise the position of the wife, by identifying her with the primary divinity Sakti herself, and making her person sacred against the least ungentle touch. I may add that our Penal Code makes no exception in favour of the husband's right to chastise the wife.

---

[1] IX, 12. [2] VIII, 299, 300. [3] Vol. II, pp. 277, 278 (5th ed.)
[4] Colebrooke's Digest, Bk. III, Ch. I, 11, note.

LECTURE IV.

In an early case, it was held that an action could not be maintained for loss of character by a wife against her husband under the *Sastra*, because a woman's husband is like unto her god, and she must remain obedient to his orders and conform to his will.[1] The correctness of this ruling is open to question. For the Hindu law not only directs the wife to revere the husband as a god, but it also directs the husband to honor the wife. But whatever doubts there might have been on this point, have now been removed. And the Indian Penal Code, however unseemly its interference may be, will not allow any husband to trifle with the reputation of his wife with impunity.

No system of law has ever surpassed our own in enjoining on the wife the duty of obedience to the husband and veneration for his person. It is inculcated by the highest authority that "though unobservant of approved usages, or enamoured of another woman, or devoid of good qualities, yet a husband must constantly be revered as a god by a virtuous wife."[2] Nor have precepts like these been without their effect. The feelings which they serve to engender, often enable the wife calmly to bear her lot however unhappy, and to try to propitiate a cruel husband; and often prevent those vain bickerings which can only embitter life.

Remedy of the husband against infringement of marital rights.

Such being the rights which the husband acquires by marriage over the wife's person, the next question is how they are to be enforced in case of infringement.

---

[1] Deokoonwur *v.* Umbaram Lala, 1 Borr., 370, cited in 1 Morley's Digest, 288, pl. 11.

[2] Manu, V, 154.

Where the wife is an infant, and the husband seeks to have her in his custody, the proper course is to proceed according to the provisions of Act IX of 1861. The husband may also by a civil suit obtain an injunction upon any person detaining his wife, to abstain from putting any obstruction in the way of the wife's returning to her husband; but no order can be made upon such person directing him to send the wife to her husband.[1]

Restitution of conjugal rights.

Where the wife is qualified by her age to perform her conjugal duties, the proper remedy for the husband is a suit for restitution of conjugal rights. It was at one time doubted whether such a suit would lie in the Civil Courts of India, and the ground for such doubt was the difficulty of enforcing the performance of conjugal duties in their detail; but the point has been settled by the decision of the Privy Council in the case of *Moonshee Buzloor Ruheem* v. *Shumsoonnissa Begum.*[2] In that case the Judicial Committee observed: "Upon authority then, as well as principle, their Lordships have no doubt that a Mussulman husband may institute a suit in the Civil Courts of India for a declaration of his right to the possession of his wife and for a sentence that she return to cohabitation, and that that suit must be determined according to the principles of the Mahomedan Law. The latter proposition follows not merely from the imperative words of Regulation IV of 1793, section 15, but from the nature of the thing. For since the rights and duties resulting from the contract of marriage vary in different communities, so, especially in India, where there is no general marriage law, they can be only ascertained by

---

[1] Lall Nath Misser *v.* Sheoburn Pandey, 20 W. R., 92. But see Hurka Shunkur *v.* Raeejee Munohur, 1 Borr., 353, 1 Morley's Digest, 288, pl. 11.

[2] 8 W. R., P. C., 3; or 11 Moore's Indian Appeals, 551.

LECTURE IV. reference to the particular law of the contracting parties." Though the case was one between Mahomedans, the rule laid down evidently applies *mutatis mutandis* to the Hindus, and it has been so applied.[1] But the form of the decree in such suits, and the mode of executing it, have been points for some controversy. It seems to have been sometimes held,[2] that the decree should direct the delivery of the wife bodily into her husband's hands, and the language of article 34 of the second schedule of the Limitation Act (1877) which provides for suits for the recovery of a wife, might perhaps be referred to as favoring such a view. But the provisions of the Limitation Law are no safe guide in such matters; and it may now be taken as settled that the proper form of the decree should be this: "that the plaintiff is entitled to his conjugal rights, and that his lawful wife, the defendant, be ordered to return to his protection."[3]

Regarding the mode of execution of such a decree, there was some difference of opinion in the Indian Courts. While it was held by the High Court of Bengal in the case of *Gatha Ram Mistree* v. *Moohita Kochin Atteah Domoonee*,[4] that the decree in such cases could only have the effect of a declaratory decree, and was incapable of enforcement by any coercive process against the wife, the Bombay High Court ruled,[5] that in case of disobedience, the decree could be enforced by imprisonment of the wife under section 200 of Act VIII of 1859. The question has now been settled

---

[1] Kateeram Dokanee *v.* Mussamut Gendhenee, 23 W. R., 178.

[2] Hurka Shunker *v.* Raeejee Munohur, 1 Borr., 353, cited in 1 Morley's Digest, 288, pl. 11.

[3] Koobur Khansama *v.* Jan Khansama, 8 W. R., 467; Chotun Bebee *v.* Ameer Chund, 6 W. R., 105.

[4] 3 W. R., 179.

[5] Yamuna Bai *v.* Narayan Moreshvar Pendse, I. L R., 1 Bom., 164.

by Act X of 1877 (section 260), which provides that a decree for restitution of conjugal rights may be enforced by the imprisonment of the person and the attachment of the property of the party against whom such decree is made. But though no longer regulating the procedure in such cases, the judgment of Mr. Justice Markby, in the Bengal case just referred to, is highly instructive; and I think it may be useful to quote the following passages from it:—

"It appears to have been at one time thought that in this country the duty of cohabitation should be enforced by seizing and making over the recreant party bodily to the claimant, and cases are mentioned in which this has been directed in the case of a wife refusing to return to her husband. I am not aware of any case in which it has been suggested that similar violent measures should be taken against a husband refusing to receive his wife; and the cases in which a wife has been so treated are obviously based upon the notion that the husband purchases the wife at marriage, and that she thereby becomes an article of his property. Widely as this notion has prevailed in the world, I need scarcely say, that it is wholly abhorrent to the Hindoo law.

* * * * *

"I do not, indeed, think it likely that any one will contend that the bare declaration of the existence of the relation, even if not 'relief' in the technical sense of that term, is not of the greatest value and assistance to the parties: what seems to be considered is that the Courts *must*, in order to be logically consistent, follow up this declaration with all the powers which they possess.

"That the Courts, however, are not hemmed in by any such necessity is, I think, indisputable. The simplest and

LECTURE IV. most direct, and indeed the only really effectual, mode of enforcing the obligation, and, therefore, the one to be adopted, if the Courts have no discretion in the exercise of their power, is to bring the parties together by force. But this has been universally repudiated, not only in India, as is above shown, but in every other country as shocking to our feelings of humanity. The alternative of forcing the recusant party into compliance by imprisonment is a course which to my mind has little to recommend it by comparison, and though not quite as universally condemned has also been very generally repudiated. During the anxious enquiry, which I have thought it my duty to make upon this subject, I have ascertained that, upon the continent of Europe, the right both of the husband and of the wife to cohabitation (in the etymological sense), the husband selecting the place of residence, is everywhere considered as altogether beyond dispute. So also is the right to proceed against and to punish any third person who detains a wife from her husband: so also is the right of the husband to maintain a suit against the wife if she refuses to acknowledge the marital rights. But all attempts at enforcing this duty by compulsion have been abandoned or very nearly so. The only trace of compulsion which I have found is in some smaller states of Germany, where a very small fine or a few days' simple confinement of the woman appears to be allowed. If this produces no effect, no further punishment can be inflicted. The Prussian Courts have expressly decided that no direct compulsion whatever can be applied. The matter has been the subject of considerable discussion in Austria and in France. In the latter country I am informed on the highest authority that the question has been settled against the use of compulsion. In Austria I am not sure that the question has been finally set at rest, but I have reason to believe that the leaning is strongly against the use of any such means. LECTURE IV.

"If we consider the law of England, I think the difficulties about the Civil Court attempting to enforce by compulsion the observance of conjugal duties are in no way lessened. Perhaps some persons would be inclined at first sight to treat the law of England as affording an example of the almost unbounded exercise of judicial power in this direction: and if we look to forms and words only, it is so. The old ecclesiastical Courts, that is, the Church, claimed to have power to enforce specifically the performance of conjugal duties in their minutest particulars, and gave decrees accordingly. But inasmuch as these Courts soon found that they had no effectual independent power of enforcing their decrees when pronounced (3 Black. Comm., 101), this claim was not so substantial as at first sight appears. I am unable to find any exact information in any books available to me as to the exact proceedings which could be taken upon the decree of an ecclesiastical Court for the restitution of conjugal rights. Undoubtedly, the ecclesiastical Courts had a right to call in the ordinary civil power in aid of its own weak authority (Black., *ubi supra*), but whether from the difficulty of the procedure, or the contempt entertained for those who invoked the assistance of the Court for such purposes (3 Black., 94), such extremities were, I believe, very rarely proceeded to. No doubt, the Court which now exercises jurisdiction in matters matrimonial in place of the old ecclesiastical Courts has the same power of enforcing its decrees as the Court of Chancery, but I can only find three cases in the reports since the new Court was established in which writs have been actually issued. It is

LECTURE IV. significant that, in two of these cases, the recusant party had already escaped out of the country.

"But surely when we look to the law of England for a guide, it is where that law is in harmony with the general principles of equity and jurisprudence that we should adopt it; not where it is exceptional. That the English law on the subject of enforcing conjugal rights is exceptional, I have no manner of doubt. It is based on the canon law or the law of the Church, and as far as I can gather, the following are the propositions which that law maintained:—(1) that all sexual intercourse, except between husband and wife, is a mortal sin; (2) that marriage is a divine institution entirely under the control of the Church; (3) that all marriages not sanctioned by the Church are unlawful; (4) that divorce is impossible; (5) that the Church can release the parties from their conjugal duties; and (6) that they can enforce these duties in the minutest particulars. The law of England has, in modern days, to a very great extent, rejected these pretensions and modified these views, but they have not as yet been radically removed: rather, however, in my opinion, because they produce but small practical evils, than from any approval of the principles on which they rest."

We have hitherto considered only the case of the husband seeking to enforce his conjugal rights; but the same rules apply where the wife is the wronged party, and seeks redress.

Cases in which restitution of conjugal rights is not allowed.

Though, as a rule, either spouse is entitled to a decree for restitution of conjugal rights against the other, there are cases in which such decree will not be granted. Thus, where a custom binding upon a particular class or caste is established, by which the husband is not to cohabit with his wife until a second ceremony is gone through after marriage, a claim for restitution of conjugal rights will not be enforced where such ceremony has been neglected.[1] LECTURE IV.

How far cruelty and ill-treatment would be an answer to a suit for restitution of conjugal rights is an important practical question. Judging from the precept of Manu that even the worst husband is to be revered as a god,[2] it might seem that cruelty and ill-treatment would not excuse a wife's non-performance of conjugal duties. But the Hindu law is not really so cruel. It excuses a wife who is averse from a husband who is a lunatic, or a deadly sinner, or an eunuch, or a person afflicted with any loathsome disease.[3] Following this spirit of the Hindu law, the High Court of Bombay in one case[4] refused to decree restitution of conjugal rights in favor of a husband who was suffering from leprosy and syphilis.

It is not every unkind act that would disentitle a husband to enforce his marital rights. The mere taking of a wife's jewels, or the marrying of a second wife, has been held to be no bar to a Hindu husband's claim for restitution of conjugal rights.[5] In *Moonshee Buzloor Ruheem* v. *Shumsoonissa Begum*, their Lordships of the Privy Council observed: "It seems to them clear that if cruelty in a degree rendering it unsafe for the wife to return to her husband's dominion were established, the Court might refuse to send her back. It may be, too, that gross failure by the husband of the per-

---

1 Bool Chand Kalta *v.* Mussamut Janokee, 24 W. R., 228; 25 W. R., 386.

2 V, 154.

3 Manu, IX, 79.

4 Bai Premkuvar *v.* Bhika Kallianji, 5 Bom., A. C. J., 209.

5 Jeebo Dhon Banyah *v.* Mussamut Sundhoo, 17 W. R., 522; see also Verasvami Chetti *v.* Appasvami Chetti, 1 Mad., 375; Sitanath Mookerjee *v.* Sreemutty Haimabutty Dabee, 24 W. R., 377.

LECTURE IV. formance of the obligations which the marriage contract imposes on him for the benefit of the wife, might, if properly proved, afford good grounds for refusing to him the assistance of the Court. And as their Lordships have already intimated, there may be cases in which the Court would qualify its interference by imposing terms on the husband."[1]

The question, what constitutes legal cruelty sufficient to bar a claim for restitution of conjugal rights, has been very fully discussed by Mr. Justice Melvill in *Yamuna Bai* v. *Narayan Moreshvar Pendse*,[2] and the conclusion arrived at is, that the Hindu law on the question of what is legal cruelty between man and wife would not differ materially from the English law; that to constitute legal cruelty there must be actual violence of such a character as to endanger personal health or safety, or there must be reasonable apprehension of it; and that mere pain to the mental feelings, such for instance as would result from an unfounded charge of infidelity, however wantonly caused, or keenly felt, would not come within the definition of legal cruelty.

Where a husband had ill-treated a wife on account of a favorite mistress, and had agreed to separate from the wife, and had refused her maintenance during the period of separation, it was held that he was not entitled to insist upon restitution of conjugal rights.[3]

Conjugal infidelity in a wife would bar her claim for restitution of conjugal rights. The Hindu law allows a disloyal wife to be forsaken.[4]

---

[1] 11 Moore's Indian Appeals, 615; 8 W. R., P. C., 15.

[2] I. L. R., 1 Bom., 164.

[3] Moola v. Nundy and Mussumat Poonia, 4 N. W. P., 109.

[4] Colebrooke's Digest, Bk. IV, 79, 80.

Effect of change of religion on the claim for restitution of conjugal rights.

A party who has renounced Hinduism is not entitled to enforce a claim for restitution of conjugal rights against a husband or a wife who remains a Hindu. The Hindu law allows one to forsake a degraded husband, or a degraded wife,[1] and degradation from caste is a natural consequence of apostacy. Act XXI of 1850 by enacting that loss of caste or change of religion shall not inflict on any person forfeiture of *rights* or property, seems to throw some doubt on the point. But the remarks of Mr. Justice Campbell in *Muchoo* v. *Arzoon Sahoo*[2] go a great way in support of the rule stated above. After holding that the right to the custody of children is a right within the meaning of Act XXI of 1850, the learned Judge observed:

"The pleader for the appellant further argued that no one can be permitted so to use his right as to deprive any other person or persons of *their* rights. For instance, he says, a husband who becomes a Christian will not be permitted to claim the person of a wife who remains a Hindoo. This is so far true; and in this case, the claim to the wife was rightly dismissed, but was, I think, dismissed simply for the reason that, admitting the husband's *primâ facie* claim to the custody of the wife, that claim may be defeated by a reasonable plea. If a wife pleads that her husband beats and ill-uses her in such a way that she cannot reasonably be required to live with him, and that plea is made out, doubtless the Court will not enforce a restitution of conjugal rights. So also, if she pleads that the husband, by change of religion, has placed himself in that position that she cannot live with him without doing extreme violence to her religious opinions and the social feelings in which she

[1] Colebrooke's Digest, Bk. IV, 58, 62, 151.

[2] 5 W. R., 235.

LECTURE IV. has been brought up, and in the enjoyment of which she married, that plea would also be a good plea."

So, Sir Adam Bittleston on one occasion said:[1]

"So far, however, as Hindoo law is concerned, it seems to me enough to say that, in my opinion, a Hindoo married woman who deserts her husband, becomes a convert to Mahomedanism, and adopts the habits and lives as the wife of a Mussulman, is altogether out of the pale of Hindoo law; that she ceases to have any recognized legal *status* according to that law, which counts her as one dead, or at least recognizes her existence only as an object of charity. This is not inconsistent with such passages as that cited from Manu: 'That neither by sale nor desertion can a wife be released from her husband;' which certainly have reference to persons still within the pale of Hindoo law. It seems to me, however, at variance with the spirit of Hindoo law, to hold that it concerns itself with a woman in such case, as far as to impose on her any obligation not to marry again, *provided the second husband be not a Hindoo*; and if she does marry again, the validity of that marriage must, I think, depend upon the law of the sect to which she has become a convert."

But I must tell you that the decisions of our Courts have not been uniform on this point. Thus in one case,[2] Sir W. Burton is reported to have ordered the wife of a converted Brahman to be restored to him upon *habeas corpus*; and in another case,[3] the Agra Sudder Court held that loss of caste by a husband could not dissolve his marriage, or bar his claim to the possession of the wife's person.

[1] Rahmed Beebee *v.* Rokeya Beebee, 1 Norton's Leading Cases on Hindu Law, 12.

[2] *In re* the Wife of P. Streenevassa, 1 Norton's Leading Cases on Hindu Law, 13.

[3] Mussumat Emurtee *v.* Nirmul, N. W. P. Rep., 1864, p. 583.

Considering, however, the feelings of those who really profess the Hindu faith, it would be a matter of extreme hardship, to say the least, to enforce restitution of conjugal rights in such cases; and I should therefore venture to affirm that the view taken by Mr. Justice Campbell is the proper view of the matter. **LECTURE IV.**

Act XXI of 1866. The case in which a Hindu husband or wife becomes a convert to Christianity, is provided for by Act XXI of 1866. Under that Act, a convert can sue a native husband or wife for conjugal society, and in case of refusal by such husband or wife to cohabit with the convert, on the ground of change of religion, the marriage between the parties shall be declared dissolved.

For suits for the restitution of conjugal rights, the period of limitation is two years, from the time when such restitution is demanded and refused, the party refusing being of full age and sound mind.[1]

Adultery. Adultery in Hindu law is both a deadly sin and a heinous crime; and both the adulterer and the adulteress are liable to punishment: moreover, the punishment for every act of adulterous inclination, such as talking with the wife of another man in a secluded place, or touching her apparel and ornaments, is most minutely laid down.[2] The Indian Penal Code, while it makes adultery an offence, exempts the female offender from punishment. The reason for this indulgence to her is thus stated by the Law Commissioners:

"Though we well know that the dearest interests of the human race are closely connected with the chastity of women and the sacredness of the nuptial contract, we cannot but

---

[1] Act IX of 1872, 2nd Schedule, No. 42; Act XV of 1877, 2nd Schedule, No. 35.

[2] Manu, V, 164; XI, 177; VIII, 371—385, 352—362.

LECTURE IV. feel that there are some peculiarities in the state of society in this country, which may well lead a humane man to pause, before he determines to punish the infidelity of wives. The condition of the women of this country is unhappily very different from that of the women of England and France. They are married while still children. They are often neglected for other wives while still young. They share the attentions of a husband with several rivals. To make laws for punishing the inconstancy of the wife, while the law admits the privilege of the husband to fill his zenana with women, is a course which we are most reluctant to adopt."

Adultery and acts of adulterous inclination being crimes in Hindu law, it is maintained by Macnaghten, Colebrooke, and Ellis, that an action for damages will not lie against the wrong-doer.[1] The last-named authority observes that though it is no doubt equitable to allow the husband to recover his marriage expenses against the seducer, yet there is no such remedy prescribed by the Hindu law, and that such cases ought to be governed only by that law. Sir T. Strange was, however, of a contrary opinion. According to him, a civil action for criminal conversation would lie, the case not being one which is to be governed by the Hindu law.[2] He cites a case in which the Pandit's opinion allows the plaintiff to recover his marriage expenses from the adulterer.[3] The Bombay Sadr Court in one case awarded damages to the plaintiff who sought to recover his wife from the defendant who had enticed her way;[4] and in *Soodasun Sain* v. *Lockenauth*

---

[1] Macnaghten's Principles of Hindu Law, p. 61; 2 Strange, pp. 40—44.

[2] 1 Strange's Elements of Hindu Law, p. 46.

[3] 2 *Ibid*, 41.

[4] Hurka Shunkur *v.* Raeejee Munohur, 1 Borr., 353, cited in 1 Morley's Digest, 288, pl. 11.

Mullick, reported in Montriou's Cases of Hindu Law, p. 619, the Supreme Court of Calcutta held, that a civil action for criminal conversation was maintainable between Hindu parties. With reference to the special damage to be alleged in such cases, the learned editor in a note remarks: "It was suggested that in the case of a Hindu plaintiff, the loss of caste, or pollution of the zenana, and the like, might be laid as special damage in the declaration. In the instance of a koolin brahmin with 100 wives, some of whom he may never have seen more than once, the allegation of the loss of the wife's society would not perhaps be strictly applicable."

Effects of marriage on personal capacity.

I come now to consider the effects of marriage on the personal capacity of the parties.

By marriage a Hindu enters the second order, or the order of householder. It was permitted to the men of the twice-born classes, only after the completion of their studentship. It would seem, therefore, that originally marriage marked the period when a man was released from the authority of his father or other guardian, and entered upon the management of his own affairs, both temporal and spiritual. Some trace of this is still to be found in the fact that the *nandimukh sraddha*, or the invocation of ancestors on auspicious occasions in relation to a man, is, after his marriage, required to be performed not by his father but by himself.[1]

Marriage so far unalterably fixes the relation of a man in his own family, that after that ceremony, even a Sudra cannot pass by adoption into another family.[2]

---

[1] See Raghunandan's Sraddhatattwa Institutes, Vol. I, p. 196; see also Manu, Ch. III, 78—82.

[2] Dattaka Chandrika, II, 29; 1 Strange, 91; Macnaghten's Principles of Hindu Law, p. 72. In Western India, however, a *sagotra* relation among the Sudras has been held eligible for adoption even after marriage; see Nathaji Krishnaji *v.* Hari Jagoji, 8 Bom., A. C. J., 67.

LECTURE IV.

Remarriage. The next point for notice is the capacity of parties to marry again during the continuance of a former marriage. In this respect the Hindu law is, no doubt, very much in favor of the stronger sex.

It prohibits the wife to marry again during the lifetime of the husband; and even after his death, she was not, until the passing of the Widow Marriage Act, considered competent to remarry.[1] And even where there is a custom among the lower castes for a wife to contract a second marriage, called a *natra* or *pat*, during the lifetime of the husband, on permission obtained from a *punchayet* of her own caste, the Courts of British India have refused to recognize such custom, on account of its being immoral and opposed to the spirit of the Hindu law, and have held the parties to such remarriage liable to punishment under the Indian Penal Code, as guilty of offences relating to marriage.[2] Where, however, a Hindu married woman deserts her husband, becomes a convert to Mahomedanism, and marries again, her case will not be governed by the Hindu law which regards her as dead.[3] So where either party becomes a convert to Christianity, and is repudiated by the other, the convert may obtain a decree declaring the marriage dissolved, and then by Act XXI of 1866, section 19, the wife, whether a convert or a Hindu, shall be competent to marry again, and the issue of such remarriage is declared to be legitimate, notwithstanding any provision of the Hindu law to the contrary.

---

[1] See the texts cited in Vidyasagar's 2nd Tract on Polygamy, pp. 100—109, 199—204; see also Udvahatattwa, Inst. of Raghunandana, Vol. II, pp. 62, 63; Shama Churn's Vyavastha Darpana, p. 647; Manu, V, 157.

[2] See Steele, pp. 159, 168; Reg. *v.* Karsan Goja, 2 Bom., 124; Uji *v.* Hathi Lalu, 7 Bom., A. C. J., 133; Reg. *v.* Sambhu Raghu, I. L. R., 1 Bom., 347.

[3] See Rahmed Beebee *v.* Rokeya Beebee 1 Norton's Leading Cases, p. 12.

A Hindu husband is always permitted to marry again during the lifetime of his wife, though such marriage, if contracted without just cause, is strongly disapproved.[1] "The first is the wife married from a sense of duty," and the others are regarded as married from sensual motives.[2] "With sorrow," says Daksa feelingly, "does he eat who has two contentious wives; dissention, mutual enmity, meanness, and pain distract his mind;"[3] but his commentator Jagannath, who lived at a time when *kulinism* and polygamy were widely prevalent, tries to soften the effect of the text, by showing that if the wives be complacent, none of the evil consequences would follow. The causes which justify supersession of the wife and remarriage during her lifetime, are barrenness, ill-health, ill-temper, and misconduct of the wife.[4] LECTURE IV.

Supersession.

It should be observed that supersession (which is *adhivedana* in Sanskrit) here means, as explained in the Mitakshara and the Subodhini, merely the contracting of a second marriage while the first wife lives; and it does not imply that the first wife is actually forsaken, or that her place is taken by the second, in respect of any matter except perhaps the husband's affection.[5] It is true that Vijnaneswara in one place uses supersession and desertion as synonymous, but Sulpani, another high authority, uses the term in the sense given above, and Jagannath appears to follow the latter.[6] This view is further confirmed by the rules

---

[1] Virasvami Chetti *v.* Appasvami Chetti, 1 Mad., 375.

[2] Colebrooke's Digest, Bk. IV, 51; Manu, III, 12, 13.

[3] Colebrooke's Digest, Bk. IV, 55.

[4] *Ibid*, 62—70; Manu, IX, 80, 81.

[5] Mitakshara, Ch. II, Sec. XI, 2 (note), and 35; see also Yajnavalkya, I, 73, and commentary on that text in the Mitakshara.

[6] Colebrooke's Digest, Bk. IV, 71, 72, commentary.

LECTURE IV. regarding precedence among wives, which is settled by law with a view to prevent disputes.

Formerly when intermarriage between different castes was allowed, a wife of equal class with the husband was entitled to precedence over those of a different class.[1] When there are several wives of the same class with the husband, the eldest, that is the one first married, should be associated with him in performing acts of religion, even though his younger wives be dearer to him.[2] One of the most important of these acts, which has also a legal aspect, is the taking of a child in adoption. The wife who is associated with the adopter in that act, becomes the mother of the boy adopted, and her ancestors become the maternal ancestors of the adopted son.[3] I need hardly add that this rule of precedence is merely a moral injunction, and is often violated out of partiality to a favorite wife.

Present on supersession.

If a wife is superseded without just cause, Hindu law allows her some compensation for the wrong, inadequate though it be. The measure of the compensation is given by Yajnavalkya somewhat obscurely in these words:— "To a woman whose husband marries a second wife, must be given an equal sum on account of the supersession, provided no separate property have been bestowed on her; but if any have been assigned, let him allot half."[4] Commentators are not unanimous as to the interpretation of this text. According to Vijnaneswar, "equal" here means 'equal to the sum expended for the second marriage;' according

[1] Colebrooke's Digest, Bk. IV, 47, 48.

[2] *Ibid*, 49, 51.

[3] Dattaka Mimansa, VI, 50; *Ibid*, III, 17; Colebrooke's Digest, Bk. V, p. 273, commentary, Madras ed., Vol. II, p. 394; Vyavastha Darpana, 868.

[4] II, 148.

to Srikrishna Tarkalankar, it signifies 'as much as is given to the second wife;'[1] while according to a third interpretation it means 'as much as is promised.' Jagannath considers the first two interpretations to be unsatisfactory, and concludes that a rule on the subject remains yet to be framed, on due consideration of the difficulties attending the interpretation of the text.[2] All are agreed, however, as to this, that in estimating the value of the present, account is to be taken of what has been given to the woman as her separate property; and that the word 'half' (*ardham*) in the above text means, not an exact half, but a part generally, or so much as taken together with the separate property already given, would be equal to the prescribed amount of compensation.[3] Colebrooke accepts the interpretation of Vijnaneswar as the correct one.[4]

The present on supersession is called the *adhivedanika*, and forms one of the different kinds of *stridhan*, or woman's property. It will be considered again in a future Lecture.

Remarriage of a convert to Christianity relapsing to Hinduism.

A somewhat curious case once arose regarding a Hindu's right of remarriage. A Hindu who had become a convert to Christianity, and had married according to the Christian form, became again a professing Hindu, and married a Hindu woman in the Hindu form; and the question was raised whether for this he had been rightly convicted of bigamy. The High Court of Madras answered this question in the negative, on the ground that the second marriage was not void by reason of the wife by the first marriage being still alive, as the Hindu law which governed

---

[1] Mitakshara, Ch. II, Sec. XI, 35; Dayakrama Sangraha, Ch. VI, 31.

[2] Colebrooke's Digest, Bk. V, 466, commentary.

[3] Mitakshara, Ch. II, Sec. XI, 35; Colebrooke's Digest, Bk. V, 87, commentary; Vyavahara Mayukhu, Ch. IV, Sec. X, 3; Vivada Chintamani, Tagore's translation, p. 258. But see Dayakrama Sangraha, Ch. VI, 28.

[4] See 2 Strange's Hindu Law, 51.

S

LECTURE IV. the prisoner's second marriage, would ignore the first marriage altogether.[1]

Man and wife one person in Hindu law only for religious purposes.

The Hindu law, while it yields to no system in maintaining the unity of man and wife, is more equitable than other systems such as the English, as it leaves to women a much larger share of freedom in the exercise of their rights during coverture. Marriage according to the Vedas is a union of flesh with flesh and bone with bone.[2] Accordingly Brihaspati says: "In scripture and in the code of law, as well as in popular practice, a wife is declared to be half the body of her husband, equally sharing the fruit of pure and impure acts."[3] So Manu: "The husband is even one person with his wife for all religious, not civil, purposes. Neither by sale nor desertion can a wife be released from her husband"[4] You will thus observe that the identity of person between man and wife does not extend to civil purposes; and that therefore, the peculiar and often embarrassing consequences of the legal identity of husband and wife in the English law, such as that the husband cannot make a gift to the wife, and that the wife cannot sue or hold property alone,[5] do not exist in our law. A Hindu married woman may, during coverture, hold and enjoy property in her own right independently of her husband.[6] It is true that Manu says: "Three persons—a wife, a son, and a slave—are declared by law to have in general no wealth exclusively their own: the wealth which they may earn is regularly acquired for

[1] 3 Mad., App. (Criminal Cases), vii.

[2] Dayabhaga, Ch IV, Sec. II, 14.

[3] *Ibid*, Ch. XI, Sec. I, 2.

[4] IX, 45, 46.

[5] Stephen's Commentaries, Bk. III, Ch. II.

[6] Colebrooke's Digest, Bk. V, 475, 478; Dayabhaga, Ch. IV, Sec. I, 21; Ramasami Padeiyatchi *v.* Virasami Padeiyatchi, 3 Mad., 272.

the man to whom they belong."[1] But commentators have restricted the application of this text so far as it relates to the wife, to such wealth only as is earned by mechanical arts and the like.[2] A married woman may also obtain property by gift from her husband.[3] It may be observed that the tendency of modern legislation has been to remove all personal disqualifications for holding or enjoying property, arising from coverture. Thus the Indian Succession Act (section 4) provides that no person shall by marriage become incapable of doing any act in respect of his or her own property which he or she could have done if unmarried.

Wife may contract.

Coverture in Hindu law does not disqualify a woman from entering into contracts. "A Hindu female," observed Justice Nanabhai Haridas, "is not, on account of her sex, absolutely disqualified from entering into a contract. In the enumerations of persons incompetent to contract given by Manu, Yajnavalkya, Katyayana, and Gotama,[4] a woman, as such, is not included; and marriage, whatever other effect it may have, does not take away or destroy any capacity possessed by her in that respect."[5] And Yajnavalkya and Katyayana by declaring that the wife is bound to pay the debts contracted by her, clearly recognize her power to contract.[6] A Hindu married woman is, therefore, under the Indian Contract Act (section 11), competent to contract, if not disqualified by reason of minority or unsoundness of mind.

---

[1] VIII, 416.

[2] Vyavahara Mayukhu, Ch. IV, Sec. X, 7; Viramitrodaya, Chapter on Stridhana; Smriti Chandrika, Ch. IX, Sec. I, 16.

[3] Colebrooke's Digest, Bk. V, 475.

[4] *Ibid*, Bk. II, Ch. IV, 57, 58, 61, 66.

[5] Nathubhai Bhailal *v.* Javher Raiji, I. L. R., 1 Bom. 121; see also 1 Strange. 276.

[6] Colebrooke's Digest, Bk I, Ch. V, 210, 211.

LECTURE IV.

She may sue and be sued.

A Hindu married woman may sue and be sued alone and in her own name.[1] She may also sue and be sued by her husband, though such suits are discreditable and ought not to be encouraged.[2]

English law, while it disqualifies a *feme covert* as a rule from managing her own property, entering into contracts, and suing in her own name, gives her as a compensating advantage, exemption from liability to be sued alone except in certain cases.[3] The position of the Hindu wife is less advantageous in this respect, and so it ought to be. For, if the law allows her to manage her own property, to enter into contracts on account of herself, and to carry on her own suits, it is but fair that it should make her alone answerable for her own liabilities.

She is not exempt from arrest in execution of civil process.

Under the Civil Procedure Code of 1859, though a Hindu female, by reason of her not appearing in public, was exempt from personal appearance in Court as a party or a witness, yet such exemption was held[4] not to protect her from liability to arrest in execution of decree; and in the present Code of Civil Procedure (section 640) it is expressly provided that women who are exempt from personal appearance in Court, are not on that account to be deemed exempt from arrest in execution of civil process. And though the present Code (Chapter XLIX) exempts certain classes of persons from arrest, married women as a class are not mentioned among them.

Husband and wife competent witnesses for or against each other.

As a consequence of the legal identity of husband and wife, and with a view to prevent as much as possible all occa-

[1] Bhoyrubchunder Doss and another *v.* Madhubchunder Poramanic and others, 1 Hyde, 281.

[2] Colebrooke's Digest, Bk. IV, Ch. I, Sec. I; 2 Strange, 59, 60; G. *v.* K., 2 Morley's Digest, 234.

[3] Broom's Commentaries, p. 123 (5th ed.)

[4] Maharanee Udhee Ranee Narain Coomaree *v.* Sreemuttee Burroda Soonduree Dabee, 10 W. R., F. B., 21.

sions for domestic dissension and distrust, it was at one time a fundamental rule of English law that a husband or a wife could not be a competent witness for or against each other. The unsoundness of this rule has, however, been fully exposed by Bentham.[1]

The Hindu law of evidence, which in many respects was much in advance of its age, and which has been justly admired by Sir T. Strange,[2] never recognized any such strict rule. It is true that women were generally regarded as incompetent witnesses, and husband and wife according to some authorities were considered incompetent to be witnesses for each other; but Manu says that on failure of witnesses duly qualified, evidence may be given by a woman, a child, and others.[3]

Before the Evidence Act of 1872, it was provided by Act II of 1855, section 20, that a husband or a wife should be competent to give evidence for or against each other in civil cases, but that communications made by the parties to each other during marriage should be deemed privileged. In the case of *Queen v. Khyroollah*,[4] the question was raised whether a husband or a wife could give evidence for or against each other in a criminal case, and it was answered in the affirmative by a majority of the Full Bench before which the case was heard. And now by Act I of 1872, (sections 120, 122) it is laid down broadly that the husband or wife of any party to any proceeding, whether civil or criminal, shall be a competent witness in such proceeding, but

---

[1] Rationale of Judicial Evidence, Bk. IX, Part IV, Ch. V, Sec. IV.

[2] 1 Strange, 311.

[3] Mitakshara, Macnaghten's Hindu Law, 244; Virada Chintamani, p. 312; Manu, VIII, 70.

[4] 6 W. R., Cr., 21.

LECTURE IV. communications made by either spouse to the other during marriage shall not be ordinarily permitted to be disclosed.

Husband and wife in Hindu law are not competent to be sureties for each other.[1] As, however, the relation of principal and surety is governed, not by the Hindu law, but by the Contract Act, which does not declare their incompetency in this respect, this rule is now of little practical value.

Effects of marriage on the property of the husband and of the wife.

The effect of marriage on the property of either spouse next claims our attention. With a view to aid the fusion of two lives into one, and to promote domestic prosperity by the united exertion of both, the husband and the wife ought, it is said, to enjoy their property in common; and it is upon this principle that the English law on the subject seems to be based. The rule of English law is, however, obviously inequitable; for though all that belongs to the wife becomes the property of the husband, it is not provided that what belongs to him should also become her property. But, as I have just remarked, the tendency of modern legislation has been to restore equality, by allowing the parties to hold separate property: thus the Indian Succession Act (section 4) provides that no person shall by marriage acquire any interest in the property of the person whom he or she marries; and the Married Woman's Property Acts (33 & 34 Vict., cap. 93, for England, and Act III of 1874 for India) permit married women to hold some kinds of property separately and exclusively. While the English law as it originally stood gives you one extreme, namely, absolute community of interest in favor of the husband, the Mahomedan law gives the other extreme of absolute diversity of interest in the parties; and, I think, it would not be showing any undue partiality to our own system, if I say that the

[1] See Vivada Chintamani, Tagore's translation, p. 312.

Hindu law adopts the just mean between the two. It recognizes, as you will see, mutual community of interest, and at the same time allows the parties to hold separate property.

You have seen that a text of Manu[1] declares that the wife and certain other persons have no property in the wealth acquired by them, and that such wealth is acquired for the man to whom they belong; and you have also seen that it is explained by commentators as relating only to wealth earned by the mechanical arts and the like. This text might perhaps have been, in Manu's time, the relic of an earlier and a more archaic system, in which the patriarchal head of the family owned all the wealth earned by the wives, the sons, and the slaves belonging to it. But in later Hindu law, the independent ownership of the wife over certain kinds of property (which will be more fully treated of hereafter under the head of *stridhan*) is clearly recognized. The sages have defined these different kinds of property;[2] and though there is some difference of opinion among the different schools as to what constitutes *stridhan*, or woman's separate property, a question which will be discussed in its proper place, they all admit the independent right of the wife over such property.[3] Accordingly it has been held that the proposition, that whatever is acquired by a married woman during coverture belongs to her husband, has no foundation in the Hindu law.[4] But

---

[1] VIII, 416.

[2] Colebrooke's Digest, Bk. V, 462—473.

[3] See Mitakshara, Ch. II, Sec. XI, 32, 33; Dayabhaga, Ch. IV, Sec. I, 19—25; Vivada Chintamani, 263—266; Vyavahara Mayukhu, Ch. IV, Sec. X, 7—10; Smriti Chandrika, Ch. IX, Sec. II, 14; see also *Doe dem* Kullammal *v.* Kuppu Pillai, 1 Mad., 85.

[4] Ramasami Padeiyatchi *v.* Virasami Padeiyatchi, 3 Mad., 372.

though the wife has independent ownership over her *stridhan*, the community of interest of the parties is so far recognized as to allow the husband to use the wife's *stridhan* in times of pressing need, making repayment optional with him. The leading authorities of all the schools are agreed as to this.[1]

The right to use the wife's *stridhan* in times of need is, however, personal in the husband, and it has been held that the wife's ornaments are not liable to be seized in execution of a decree against the husband, though he might have applied them if he had no other means, to obtain his discharge from legal custody.[2]

On the other hand, the wife's interest in the property of her husband is recognized with equal clearness. Apastamba says: "Partition does not take place between a wife and her lord. From the time of taking her hand in marriage her aid in all acts is required, as well as her participation in the pure and impure fruit of action, and her concurrence in the receipt of wealth: Sages do not deem it a theft, if a gift be made by a wife for a just cause during the absence of her husband."[3]

The question how far a husband or a wife is guilty of theft for taking each other's property, has been sometimes raised. In a case decided before the passing of the Indian Penal Code, it was held that a Hindu husband could not be convicted of robbing his wife, she being according to law completely under his control.[4] Whether under the Penal Code such a decision would be correct or not has been a

---

[1] See the references cited in note 3 of the preceding page.

[2] See 1 Strange, 27; 2 Strange, 23; Tukaram bin Ramkrishna *v.* Gunaji bin Mhaloji, 8 Bom., A. C. J., 129.

[3] Colebrooke's Digest, Bk. V, 89.

[4] Case of Ootumram Atmaram, 3 Morley's Digest, 129, pl. 185.

matter of some doubt.[1] One thing, however, is clear, that section 27 of the Code will not protect the husband; for, the wife's possession is his possession only when she holds the property in question on his account, and evidently she does not hold her *stridhan* on account of her husband. If he takes the property of his wife without her consent, under the exceptional circumstances of necessity which justify his use of it, he would not be guilty of any offence, the element of dishonesty being wanting; if he exceeds those limits, he would, I apprehend, be guilty. LECTURE IV.

A Hindu wife, who removes from the possession of her husband, and without his consent, her *palla* or *stridhan*, has been held not to be guilty of theft.[2]

The question of the rights of the husband and the wife over each other's property has been only incidentally touched upon here. The subject will be resumed in a future Lecture.[3]

Wife entitled to a share on partition.

That the wife has an interest in the property of her husband, is further shown by the fact that she is entitled to a share of it at the time of partition. There is some difference of opinion among the different schools as to the manner in which such share is to be allotted.

The leading text on this point is one of Yajnavalkya, which runs thus:

"If he make the allotments equal, his wives, to whom no separate property has been given by the husband or the father-in-law, must be rendered partakers of like portions."[4]

From this text, the Mitakshara[5] deduces the following rules:—

I. When the father makes the sons partakers of equal

---

[1] 1 Norton's Leading Cases on Hindu Law, 11.

[2] Reg. v. Natha Kalyan and Bai Lakhi, 8 Bom. Crown Cases, 11.

[3] See Lecture VIII. [4] II, 115. [5] Ch. I, Sec. II, 8—10.

LECTURE IV. shares, his wives must each get a share equal to that of a son, if they have received no *stridhan* from their husband or father-in-law, or equal to half of a son's share, if they have received any *stridhan*. (The latter part of the rule is deduced from the text of Yajnavalkya relating to presents on supersession;[1] and the word 'half' (*ardham*) is defined to mean here not an exact half, but so much as would, together with the *stridhan* assigned, amount to the prescribed share.[2])

II. When a father makes an unequal partition, giving a superior allotment to the eldest son, and unequal shares to the others, his wives divide equally with his sons the amount left after deducting the distinctive portions, namely a twentieth part, &c., for the several sons (according to Ch. I, Sec. II, para. 4); and they take also their own distinctive portions, *viz.*, the furnitures of the house and their ornaments.

The Vyavahara Mayukhu, which in addition to the Mitakshara is one of the leading authorities in the Bombay school, adopts the first of the above two rules, but is silent as to the share of the wife in the case of unequal partition, for this reason, that it holds such partition prohibited in the *Kali* age.[3]

In the Dravida school, the Smriti Chandrika gives the following exposition of Yajnavalkya's text—"The meaning of this text is, that where a father, even where he is old, chooses to render all, inclusive of himself, partakers of equal portions, then he ought to take, on account of *each* of his wives, a share equal to that taken by himself. Hence, the doubt, whether the above text of Yajnavalkya is not opposed to a passage of Harita, which declares

---

[1] II, 148, already cited. [2] Mitakshara, Ch. II, Sec. XI, 35.
[3] Ch. IV, Sec. IV, 15, 11.

'Partition does not take place between a wife and her lord,' is also removed. Thus everything is rendered right."[1]

You will observe that according to this authority the wives do not get any shares separately assigned to them, but their husband takes a share on account of each of them. But the Parasara Madhavya, another high authority in Southern India, does not recognize this qualification as to the mode in which the wife's share is to be held.[2]

In the Vivada Chintamani, one of the leading authorities of the Mithila school, the rule is substantially the same as that in the Mitakshara in the case of equal partition by the father; but in the case of unequal partition, which for the present purpose according to Vachaspati Misra is where the father, giving smaller shares to his sons, takes the largest portion for his own use, he must give equal shares to his wives out of his own property.[3]

In the Bengal school, where the father is the absolute owner of all his property, whether ancestral or self-acquired,[4] he can make a partition in any way, or withhold it at his pleasure. Where he makes an equal partition among his sons, according to the Dayabhaga,[5] the Dayakrama Sangraha,[6] and the Dayatattwa,[7] his sonless wives are each entitled to a share equal to that of a son, or to half of such share, according as they are unprovided or provided with *stridhan*. You will observe that there is a material point of difference between the Bengal school and the other schools. These latter allow shares to all the wives, while the former gives them to those only that are sonless. The Bengal rule is based upon a text of Vyasa, and the

---

[1] Ch. II, Sec. I, 39.

[2] Dayavibhaga (Burnell's translation), p. 8.

[3] Pp. 230, 231.

[4] See Jotendro Mohun Tagore *v.* Ganendro Mohun Tagore, 18 W. R., 359.

[5] Ch. III, Sec. II, 31, 32.

[6] Ch. VI, 22—28.

[7] Ch. II, 13—18.

LECTURE IV. reason for it is probably this: that the wives who have sons would be supported by those sons out of the shares received by them, and it is only the sonless wives who stand in need of support, and ought to be the peculiar objects of their husband's care in this respect. The Bengal school differs from the others in another point also, namely, in maintaining that the share of the wife who has got *stridhan*, is an exact half of a son's share, and not merely as much as would, when added to such *stridhan*, make up her prescribed share. Jagannath, however, in one place,[1] gives to the word half (*ardha*) the general signification assigned to it in the Mitakshara.

It should be noticed that the wife has no right to compel partition, and that her right to a share arises only when a partition is made by her husband; and even then it is maintained by some[2] that her share is not to be assigned to her separately, but is to be held by her husband on her account. The truth seems to be that the wife's share on partition was originally intended as a provision for her maintenance.

The law on the subject of the wife's share on partition is not free from difficulty. You will find an elaborate though not very lucid disquisition upon it by Jagannath, in his commentary on texts 86 to 89 of Book V of his Digest, where the opinions of the leading writers on the subject have been examined.

As a general rule, it may be stated that when an equal partition is made by the father among his sons, under the Bengal school, his sonless wives get each a share which is

---

[1] Colebrooke's Digest, Bk. V, 87, commentary, Mad. ed., Vol. II, pp. 248, 249.

[2] See Smriti Chandrika, Ch. II, Sec. I, 39; Vivada Chintamani, 312; Colebrooke's Digest, Bk. V, 89; 1 Strange, 189.

equal to, or half of, that of a son, according as they are unprovided or provided with *stridhan*; and in the other schools, all his wives get each a share, which together with her *stridhan* (received from her husband's family), if any, is equal to a son's share.

It has been held by the High Court of Bengal in the case of *Lalljeet Singh* v. *Raj Coomar Singh*,[1] that under the Mitakshara, the wife being entitled to a share on partition, a suit for partition can not be maintained by the sons against their father, without making the mother a party to it.

The extent of the wife's interest in the share allotted to her on partition will be considered hereafter.[2]

Wife entitled to maintenance.

The duty of maintaining the wife and other dependent members of the family who are in want, is strictly enjoined by the Hindu law, and even censurable acts, such as receiving presents from a low person, are excused if done with a view to provide maintenance for them.[3] The maxim that one must be just before he can be allowed to be generous, is beautifully expressed by Manu, thus :—

"He who bestows gifts on strangers with a view to worldly fame, while he suffers his family to live in distress, though he has power to support them, touches his lips with honey, but swallows poison: such virtue is counterfeit." (XI, 9.)

The wife can enforce her claim for maintenance if it is denied,[4] and such claim is not affected by her supersession.[5]

---

[1] 20 W. R., 336.

[2] See Lecture VIII.

[3] Manu, III, 55—59; IV, 251; IX, 74, 95.

[4] Dayabhaga, Ch. II, 23; Ch. IV, Sec. I, 25; Vyavahara Mayukha, XX, 1; Colebrooke's Digest, Bk. IV, 74; Macnaghten's Precedents of Hindu Law, Ch. II, Cases i and ii.

[5] Colebrooke's Digest, Bk. IV, 74.

LECTURE IV. A wife forsaken without fault may, according to Yajnavalkya, compel her husband to pay her a third part of his wealth, or if poor, to provide maintenance for her.[1] From the alternative provisions of this rule, it would seem that the third part of the deserting husband's estate is mentioned as the ultimate measure of the wife's maintenance, and is directed to be given to her in lieu of maintenance, and also as a sort of punishment for the offending husband. Though according to some opinions,[2] an unjustly deserted wife may claim and recover a third of her husband's wealth, yet there are opinions to the contrary;[3] and considering the perpetual dependence of woman, and the possibility of the husband and the wife being reconciled to each other at any time, the penal provision in Yajnavalkya's text would not, I think, be enforced by our Courts; and the wife would be allowed maintenance only, though in assessing its amount, the husband's means and conduct would be taken into due consideration.

From whom. As a rule, the wife is entitled to maintenance from the husband alone; and so long as he is alive, neither his nor her relations are bound to support her.[4] Where, however, a husband deserts his wife, and is not heard of for some years, it has been held that though his relations are not under any personal liability to support her, yet if they have property of the husband in their hands, and the proceeds thereof are not accounted for by them, the wife

[1] Colebrooke's Digest, Bk. IV, 72.

[2] See 2 Strange, 45, 48, 51.

[3] Macnaghten's Precedents of Hindu Law, Ch. II, Case iii.

[4] Iyagaru Soobaroyadoo v. Iyagaru Sashama, Mad. S. D. R. for 1856, p. 22; and Rangayian v. Kalyam Ummall, Mad. S. D. R. for 1860, p. 86; cited in 1 Norton's Leading Cases, p. 39.

is entitled to receive maintenance from those proceeds to an extent not exceeding one-third of the amount.[1] LECTURE IV.

So, where the husband is excluded from inheritance by reason of disqualification, his sonless wives, if chaste, are entitled to maintenance from those who inherit to the exclusion of their husband. This right to maintenance is founded on a text of Yajnavalkya,[2] which is adopted by the commentators of all the schools.[3] No express provision is made for the wives who have sons, because in their case, these sons themselves being the heirs to the exclusion of their father,[4] there would be no difficulty in their being supported by the heirs.

Maintenance when allowed to a wife living apart.

The wife's right to maintenance and her conjugal duty of obedience to her husband, stand in a reciprocal relation to each other, and the wife can have no claim to maintenance if she refuses to live with her husband without just cause.[5] In *Sitanath Mookerjee* v. *Sreemutty Haimabutty Dabee*,[6] in which a wife living apart from her husband on account of unkind treatment claimed maintenance, Sir Richard Garth, C. J., observed:

"Now what is the Hindu law upon this subject?

"It is clear that, according to that law, a wife's first duty to her husband is to submit herself obediently to his authority, and to remain under his roof and protection; and although it might be very difficult to deduce from the authorities at

[1] Ramabai v. Trimbak Ganesh Desai, 9 Bom., 283. [2] II, 142.

[3] Mitakshara, Ch. II, Sec. X, 14, 15; Dayabhaga, Ch. V, 19; Vyavahara Mayukha, Ch. IV, Sec. XI, 12; Vivada Chintamani, p. 244; Smriti Chandrika, Ch. V, 43.

[4] Yajnavalkya, II, 141; Mitakshara, Ch. II, Sec. X, 9—11; Dayabhaga, Ch. V, 19.

[5] Virasvami Chetti v. Appasvami Chetti, 1 Mad., 375; Kullyanessuree Debee v. Dwarkanath Chatterjee, 6 W. R., 116; Colebrooke's Digest, Bk. IV, 57, 63. [6] 24 W. R., 377.

LECTURE IV. the present day any definite rule as to the causes which would justify a wife in leaving her husband's house, it may safely be affirmed that mere unkindness or neglect short of *cruelty* would not be a sufficient justification.

"That the law of modern times does recognize the right of the wife to leave her husband in certain cases of cruelty is apparent from the provision introduced into the first Code of Criminal Procedure in the year 1861, and reproduced in the existing Code in Section 536, which provides that a man may be ordered to maintain his wife who refuses to live with him if the Magistrate be satisfied that the husband is 'living in adultery, or *has habitually treated his wife with cruelty.*' But it is further enacted by the same Section, that no wife shall be entitled to receive this allowance from her husband if she is living in adultery, *or if, without any sufficient reason, she refuses to live with her husband, or if they are living separately by consent.*

"We are not at all prepared to say that the jurisdiction or powers of the Civil Courts are bound or limited in any degree by this Section of the Criminal Code; but we do consider that in such a case as the present these provisions may be usefully regarded as a guide to what the Legislature considered to be the correct law upon the subject; and unless we can see that the husband in this instance has refused to maintain his wife in his house, or has been guilty of acts of cruelty, which would justify her in leaving his protection, she is not entitled to the relief for which she prays."

What causes would justify the wife's refusal to live with her husband, I have already to some extent considered, when treating of restitution of conjugal rights. When any of these justifying causes (which consist of cruelty or ill-treatment in any aggravated form) exists, the wife is entitled to live apart from her husband, and to claim separate maintenance from him. This separate living at the expense of the husband, corresponds to what is called judicial separation in the English law; and as the Hindu law does not recognize divorce, this is the only remedy that the Hindu wife has against marital injustice and oppression. LECTURE IV.

Where a Hindu husband keeps a Mahomedan mistress, and by such conduct compels his wife, under her religious feelings, to leave the house, and she lives apart and chastely, she is entitled to claim maintenance from him.[1] Indeed, Colebrooke and Ellis go further, and maintain that the mere entertaining of a concubine is a justification for the wife's living apart, and would subject the husband to the obligation of maintaining her separately.[2] But such a broad rule would be contrary to the precept of Manu,[3] and its correctness has since been questioned.[4]

So where a Hindu wife had left her husband's house, and carried on an independent calling, and the husband did not object to the calling, or give her notice to return, it has been held that if she is subsequently desirous of returning to her husband's house, and he declines to maintain her, she is entitled to maintenance.[5]

Maintenance when forfeited.

Conjugal infidelity would of course bar a wife's claim for maintenance. Yajnavalkya says: "Let a man keep a disloyal wife deprived of her rights, squalid, maintained on a ball of grain alone, subdued and only suffered to repose on the meanest bed."[6] So Narada prescribes 'the

---

[1] Lalla Gobind Pershad *v.* Dowlut Butee, 14 W. R., 451.
[2] 2 Strange, 46, 47.
[3] V, 154.
[4] See Yamunabai *v.* Narayan Moreshvar Pendse, I. L. R., 1 Bom., 173.
[5] Nitye Laha *v.* Soondaree Dossee, 9 W. R., 475.
[6] Colebrooke's Digest, Bk. IV, 82.

LECTURE IV. lowest bed, the meanest food, the worst habitation' as a punishment for the disloyal wife; and Manu permits the husband either to forsake her, or to subject her to penance and mortification.[1] Accordingly it has been held by the Courts of India that an unchaste wife is not entitled to maintenance.[2]

But be it said to the credit of our law, that whilst showing the utmost abhorrence towards unchastity, it does not condemn the unchaste wife to die of starvation, or to be forced by absolute necessity to lead a life of shame and misery for one false step. Though it bars her right to maintenance as a source of wealth, it allows her what has been styled *starving maintenance*, that is, bare food and raiment, as the very texts cited above will show. Though an opposite rule has, it seems, been sometimes followed,[3] yet the true humane spirit of the Hindu law has been generally recognized.[4]

Rate of maintenance.

The Civil Courts, it has been held, have power to fix the rate of maintenance payable by the husband to the wife, in cases where for lawful cause she is residing apart from him, and also power to make an order that maintenance at that rate shall be paid in future, subject to any modification that future circumstances may require.[5] The minimun rate of maintenance is prescribed by the Hindu law with some precision,[6] but the rule had reference to a

[1] Colebrooke's Digest, Bk. VI, 80, 81.

[2] Ilata Shavatri v. Ilata Narayanan Nambudiri, 1 Mad., 372; 2 Strange 39.

[3] Ragava Chary v. Seedumall, 2 Mad. Sel. Dec., 20, cited in 1 Norton's Leading Cases on Hindu Law, 37.

[4] 1 Strange, 172; 2 Strange, 39; Honamma v. Timannabhat, I. L. R., 1 Bom., 559.

[5] Nubo Gopal Roy v. Sreemutty Amrit Moyee Dossee, 24 W. R., 428.

[6] Smriti Chandrika, Ch. XI, Sec. I, 39,40; Macnaghten's Precedents, Ch. II, Case iv note, p. 111.

different state of society, and is not of much practical value now. At the present day, the rate will have to be determined by the Court after considering the means of the husband and other circumstances in each case.

LECTURE IV.

Arrears of maintenance.

It was held by the Madras Sadr Court in some cases that arrears of maintenance could not be recovered; but those decisions have since been dissented from, as there is no authority in the Hindu law to support them.[1] The only bar to the recovery of such arrears is lapse of time. Under the present Limitation Law (Act XV of 1877, Schedule II, No. 128), a claim for arrears of maintenance is not barred if brought within twelve years.

Recovery of maintenance under the Code of Criminal Procedure.

Besides a civil suit, there is another mode, more simple and less expensive, by which a wife may recover maintenance from her husband. Section 536 of the Code of Criminal Procedure, which corresponds to section 316 of the old Code of 1861, provides that if a person having sufficient means neglects or refuses to maintain his wife, a Magistrate having jurisdiction may, upon due proof thereof, order such person to pay from the date of such order, maintenance at such rate not exceeding fifty rupees a month as such Magistrate may think reasonable. The section further enacts,—

"If such person wilfully neglects to comply with this order, such Magistrate may, for every breach of the order, by warrant, direct the amount due to be levied in the manner provided for levying fines; and may order such person to be imprisoned, with or without hard labor, for any term not exceeding one month, for each month's allowance remaining unpaid:

"Provided that if such person offers to maintain his wife

[1] Venkopadhyaya v. Kavari Hengusu, 2 Mad., 36.

LECTURE IV. on condition of her living with him, and his wife refuses to live with him, such Magistrate may consider any grounds of refusal stated by such wife; and may make the order allowed by this section notwithstanding such offer, if he is satisfied that such person is living in adultery, or that he has habitually treated his wife with cruelty.

"No wife shall be entitled to receive an allowance from her husband under this section if she is living in adultery, or if, without any sufficient reason, she refuses to live with her husband, or if they are living separately by consent."

It has been held,[1] however, that up to the time when the father allows his daughter to go to the house of her husband, and when, by the custom of Hindu society, she would probably go, the husband incurs no liability in respect of her maintenance under this section.

A Christian wife of a Christian convert is entitled to claim maintenance under the Code of Criminal Procedure, notwithstanding that her husband renounces Christianity, and reverts to Hinduism and marries a second wife.[2]

Maintenance of concubines.

Though the Hindu law does not, like the Roman law,[3] allow concubinage, yet according to some authorities, a concubine of a Hindu is entitled to maintenance.[4] But a woman living in adultery cannot claim maintenance from the adulterer.[5]

Husband and wife how far bound by each other's contracts.

We have seen above, that a Hindu married woman is not incompetent to enter into contracts. It remains to be seen

---

[1] Mussamut Somree v. Jitun Sonar, 22 W. R., Cr., 30.

[2] 4 Mad., Criminal Cases, iii.

[3] Mackenzie's Roman Law, p. 105.

[4] Mitakshara, Ch. II, Sec. I, 28; Dayabhaga, Ch. XI, Sec. I, 48; 1 Strange, 71; Vyavahara Mayukha, Ch. IV, Sec. VIII, 5; 1 W. & B., 93; Khemkor v. Umiashankar, 10 Bom., 381; Vrandavandas Ramdas v. Yamunabai, 12 Bom., 229.

[5] Sikki v. Vencatasamy Gounden, 8 Mad., 144.

how far the husband and the wife are bound by each other's contracts. Under the English law, a *feme covert* as a rule is incapable of contracting except as her husband's agent; but her contracts for supplying herself with necessaries suitable to her station in life, are binding on her husband.[1] In the Hindu law, according to Yajnavalkya:

"Neither shall a wife or mother be in general compelled to pay a debt contracted by her husband or son, nor a father to pay a debt contracted by his son, unless it were for the behoof of the family; nor a husband to pay a debt contracted by his wife."[2]

Narada declares: "A debt contracted by the wife shall by no means bind the husband, unless it were for necessaries at a time of great distress."[3] And so Katyayana: "A debt which is contracted by a wife or mother for the behoof of the family, when her husband or son is gone to a foreign country, after authorizing the loan, must be paid by the husband or son."[4] Thus you will observe that a Hindu husband is bound by the contracts of his wife, when they are entered into by her with his authority, express or implied, or for the support of his family under necessity. A special rule is laid down by Yajnavalkya for certain cases: "If the wife of a herdsman, a vinter, a dancer, a washerman, or a hunter, contract a debt, the husband shall pay it; because his livelihood chiefly depends upon the labor of such a wife."[5] And there are also texts of Brihaspati and Narada to the same effect. Upon these texts Jagannath has the following commentary:—

"Here 'washer' and the rest are mentioned indetermin-

---

[1] Stephen's Commentaries, Bk. III, Ch. II.

[2] Colebrooke's Digest, Bk. I, Ch. V, 207.

[3] *Ibid*, 209. [4] *Ibid*, 219. [5] *Ibid*, 216.

LECTURE IV. ately. In fact, whatever be his class, if the husband's livelihood depend chiefly on the labor of his wife, he must discharge a debt contracted by her, whether he be a priest or a washer: but he whose livelihood does not depend on his wife, whether he be a washer or a priest, shall not pay his wife's debt. This is noticed by Misra: *he says,* 'in other cases also, wherever the wife has the chief management, there is no restriction of class; the wife alone conducts all affairs, the husband is absolutely ignorant of every transaction.' Accordingly it is observed, that in the province of *Cámarúpa,* almost every civil transaction is now conducted by women.

"But this is merely a vague description; for a debt contracted by the wife of a *Bráhmana,* and so forth, for the support of the family, must also be paid by the chief of that family. From the reason assigned, "because his livelihood chiefly depends on the labour of such a wife," it appears that any other persons of whom the livelihood depends on the labour of their wives, must pay the debt contracted by those wives. This is admitted in the *Mitakshara.* Chandéswara also makes the same observation,—'The circumstance of his livelihood depending on the labour of his wife is particularly intended; not any restriction of class.' "[1] The special cases, therefore, come under the general rule, as cases of implied authority.

In cases not coming within the rule, the wife alone is bound to pay the debts contracted by her.[2]

The Hindu law on this subject has been thus summed up by Sir Colley Scotland in *Virasvami Chetti* v. *Appasvami Chetti:*[3] "On this question the Hindu law appears to rest

---

[1] Colebrooke's Digest, Bk. I, Ch. V, 218, commentary.
[2] *Ibid,* 210, 211. [3] 1 Mad., 375.

upon pretty much the same grounds as the English law. A person dealing with a wife and seeking to charge her husband must shew either that the wife is living with her husband and managing the household affairs—in which case an implied agency to buy necessaries is presumed—or, he must shew the existence of such a state of things as would warrant her in living apart from her husband and claiming support or maintenance—when of course the law would give her an implied authority to bind him for necessaries supplied to her during such separation, in the event of his not providing her with maintenance." LECTURE IV.

Though matters of contract, when not provided for by the Contract Act, are to be governed, not by the Hindu law, but by principles of justice, equity, and good conscience,[1] yet, as on the point in question, that law is in conformity with justice, equity, and good conscience, it has been generally consulted by our Courts in determining the liability of the husband for the acts of the wife.[2]

Where a wife voluntarily separates from her husband without any justifying cause, she, and not her husband, is liable for debts contracted by her (even for necessaries), but her liability has been declared not to be personal, but to be limited to the extent of any *stridhan* she may have.[3] The reason for this limitation is not however very clearly stated.

According to the Vyavahara Mayukha, he who takes the wife of a deceased person, is bound to pay the debts of such Bombay Act VII of 1866.

---

[1] See Deen Doyal Poramanik *v.* Kylas Chunder Pal Chowdhry, I. L. R., 1 Cal., 92, and the authorities cited there.

[2] Macnaghten's Precedents of Hindu Law, Ch. X, Case iv; Nathubhai Bhailal *v.* Javher Raiji, I. L. R., 1 Bom., 121.

[3] Nathubhai Bhailal *v.* Javher Raija, I. L. R., 1 Bom., 121.

LECTURE IV. person on failure of those who take his assets.[1] This rule, which obtained in the Bombay Presidency, and was an evident hardship upon any one marrying a Hindu widow, has been now abrogated by the Bombay Hindu Heirs' Relief Act (Bombay Act VII of 1866, section 4).

A Hindu wife is not bound by her husband's acts in relation to her property. He has no power to part with her property without her consent, or to affect her interest in her own property by any document that he may execute.[2]

Husband or wife entitled to compensation under Act XIII of 1855.

When the death of any person is caused by an actionable wrong, the husband or wife of such person is, under Act XIII of 1855, one of the parties entitled to compensation for the loss occasioned.

Effects of marriage on offspring—Legitimacy.

I come now to the effects of marriage on the offspring of the parties. The most important among these is the status of legitimacy, which belongs to children of lawfully united parents. The rules of legitimacy are different in different systems. By the Roman law, and the laws of France and Scotland, which on this subject are based upon that law, the marriage of the parents at any time legitimizes all their children whether born before or after such marriage.[3] The Mahomedan law goes even further, and makes acknowledgment by the father under certain qualifications sufficient to legitimate the issue.[4] Under the English law, a child to be legitimate must be born, though not begotten, in lawful wedlock;[5] and indeed, so jealous is

---

[1] Ch. V, Sec. IV, 16, 17.

[2] Sooda Ram Doss v. Joogul Kishore Goopto, 24 W. R., 274; Mohima Chunder Roy v. Durga Monee, 23 W. R., 184.

[3] Institutes of Justinian, Lib. I, Tit. X, 13, and note by Sandars; Mackenzie's Roman Law, pp. 130—134; Code Napoleon, arts. 331—333.

[4] Hedaya (Grady's ed.), p. 439; Nubo Kant Roy Chowdhry v. Mahatab Bibee, 20 W. R., 164.

[5] Birtwhistle v. Vardill, 7 Clark and Finnelly, 895.

that law in this respect, that it will not allow a person, though legitimate by the law of his domicile, to inherit real property in England, unless he is legitimate by the law of that country, as has been finally settled by the House of Lords in *Birtwhistle* v. *Vardill.*[1] Blackstone justly praises the law of his own country, as tending to promote good morals and prevent illicit cohabitation, at the same time that it makes due allowance for the frailties of human nature.[2]

The Hindu law of legitimacy is more strict than even the English law. Manu defines the *aurasa* son or son of the body, thus:—

"Him whom a man has begotten on his own wedded wife, let him know to be the first in rank, as the son of his body." (IX, 166.) And to the same effect are the texts of Vasistha, Devala, Baudhayana, Apastamba, and Yajnavalkya.[3] According to the Hindu sages, therefore, in order to constitute legitimacy, there must be not only birth but also procreation in lawful wedlock; and some of the leading commentators, such as Kulluka, Vijnaneswar, and Nilkantha, confirm this view of their texts.[4] The Privy Council have however, taken a different view. Sir Barnes Peacock in delivering the judgment of the Judicial Committee in the case of *Pedda Amani* v. *Zemindar of Marungapuri,*[5] observed: "The point of illegitimacy being established by proof that the procreation was before marriage, had never suggested itself to the learned Counsel for the Appellant at the time of the trial, nor does it appear from the authorities

[1] 7 Clark and Finnelly, 895.

[2] Stephen's Commentaries, Bk. III, Ch. III, Vol. II, pp. 296, 297, 5th ed.

[3] Colebrooke's Digest, Bk. V, 193, 195, 196, 199, and 200.

[4] Mitakshara, Ch. I, Sec. XI, 2; Vyavahara Mayukha, Ch. IV, Sec. IV, 41.

[5] 1 L. R., I. A., 293.

LECTURE IV. cited to have been distinctly laid down that, according to Hindu law, in order to render a child legitimate, the procreation as well as the birth must take place after marriage. That would be a most inconvenient doctrine. If it is the law that law must be administered. Their Lordships, however, do not think that it is the Hindu law. They are of opinion that the Hindu law is the same in that respect as the English law." This decision, so long as the Privy Council do not think it fit to re-consider the point, must be received as the law on the subject. But with every respect that is due to the decision of the highest tribunal for India, I may be permitted to say that the doctrine that procreation in lawful wedlock is necessary to constitute legitimacy, is not only supported by the language of the texts cited above, but is also in accordance with the general spirit of the Hindu law, by which the nuptial rites are primarily meant only for virgins;[1] while the necessity of marrying girls before puberty, reduces the practical inconvenience of the doctrine within the narrowest possible limits.

I may observe that by a custom in the Tipperah Raj, the Raja can legitimize his children born of a *kachooa*, or kept woman, by subsequently going through the ceremony of marriage with her.[2]

Effect of marriage in a different caste on legitimacy.

The effect of marriage in a different caste on legitimacy may be next considered.

In former ages, as you have seen in a previous Lecture,[3] a man was permitted to marry a woman of an equal or an inferior class, but not one of a superior class.[4] The distinction between these two forms of intermarriage arose out of

---

[1] Manu, VIII, 226.

[2] Chuckrodhuj Thakoor *v.* Beer Chunder Joobraj, 1 W. R., 194.

[3] Lecture II.

[4] See Manu, III, 12, 13.

a feeling which identifies the honor of a family with that of its female members, and regards the family as raised or lowered in rank, according as its female members are married in superior or inferior families. The offspring of the former or allowable kind of intermarriage were called *anulomaja*;[1] that is, born in the direct order of the tribes, and were allowed to inherit their father's property, though in inferior shares;[2] and the issue of the prohibited form of intermarriage were called *pratilomaja*, that is, born in the inverse order of the tribes, and had no claim upon the father except for maintenance.[3] LECTURE IV.

In the *Kali* age, intermarriage between different castes is prohibited;[4] and though the authorities are not unanimous as to how far this prohibition extends to intermarriage between different castes of the Sudra class, in Bengal, as you have already seen, their preponderance is in favor of holding such prohibition to be universal and unqualified.[5]

Now let us see in the first place how the law of legitimacy stands, apart from the prohibition against intermarriage. Baudhayana defines a legitimate son thus: "A son who was begotten by a man himself on his wedded wife of equal class, let him know to be the legitimate son of his body."[6] Kulluka Bhatta in his gloss on the text of Manu[7] quoted above, says, that the wedded wife means the wedded

---

[1] *Anuloma* literally means *in the direction of the hair*; i. e., in a regular course; and *pratiloma* means *against the hair*, i. e., contrary to the regular course. See Manu, X, 5—29.

[2] Mitakshara, Ch. I, Sec. VIII; Dayabhaga, Ch. IX.

[3] Colebrooke's Digest, Bk. V, 171, commentary.

[4] See Udvahatattwa, Inst., Vol. II, p. 62; Manu, General Note, VI; Vyavastha Darpana, pp. 14, 15.

[5] See Narain Dhara v. Rakhal Gain, 23 W. R., 334, I. L. R., 1 Calc., 1, and the cases cited there.

[6] Colebrooke's Digest, Bk. V, 196. [7] IX, 166.

LECTURE IV. wife of equal class. Yajnavalkya defines a legitimate son to be a son procreated on the lawful wedded wife, and 'the lawful wedded wife'[1] (*dharma patni*) is explained in the Mitakshara[2] to mean a woman of equal tribe legally espoused, though in another place[3] in the same commentary, a son by a wife of an inferior class is also considered legitimate. The Viramitrodaya takes this latter view; while according to Chandeswar and the Parijata, 'a woman of equal class' means a woman of the twice-born class for a twice-born man, and a Sudra woman for a man of the Sudra class.[4] Balambhatta explains 'lawful' in Yajnavalkya's text to imply exclusion of a woman of a superior class, who cannot be legally taken in marriage;[5] so that according to this authority, the offspring of intermarriage between different castes would not be illegitimate, except where such intermarriage is illegal by reason of the woman belonging to a superior tribe. The son of a twice-born man by a Sudra woman has however a very inferior right to inherit the property of his father.[6] The opinion of Balambhatta seems to be the one that accords best with reason; for legality of marriage and legitimacy of issue ought always to be connected as cause and effect.

In the next place, marriage between persons of different castes being now prohibited, it would follow from what has been just said, that the issue of such marriage must be illegitimate. Some writers maintain that though equality of caste is essential to a legal marriage, it is not essential

---

[1] II, 128. [2] Ch. I, Sec. XI, 2. [3] *Ibid*, 41.

[4] See Mitakshara, Ch. I, Sec. XI, 2 note; Colebrooke's Digest, Bk. V, 200, commentary.

[5] Mitakshara, Ch. I, Sec. XI. 2 note.

[6] Mitakshara, Ch. I, Sec. VIII, 10; Dayabhaga, Ch. IX, 22—27.

to the legitimacy of the issue.[1] This, however, is supported neither by reason nor by authority. The definitions of legitimacy examined above, all require a legal marriage as a necessary condition; and where that is wanting, it is hard to see how the issue can be legitimate.

There is one point connected with the present topic which ought not to be passed over altogether. The heritable rights of sons by women of different tribes is treated of at great length in the Mitakshara[2] and the Dayabhaga;[3] and as both these works have been written in the *Kali* or the present age, it might be inferred that such sons are now so far legitimate as to be entitled to share the heritage. Such inference, however, would not be well founded. The Mitakshara is a running commentary on Yajnavalkya; and as the *Sanhita* of that sage contains texts declaratory of the rights of sons by women of different classes, the commentator merely gives his gloss upon them; but that does not warrant the inference in question. Touching the Dayabhaga, it is true that the same explanation cannot be given; but it should be borne in mind that the Dayabhaga is a speculative treatise, and that everything that it contains was not necessarily the law that obtained when it was written. And the remarks of Jagannath and Devananda Bhatta,[4] to the effect that intermarriage between different castes being prohibited in the *Kali* age, discussion on the subject of partition among sons of unequal classes would only swell their works unnecessarily, go a great way to negative the inference in question.

Presumption of legitimacy.

The law is always in favor of presuming marriage and legitimacy, and the Privy Council have held[5] that a marriage

[1] 1 Strange, 40. [2] Ch. I, Sec. VIII. [3] Ch. IX.

[4] Colebrooke's Digest, Bk. V, 172, commentary; Smriti Chandrika, Ch. X, 7.

[5] Ramamani Ammal v. Kulanthai Nauchear, 17 W. R., 5.

LECTURE IV. *de facto* being established, and the children being recognized by their father as legitimate, it would require the very strongest evidence to show that the law denied to these children their presumable legal status, on the ground of their mother's incapacity to contract a marriage.

Bastard's right to inherit.

The position of illegitimate children in the Hindu law is somewhat different from their position in the English law. In the latter system, the bastard is regarded as a *filius nullius*, a son of nobody; and for purposes of inheritance, he has no legal relationship with any one in the ascending or the collateral line, and his only relations are his own legitimate descendants.[1] In the Hindu law the illegitimate son of a regenerate man is always excluded from inheritance; but in the case of a Sudra, the illegitimate son of a particular description, namely, the son born of an unmarried female slave or slave's female slave, inherits his father's property.[2] This special rule in the case of Sudras, which Sir T. Strange[3] attributes to the contempt in which they are held by the Hindu law, is deduced by the leading commentators of all the schools from the following texts:—

"A son begotten by a man of the servile class on his female slave, or on the female slave of his slave, may take a share of the heritage if permitted: thus is the law established. (Manu, IX, 179.)

"Even a son begotten by a Sudra on a female slave may take a share by his father's choice." (Yajnavalkya, II, 133.)

---

[1] Stephen's Commentaries, Bk. III, Ch. III, 5th ed., Vol. II, 311.

[2] Mitakshara, Ch. I, Sec. XII, 1—3; Dayabhaga Ch. IX, 28—31; Vyavahara Mayukha, Ch. IV, Sec. IV, 29—32; Macnaghten's Precedents of Hindu Law, p. 15 note; Chuoturya Run Murdun Syn *v.* Sahub Purlu-had Syn, 4 W. R. (P. C.), 132; 1 Morley, 310, pls. 44—47; Datti Parisi Nayudu *v.* Datti Bangaru Nayudu, 4 Mad., 204.

[3] 1 Strange, 69.

It has been sometimes maintained that the authorities would support the broad proposition that a Sudra's illegitimate son of every description would inherit to his father;[1] and a slight inaccuracy which occurs in Colebrooke's translation of the Dayabhaga (Chap. IX, 29) favors such a view. But Mr. Justice Romesh Chunder Mitter, in his elaborate judgment in *Narain Dhara* v. *Rakhal Gain*,[2] has clearly pointed out this error, and deduced the correct rule given above, after a full examination of the authorities on the subject.

The meaning of the term female slave (*dasi*) in the above rule, has been the subject of much contention in our Courts, and the authorities are not unanimous on the subject. They seem, however, to favor the view that a "*female slave*" here means not necessarily a *slave* bought or taken captive, but includes a continuous concubine, provided that the intercourse is neither adulterous nor incestuous.[3] The case of *Rahi* v. *Govinda Valad Teja*[4] may be referred to for a full exposition of the meaning of the term *dasiputra*, and of the law relating to the rights of an illegitimate son.

The question how far one illegitimate branch can inherit from another was raised in the case of *Myna Bai* v. *Uttaram*. The facts of that case were somewhat anomalous. An Englishman had two sons by a Brahman married woman who had deserted her husband and lived in

---

[1] 1 Strange, 69; Pandaiya Telaver *v.* Puli Telaver, 1 Mad., 478; but see the judgment of the Privy Council in that case, 12 W. R. (P. C.), 41.

[2] 23 W. R., 334; I. L. R., 1 Calc., 1.

[3] Muttusamy Jagavira Yettapa Naikar *v.* Venkatasubha Yettia, 2 Mad., 293; and the same case on appeal to the Privy Council, 11 W. R. (P. C.), 6; Datti Parisi Nayudu *v.* Datti Bangaru Nayudu, 4 Mad., 204; Vencatachella Chetty *v.* Parvatham, 8 Mad., 131.

[4] I. L. R., 1 Bom., 97.

LECTURE IV. adultery with him; and upon the death of one of these sons, the other claimed his estate as his heir. The Privy Council held[1] that the parties had been rightly considered to be Hindus, but remitted the case to India for further investigation as to collateral heirship under the peculiar circumstances of the case. Thereupon the High Court of Madras[2] held that illegitimate sons could inherit the property of their mother and of one another.

Maintenance of children.

That a man should be bound to maintain his legitimate children is natural and obvious; and the same texts that enjoin him to support his wife, may be cited also for the present purpose.[3]

It is equally clear that a man is bound to maintain his illegitimate children. If illicit cohabitation is sinful, the denying of support to the innocent offspring of such cohabitation would only aggravate the offence. Nor is authority wanting in support of the bastard's right to maintenance. Jimuta Vahana,[4] Nilkantha,[5] and Vijnaneswara,[6] more or less, allow such right in the case of a son by an unmarried Sudra woman; and the Privy Council in the case of *Chuoturya Run Murdun Syn* v. *Sahub Purluhad Syn*,[7] following the last-named commentator, held that an illegitimate son of a twice-born man is entitled to maintenance out of his father's estate. In the case of Sudras, the illegitimate son is entitled in some cases to a share of the heritage, as you

---

[1] 2 W. R. (P. C.), 4.

[2] 2 Mad., 196.

[3] Manu, IX, 108; XI, 9, 10; Colebrooke's Digest, Bk. V, 77; *Ibid*, II, Ch. IV, 11, 12: see also 1 Strange, 67; Macnaghten's Precedents of Hindu Law, 114; Ayyavu Muppanar *v.* Niladatchi Ammal, 1 Mad., 45.

[4] Dayabhaga, Ch. IX, 28.

[5] Vyavahara Mayukha, Ch. IV, Sec. IV, 30.

[6] Mitakshara, Ch. I, Sec. XII, 3.

[7] 4 W. R. (P. C.), 132; see also Pershad Singh *v.* Ranee Muhesree, 3 Sel. Rep. (new ed.), 176.

have just seen, and in other cases to maintenance;[1] nor is it necessary in this latter class of cases that the mother of the illegitimate child should be a concubine possessing any peculiar status in the family of the father.[2] The maintenance of an illegitimate son has been held to be a charge on the estate of his father.[3] LECTURE IV.

The claim of an illegitimate son for maintenance has been held not liable to be defeated by the fact of his being the issue of adulterous intercourse.[4]

The foregoing rules apply to claims by illegitimate children for maintenance out of the estate of their father after his death, and are based upon the general principle of the Hindu law, that persons excluded from inheritance by reason of certain disqualifications (of which illegitimacy may be regarded as one) are entitled to maintenance out of the estate they are excluded from.[5] The reported decisions are all under the law of the schools that follow the Mitakshara; but there is no reason to suppose that a different rule would be followed under the law of Bengal.

During the father's lifetime, children, whether legitimate or illegitimate, are entitled to maintenance from him, only so long as they are young and unable to provide for themselves.

---

[1] Inderun Valungypooly Taver *v.* Ramasawmy Talaver, 12 W. R. (P. C.), 41.

[2] Muttusawmy Jagavira Yettapa *v.* Venkatasuba Yettia, 2 Mad., 293; and the judgment of the Privy Council in the same case in 11 W. R. (P. C.), 6.

[3] Coomara Yettapa Naikar *v.* Venkateswara Yettia, 5 Mad., 405.

[4] Rahi *v.* Govind Valad Teja, I. L. R., 1 Bom., 117; Veraramuthi Udayan *v.* Singaravelu, I. L. R., 1 Mad., 306.

[5] Mitakshara, Ch. II, Sec. X, 5; Dayabhaga, Ch. V, 11, 14—16; Smriti Chandrika, Ch. V, 10—14, 20; Veraramuthi Udayan *v.* Singaravelu, I. L. R., 1 Mad., 306.

In addition to the remedy by civil suit, the same summary mode (Act X of 1872, section 536) is prescribed for children, whether legitimate or illegitimate, as that for the wife, to enable them to recover maintenance from their father.

The minority of the father would be no ground for excusing him from the necessity of providing support for his child, whether legitimate or illegitimate; but before any order for maintenance can be made, the law requires it to be proved that the father has sufficient means.[1]

Under what circumstances a father is bound to maintain his child, it is not very easy to define. By the English law, a father is bound to maintain his children, of whatever age, when in want, and unable through infancy, disease, or accident, to provide for themselves.[2] Our Code of Criminal Procedure enacts that children are entitled to maintenance if unable to maintain themselves; and as the grounds of inability are not specified in the Code, it would follow that inability from any cause, such as infancy, disease, or the like, would entitle a child to maintenance. Nor is the spirit of the Hindu law different from this, as may be seen from the following text of Yajnavalkya:[3]—

"After assigning a sufficient support to infants, to a married daughter residing in the house of her father, to aged persons, pregnant women, persons afflicted with disease, damsels yet unmarried, guests and servants, the husband and wife may enjoy the residue."

The High Court of Bengal has, however, held that, under the Hindu law, a father is not bound to maintain a

---

[1] The Queen on the information of Mussamut Narain Koer v. Roshun Lall, 4 N. W. P., 123.

[2] Stephen's Commentaries, Bk. III, Ch. III, Vol. II, 302, 5th ed.

[3] Colebrooke's Digest, Bk. V, 77.

grown up son, even if he is laboring under a temporary disorder.[1] At what age a child should be deemed grown up, does not appear. Ordinarily the claim for maintenance would last till majority is attained, though long before that time many persons begin to earn their own livelihood. But it should be remembered that children are entitled to maintenance only when they are in want and unable to maintain themselves. LECTURE IV.

Under the Mitakshara law, which recognizes the joint ownership of the father and the son in ancestral property,[2] the son, if unable to enforce partition by reason of such property being in any case impartible, can sue his father for maintenance; and this right of the son is not, it seems, affected by the fact of his having attained maturity, or of his not being in want.[3] Where a son or other member of an undivided Hindu family is competent to sue for partition, a suit for maintenance will not lie.[4]

Custody of children.

The father is the natural guardian of his legitimate children, and is entitled to the custody of their persons in preference to all others until they attain majority.[5] But in the case of a female child, the father's right, as you have seen, ceases after her marriage, when she comes under the guardianship of her husband. So long as the father, not being himself a minor, is alive, the law dispenses with the appointment of any guardian of the persons of his minor children.[6]

---

[1] Prem Chand Pepara *v.* Hoolas Chand Pepara, 12 W. R., 494.

[2] Mitakshara, Ch. I, Sec. V.

[3] Himmatsing Becharsing *v.* Gunpatsing, 12 Bom., 94.

[4] 12 Bom., 96 note.

[5] Colebrooke's Digest, Bk. V, 452, 453; Macnaghten's Principles of Hindu Law, pp. 103, 104; 1 Strange, 71; In the matter of Himnauth Bose, 1 Hyde, 111.

[6] Act XL of 1858, s. 27.

LECTURE IV. The mother's right to the guardianship and custody of her children is inferior only to that of the father, though for certain purposes, such as giving a daughter in marriage, and the like, the Hindu law subjects her, to some extent, to the control of her husband's kinsmen.[1]

In some cases the mother may be entitled to the custody of the children in preference to the father. The nurture of children is, by nature as well as by our law,[2] the peculiar duty of the mother; and so where they are of extremely tender age, and the mother, in consequence of the father's profligacy or misconduct, is compelled to live apart from him, it is as necessary for the children that they should be placed under their mother's care, as it is just to the mother that she should not be deprived of the solace of having the custody of her children.

A Hindu father's change of religion would not, however, bar his right to the custody of his infant children, though, if they have attained years of discretion, their wishes in the matter would be consulted by the Court.[3]

The custody of illegitimate children in other systems of law belongs to the mother.[4] The rule is based upon obvious grounds of necessity and convenience, and there is no reason why a different rule should be followed in the Hindu law in the absence of any express provision to the contrary.

Claims to the custody of minors are to be enforced according to the provisions of Act IX of 1861. And a person

---

[1] 1 Strange, 72; Colebrooke's Digest, Bk. V, 453, commentary; Ram Dhun Doss v. Rum Ruttun Dutt, 10 W. R., 425; S. Namasevayam Pillay v. Annammai Ummal, 4 Mad., 339.

[2] Manu, IX, 27.

[3] Muchoo v. Arzoon Sahoo, 5 W. R., 235.

[4] See Stephen's Comm., Bk. III, Ch. III, Vol. II, p. 309, 5th ed.

who kidnaps from lawful custody a minor under fourteen years if a male, or sixteen years if a female, is liable to be punished under section 363 of the Indian Penal Code.

Right to give or take a son in adoption.

Though the custody of children may sometimes belong to the mother, the right of giving a son in adoption belongs exclusively to the father; and if the mother sometimes does exercise this right, it is only with the permission of her husband.[1] So also the right of taking a son in adoption in the *dattaka* form can be exercised by a woman only with the permission of her husband, or, according to the law in some parts of India, with the permission of his kinsmen after his death.[2]

Paternal power under the Hindu law.

This brings us to the consideration of the paternal authority under the Hindu law. Much of the power which in advanced and well-organized society is placed in the hands of the State, was, in feebly-organized primitive society, exercised by the head of each family within his own domestic circle; and accordingly, in ancient law, the authority of the father was almost unbounded. In the Roman law it is called the *patria potestas*, and originally included the power of life and death.[3] The Hindu law, as far as tradition tells us was never so inhuman as that, though traces of the existence of an unlimited power in other respects are still evident. Thus Vasistha, after premising that the son owes his existence to his parents, observes: "Both parents have power, for just reasons, to give, to sell, or to desert him; but let no man give or accept an only son, since he must remain to raise up a progeny for the obsequies of ancestors."[4] But

[1] Manu, IX, 168; Dattaka Mimansa, I, 15; Dattaka Chandrika, I, 31.

[2] The Collector of Madura *v.* Muttu Ramalinga Satthupathy, 10 W. R. (P. C.), 17.

[3] Institutes of Justinian, Lib. I, Tit. IX, and note by Sandars; Maine's Ancient Law, p. 138.

[4] Colebrooke's Digest, Bk. V, 273.

LECTURE IV. you will observe from this very text, that ancestor-worship and the spiritual necessity of having a son, helped to raise the position of the son in the Hindu law. Other sages also have prohibited the sale or gift of a son.[1]

A text of Manu[2] says that the son is one of the three persons declared by law to have in general no wealth exclusively their own. But the effect of this rule has been more than counteracted by a text of equal authority,[3] which declares the ownership of the father and the son to be equal in ancestral property. This text of Yajnavalkya, which has been elaborately developed in the Mitakshara,[4] has for a long time been the prevailing rule of Hindu law. This doctrine of equal ownership of the father and the son, which creates restraint on alienation, may not be a very convenient one in advanced society; but it has served to soften the rigor of paternal authority under the Hindu law, and it is owing to this perhaps as much as to the goodness of Hindu fathers, that paternal power under that law has not that stern character which it wears in other archaic systems. Practically, therefore, the father's power in our law is similar to that under any advanced modern system: indeed it is not so great with us as it is under the Code Napoleon.[5]

The Hindu father's power over his son may be shortly summed up thus: He can inflict moderate correction with a rope or a shoot of a cane,[6] as long as the son is under sixteen years; after that age the son is to be treated as a friend. He can have the son in his custody as long as the son is a minor. He has the right to dispose of his child

[1] Colebrooke's Digest, Bk. II, Ch IV, 7, 16.
[2] VIII, 416.
[3] Yajnavalkya, II, 121.
[4] Ch. I, Sec. V.
[5] See arts. 371—387.
[6] Manu, VIII, 299.

in marriage during minority.[1] He is also entitled to a share in the son's acquisitions.[2] But a great deal of the Hindu father's actual authority is based upon moral injunctions; and nowhere has filial duty been more strictly enjoined than in the Institutes of Manu.[3]

I need hardly add that the exercise of paternal authority is not merely allowable as a sort of compensation to the father for his trouble and anxiety in bringing up his children, but is absolutely necessary to protect the interests of these last, against the errors and indiscretion of infancy. Unlike other rights, these rights of the father inure not so much for the benefit of the person possessing them, as for the good of the person over whom they are exercised.

Maintenance of parents.

In the Hindu law, the son is as much bound to maintain his aged parents, as the father is, to support his infant children.[4]

If the latter duty is necessary to be enforced for the preservation of our race, the former is equally necessary to be enforced for its happiness. The comprehensive character of the Hindu law of maintenance, which extends its protection not merely to the wife, the children, and the parents, but also to a number of other relations, has been sometimes cried down as inevitably tending to foster habits of indolence and dependence. But competent judges have justly commended it; and apart from sentimental considerations, it should be borne in mind that it is this law and the morality by which it is supported, that have saved our Government the trouble of enforcing that complicated system of poor laws, which is a social necessity in other countries.

[1] Macnaghten's Precedents of Hindu Law, 204.

[2] Dayabhaga, Ch. II, 65.

[3] II, 227—235.

[4] Colebrooke's Digest, Bk. V, 77; Macnaghten's Precedents of Hindu Law, 113—115.

LECTURE IV.

Rules for women whose husbands are away.

I pass over that chapter of our law which treats of the rules relating to the conduct of women whose husbands are away, as they are mostly in the nature of mere moral injunctions. It will be sufficient here to say that the husband is required to provide support for the wife, and the wife is required to reside with his or her own relations.[1]

Appointment of a wife to raise up offspring.

Notwithstanding the strict rules about chastity and the strong condemnation of unchastity even in thought, the spiritual necessity for a son has introduced into the Hindu law the anomalous provision of the appointment of a wife to raise up offspring in the event of the husband's incapacity or death.[2] This provision is not peculiar to the Hindu law, but is to be found in other ancient codes, such as the Jewish.[3] The son thus produced is called the *kshetraja* son, or the son of the wife, and is one of the twelve kinds of sons enumerated by the sages; and in ancient times he was entitled to a share of the heritage.[4] The practice was strictly guarded by rules, and was never allowed to be made a source of sensual gratification; and in Manu's time, though permitted, it was greatly discountenanced.[5] In the present age it is altogether forbidden;[6] and it exists in certain places, such as Orissa, only as a local custom.[7]

---

[1] Colebrooke's Digest, Bk. IV, Ch. II, Sec. II.

[2] Colebrooke's Digest, Bk. IV, Ch. IV, Sec. I; Bk. V, Ch. IV, Sec. IV.

[3] Deuteronomy, XXV, 5—10.

[4] Manu, IX, 158—160, 164, 165, 180.

[5] Manu, IX, 58—68; V, 156—166.

[6] General Note to Manu.

[7] Macnaghten's Principles of Hindu Law, p. 102 (3rd ed.); note to Mussummaut Sutputtee *v.* Indranund Jha, 2 Sel. Rep., 224 (new ed.)

LECTURE V.

DISSOLUTION OF MARRIAGE—WIDOWHOOD.

Duration of the conjugal relation—Divorce—Its different forms—Its effects—Divorce when allowable—Grounds of divorce in different systems of law—Divorce in the ordinary sense unknown to the Hindu law—Divorce allowed by custom in some cases—Grounds of such divorce—Distinction between divorce and dissolution of marriage in Hindu law—and between desertion and supersession — Judicial separation — Grounds which justify supersession — Grounds which justify desertion of a wife—Grounds which justify desertion of the husband—Change of religion a ground for desertion—Act XXI of 1866—Position of the wife who deserts, or is deserted by, her husband—Position of the woman whose marriage is void *ab initio*—Widowhood—Duties of the widow—*Sati*—Origin of the practice—Supposed *Vaidik* authority for it—Duties of a widow surviving her husband—Rights of the widow—Maintenance—Amount of maintenance—Widow's maintenance how far a charge on her husband's estate—Heir not liable for widow's contracts for necessary supplies—Widow entitled to maintenance though not living in her husband's house—Widow how far entitled to maintenance from relations other than her husband's heirs—Right to maintenance not saleable—Maintenance forfeited for unchastity—Suits for maintenance—Widow entitled to reside in the family dwelling-house—She is entitled to a share on partition—Widow entitled to inherit in certain cases—But she takes a qualified estate—Succession of several widows—Perpetual widowhood—Act XV of 1856.

HAVING considered between what parties and in what modes marriage may be contracted, and what rights and duties arise out of it, I come now to consider how, if at all, the contract may be dissolved. I may here premise a few general observations before entering into the details of the Hindu law on the subject.

Duration of the conjugal relation.

Excepting the Mahomedan law, which sanctions temporary marriages, no other polished system of law permits parties to settle for themselves the duration of their conjugal relation. The duration is fixed for them by law, and is in most civilized countries the period of their joint lives. Our system goes further, and maintains that, as regards the woman, even the death of her husband does not dissolve the marriage-tie. Such being the spirit of our law,

LECTURE V. a contract between the parties to a marriage to the effect that their marriage would become dissolved on the happening of any specified contingency, has been declared to be void, as being opposed to the policy of that law.[1]

The reasons for making marriage a life-long union are obvious. Man may contract a temporary marriage for the gratification of a transient passion; but to the woman the pleasures of matrimony are soon followed by the cares of maternity; and if she is not able to reckon with certainty upon the help and co-operation of her husband, her condition, as well as that of her infant child, would be really miserable. This co-operation, which the proper care and nurture of a single child would necessitate for a number of years, would have to be prolonged indefinitely by the births of successive children, till at last neither party would have much inducement to separate from the other. Thus ordinary foresight would show that marriage for life is the best form of marriage. But as the best interests of society are here involved, lest that foresight be ever blinded by the impulse of passion, the law interposes in most countries, and declares marriage to be a union for life.

Divorce—Its different forms.

But though this may be a very wholesome rule in general, exceptional cases may arise in which the continuance of the union would be a source of lasting misery to either or both of the parties. To meet these contingencies, divorce in some form or other is prescribed by most systems of law. The different forms of divorce may be classed under either of two heads,—first, dissolution of marriage; and second, separation of the husband and wife in bed and board, their marriage-tie still subsisting. The former is resorted to when

---

[1] Seetaram *v.* Mussamut Aheeree Heeranee, 20 W. R., 49.

owing to some circumstance affecting the validity of the marriage, or owing to disagreement of a lasting nature between the parties, it is thought improper that they should continue as husband and wife; while the latter is the remedy in cases in which, owing to some present cause of disagreement, such as ill-treatment or the like, it becomes necessary that the parties should live separate, though there may be hope of future reconciliation between them. The former mode has been called divorce *á vinculo matrimonii,* or divorce simply, or dissolution of marriage; and the latter has been styled divorce *á mensa et thoro,* or judicial separation.

Its effects.

In the former case, the effect of divorce is to dissolve the marriage-tie completely, and to leave the parties free to marry again; and when the ground of the divorce is the invalidity of the marriage, its effect is to declare the marriage void *ab initio,* and, except for some purposes in certain cases, to bastardize the issue of such marriage. In the latter case, the effect is to permit the husband and the wife to live separately, and to prevent either party from enforcing restitution of conjugal rights against the other; though, if they both agree, there would be no bar to their living together again as man and wife.

Divorce when allowable.

The grounds upon which a marriage may be declared void *ab initio,* depend upon the rules relating to the qualifications of parties to marriage, and the formalities required for contracting it, in each particular system.

The determination of the proper grounds for allowing dissolution of marriage not void *ab initio,* is one of the most difficult problems for the legislator. If, on the one hand, to deny divorce universally would involve a grievous wrong to individuals in some cases, on the other hand, to allow it freely would be equally grievous in its consequences to society;

LECTURE V. for it needs hardly to be pointed out that it is upon the indissolubility of marriage that the integrity of the family, the proper rearing of the next generation, and the cultivation of domestic virtues depend. The grounds which are usually insisted upon as justifying divorce, may be classified under two heads,—namely, consent of both parties, and misconduct of either or of both. At first sight, the former ground seems to be so natural and so little open to objection, that one is apt to wonder why it has not been universally adopted, and why, on the contrary, collusion between the parties should form a ground for rejecting an application for divorce.[1] The propriety of allowing divorce upon consent of both parties has been discussed at some length by Jeremy Bentham in his Principles of the Civil Code,[2] and his opinion is decidedly in its favor. It would carry me much beyond the scope of the present lecture to examine the question in detail. Generally speaking, one reason why this ground of divorce, which is apparently so unobjectionable, is rejected in most systems, is, because it is thought that the disagreement and the consequent separation which we may bring about by our own choice, may as well be prevented by some care and self-sacrifice on our part, if we know that there is no choice in the matter. Another reason is, that it is apprehended, that marriage will be thoughtlessly contracted if it can be dissolved by mutual consent. The admissibility of the grounds of the latter class rests upon a very different consideration. When the conduct of either of the parties has been such that it would be cruel to the other to allow the matrimonial relation to subsist between them, divorce is the only remedy for the wrong. But it ought to be granted

---

[1] See for instance Act IV of 1869, s. 13.

[2] Ch. V, Sec II.

only at the instance of the wronged party, and the misconduct for which it should be granted, ought to be such that no one would be likely to permit it to be imputed to him merely for the purpose of obtaining divorce. It is upon grounds of the latter class,—that is, misconduct of the parties,—that divorce is allowed in most civilized countries.

Grounds of divorce in different system of law.

The Roman law allowed divorce by the mutual consent of parties, or at the choice of either of them if the other was guilty of conjugal infidelity.[1] The Mahomedan law goes further, and permits divorce, not only by the consent of both parties, but also at the mere will and pleasure of the husband.[2] The Code Napoleon allows divorce by mutual consent in a certain limited class of cases under very stringent restrictions. It also authorizes divorce on the ground of adultery by the wife, or by the husband if he keeps his concubine in the common dwelling-house; or of ill-treatment; or of condemnation of either party to an infamous punishment.[3] By the law of Scotland, either spouse can divorce the other on the ground of adultery or wilful desertion.[4] By the English law and the Indian Divorce Act (IV of 1869) for Christians, divorce can be obtained by the husband on the ground of adultery by the wife; and by the wife on the ground of adultery by the husband, coupled with certain aggravating circumstances, such as incest, cruelty, or the like.[5] The Indian Act also allows the wife to obtain a divorce on the ground of her husband's change of religion and subsequent marriage with another woman.

[1] Sandars's Justinian, Lib. I, Tit. X, 12, note.

[2] Hedaya, Grady's edition, pp. 72, 112.

[3] Arts. 229—233.

[4] Mackenzie's Roman Law, 4th ed., p. 128.

[5] Stephen's Commentaries, Vol. II, pp. 291—294, 5th ed.; Act IV of 1869, s. 10.

*

LECTURE V.

You will observe that, while conjugal infidelity in the wife is always a ground of divorce in all these systems, the same offence in the husband would not, according to some of them, authorize divorce, unless it be coupled with some aggravating circumstance. Morally the offence is the same by whichever party it is committed; but from a social point of view, the consequences of infidelity in the wife are far more seriously embarrassing to the matrimonial union than those of infidelity in the husband; and this seems to be the only ground of justification for this unequal legislation.

Divorce in the ordinary sense unknown to the Hindu law.

The provisions of the Hindu law on this important subject are not altogether satisfactory. By that law, marriage is regarded as a sacrament and an indissoluble union; and accordingly Manu declares,[1]—"Neither by sale nor desertion, can a wife be released from her husband;" and in another place he says,—"'Let mutual fidelity continue till death;' this in few words may be considered as the supreme law between husband and wife."[2] So far our law deals equally with both parties. But it goes further. While, as you have seen, it allows a man to have a plurality of wives, it forbids the second marriage of a woman even after the death of her first husband. It is true that some authorities permit a woman to take a second husband under certain circumstances. Thus Parasara in his celebrated text declares,—"If the husband be missing, or dead, or retired from the world, or impotent, or degraded, in these five calamities a woman may take another husband."[3] And Narada[4] and Devala[5] lay down rules to the same effect. But these rules, either

---

[1] IX, 46. [2] IX, 101.

[3] Ch. IV, quoted in Vidyasagara's Marriage of Hindu Widows, p. 7.

[4] XII, 97–101. [5] Colebrooke's Digest, Bk. IV, 151–153.

like the practice of raising up issue by a kinsman on an appointed wife, relate to a primitive stage of Hindu society in which rapid multiplication of the race was deemed an important object, or they merely show the existence of some difference of opinion among the Hindu sages on a point on which absolute unanimity of opinion can hardly be expected. The prevailing sentiment of Hindu society has for a long time been repugnant to the second marriage of a woman. Manu says, "The holy nuptial texts are applied solely to virgins,[1] and nowhere on earth to girls who have lost their virginity; since those women are in general excluded from legal ceremonies."[2] And in another place he declares, "Nor is a second husband allowed in any part of this code to a virtuous woman."[3] Indeed a twice-married woman *(punarbhu)* and a disloyal wife *(swairini)* are considered as belonging to classes not very far removed from one another. Thus Narada says:[4] LECTURE V.

"Others are women who had a different husband before *(parapurvá)*; they are declared to be of seven kinds, in order as enumerated: among these, the twice married woman is of three descriptions, and the disloyal wife of four sorts."

Their husbands are, according to Manu, 'to be avoided with great care;'[5] their children, says Harita, 'should not be admitted to social meetings;'[6] neither they, nor their daughters, are to be taken in marriage;[7] and their sons, called the *paunarbhava*, though formerly allowed to inherit in default of legitimate sons, as coming under one of the twelve

[1] The word in the original is *Kanya*, which has been explained to mean 'a girl not deflowered, nor given in marriage.' See Colebrooke's Digest, Bk. IV, 168, commentary.

[2] VIII, 226. [3] V, 162. [4] XII, 46—54. [5] III, 166.

[6] Colebrooke's Digest, Bk. IV, 162. [7] *Ibid*, 165.

LECTURE V. descriptions of sons,[1] are in the present age declared unfit to have any share of the heritage.[2]

Thus, while the practice of polygamy renders dissolution of marriage unnecessary for the husband, the prohibition of the second marriage of a woman renders divorce useless for the wife. Accordingly, as a rule, divorce in the ordinary sense of the word has been unknown in Hindu society.

Sir T. Strange says,[3] that the right of divorce in the Hindu law is marital only; but this is not correct. If by divorce is meant dissolution of marriage, it is not obtainable even by the husband, for, according to Manu (IX, 46), a wife can never be released from her husband; and if by the right of divorce is meant the right of either spouse to desert or to live separate from the other, such right, as you will presently see, belongs, under certain circumstances, to the wife as well as to the husband.

Divorce allowed by custom in some cases.

But though not allowed by the general Hindu law, divorce and remarriage of a divorced wife are in some cases permitted by custom.[4] Such custom, however, prevails only among the inferior classes, especially in the Bombay Presidency;[5] and disputes concerning this subject are generally settled by *punchayets* or caste assemblies. But it has been held that the Courts are not bound to recognize the authority of the caste to declare a marriage void, or to give permission to a woman to remarry.[6]

---

[1] Manu, IX, 158—160.

[2] General Note to Manu, VI, 8; Dattaka Mimansa, I, 64; see also Mohun Sing *v.* Chumun Rai, 1 Sel. Rep., 37; Vencatachella Chetty *v.* Parvatham, 8 Mad., 142.

[3] 1 Strange, 52.

[4] See Kudomee Dossee *v.* Joteeram Kolita, I. L. R., 3 Calc., 305.

[5] 1 Strange, 52.

[6] Reg. *v.* Sambhu Raghu, I. L. R., 1 Bom., 352.

The ground upon which such divorce is most commonly granted, is the mutual consent of the husband and the wife, the former granting the latter a *char chitti*, or letter of release.[1] Other grounds are mentioned by Steele[2] as justifying divorce among the inferior castes in Bombay, and these grounds are, impotence of the husband, continual quarrel, habitual ill-treatment, and any irregularity rendering the marriage *ab initio* null and void. Our Courts have accordingly held that with some castes divorce is allowable in case of ill-treatment.[3]

LECTURE V.

Grounds of such divorce.

But the prevailing practice has been not to recognize the validity of any divorce obtained without the consent of the husband.[4] In *Reg.* v. *Karsan Goja*,[5] which is the leading case on the point, the prisoner Karsan Goja had married and cohabited with one Rupa, a married woman, who had repudiated her former husband without his consent. Thereupon Karsan was tried for adultery, and Rupa for marrying again in her husband's lifetime, and their defence was, that by the custom of their caste, a woman might, without the consent of her husband, leave him and contract a valid marriage, called *natra*, with another man. They were both convicted, and the High Court of Bombay, in upholding the convictions, observed: "We are of opinion that such a caste custom as that set up, even if it be proved to exist, is invalid, as being entirely opposed to the spirit of the Hindu law; and we hold that a marriage entered into in accord-

[1] Steele. p. 169. [2] *Ibid*, pp. 168, 169.

[3] See Kaseeram Kriparam *v.* Umbaram Huree Chand, 1 Borr., 387; Kasee Dhoollub *v.* Ruttun Baee, *Ibid*, 410, cited in 1 Morley's Digest, 289, pls. 14, 14*a*

[4] See Dyaram Doolubh *v.* Baee Umba, 3 Morley's Digest, 181, pl. 1; 1 W. & B., 92. [5] 2 Bom., 117.

ance with such a custom is void." The same principle has been followed in several subsequent cases.[1]

Distinction between divorce and dissolution of marriage in Hindu law,

Though the Hindu law does not allow divorce, it is not so unreasonable as to compel married parties to live together as man and wife under all possible circumstances. In certain cases, as you have seen already, either spouse is permitted to resist the claim of the other for restitution of conjugal rights. This separation, called in Hindu law desertion (*tyag*), differs from divorce as ordinarily understood, in this,—that however grave or permanent the cause of the desertion, and however solemnly and irrevocably it may take place, it can never have the effect of dissolving the marriage tie completely, so long as both parties remain Hindus.[2]

and between desertion and supersession.

Supersession of one wife by another, which is not unfrequently a motive for divorce in monogamic societies, differs from desertion under the Hindu law in this,—that the superseded wife does not lose her claim for restitution of conjugal rights, nor indeed any of her rights as wife.

Yajnavalkya declares: "But a superseded wife must be maintained, else a great offence is committed."[3] And Vijnaneswar commenting on this text observes: "Though superseded by another wife, she must be treated with courtesy, and receive gifts and respect as before, &c."[4]

Judicial separation.

Where a wife is deserted for any cause not affecting her caste, or the validity of her marriage, and the desertion is in consequence not irrevocable in its nature, such

---

[1] Khemkor *v.* Umia Shankar, 10 Bom., 381; Rahi *v.* Govind, I. L. R., 1 Bom., 116; Narayan Bharthi *v.* Laving Bharthi, I. L. R., 2 Bom., 140.

[2] See Manu. IX, 46.

[3] I, 74.

[4] Mitakshara Acharadhyaya, leaf 9 (Sanskrit).

desertion resembles what is called judicial separation in other systems.

Grounds which justify supersession.

Polygamy being generally permitted, any enquiry into the grounds which justify supersession, would be mere matter of curiosity. Manu has the following rules on the subject:

"A wife who drinks any spirituous liquors, who acts immorally, who shows hatred *to her lord*, who is *incurably* diseased, who is mischievous, who wastes his property, may at all times be superseded by another wife.

"A barren wife may be superseded by another in the eighth year; she whose children are all dead, in the tenth; she who brings forth *only* daughters, in the eleventh; she, who speaks unkindly, without delay.

"But she who, though afflicted with illness, is beloved and virtuous, must never be disgraced, though she may be superseded by another wife with her own consent."[1]

You will here observe that by permitting the immediate supersession of a wife who speaks unkindly, Manu has practically permitted supersession in all cases.

The consideration of the grounds which justify desertion is of much greater importance in practice. I have to some extent already touched upon them when considering the subject of restitution of conjugal rights.

Grounds which justify desertion of a wife.

A wife may be always deserted for conjugal infidelity. Manu says, "That a woman who follows her own will should be forsaken, is ordained by the law; but let not a man slay his wife, nor mutilate her person: Vivaswat declared that a woman wilfully disloyal should be forsaken, not slain, nor disfigured; a man should avoid the slaughter of women."[2]

---

[1] IX, 80—82.

[2] Colebrooke's Digest, Bk. IV, 80.

LECTURE V. A man may also forsake a wife who treats him with aversion,[1] or who is disobedient and self-willed,[2] or who commits any sin in the first degree[3] (such as killing a Brahman, drinking forbidden liquor, stealing gold, &c.[4]) In this last case, under the old Hindu law, the delinquent used to be formally degraded and excommunicated, and thenceforth, till expiation, to be regarded as civilly dead.[5] Hindu society is become more tolerant now, and this practice of formal excommunication is falling into disuse; and indeed, upon a literal construction of Act XXI of 1850, section 1, which provides that loss of caste or excommunication shall no longer occasion any forfeiture of rights, it might seem as if a degraded or excommunicated wife was not any longer liable to be deprived of her conjugal rights. But this Act must receive a more limited construction in order to be reconciled with reason and justice. As has been well observed in *Muchoo* v. *Arzoon Sahoo*,[6] though a person who is excommunicated is not on that account to be deprived of his or her rights, yet such person must not be empowered to deprive others of their right to the freedom of conscience, and the liberty of withholding communion with interdicted persons.

There is one other class of grounds which ought to be noticed, and which not only justify but necessitate desertion of the wife. If the wife is related within the prohibited degrees, or if she belongs to the same *gotra*, she is required to be forsaken as soon as the fact is discovered, and the husband is required to perform penance.[7]

---

[1] Manu, IX, 77.
[2] Colebrooke's Digest, Bk. IV, 80.
[3] Yajnavalkya, I, 72.
[4] Yajnavalkya, III, 227; Manu, XI, 55.
[5] Manu, XI, 182—186, 189.
[6] 5 W. R., 235.
[7] See Kulluka Bhatta's Commentary on Manu, III, 5 and 11; and Udvahatattwa, Institutes of Raghunandana, Vol. II, p. 82.

LECTURE V.

Grounds which justify desertion of the husband.

It remains now to see on what grounds a husband may be deserted. As a rule, "though unobservant of approved usages, or enamoured of another woman, or devoid of good qualities, yet a husband must be constantly revered as a god by a virtuous wife." Such is the law laid down by the highest authority.[1] But the same authority has also said:

"But she who is averse from a mad husband, or a deadly sinner, or an eunuch, or one without manly strength, or one afflicted with such maladies as punish crimes, must neither be deserted nor stripped of her property."[2] This text, however, does not, as Macnaghten[3] thinks, authorize desertion of the husband under the circumstances mentioned. For what Manu excuses here is *aversion*, which according to Kalluka and Jagannath[4] means want of diligent attention, not absolute desertion.

There are passages in the writings of the sages which are more directly in point. Thus Devala says: "A husband may be forsaken by his wife, if he be an abandoned sinner, or an heretical mendicant, or impotent, or degraded, or afflicted with phthisis, or if he have been long absent in a foreign country;" and he goes even further and ordains, that in these cases the wife may take another husband for the sake of obtaining progeny, not through female independence.[5] And Parasara and Narada (in the texts referred to above[6]) by allowing a woman to take a second husband if the first be impotent, or degraded, or retired from the world, or long absent, *à fortiori*, permit desertion of the husband in such cases.

---

[1] Manu, V, 154.

[2] Manu, IX, 79.

[3] Principles of Hindu Law, p, 62.

[4] Colebrooke's Digest, Bk. IV, 57, commentary.

[5] *Ibid*, Bk. IV, 151, 152.

[6] See *ante*, p. 182.

LECTURE V. The periods of absence which would justify desertion in different cases are also laid down by Devala,[1] being eight, six, four, and (presumably) two years, for the sacerdotal, military, commercial, and servile classes respectively, or half the period in each case where the wife has borne no child. I may here observe that, by the English law[2] and by Act IV of 1869 (section 22), desertion for two years is made a ground for judicial separation. According to Manu and Vasistha, however, an absent husband is not to be deserted by the wife; but she is to follow after she has waited for some time.[3]

The remarriage of the wife, which is allowed by Devala, Parasara, and Narada, being generally held to be prohibited in the present age, the rules authorizing the desertion of her husband have become obsolete for want of sufficient lawful inducement for such desertion; and the only grounds which, according to the opinion of modern writers,[4] and the prevailing sentiments and practice of Hindu society, justify desertion of the husband, are his degradation and loss of caste.[5]

The above rule calls for some explanation. You may ask, what offences lead to degradation or loss of caste. The answer to this is not very easy. It is true that these offences are enumerated by Manu[6] and Yajnavalkya[7] with sufficient minuteness; but many of them would hardly be considered as offences in the present altered state of Hindu society. As specimens of the law on the subject, I may

---

[1] Colebrooke's Digest, Bk. IV, 153.
[2] Stephen's Commentaries, Vol. II, p. 292 (5th ed.)
[3] Colebrooke's Digest, Bk. IV, 154, 155.
[4] See Shama Churn's Vyavastha Darpana, pp. 677, 678.
[5] Colebrooke's Digest, Bk. IV, 58; Steele, 32.
[6] XI, 55—71.
[7] III, 227—233.

quote the following texts of Manu, which enumerate some of the graver offences :— LECTURE V.

"Killing a Brahman, drinking forbidden liquor, stealing gold from a priest, adultery with the wife of a father, natural or spiritual, and associating with such as commit those offences, wise legislators must declare to be crimes in the highest degree." (XI, 55.)

"False boasting of high tribe, malignant information before the king, of a criminal who must suffer death, or falsely accusing a spiritual preceptor, are crimes in the second degree, and nearly equal to killing a Brahman." (XI, 56.)

"Carnal commerce with sisters by the same mother, with little girls, with women of the lowest mixed class, or with the wives of a friend, or of a son, the wise must consider as nearly equal to a violation of the paternal bed." (XI, 59.)

Most of these offences are expiable by penance, and after expiation, a sinner is allowed to mix in society, and he would therefore, it seems, be entitled to claim restitution of conjugal rights.[1] But the gravest offences, such as violation of the paternal bed, and the like, can be expiated only by death.[2] It is difficult to say, however, which of these offences require expiation at the present day to prevent degradation or loss of caste.

So long as a man, however vicious or abandoned he may be, is not formally excommunicated, he would, it seems, be entitled to claim the conjugal society of his wife. And even after formal excommunication, he would not necessarily forfeit his marital rights. For, as the propriety of every excommunication is open to be questioned before a Court of Justice,

[1] Manu, XI, 190. [2] Manu, XI, 100—104.
[3] Gopal Gurain v. Gurain, 7 W. R., 299; see also Sudaram Patro v. Soodha Ram, 11 W. R., 457.

LECTURE V. the mere fact of degradation from caste would not disentitle a man to claim restitution of conjugal rights, unless such degradation be for a cause which the Courts would accept as legitimate.

Among other causes which justify desertion of the husband by the wife, may be mentioned cruelty of the husband, and his laboring under loathsome and contagious disease.[1] These have already been considered in the preceding lecture.

Change of religion a ground for desertion.

Change of religion in either spouse would justify desertion by other, and Act XXI of 1850, as I have already explained, would not interfere with such desertion.[2] In such cases, the convert partner is regarded in Hindu law as civilly dead.[3] In the converse case, which is extremely rare, of a Hindu convert to Christianity or other faith, returning back to Hinduism on performance of the necessary expiation, it has been held that the Hindu law would altogether ignore the marriage of the party, contracted while a convert, and would authorize his marriage with a Hindu wife.[4] This decision, we are told by Sir Henry Maine[5] in his speech on the Indian Divorce Bill, has been the cause of the insertion of the provision in Act IV of 1869 (section 10) to the effect that a Christian wife may obtain divorce from her husband by reason of his change of religion and subsequent marriage with another woman.

Act XXI of 1866.

Act XXI of 1866 has made some important provisions for dissolution of marriage when either spouse becomes a

[1] See Yamuna Bai *v.* Narayan Moreshvar Pendse, I. L. R., 1 Bom., 164; Bai Prem Kuvar *v.* Bhika Kalliranji, 5 Bom., A. C. J., 209.

[2] See Muchoo *v.* Arzoon Sahoo, 5 W. R., 235.

[3] Rahmed Beebee *v.* Rokeya Beebee, 1 Norton's Leading Cases on Hindu Law, 12.

[4] 3 Mad. (Criminal Cases), App., vii.

[5] See Supplement to the *Gazette of India* for March 6, 1869, p. 295.

convert to Christianity. It authorizes the convert to sue his or her non-converted partner for conjugal society, and it gives the latter the option of agreeing or refusing to cohabit with the former; and in case of his or her refusal on the ground of change of religion, it directs the Court to declare the marriage dissolved.

Position of the wife who deserts or is deserted by her husband.

The position of the wife who lawfully deserts her husband, or is lawfully deserted by him, is in some respects rather anomalous. So long as both parties remain Hindus, desertion does not dissolve their marriage.[1]

In the case of desertion of the husband by the wife, she must remain under the care of her grown-up sons, if any, or under the care of other kinsmen; for her state is one of perpetual tutelage.[2] As a rule, she is entitled to maintenance from her husband. Where degradation of the husband is the cause of desertion, the Hindu law, which excludes the degraded husband from inheritance, imposes upon the person taking his share of the patrimony the obligation of maintaining his wife if chaste;[3] and now as by Act XXI of 1850 degradation or loss of caste no longer occasions any forfeiture of rights or property, it would follow that the wife is entitled to maintenance from her degraded husband, though she may not live with him.

When change of religion by the husband is the cause of desertion, the case seems to stand on somewhat different grounds. Change of religion, as observed by the Judicial Committee in *Abraham* v. *Abraham*,[4] would release the convert from the trammels of the Hindu law; and his rights and duties would have mainly to be determined by

---

[1] Manu, IX, 46. [2] Manu, IX, 3.
[3] Mitakshara, Ch. II, Sec. X, 14; Dayabhaga, Ch. V, 19.
[4] 1 W. R. (P. C.), 5.

LECTURE V. the law of the sect to which he becomes a convert; and such law in some cases, as where the conversion is to Mahomedanism, would declare the former marriage dissolved.[1] Nevertheless, the adoption of a new religion ought not to have the effect of sweeping away all existing obligations. Considering that, by Act XXI of 1850, the Hindu convert is no longer to be deprived of his rights or property by reason of change of faith, and considering the feelings and the helpless condition of the Hindu wife, and the prohibition against her remarriage, it would be a matter of extreme hardship if she is to be deprived of her right to claim maintenance from her husband, whom, owing to her religious feelings, she may be obliged to forsake. The question is not one of Hindu law, but involves important general principles. The decision of the Madras High Court reported in 4 Mad. H. C. Rep., page iii, may be referred to, as favoring the wife's claim in such cases.

The case of conversion of the husband to Christianity has been expressly provided for by the Legislature. You have seen that the convert husband may, under Act XXI of 1866, sue the Hindu wife for conjugal society, and in the event of her persistent and voluntary refusal to cohabit with him on the ground of his change of faith, a decree may be passed declaring their marriage dissolved. After such decree, the wife, it seems, can have no claim for maintenance against her husband. The Act, however, on the whole, deals equally with both parties, and it contains the following important provision:—

"When any decree dissolving a marriage shall have been passed under the provisions of this Act, it shall be as lawful for the respective parties thereto to marry again as if the

[1] See Hedaya, Bk. II, Ch. V.

prior marriage had been dissolved by death, and the issue of any such remarriage shall be legitimate, any Native law to the contrary notwithstanding. Provided always that no minister of religion shall be compelled to solemnize the marriage of any person whose former marriage may have been dissolved under this Act, or shall be liable to any suit or penalty for refusing to solemnize the marriage of any such person." (Section 19.)

This, you will observe, is the only case in which a Hindu wife can obtain a complete divorce, being permitted not only to forsake her husband, but also to contract a valid and legal remarriage. But as such marriage cannot possess the sacramental character of the nuptial rite in the eye of the Hindu, and as the reproach of being a twice-married woman would still attach to the wife, this permission of re-marriage is seldom if ever availed of.

A wife deserted by her husband is still entitled to some maintenance, even when the cause of desertion is her infidelity to the marriage-bed. But in this last-mentioned case, her maintenance is limited to what has been called a *starving maintenance*, being mere food and raiment,[1] and is allowed only when she ceases to live in adultery.

If she is deserted by reason of her degradation, she is directed to dwell in a hut near the family house.[2] When her change of religion is the cause of desertion, she would no longer be bound by the rules of the Hindu law, and her legal position is to be determined by the law of the sect to which she becomes a convert.[3] If she

---

[1] See Colebrooke's Digest, Bk. IV, 81—83; Honamma v. Timanna Bhat, I. L. R., 1 Bom., 559.

[2] Manu, XI, 189.

[3] See Rahmed Beebee v. Rokeya Beebee, 1 Norton's Leading Cases on Hindu Law, 12.

LECTURE V. embraces Christianity, the provisions of Act XXI of 1866 would enable her to marry again, after obtaining a decree for dissolution of her former marriage.

Position of the woman whose marriage is void *ab initio.*

The position of the woman whose marriage is void *ab initio*, seems to be singularly unfortunate under the Hindu law. The causes which render a marriage void *ab initio* are, first, difference of caste in the contracting parties; and second, identity of *gotra*, or relationship within the prohibited degrees. In the former case, according to some authorities, if the error is discovered before *garbhadhan*, the girl is to perform expiation, and may be married again; but after *garbhadhan*, she is no longer eligible for remarriage, and if of a lower caste, she is liable to be repudiated by her husband, though she is entitled to be maintained, and her issue would be considered illegitimate.[1] In the latter case, on the error being discovered, the husband is directed to perform penance and repudiate the wife; but he is required to support her.[2] Her remarriage, however, is nowhere allowed, even though the repudiation take place before consummation. The doctrine of the Hindu law is, that a girl is blemished by the mere ceremony of marriage, and if married again, the reproach of being a twice-married woman (*punarbhu*) would attach to her, even if she be a *virgo intacta*.[3] This is hardly just. Even the virgin widow has one consolation for her hard lot, that it is due to a cause which no human foresight could prevent. But the condition of the repudiated virgin wife, who is condemned to a life of virtual widowhood for the error of a reckless guardian, is truly pitiable. A far more rational rule, and one not wholly

[1] See Steele, pp. 29, 30, 166.

[2] Manu, III, 5 and 11, Note by Kulluka; Colebrooke's Digest, Bk. V, 339, 340.

[3] Colebrooke's Digest, Bk. IV, 158—169; Manu, VIII, 226, 227.

against the spirit of our law, would be to allow remarriage in such cases, where the wife is repudiated before consummation. For here the girl is free from blemish by intercourse; and as for the blemish by reason of the nuptial ceremony, such ceremony being performed under a mistake of fact, may, by a principle not altogether unknown to the Hindu law,[1] be regarded in law as not performed at all. Such a rule seems also to receive some support from the decision of the High Court of Bengal in *Anjona Dossee* v. *Proladh Chunder Ghose*,[2] in which the Officiating Chief Justice Norman, in delivering the judgment of the Court upon the question whether a suit for declaration of the nullity of a Hindu marriage would lie, observed:—

"If the marriage is in fact no marriage, unless she can obtain a declaration from a Court of Justice that the marriage is null and void, unless she can obtain the protection which such Court can give her, she may be obliged to live with the defendant in a state of concubinage, or at least she will be prevented from marrying any one else. The rights which a decree in this suit may protect—with which the defendant may be restrained from interfering—the preservation of the personal purity of the infant plaintiff and her right and power to contract a valid marriage—are amongst the highest rights which a human being can possess; and it would be a matter deeply to be lamented if the Court had no power to protect and defend them."

Happily, however, in practice the strictness with which relationship and other particulars are enquired into before

---

[1] In the somewhat analogous case of a thing given by mistake, Narada declares that it must be considered as not given. See Colebrooke's Digest, Bk. II, Ch. IV, 53; Narada, IV, 8.

[2] 14 W. R., 403.

LECTURE V. making the nuptial contract, reduces the evil here complained of within the narrowest possible limits.

Widowhood. Connected with divorce or desertion, which is separation of the married pair by voluntary act, is widowhood or the state of separation by death; and it therefore deserves in this place a passing notice. The position of the Hindu widow is in many respects so unique in jurisprudence, and the law relating to her rights and status is of such wide extent and vast practical importance, that you can hardly expect anything like an adequate treatment of the subject in a single lecture. All I can do here will only be to give you a rough outline of that law.

The institution of widowhood with all its hardships and disadvantages, is a result of that unequal legislation for the two sexes, which characterizes all archaic systems. In primitive society, women, like slaves, are always regarded as articles of property; and just as provision is made for succession to a man's other property on his death, similarly provision is also made in primitive law with regard to his wives; by which they are to pass to his brothers. This system of Levirate, Sir John Lubbock tells us, is widely distributed, and he shows its prevalence among several barbarous and semi-barbarous nations at the present day.[1] The practice prevailed among the Jews;[2] and the law of polished Athens went even further, and permitted the husband to bequeath his wife to any man whom he might choose for his successor.[3]

Traces of this leviratical system may be found in our own law. "The damsel indeed," says Manu, "whose husband shall die after troth verbally plighted, but before

[1] Origin of Civilisation, pp. 135, 136.
[2] Deuteronomy, XXV, 5—10.
[3] See Commentary on Isæus, Sir W. Jones's Works, Vol. IV, p. 211.

consummation, his brother shall take in marriage according to this rule, &c."[1] But the practice had already become repugnant to the prevailing moral sentiments of the people in Manu's time, and accordingly it is very much discountenanced in his code.[2] With the moral progress of society, it was felt to be unjust to compel a woman to accept a second husband appointed by law; and perpetual widowhood under proper guardianship became the normal condition of the Hindu wife after her husband's death.

Duties of the widow—*Sati.*

Under the Hindu law as it stood before the year 1829, a woman, on the death of her husband, might either immolate herself on his funeral pile, or lead a life of perpetual widowhood. Thanks to the British rule, this inhuman practice of self-immolation of the widow, commonly called the practice of *Sati*, was abolished by Bengal Regulation XVII of that year, which declares the practice to be illegal and punishable by the Criminal Courts.

The rite was called *sahamarana* or *anumarana* according as the wife died on the same funeral pile with her husband, or on a different pile, as in the event of her husband dying abroad. It is extolled by some of the sages as the highest virtuous act for a woman, and minute rules are laid down for regulating the practice in different cases.[3] But as the interest attaching to the subject is purely historical now, I spare myself the not very grateful task of dwelling at length upon these rules. It is some relief to notice that mothers of infant children and pregnant women were prohibited to observe this rite.

---

[1] IX, 69.

[2] IX, 65—68.

[3] See Raghunandana's Suddhitattwa, and Colebrooke's Digest, Bk. IV, 123—131; Mitakshara, Acharadhyaya (Sanskrit), leaf 12.

LECTURE V.

Origin of the practice.

Regarding the origin of this practice, strange views have been sometimes entertained. Thus Diodorus Siculus[1] supposes it to have originated with a view to check the wicked practice of poisoning husbands. This, however, is a most unfounded conjecture. The truth is, that this practice was not peculiar to India,[2] though India is perhaps the only country in which it co-existed with a high degree of national progress. And it seems to have originated in those vague notions of a future state which are current among primitive races, and which perhaps led them to imagine that the dead ought to carry with them to the next world not only their goods and chattels (which are often buried with them), but also their wives and slaves.[3]

Supposed Vaidik authority for it.

The Aryan Hindus are supposed to have borrowed the *sati* rite from the aboriginal Tamulians. It is not mentioned among the funeral rites which are enumerated in detail in the Taittiriya Aranyaka of the Black Yajurveda,[4] nor in the Code of Manu. As for the text of the Rigveda, cited by Raghunandana as authority for this rite, Western scholars have shown that it involves a slight misquotation which has materially altered the meaning.[5]

Duties of a widow surviving her husband.

The duties of a widow surviving her husband claim our attention next. In primitive society, one of the most im-

---

[1] See Introduction to the Taittiriya Aranyaka of the Black Yajurveda, by Dr. Rajendralala Mitra, p. 9.

[2] Max Müller's Chips from a German Workshop, Vol. II, p. 264.

[3] See Spencer's Sociology, p. 203 *et seq.*

[4] See Introduction to the Taittiriya Aranyaka of the Black Yajurveda, by Dr. Rajendralala Mitra, pp. 11, 12.

[5] The question how far the *sati* rite is sanctioned by the Vedas has been discussed at some length by Professor Wilson, who was the first to point out the above error (see Wilson's Essays, Vol. II, pp. 270 to 309); and also by Professor Max Müller in his Chips from a German Workshop, Vol. II, pp. 33 to 38.

portant of these was to raise up issue for her deceased husband. But in Manu's time the practice was becoming obsolete, and it is condemned in the institutes of that sage as 'fit only for cattle.'[1] And in the present age it is absolutely prohibited.[2] LECTURE V.

The duties of a faithful widow have been thus described by Manu :—

"A faithful wife who wishes to attain in heaven the mansion of her husband, must do nothing unkind to him, be he living or dead.

"Let her emaciate her body, by living voluntarily on pure flowers, roots, and fruit; but let her not, when her lord is deceased, even pronounce the name of another man.

"Let her continue till death forgiving all injuries, performing harsh duties, avoiding every sensual pleasure, and cheerfully practising the incomparable rules of virtue, which have been followed by such women as were devoted to one only husband." (vv. 156—158.)

So Vishnu: "After the death of her husband a wife must practise austerities or ascend the pile after him."[3] There are numerous texts prescribing the number of meals a day that the widow may take, the nature of the bed she is to sleep upon, and other particulars relating to her conduct.[4] In short, she is to lead a life of pious austerity for the spiritual welfare, not of herself alone, but also of her husband; for, says Brihaspati, "A wife is considered as half the body of her husband, equally sharing the fruit of pure and impure acts."[5] Strict as the rules regulating her conduct are, and severe as is the self-denial they impose upon her, they are still

[1] IX, 66.

[2] General Note to Manu.

[3] Colebrooke's Digest, IV, 133.

[4] *Ibid*, 134—145.

[5] Colebrooke's Digest, IV, 132.

LECTURE V. observed in the main, notwithstanding the sweeping changes that have revolutionized Hindu society, and notwithstanding the fact that remarriage is now declared legal for her.

But if the Hindu law imposes such austere duties upon the widow, it also allows her important rights.

Rights of the widow.

Maintenance.

In the first place she is always entitled to maintenance from the person who inherits her husband's estate.[1] This is an important right of the widow, and our Courts have always been anxious to secure it to her in the best possible manner. The ordinary mode of enforcing it is to bring a suit for establishing the right to maintenance and for obtaining arrears of maintenance such as may be due; and then to recover all future arrears by a suit each time that an arrear falls due. But she has not been always left to this troublesome and circuitous mode of enforcing her right. In the case of *Sree Mootee Mundoodaree Dabee* v. *Joynarain Puckrassee*,[2] decided by the Supreme Court of Calcutta in the year 1801, in which separate maintenance was claimed by the widow, the defendant, her stepson, was ordered to deposit with the Accountant-General a sum sufficient to produce the monthly allowance decreed, and on his default to do so, the Master was directed to sell a competent portion of the husband's estate such as would yield the monthly sum allowed as maintenance. And in the case of *Seebchunder Bose* v. *Gooroopersaud Bose*, which was a suit for partition amongst brothers, it was ordered that before any partition be made, the Master do enquire and report what sum would be requisite for the purpose of securing to their stepmother

---

[1] Mitakshara, Ch. II, Sec. I, 7; Colebrooke's Digest, Bk. V, 405; Smriti Chandrika, Ch. XI, Sec. I., 34; 1 Strange, 171; 2 Strange, 290—296; Macnaghten's Precedents of Hindu Law, Ch. I, Sec. II, Case xii; Ch. II, Cases x and xi.

[2] Macnaghten's Considerations on Hindu Law, 60.

(a childless widow) a suitable maintenance, and it was ordered that *in the first instance* such sum be set apart for the purpose.[1] "From these decisions," says Sir Francis Macnaghten, "it clearly appears that the widow entitled to maintenance is not to be left at the mercy of him whose duty it is to maintain her, but that she may compel him to do her justice,—and although the obligation imposed upon him be indefinite, that a Court of Equity will define it, by adverting to circumstances, and aid her in the enforcement of such advantages as the possessor of her husband's wealth is bound in conscience to confer." And he further observes, that a widow entitled to maintenance may restrain the representatives of her husband from wasting or making away with his estate, or at least compel them under such circumstances to give security for due payment of a suitable maintenance.[2]

Amount of maintenance.

The minimum rate of maintenance for the widow is specified in the Hindu law with sufficient precision.[3] But as the rules on the subject refer to a state of society very different from the present, they are not now followed, and the Courts have always exercised their discretion in determining the amount of maintenance in each case.[4] The amount is not merely to be so much as is just sufficient for the widow's support, but is to include some allowance for the performance of charities and the discharge of religious obligations, and is to be assessed with reference to the value of her husband's estate; and in fixing the amount, the value of her *stridhan*

---

[1] Macnaghten's Considerations on Hindu Law, p. 63.

[2] *Ibid*, pp. 62, 63.

[3] See Smriti Chandrika, Ch. XI, S. I. 39; Macnaghten's Precedents of Hindu Law, pp. 111 and 112 note.

[4] See Mussummaut Bheeloo *v.* Phool Chund, 3 Sel Rep. (new ed.), 298; Ranee Parvata Vardani Nachear *v.* Anandai, 12 Moo. I. A., 447.

LECTURE V.

is, according to some authorities, to be taken into account.[1] But it has been held that it is not necessary that she "should be maintained in the same state as her husband would maintain her." [2]

Widow's maintenance how far a charge on her husband's estate.

As a rule, the widow's maintenance is a charge on her husband's estate. It has been held that her claim cannot be defeated by her husband's will, merely by implication.[3] Where the estate, which is chargeable with the maintenance of a widow, comes into the hands of several heirs, the widow has been held entitled to sue any one of them for her maintenance, on the ground that it is a charge upon the whole estate and therefore upon every part thereof.[4] In such cases, if any one of the heirs is made to pay the whole amount of maintenance, his remedy would be to sue the other heirs for contribution. So long as the estate which is chargeable, remains in the hands of successive heirs, the widow's claim continues to be a charge on it. Where, however, it passes into the hands of persons by some title other than inheritance, it has been a matter of some contention as to whether the charge still subsists. If the purchaser of an estate take it with notice of a widow's claim for maintenance, it is a settled rule that it continues liable for such claim.[5] The question how far it would be necessary for the widow in such cases to try in the first place to recover her maintenance from the heir-at-law before she would be entitled to follow the estate in the hands of the purchaser, has

---

[1] 1 Strange, 171 ; 2 Strange, 305.

[2] Kalee Persaud Sing *v.* Kupoor Koowaree, 4 W. R., 65.

[3] Comulmoney Dossee *v.* Rammanath Bysack, 1 Fulton, 193.

[4] Ramchandra Dikshit *v.* Savitribai, 4 Bom., A. C. J., 73.

[5] Srimati Bhagabati Dasi *v.* Kanailal Mitter, 8 B. L. R., 225 ; Hera Lall *v.* Mussumat Kousillah. 2 Agra H. C. R., 42 ; Baboo Goluck Chunder Bose *v.* Ranee Ohilla Dayee, 25 W. R., 100.

been answered by Mr. Justice Romesh Chunder Mitter in the case of *Baboo Goluck Chunder Bose* v. *Ranee Ohilla Dayee*[1] thus:—

"As regards the second question that has been argued before us, it seems to me that it is not a correct proposition of Hindoo law to say, that, in all cases, a Hindoo widow is not entitled to follow properties from which she is entitled to obtain her maintenance in the hands of the purchaser, unless she at first attempts to recover her maintenance from the heir-at-law. It may be that, in certain cases, where the defence is that sufficient property is still in the hands of the heir-at-law from which the maintenance can be recovered, the person entitled to maintenance might not be allowed to recover it from the purchaser of a small portion of the family property without first attempting to recover it from the properties in the possession of the heir-at-law. But in this case there was no such defence, and, in either of the Courts below, the objection in this form was not raised. And we do not think that we ought to allow it to be raised here for the first time in special appeal."

Where the estate is acquired by a *bonâ fide* purchaser for value without notice, the case rests upon different grounds. There is some authority apparently in support of the contention that the estate even in such cases continues liable. Thus there is a text of Katyayana, which says, "Except his whole estate and his dwelling-house, what remains after the food and clothing of his family, a man may give away, whatever it be, whether fixed or moveable; otherwise it may not be given,"[2] and which may imply that the maintenance of the late proprietor's widow, amongst

[1] 25 W. R., 100. [2] Colebrooke's Digest, Bk. II, Ch. IV, 10.

LECTURE V. others, imposes a restriction upon the heir's power of alienation. Moreover, there is the decision of the Privy Council in the case of *Mussumat Golab Koonwar* v. *The Collector of Benares*,[1] in which the widow was held entitled to maintenance out of her husband's estate, after it had been forfeited to Government by reason of her sons being implicated in an insurrection. There is also a dictum of Mr. Justice Glover in the case of *Mussamut Khukroo Misrain* v. *Jhoomuck Lall Dass*[2] to the effect that a Hindu widow's maintenance is a charge on her husband's estate into whose hands soever it may pass. But on the other hand, there are authorities in support of the opposite view.[3]

The question has been very fully considered by Mr. Justice Jackson in the case of *Adhiranee Narain Coomary* v. *Shona Malee Pat Mahadai*,[4] in which, upon a review of the authorities on both sides, the conclusion has been arrived at, that the widow's lien for maintenance does not follow her husband's estate in the hands of a *bonâ fide* purchaser without notice. As observed in that case, the text of Katyayana quoted above is far too vague to support the widow's contention; and, indeed, it may well be doubted whether the text applies to any case other than that of a gift of the whole of a man's estate; for in the case of sale it might be said that the consideration received by the heir would take the place of the property sold, and might be held answerable for the widow's maintenance. And as for the case of *Mussumat Golab Koonwar* v. *The Collector of Benares*,[5]

---

[1] 7 W. R. (P. C.), 47.

[2] 5 W. R., 263.

[3] Srimati Bhagabati Dasi *v* Kanailal Mitter, 8 B. L. R., 225; Mussamat Goolabi *v.* Ramtahal Rai, 1 All. H. C. R., 191; Lakshman Ramchandra *v.* Sarasvatibai, 12 Bom., 69; Juggernath Sawunt *v.* Maharanee Odhiranee Narain Koomaree, 20 W R., 126.

[4] I. L. R., 1 Calc., 365.

[5] 7 W. R. (P. C.), 47.

the Government, as might be expected, did not think it fit to raise any objection to the widow's claim for maintenance, and the decision of the Privy Council was, it would seem, based in a great measure upon the absence of such objection. The strongest argument in favor of the widow's claim is this, that as her maintenance is a charge on the estate, and as upon the well-known principle recognized by the Privy Council in the case of *Varden Seth Sam* v. *Luckpathy Royjee Lallah*,[1] one who owns property subject to a charge can, in general, convey no title higher or more free than his own, it lies always on the purchaser to make out a case to defeat the widow's claim. But as has been pointed out by Mr. Justice Jackson, the holder of a lien on specific property is in a different position from a person possessed of a right which constitutes a charge upon the general estate of a deceased person. The inconvenience, moreover, of allowing the widow's claim in such cases would be considerable. As observed by Mr. Justice Phear in *Bhagabati Dasi's* case, "if the heir has any power of alienation at all, it would be most unreasonable that a *bonâ fide* purchaser for valuable consideration should be subjected to the possibility of a charge springing up at any time, though it had no definite existence when he purchased."[2]

Where the widow makes any one among several co-heirs answerable for her maintenance, such person may obtain contribution from the other co-heirs; but there is not the same facility for the remedy by contribution in the case of a purchaser. For the estate might vest in a number of co-heirs, and different portions of the estate might be purchased from them by different parties, some buying with, and

---

[1] 9 Moore's I. A., 322.

[2] 8 B. L. R., 229.

LECTURE V.

some without, notice of the widow's claim; and in the event of the widow choosing to make one of the purchasers without notice liable for her claim, against whom is such purchaser to proceed for contribution, and how is the Court to apportion the liability for the same? To allow the widow to enforce her claim against a purchaser in such cases would thus lead to evident inconvenience.

The somewhat broad proposition laid down by Sir Richard Couch, when Chief Justice of Bombay, in *Ramchandra Dikshit* v. *Savitribai*,[1] that the widow's maintenance "is a charge upon the whole estate and therefore upon every part thereof," has been qualified and explained by him in the case of *Nistarini Dasi* v. *Makhunlall Dutt*,[2] where, speaking of the Bombay case, he says: "The question there was as to whether one brother could be sued alone, and it was held that he could." Nor will the adverse rule seriously affect the interests of the widow; for, in addition to other remedies, such as taking security from the heir, to which, according to Sir Francis Macnaghten, she is entitled, she can always protect herself by giving due notice of her claim. Upon reason and authority, therefore, the rule laid down in *Adhiranee Narain Coomary's* case appears to be unexceptionable.

Heir not liable for widow's contracts for necessary supplies.

Though the widow is entitled to maintenance from the person inheriting her husband's estate, her contracts for necessary supplies would not be binding on such person. In the case of *Ramasamy Aiyan* v. *Minakshi Ammal*,[3] which was a suit for money advanced to the first defendant, a widow, for her necessary maintenance, and in which the second defendant, the heir in possession of the first defend-

[1] 4 Bom., A. C. J., 73.

[2] 9 B. L. R., 27.

[3] 2 Mad., 409.

ant's husband's estate, was sought to be made liable, the Court observed—

"Now, clearly as a matter of contract, there is no liability on the part of the second defendant, nor was there on the part of her husband. The first defendant had full capacity to contract, and she alone executed the bond; and granting that the plaintiff made the advances under the *bonâ fide* belief that, as widow, the first defendant had a continuing right to maintenance out of the estate in the hands of her adopted son and his widow, the second defendant, we think there is no principle or rule of Hindu law which recognizes any authority in a widow, entitled only to maintenance, to make contracts for necessary supplies binding upon the heir in possession of the family property and liable to maintain her."

Widow entitled to maintenance though not living in her husband's house.

The question whether a widow in order to be entitled to maintenance is bound to reside with her husband's relatives, has been sometimes raised; but the point has been settled by decisions of the Privy Council, and the rule now is, that should a widow without unchaste purposes quit her husband's family house, and live with her parents or other relatives, she would still be entitled to maintenance. The case of *Rajah Pirthee Singh* v. *Ranee Raj Kower*[1] is the latest important case on the point. In that case the earlier decisions have been examined, and the Privy Council in their judgment observe: "It therefore appears that a Hindu widow is not bound to reside with the relatives of her husband; that the relatives of her husband have no right to compel her to live with them; and that she does not forfeit her right to property or maintenance merely on account of

[1] 20 W. R., 21.

her going and residing with her family, or leaving her husband's residence from any other cause than unchaste or improper purposes."

Widow how far entitled to maintenance from relations other than her husband's heirs.

We have hitherto been considering the claim of a widow for maintenance against the person inheriting her husband's estate. The question next arises how far she is entitled to be maintained by the heir when her husband leaves no property, and how far she can claim maintenance from other relatives. The Hindu sages emphatically enjoin upon every person the duty of maintaining the dependent members of his family. The following are a few of the many texts on the subject:[1]—

Manu:—"The ample support of those who are entitled to maintenance is rewarded with *bliss in* heaven; but hell is the portion of that man whose family is afflicted with pain by his neglect: therefore let him maintain his family with the utmost care."

Narada:—"Even they who are born, or yet unborn, and they who exist in the womb, require funds for subsistence; the deprivation of the means of subsistence is reprehended."

Brihaspati:—"A man may give what remains after the food and clothing of his family: the giver of more *who leaves his family naked and unfed*, may taste honey at first, but shall afterwards find it poison."

Following the spirit of the Hindu law, the High Court of Bombay has held that a Hindu widow, if destitute of means, is entitled to maintenance from her husband's relatives, although she may have shared her husband's estate, and may have supported herself for a long period by trading;[2] that the fact of her husband having been divided from the

---

[1] Colebrooke's Digest, Bk. II, Ch. IV, 11, 12, and 18.

[2] Bai Lakshmi *v.* Lakhmidas Gopaldas, 1 Bom, 13.

family would not affect her right to maintenance;[1] and that such right is not limited to obtaining food and clothing by living in the family house, but that the Court may at its discretion award her a separate maintenance.[2] LECTURE V.

But the High Court of Bengal has laid down a different rule. In the case of *Kasheenath Doss* v. *Khettur Monee Dossee*,[3] the following question was referred for the decision of a Full Bench,—namely, whether a Hindu widow refusing to live in the house of her father-in-law, can maintain a suit against him for a pecuniary allowance by way of maintenance. Sir Barnes Peacock, whose decision was affirmed on appeal, in delivering judgment, observed:

"Two questions seem to arise out of the point submitted for the opinion of the Full Bench, *viz.,—first,* whether the widow of a Hindoo refusing to live in the house of her father-in-law can sue him for a pecuniary allowance by way of maintenance, if she leave his house without reasonable cause; and *secondly,* is she entitled to maintenance if she leave on account of ill-usage or other reasonable cause?

"In the case cited from the 2nd volume of the Weekly Reporter, page 134, it was held that a daughter-in-law has a right to maintenance from her father-in-law, so long as she is chaste, whether she continues to live with him or not, and Mr. Justice Kemp is still of that opinion.

"It appears to me, however, that, according to the law as administered in Lower Bengal, a daughter-in-law has not in either case a legal ground of action to recover maintenance against her father-in-law.

---

[1] Chandrabhagabai *v.* Kashinath Vithal, 2 Bom., 323.

[2] Timmappa Bhat *v.* Parmeshriamma, 5 Bom., A. C. J., 130; Udaram Sitaram *v.* Sonkabai, 10 Bom., 483.

[3] 9 W. R., 413.

LECTURE V. "The rights of a wife or of a widow, and those of a son's widow, to maintenance, appear to me to be governed by very different principles. A son's widow has not the same legal rights against her father-in-law as a wife has against her husband, or as a widow has against the heirs of her husband who take his estate by inheritance. The father is not heir to his son in preference to the son's widow.

"A son's widow has no right in her father-in-law's estate, and, upon partition of such estate, she is not, like a daughter, entitled to a share, even though the estate was ancestral.

"The rule laid down in Ruggomonee Dassee *versus* Shib Chunder Mullick, Hyde's Reports for 1864, page 103, *viz.*, that the maintenance of a son's widow is a mere moral duty on the part of her father-in-law, and that the case is distinguishable from those in which an heir takes property subject to the obligation of maintaining persons who are excluded from inheritance, or those whom the deceased proprietor was morally bound to maintain, appears to me to be correct.

"The obligation of an heir to provide out of the estate which descends to him maintenance for certain persons whom the ancestor was legally or morally bound to maintain, is a legal as well as a moral obligation, for the estate is inherited subject to the obligation of providing such maintenance. A son who takes his father's estate by inheritance is bound to provide maintenance for his father's widow. The obligation is a charge upon the estate, which continues as long as the widow remains chaste, whether she continue to live in the family of the heirs or not."

As the Judges who composed the Full Bench were equally divided in opinion, an appeal was preferred under section 15 of the Letters Patent of the High Court, and the case finally came on for hearing before another Full Bench of seven Judges,[1] who unanimously affirmed the judgment of the Chief Justice, mainly on two among other grounds, namely, *first*, because the rules of the Hindu law on the point (such as the texts of Manu, Narada, and Brihaspati already quoted) are mere moral injunctions, as appears from their being enforced only by moral sanctions, while other rules that are meant to be rules of law are declared enforceable by fine and other temporal sanctions; and *secondly*, because it would be most unreasonale and inconvenient to allow the claim of the widow in such cases.

Upon the question whether a son's widow is entitled to be supported by her father-in-law if she resides in his house, Mr. Justice Norman observed: "If she resides in the house of her father-in-law and is an infant, and for that or other reasons is unable to maintain herself, there may be, and probably is—both according to Hindoo law and according to natural law, equity, and good conscience,—a legal obligation on the part of the father-in-law, who has taken upon himself the care of her person and the charge of entertaining her as a member of his family, and on whose protection she is dependent, to provide her with food and the actual necessaries of life."[2] Mr. Justice E. Jackson was of the same opinion. But as the question was not raised before the Court, the other Judges expressed no opinion upon it; so that it still remains an open question. Considering the constitution of Hindu society, considering the extremely helpless condition of the Hindu widow, and considering that the obligation of the father-in-law or other near relation to give her food and raiment if she resides in his

[1] See 10 W. R. (F. B.), 89. [2] *Ibid*, 95.

LECTURE V. house, is not only enjoined by precept, but is also confirmed by invariable usage, it is hoped, that should this question ever arise, it will be decided in favour of the widow.

In the judgment of Sir Barnes Peacock, you will observe that an important general rule has been laid down regarding a person's liability to provide maintenance for others. That rule is this, that the heir of a person taking his estate is legally bound to maintain all those whom the late proprietor was either legally or morally bound to maintain; for the heir takes the estate of the ancestor for his spiritual benefit. Thus, in this instance, what was a mere moral obligation in the ancestor becomes transformed into a legal obligation in his heir.

The ruling of the Bengal High Court in the case of *Kasheenath Doss* v. *Khettur Monee Dossee* has been followed by the High Court of Allahabad in the case of *Ganga Bai* v. *Sita Ram.*[1]

Right to maintenance not saleable.

The widow's right to maintenance out of the estate of her husband in the hands of his heir has been held not liable to be sold in execution of a decree against her.[2] And now by section 266 of Act X of 1877, a right to future maintenance has been declared exempt from liability to attachment and sale in execution of decee in all cases. Arrears of maintenace already due have however been held to be liable to attachment in execution of decree.[3]

Maintenance forfeited for unchastity.

A widow forfeits her right to maintenance by reason of unchastity.[4] But this rule of forfeiture has been held not

---

[1] I. L. R., 1 All., 170.

[2] Bhyrub Chunder Ghose *v.* Nubo Chunder Gooho, 5 W. R., 111.

[3] Hoymobutty Debia Chowdhrain *v.* Koroona Moyee Debia Chowdhrain, 8 W. R., 41.

[4] See Colebrooke's Digest, Bk. V, 334; Mitakshara, Ch. II, Sec. I, 7; Dayabhaga, Ch. XI., Sec. I, 48; Macnaghten's Precedents of Hindu Law,

to extend to a claim for starving maintenance,—that is, bare food and raiment.[1]

LECTURE V.

Suits for maintenance.

Suits for maintenance have been held to be cognizable by Courts of Small Causes;[2] and the decree in such a suit may provide for future maintenance, which may be recovered by process of execution.[3] But a Small Cause Court has no jurisdiction to determine the right to maintenance where that is denied.[4]

Widow entitled to reside in the family dwelling-house.

A Hindu widow is entitled to live in her husband's dwelling-house, and his heir or the purchaser from such heir has no right to turn her out without providing for her some other suitable dwelling. This rule has been laid down by the High Court of Bengal in the case of *Mungala Dabee* v. *Dinonath Bose.*[5] Sir Barnes Peacock in his judgment in that case observed: "I have very great doubt myself whether a son, whether natural born or adopted, is entitled to turn his father's widow and the other females of the family who are entitled to maintenance out of the dwelling selected by the father for his own residence, and in which he left the females of his family at the time of his death. No one who is at all acquainted with the usages and customs of Hindoos, can doubt that it would be highly injurious to the reputation of the females of a family to be turned out of the residence, at least until some other proper place has been provided for them. It is laid down by Katyayana, that

Ch. II, Case v; Maharanee Bussunt Koomaree *v.* Maharanee Kummul Koomaree, 7 Sel Rep., 168 (new ed.); Kerry Kolitanee *v.* Monee Ram Kolita (*per* Jackson, J.), 19 W. R., 405; Visalatchi Ammal *v.* Annasamy Sastry, 5 Mad., 160; 1 Strange, 172; 2 Strange, 310.

[1] See Honamma *v.* Timanna Bhat, I. L. R., 1 Bom., 559.

[2] Ramchandra Dikhsit *v.* Savitribai, 4 Bom. A. C. J., 73.

[3] Sinthayee *v.* Thanakapudayen, 4 Madras, 183.

[4] Bhugwan Chunder Bose *v.* Bindoo Bashinee Dossee, 6 W. R., 286.

[5] 12 W. R., Appeals from Original Jurisdiction, 35.

'except his whole estate and his dwelling-house, what remains after the food and clothing of his family, a man may give away, whatever it be, whether fixed or moveable; otherwise it may not be given.' 2 Colebrooke's Digest, page 133.

"The meaning of that passage is, that he must not give away his whole estate without providing food and clothing for his family, and that he must reserve 'one house, without which he himself or his family might want a dwelling.'"

The question was raised whether this text of Katyayana was a mere moral precept or a rule of law; and the Chief Justice, after some discussion, came to the conclusion that it was of the latter description.

This decision has been followed in a recent case[1] by the High Court of Allahabad.

She is entitled to a share on partition.

The widow is also entitled to a share on partition. Her right is based upon the following texts:—

"Of heirs dividing after the death of the father, let the mother also take an equal share." (Yajnavalkya.)[2]

"On the death of the father, the mother (*janani*) has a claim to an equal share with her own sons; *his* mothers (*matarah*) take the same share; and the unmarried daughters each a fourth of a share." (Brihaspati.)[3]

"Mothers take shares proportionate to the shares of sons, and so do unmarried daughters." (Vishnu.)[4]

From the foregoing text of Yajnavalkya, Vijnaneswara deduces the rule that when the heirs separate after the demise of the father, the mother takes a share equal to that of a son.[5] He does not explain whether the term mother

---

[1] Gauri *v.* Chandramani, I. L. R., 1 All., 262.
[2] II, 123.
[3] Colebrooke's Digest, Bk. V, 85.
[4] *Ibid*, 86.
[5] Mitakshara, Ch. I, Sec. VII, 2.

includes a stepmother,—that is, whether, when the sons come to a partition after their father's death, all his widows, whether having sons or not, become entitled to shares. But the leading authorities of the cognate schools, the Vivada Chintamani,[1] the Vyavahara Mayukha,[2] and the Smriti Chandrika,[3] all maintain that the word 'mother' includes a stepmother, so that, according to them, when the sons come to a partition, the farther's widows, whether sonless or having sons, are each entitled to a share equal to that of a son. LECTURE V.

The Bengal school, however, differs from the others. Jimutavahana[4] and Srikrishna[5] agree in holding that, on partition after the father's death, the stepmothers, or the father's sonless widows, are not entitled to any share; for 'mother,' in the above text of Brihaspati, which they adopt as the basis of their commentary, does not according to them include a stepmother. From this interpretation an important rule has been deduced,—namely, that the mother is entitled to a share only when her sons separate from one another, and that she is not entitled to any share when they separate from their half-brothers, if they continue joint among themselves.[6]

To illustrate this rule by an example: suppose that a man has three sons, *A*, *B*, and *C*, by his wife *X*; and four sons, *D*, *E*, *F*, *G*, by another wife *Y*. According to the Benares and the cognate schools, on partition, the property would be divided into nine equal parts, and the nine persons,—namely, the seven sons and the two widows,—would each take one part.

---

[1] Prossonna Coomar Tagore's translation, p. 240.

[2] Ch. IV, Sec. IV, 19.

[3] Ch. IV, 14.

[4] Dayabhaga, Ch. III, Sec. II, 30.

[5] Dayakrama Sangraha, Ch. VII, 3.

[6] See Srikrishna's Commentary on vv. 29—33 of Sec. II, Ch. III of the Dayabhaga; and Macnaghten's Considerations on Hindu Law, p. 54.

LECTURE V. But, according to the Bengal school, when the three brothers *A*, *B*, and *C* separate from their half-brothers *D*, *E*, *F*, and *G*, the property would be divided into seven equal parts, and the two groups of uterine brothers would respectively take three and four of these parts,—that is, three-sevenths and four-sevenths of the whole; and *X* and *Y* would take nothing. And when the sons of *X* separate from one another, they divide their three-sevenths of the whole estate into four equal parts, and each of them takes one part,—that is, three-twenty-eighths of the whole, and their mother *X* takes an equal share. And so, when the sons of *Y* come to a partition, they divide their four-sevenths of the whole estate into five equal parts, and each of them gets one part, or four-thirty-fifths of the whole estate, and their mother gets an equal share.

Where the mother has received any *stridhan* from her husband's family, her share on partition is reduced to as much as is equal to half of a son's share, according to some authorities;[1] and according to others,[2] to as much as would, together with her *stridhan*, make her share equal to that of a son. This rule is deduced by analogy from the texts of Yajnavalkya,[3] which reduce the wife's claim to a half in the cases of partition by the father and present on supersession.

Widow entitled to inherit in certain cases.

The widow is entitled to inherit her husband's estate in certain cases. When a man dies leaving no son—(the term son here includes a grandson and also a great grandson)[4] his widow, according to some of the sages, such as Yajna-

---

[1] Dayabhaga, Ch. III, Sec. II, 31; Dayatattwa, Ch. III, 4.

[2] Mitakshara, Ch. I, Sec. VII, 2; Ch. II, Sec. XI, 34, 35; Vyavahara Mayukha, Ch. IV, Sec. IV, 18.

[3] II, 115, 148.

[4] See Mitakshara, Ch. II, Sec. VIII, 1; Dayabhaga, Ch. XI, Sec. I, 34.

vaklya, Brihaspati, Vishnu, and Brihat Manu, is his next heir. But there are also texts opposed to the widow's claim, such as those of Narada, Devala, Sankha, Likhita, Paithinasi, and Yama.[1] The true reason for this conflict of authority on a question of such evident practical importance as the succession of the widow to her husband's estate, it is not very easy to ascertain. Possibly, the adverse texts relate to a time when the patriarchal family system was in full force, and are relics of an archaic system of jurisprudence; while the other texts have reference to a state of society comparatively more modern. This conflict of authorities, that in course of time have come to be regarded as equally entitled to respect, has been a source of no ordinary embarrassment to modern commentators; and it has compelled them to enter into long and intricate and often unsatisfactory processes of reasoning in order to reconcile these authorities.

The Mitakshara, which is the oldest of modern commentaries, in reconciling these conflicting authorities, effects a sort of compromise between archaic views and the more advanced notions of its own time. It holds that the texts adverse to the widow's claim apply to joint families, and deduces the rule that the widow, being chaste, takes the whole estate of a man, who being separated from his co-heirs, and not subsequently reunited with them, dies leaving no male issue.[2] But if he dies before separation or after reunion, his undivided or reunited kinsmen, and not his widow, become his heirs. To this rule of succession in a joint family, called the rule of succession by survivorship, an important qualifica-

---

[1] See Mitakshara, Ch. II, Sec. I; Dayabhaga, Ch. XI, Sec. I.

[2] Mitakshara, Ch. II, Sec. I, 39.

LECTURE V. tion has been added by the Privy Council in the Shivagunga case,[1] in which it has been held that if an undivided coparcener has any separate property of his own, his widow shall be his heir so far as such property is concerned, though his undivided kinsmen would succeed to his joint property. At the present day, the rule laid down in the Mitakshara, with the qualification introduced by the Privy Council, is the law governing all the schools except the Bengal.[2]

But Jimutavahana, the founder of the Bengal school, who evidently entertains more advanced views on jurisprudence, as may be seen from his maintaining the doctrine of *factum valet* and the distinction between legal and moral injunctions,[3] does not accept Vijnaneswara's rule. He maintains the widow's right of succession in all cases, whether her husband was separated or unseparated from, or reunited or unreunited with, his coparceners. His rule being different from that laid down in the authoritative work of Vijnaneswara, he feels the necessity of adducing a reason for it, and one that would be acceptable to his countrymen; and accordingly he avails himself of the doctrine of spiritual benefit which is sanctioned by Manu, and after an elaborate discussion showing the bearing of that doctrine upon his present purpose,[4] concludes thus: — "Since by these and other passages it is declared that the wife rescues her husband from hell; and since a woman doing improper acts through indigence causes her husband to fall (to a region of horror), for they share the fruits of virtue and of vice;

---

[1] Kattama Nauchear v. The Rajah of Shivagungah, 2 W. R. (P. C.), 31.

[2] See Vyavahara Mayukha, Ch. IV, Sec. VIII, 1—9 ; Smriti Chandrika, Ch. XI, Sec. I, 23—25 ; Dayavibhaga (Burnell's translation), p. 32 ; Vivada Chintamani (Tagore's translation), p. 291.

[3] See Dayabhaga, Ch. II, 28—30.

[4] See Ch. XI, Sec. I, 31—43.

therefore the wealth devolving on her is for the benefit of the former owner; and the wife's succession is consequently proper."[1] You will observe that this application of the doctrine of spiritual benefit, though perhaps not wholly uninfluenced by sacerdotal considerations, was meant by the founder of the Bengal school to serve one good purpose at least,—namely, the recognition and advancement of the proprietary rights of women. I do not mean to say anything in commendation of the Brahmanical lawyers, or their favorite doctrine. But I may say that the opinion which has been generally entertained, that sacerdotal influence has been invariably hostile to the rights of the Hindu female, is in the present instance not wholly correct.[2]

Here I may call your attention to the fact that, in treating of the widow's succession, Hindu lawyers draw a distinction between a *patni*, or wife lawfully wedded in one of the approved forms of marriage, and a woman espoused but not holding the rank of *patni*; and commentators explain away some of the texts apparently adverse to the widow's claim by showing that they relate to women espoused and not to the *patni*.[3] It is pointed out in the Smriti Chandrika,[4] upon the authority of Panini,[5] that the term *patni*, anomalously derived from *pati* (husband), means the wife who can be associated with her husband in the performance of religious sacrifices.

---

[1] See Ch. XI, Sec. I, 44.

[2] See Maine's Early History of Institutions, pp. 325—336; Maine's Village Communities, pp. 54, 55.

[3] See Mitakshara, Ch. II, Sec. I, 5, 28, 29; Dayabhaga, Ch. XI, Sec. I, 47, 48.

[4] Ch. XI, Sec. I, 9—12.

[5] IV, i, 33.

LECTURE V.

But she takes a qualified estate.

The extent of interest which a widow has in the estate inherited from her husband was at one time a subject of some contention; but the question has now been settled by decisions of the highest authority. I shall have to consider this subject again under the head of *stridhan*, and I need not dwell upon it at any length here. It will be sufficient for my present purpose to say that it has been held generally that the widow takes a special and qualified estate with a limited power of alienation, she being competent to alienate it only under certain circumstances and for certain purposes. This is the rule laid down by the Judicial Committee, in the case of *The Collector of Masulipatam* v. *Cavaly Vencata Narainapah*, in which it was further observed:—"Their Lordships are of opinion that the restrictions on a Hindu widow's power of alienation are inseparable from her estate, and that their existence does not depend on that of heirs capable of taking on her death. It follows that if, for want of heirs, the right to the property, so far as it has not been lawfully disposed of by her, passes to the Crown, the Crown must have the same power which an heir would have of protecting its interests by impeaching any unauthorized alienation by the widow."[1]

There is distinct authority in the Dayabhaga,[2] the Smriti Chandrika,[3] and also in the Vivada Chintamani[4] (so far as immoveable property is concerned), for the position that the widow's interest is a limited one. But there being no such provision in the Mitakshara, it was contended in the case of *Mussamut Thakoor Dayhee* v. *Rai Baluck Ram*,[5] that, in the

[1] 2 W. R. (P. C.), 61.
[2] Ch. XI, Sec. I, 56—62. [3] Ch. XI, Sec. I, 29—32.
[4] Tagore's translation, pp. 261—263, and 292.
[5] 10 W R (P. C.), 3.

Benares school, the widow's estate in her husband's property was absolute; but the Privy Council observed: "The result of the authorities seems to be that although, according to the law of the Western schools, the widow may have a power of disposing of moveable property inherited from her husband, which she has not under the law of Bengal, she is, by the one law as by the other, restricted from aliening any immoveable property which she has so inherited; and that, on her death, the immoveable property and the moveable, if she has not otherwise disposed of it, pass to the next heir of her husband." The question whether the widow has the power of alienating moveable property, which was left undecided in this case, was raised in the case of *Bhugwandeen Doobey* v. *Myna Baee*,[1] but the Judicial Committee answered it in the negative, observing: "The reasons for the restrictions which the Hindoo law imposes on the widow's dominion over her inheritance from her husband, whether founded on her natural dependence on others, her duty to lead an ascetic life, or on the impolicy of allowing the wealth of one family to pass to another, are as applicable to personal property invested so as to yield an income, as they are to land. The more ancient texts importing the restriction are general. It lies on those who assert that moveable property is not subject to the restriction to establish that exception to the generality of the rule. The diversity of opinion amongst the Benares Pandits is sufficient to show that the supposed distinction between moveable and immoveable property is anything but well established in that school." This is the law of the Benares school. But, according to the Hindu law as it obtains in the Presidency of Bombay, the widow has been held to possess

[1] 9 W. R (P. C.), 23.

LECTURE V.

absolute right over moveable property inherited from her husband.[1]

Though generally incompetent to alienate the property inherited from her husband, the widow may yet effect a vaild alienation with the consent of all her husband's kindred who are likely to be interested in disputing the transaction.[2]

Succession of several widows.

When there are several widows, the eldest or the first, according to Sir Thomas Strange,[3] succeeds to the estate, and the others are entitled to maintenance; but according to Macnaghten,[4] they all jointly inherit their husband's estate. In this conflict of opinion, Mr. Justice Kemp in one case[5] observed, that it was a moot point whether, under the Mitakshara, the elder widow inherits the whole estate, the younger receiving maintenance, or whether the rights of the two widows are equal. Considering that by the term *patni* is meant the wife who has the right to be associated with her husband in his religious rites,[6] and considering that according to Yajnavalkya, Vishnu, Katyayana, and Daksha,[7] that right belongs only to the eldest wife, Sir T. Strange's opinon is not altogether without authority; but the balance of authority is decidedly in favor of the opposite view.

In the Mitakshara there is a passage which seems to have been inadvertently omitted by Colebrooke in his translation, but which ought to come between verses 5 and 6 of

---

[1] Pranjivandas Tulsidas *v.* Devkuvarbai, 1 Bom., 130.

[2] See Rajlukhee Debia *v.* Gokool Chunder Chowdhry, 12 W. R. (P. C.), 47

[3] 1 Strange, 56.

[4] Principles of Hindu Law, pp. 20, 21.

[5] Judoobunsee Koer *v.* Girblurun Koer, 12 W. R., 158.

[6] See Smriti Chandrika, Ch. XI, Sec. I, 9.

[7] Colebrooke's Digest, Bk. IV, 48—51.

Section I of Chapter II of his translation, and which runs thus:— LECTURE V.

" The singular number is intended to indicate (identity of) class. Hence if there be many (wives) of the same and different classes, they take the estate after dividing it according to their due shares."

This is clear authority in favor of their joint right.

The author of the Subodhini supports the view that there may be more *patnis* than one.[1]

The Vyavahara Mayukha[2] and the Smriti Chandrika[3] also expressly provide that if there be several widows they inherit jointly.

The Dayabhaga and the Dayatattwa are not very explicit on this point, though Jagannatha thinks that, according to Jimutavahana, the eldest widow alone succeeds.[4] But, as has been pointed out,[5] the seniority of which Jimutavahana[6] and Raghunandana[7] speak, is evidently seniority in point of class, and not seniority among several wives of the same class.

The authority of reported decisions[8] is almost uniformly in favor of the rule that when there are several widows they all succeed to their husband's estate jointly. One of the latest cases on the point is that of *Gajapathi Nilamani* v. *Gajapathi Radhamani.*[9]

---

1 Mitakshara, Ch. II, Sec. I, 5 note.

2 Ch. IV, Sec. VIII, 9.

3 Ch. XI, Sec. I, 57.

4 Colebrooke's Digest, Bk. V, 414, commentary (Vol II, Mad. ed., p. 540).

5 Shama Churn's Vyavastha Darpana, pp. 41, 42.

6 Ch. XI, Sec. I, 47.

7 Dayatattwa, Ch. XI, 19, 20.

8 See *Doe dem* Baugbutty Raur *v.* Radakisnoo Mookerjee, Montriou's Cases, 314 ; Sreemutty Berjessory Dossee *v.* Ramconny Dutt, East's Notes, Case 54, 2 Morley's Digest, p. 80 ; 1 W. and B., 89 ; Ramia *v.* Bhagi, 1 Bom., 66 ; Jijoyiamba Bayi Saiba *v.* Kamakshi Bayi Saiba, 3 Mad., 424.

9 I. L. R., 1 Mad., 290.

LECTURE V.

Effect of unchastity.

A widow, in order to be entitled to succeed to the estate of her husband, must be chaste at the time when the succession opens. This is clearly laid down by all the commentators,[1] and has never been questioned. But the question whether subsequent unchastity in a widow would divest her of the estate already vested in her, has not been altogether free from doubt. It was recently raised before the High Court of Bengal, in the case of *Kerry Kolitanee* v. *Monee Ram Kolita*,[2] which was heard before a Full Bench consisting of all the Judges, and in which it has been held by the majority of the Court that a widow, who has once inherited the estate of her husband, is not liable to forfeit it for subsequent unchastity. An appeal having been preferred to Her Majesty in Council against this decision, the question remains to be finally settled by the Privy Council.

Perpetual widowhood—Act XV of 1856.

One peculiarity of widowhood in the Hindu law is its perpetual character, it being incapable of being terminated otherwise than by death. But this rule has now been abrogated by Act XV of 1856, which permits the remarriage of Hindu widows.

---

[1] See Mitakshara, Ch. II, Sec. I, 39; Vyavahara Mayukha, Ch. IV, Sec. VIII, 2; Dayabhaga, Ch. XI, Sec. I, 43, 56: see also Kerry Kolitanee v Monee Ram Kolita, *per* Jackson, J., 19 W. R., 405.

[2] 19 W. R., 367.

LECTURE VI.

CERTAIN CUSTOMARY AND STATUTORY FORMS OF MARRIAGE.

Scope of the present Lecture—Conditions requisite for validity of custom—It must be ancient—continuous—and certain—It must not be immoral, nor opposed to the general spirit of the law—Burden of proof where custom is pleaded—Forms of marriage according to family usages—Custom in the Tipperah Raj—Custom among Uriya Chiefs—Forms of marriage according to local, tribal, and caste customs—Customs of Bengal—Tribes of Assam—The Koch—The Santals—Tribes of Chota Nagpore—Customs of the North-West and the Punjab—Customs of the Bombay Presidency—Parties to marriage—Betrothment—Divorce—Remarriage—Customs of Southern India—Prohibited degrees—Different forms of marriage—Malabar law—Canarese law—Divorce and remarriage—Forms of marriage according to sectarian customs — Vaishnavas—Gosavis—Buddhists—Jainas—Sikhs—Brahmos—Remarriage of widows—Act XV of 1856—Remarks on its provisions—Act III of 1872.

Scope of the present Lecture.

We have hitherto been considering the Hindu law of marriage strictly so called,—that is, the law as laid down by the sages and the commentators. But that is not the whole of the law on the subject. There are Hindu tribes, Hindu families, and Hindu sects, which, from differences in habits, sentiments, and doctrine, and from other causes, are found to observe practices in relation to marriage widely different from those enjoined by the Hindu *sastras*; and, from the position assigned to custom as a source of law in Hindu jurisprudence,[1] these practices are regarded as legal, and the rules regulating them form an important supplement to the Hindu law. The British Indian Legislature, too, has legalized certain descriptions of marriage, with a view to meet the growing wants of Hindu society. In the present Lecture I shall notice briefly, first, some of these customary

---

[1] See The Collector of Madura *v.* Muttu Ramlinga Sathupathy, 10 W. R. (P.C.), 21.

LECTURE VI. forms of marriage, and, secondly, the forms that have been declared legal by statute law.

Conditions requisite for validity of custom.

An account of the customary forms of Hindu marriage may be prefaced with a few words explanatory of the conditions necessary for the validity of custom in Hindu law.

Under the English law, a custom in order to be valid must be ancient, invariable, reasonable, and certain. Similar qualifications apply more or less to custom under the Hindu law.

It must be ancient,

The most important of these qualifications is, that a custom must be ancient in order that it may have the force of law. "Immemorial custom," says Manu,[1] "is transcendent law, approved in the scripture, and in the codes of divine legislators."

So the text of the Vamana Purana, quoted by Vachaspati and Raghunandana, declares: "A man should not neglect the approved customs of districts, the equitable rules of his family, or the particular laws of his race. In whatever country, whatever usage has passed through successive generations, let not a man there disregard it; such usage is law in that country."[2]

These texts require that a custom must be ancient in order that it may be binding. There is, however, no definite rule in Hindu law as to how old a custom must be, in order that it may have the force of law. Sir Charles Grey, C. J., in an early case, is reported to have observed that a custom to be valid, as regards Calcutta, must have existed from before the year 1773, and as regards the Mofussil, from before the year 1793;[3] and the reason assigned for this rule is, that, since

---

[1] I, 108. [2] Colebrooke's Digest, Bk. I, 98, 99,

[3] See the extract from the judgment of Sir C. Grey, in Shama Charan's Vyavastha Darpana, p. 314 note; see *ante*, p. 14.

these dates, the power of making laws having become vested in the British Legislature, no change can be effected in the Hindu law by any other agency. The correctness of this rule, however, is in some cases open to question. Hindu law, though it has now lost its vitality considerably, is, nevertheless a growing system, susceptible of change from within; and it may well be urged that the legislature, when it declares that the Hindu law shall be the rule of decision in certain cases, refers to the living Hindu law at the time, and not to the obsolete Hindu law of any definite epoch. We may, at any rate, fairly say, that, in the Hindu law, not only is it unnecessary to trace back the existence of a custom to any definite date, but even the indefinite condition of being ancient may, in favor of some classes of customs, have to be dispensed with. Thus, suppose that a new Hindu sect comes into existence, and, from religious scruples, adopts a form of marriage somewhat different from the orthodox form; it would be going too far to hold that these marriages are void, and thus to bastardize a whole community, simply because the sect and its practices are of recent origin. Generally speaking, other conditions being fulfilled, a custom ought to be recognized as valid, when, either from observance for a long time, or from adoption by a considerable and organized body of persons, it has influenced the conduct of people to such an extent, that to disregard it, would be to disappoint well-grounded and reasonable expectations of men.

Another qualification which follows from the preceding, is, that a custom must be continuous; and it has been held[1] that well-established discontinuance would destroy a custom, though at one time it might have existed. continuous

[1] Rajah Raj Kissen Singh v. Ramjoy Surma Mozoomdar, 19 W. R., 8.

LECTURE VI.

and certain.

Certainty is another condition necessary for the validity of custom; and a custom that is fluctuating and uncertain is no custom at all.[1]

It must not be immoral, nor opposed to the general spirit of the law.

Another condition for the validity of custom, which forms the subject of some discussion in Hindu jurisprudence, is, that it must not be immoral, nor opposed to the general spirit of the Hindu law. Jagannatha has some pertinent, though somewhat quaintly expressed, observations on this point: "The use of law," says he, "is only to prevent the introduction of multiform practices at the will of men of the present generation. Where many texts of law are inconsistent, or many interpretations of the same text are contradictory, usage alone can be received as a rule of *conduct:* and practice, which differs in some respects from positive ordinances, but is not remote from ancient legislation, can only be confirmed by its *general* connection with law. Consequently, that practice which is conformable to law is best, but that which is inconsistent therewith must be abolished; yet, if that may not be, practice inconsistent with law must be nevertheless retained. But where no *positive* ordinance is found, there is nothing inconsistent with any known law, and in that case approved usage alone must regulate *proceedings.*"[2]

The truth is, that custom, from its very nature, must be inconsistent with the general rule of law, if there is any rule on the subject; and, therefore, the condition under notice ought to be regarded as sufficiently complied with, if there is, as Mr. Justice West expresses it, a general congruity with the Vedic system.[3] The fulfilment of this condition has been always insisted upon by the Courts. Thus the

[1] Luchmun Lall *v.* Mohun Lall Bhaya Gayal, 16 W. R., 179.
[2] Colebrooke's Digest, Bk. I, 50, commentary.
[3] Bhau Nanaji Utpat *v.* Sundrabai, 11 Bom., 266.

High Court of Bengal has held, that an agreement to dissolve a marriage on the happening of a certain contingency is void as being opposed to the policy of the law;[1] and the High Court of Bombay refused to recognize a custom by which a wife could obtain divorce and marry again without the consent of her husband, on the ground of its being an immoral custom, and its being entirely opposed to the spirit of the Hindu law.[2]

But here an important distinction ought to be observed. Conformity with the general spirit of the Hindu law is to be insisted upon as a necessary condition, only in those cases where the custom pleaded is one obtaining among people who are Hindus properly so called, and who follow that law in the main. But this condition is not applicable to the customs of people such as the Nairs and the Maravars of Southern India, who observe practices widely different from those of real Hindus, and who can be called Hindus only because of the indefinite character of Hinduism. To make the validity of their customs depend upon conformity with the general spirit of the Hindu law, would be to abrogate those customs altogether, and either to leave these people without law, or to force upon them the Hindu law of the sages and the commentators. The truth is, that the bodies of customs governing these tribes and classes are not in the nature of exceptions to the general Hindu law, for that law has never been the rule with them; but they are distinct bodies of law in themselves, co-ordinate with that larger body which has been reduced to writing, and is known as the Hindu law properly so called.

---

[1] Seetaram v. Mussamut Aheeree Heeranee, 20 W. R., 49.

[2] Reg. v. Karsau Goja, 2 Bom., 117; Uji v. Hathi Lalu, 7 Bom., A. C. J., 133.

LECTURE VI.

Burden of proof where custom is pleaded.

Custom being usually in the nature of an exception to the general law, the rule is, that a party who pleads a custom as obtaining in any particular community or family of Hindus, in derogation of the ordinary Hindu law, must prove its existence by evidence; that, in the absence of such evidence, the general law shall prevail.[1] Generally speaking, the correctness of this rule is undeniable. But the application of this rule to some cases may call for a word of explanation. Thus, in the case of *Lalla Mahabeer Pershad* v. *Mussamut Kundun Koowar*[2] (which has been followed in Bombay[3]) it has been held by the High Court of Bengal that, in the absence of evidence to show that the law of the sect called the Jainas is different from the ordinary Hindu law, this latter law shall be deemed applicable to them. Now this view can be supported only on the ground that the Jainas, before their schism, were true Hindus, and as such were governed by the Hindu law; so that it may be presumed, in the absence of evidence to the contrary, that the same law governs them still. And in the case of tribes that have never been true Hindus, and are only nominally within the pale of Hinduism, though really observing practices widely at variance with it, the propriety of following the rule under notice seems open to question.

Where a custom does not govern a tribe or a community, but is peculiar only to a single family, the above rule is more strictly enforced than ever. The Courts look with a jealous eye upon attempts by a single family to make a

---

[1] See Serumah Umah *v.* Palathan Vitil Marya Coothy Umah, 15 W. R. (P. C.), 47; Rama Lakhmi Ammal *v.* Sivanantha Perumal, 17 W. R., 553; Narayan Babaji *v.* Nana Manohar, 7 Bom., A. C. J., 175.

[2] 8 W. R., 116.

[3] Bhagvandas Tejmal *v.* Rajmal, 10 Bom., 241.

law for itself; and in some cases[1] they have gone even so far as to deny the validity of family customs in derogation of the general law, except as regards Rajas and Chiefs.

I may observe that, in the absence of evidence to the contrary, it is a presumption of Hindu law that a family, migrating from one province to another, retains its old customs;[2] and this presumption is founded upon the fact that, notwithstanding any change of domicil, the Hindus, as a rule, tenaciously cling to their old usages. It is perhaps partly owing to this fact, that in one and the same locality different customs may be observed to prevail in different families, while in places widely distant from one another, the same customs may be found to exist.

A custom may be either peculiar to a single family, or it may be common to a group of families, the common bond of union being residence in a particular locality, or unity of tribe or caste, or unity of creed. So that, the customary forms of marriage in Hindu law may, for convenience of treatment, be divided into the following classes: those according to family customs; those according to local, tribal, or caste customs; and those according to sectarian customs. These will be considered separately, and in the order given above.

Forms of marriage according to family usages.

I begin with the customary forms of Hindu marriage which are sanctioned by the usages of particular families. Here the first question that arises is, how far such usages, in derogation of the ordinary law, are entitled to be recognized by the

---

[1] Basvantrav Kidingappa *v.* Mantappa Kidingappa, 1 Bom., App., xlvii; Tara Chand *v.* Reeb Ram, 3 Mad., 57; Madhavrav Raghavendra *v.* Balkrishna Raghavendra, 4 Bom., A. C. J., 113; but see Bhau Nanaji Utpat *v.* Sundrabai, 11 Bom., 249.

[2] See Rutcheputty Dutt *v.* Rajunder Narain, 2 Moo. I. A., 132; Ootum Chunder Bhuttacharjee *v.* Obhoychurn Misser, Suth., F. B. R., 67; Koomud Chunder Roy *v.* Seeta Kanth Roy, *ib.*, 75; Sooreudro Nath Roy *v.* Mussamut Heeroomonee Burmonee, 10 W. R., (P. C.), 35.

LECTURE VI. Courts. The question has been raised in connection with the subject of inheritance; and though in the case of great families, such as those of Rajas and Chiefs, the authorities are unanimous in upholding the validity of well-established ancient *kuláchár*, or family custom,[1] there appears to be some difference of opinion about the validity of custom prevailing in a petty family. Thus, the High Court of Bombay, on one occasion, observed, that "it would be a dangerous doctrine that any petty family is at liberty to make a law for itself, and thus to set aside the general law of the country;"[2] and the same view was adopted both in Madras and in Bombay in subsequent cases.[3] But in a recent case,[4] Mr. Justice West, after a full examination of the authorities on the subject, has come to the conclusion that a family custom of proved antiquity, is entitled to be recognized by the Courts, irrespective of the position and rank of the family; and this rule is, no doubt, in accordance with the texts of Hindu law, which make no distinction between great and petty families. The truth is, that a petty family is not likely to be able to trace its customs very far back, and that a family must be of some position and eminence, in order to be able to establish the antiquity of its customs; so that practically, in the majority of cases, *kuláchár*, such as should have the force of law, can be established only in regard to great families.

Forms of marriage differ in their minor details according

---

[1] See Rajah Baidyanand Singh *v.* Rudranand Singh, 5 Sel. Rep., 198; Rawut Urjun Singh *v.* Rawut Ghunsiam Singh, 5 Moo. I. A., 169; Babu Gonesh Dutt Singh *v.* Maharaja Moheshur Singh, 6 Moo. I. A., 164.

[2] Basvantrav Kidingappa *v.* Mantappa Kidingappa, 1 Bom., App., xlvii.

[3] Tara Chand *v.* Reeb Ram, 3 Mad., 50; Madhavrav Raghavendra *v.* Balkrishna Raghavendra, 4 Bom., A. C. J., 113.

[4] Bhau Nanaji Utpat *v.* Sundrabai, 11 Bom., 249.

to the usages of different families. These points of difference it would be useless to enumerate, were it indeed possible to do so. Even the usages of great families, involving important points of departure from the general Hindu law, however valuable as a collection of facts, is hardly entitled to detailed enumertion in a course of lectures like the present. Such usages, when contested, shall have to be proved by evidence. I shall notice here only a few of the customs relating to marriage in great families, which have been judicially recognized.

Custom in the Tipperah Raj.

In the Tipperah Raj family, in addition to the orthodox form of marriage, there is another form called the *santigrihita*, which is sanctioned by custom, and which is celebrated by the worship of the goddess Tripura, and the taking of *santi* (benediction) water.[1] This form is sometimes identified with the *gandharba* form. A woman married by the Raja in this inferior form is called a Kachua Ranee, and is styled simply a Devi, while women married by him in the proper form are designated Maharanees and Mahadevis. Mr. Justice Morris, in his judgment in the *Tipperah Raj* case, observes:—[2] "It is manifest that the people of Tipperah, from the Rajah downwards, are very primitive, and that, in their manners and customs, they by no means follow the strict tenets of the Hindu religion. The *gandharva* or *santigrihita* form of marriage is commonly adopted. It is simple in character and requires little ceremony. At the same time a marriage in this form is binding and perfectly valid. The Rajahs do not appear to have been particular in their choice of wives. In page 266, we learn that

[1] See Chuckrodhuj Thakoor *v.* Beer Chunder Joobraj, 1 W. R., 194.

[2] Rajkumar Nobodip Chundro *v.* Rajah Birchundera, 25 W. R., 414.

LECTURE VI. a previous Rajah, Ramganga Manikhya, was the son of a slave girl (or Kachua)."

In *Rajah Nugendur Narain* v. *Rughoonath Narain Dey*,[1] the plaintiff, as the eldest son of the Rajah of Foolkoosunah, in the district of Manbhum, claimed the estate of his late father. The defendant, a younger son of the late Rajah, resisted the claim on the ground that the plaintiff's mother was a *begurbhati* wife of the late Rajah,—that is, one in whose hands the Rajah would not take cooked rice, owing to the inferiority of her father's family; and that, by a custom of the family, the son by such a wife was not entitled to the estate. The High Court of Bengal considered the custom not proved, and held that there was no distinction between legitimate children born of mothers belonging to the same great caste of Kshatriyas. It would appear from this case that it is customary with the Rajahs in the Jungle Mehals to marry women belonging to inferior grades of the Kshatriya caste, who are styled Ranees and regarded as lawful wives in every respect.

Custom among Uriya Chiefs.

The marriage customs of the Uriya Rajahs and Chiefs, are given in the compilation known as the Pachis Sawal, or twenty-five questions, put by the Superintendent of the Tributary Mehals in 1814 to the leading Rajahs in the Tributary Mehals, with their answers to the same. The following is the substance of these customary rules:—

The Rajahs may have a plurality of wives, there being sometimes as many as seven, the first being styled the Pat Ranee, or Bara Pat Maha Daee, and the others simply Ranees.[2]

---

[1] W. R. (1864), 20.

[2] Pachis Sawal, Q and A., I and II.

A Rajah generally marries in his own caste; but when marriage in the same caste is not procurable, he may marry a girl of a different caste in the *phulbiha* form,—that is, a form of marriage contracted by the ceremony of putting a garland round the neck of the woman, or by exchange of garlands.[1] A woman married in this form is called a *Phulbibahi* as distinguished from a Ranee.

In some *killahs* or states, the son of the Pat Ranee is the preferential heir to the Raj, and in his default, the eldest among the sons of the other Ranees succeeds. But in other *killahs* the eldest son of the late Rajah, whether he be born of the Pat Ranee or of any other Ranee, succeeds to the Raj.[2]

In the former class of states,—that is, those in which the son of the Pat Ranee is preferred to the sons of other Ranees,—the son born of the *phulbibahi* wife succeeds in default of sons by Ranees; and even the son born of a concubine is entitled to succeed in the absence of certain male relations in the agnatic line. But in the latter class of states, the succession of the *phulbibahi's* son is postponed in favour of the brother, his son, and certain other males in the agnatic line, while the son of the concubine has no claim to the succession.[3]

Formerly it was usual for the Ranees to become *satis*. The surviving Ranees are entitled to maintenance, but never to the succession.[4]

The Pachis Sawal has been always received as an authority, and upon the basis of such authority, the validity of the *phulbiha* form of marriage, and the rights of the sons of

---

[1] Pachis Sawal, Q. and A., VII and VIII.

[2] *Ibid*, Q. and A., IV and V.

[3] *Ibid*, Q. and A., X and XII.

[4] *Ibid*, Q. and A., IX.

LECTURE VI. the *phulbibahis* and of concubines, have been recognized by our Courts.[1]

Forms of marriage according to local, tribal, and caste customs.

I shall now consider the different forms of marriage according to local, tribal, and caste customs. These also are too numerous to admit of an exhaustive enumeration. Nor are they all necessary to be noticed in a course of lectures on the Hindu law of marriage, for several of the half-civilized Indian tribes do not at all come within the pale of Hinduism, and are never regarded as Hindus. I shall only notice some of the most important of these forms, which obtain among people who are Hindus or who have adopted Hindu practices more or less. I may tell you that, as a general rule, deviations from the ordinary Hindu law of marriage are to be found only among the aboriginal tribes and the lower classes of Aryans; and they are to be met with among the higher castes of Aryans, only where (as in Southern India) they are surrounded by non-Aryan influence.

Customs of Bengal.

To begin with Bengal. Here custom takes the place of the general law, chiefly in Assam, Kuch Behar, the Santal Parganas, and Chota-Nagpore, and occasionally among certain tribes in other parts of the country. The Assam valley, which has been rendered sacred by the famous temple of Kamakhya, has long been the seat of Hindu influence; and according to Wilson,[2] it has been in a great degree the source from which *Tantrik* innovations have proceeded. Nevertheless it has retained its primitive customs in regard to marriage. Among the agricultural classes of some tribes,

Tribes of Assam.

---

[1] See Prandhur Roy *v.* Ramchender Mongraj, S. D. A. R. for 1861, p. 16; Durrap Singh Deo *v.* Buzzurdhur Roy, 2 Hay, 335; Rungadhur Nurendra *v.* Juggurnath Bhromurbor Roy, 1 Joygobind Shome's Law Reporter, 92.

[2] Preface to the Vishnu Purana, p. lvii.

who are not very particular in following the Brahmanical ritual, the interchange of the *pan*-leaf constitutes the ceremony of marriage, and the tearing of a *pan*-leaf by the husband and the wife indicates dissolution of their union.[1] Among some tribes, there is a mock fight for the bride, between her party and the bridegroom's, which ends in the success of the latter, and then the bridegroom pays a price for the bride, in the shape of a present to her father.[2] The marriage-tie is rather lax in this part of the country; and there is a reported case from Assam,[3] in which it seems to have been held that, according to the custom of the community to which the parties belonged, a girl might marry again in the lifetime of her husband, if he failed to perform a second ceremony called *santibia*, corresponding to the ceremony of *garbhadhan*, and neglected her for a long time. LECTURE VI.

Among the Koch, who claim kindred with the Aryan Hindus, but are really a tribe of non-Aryan origin, marriages are usually settled by the mothers, and not by the fathers, when the parties are young; and widows are permitted to remarry.[4] The Koch.

Among the Santals, who can hardly be called Hindus, and who only in certain places have partially adopted Hindu practices, the marriage customs have very little in common with those of the Hindus. The practice of child-marriage is strongly condemned; boys are seldom married before sixteen; and the ordinary nubile age for a girl is fifteen. Young men and maidens freely mix with one another, and freedom of selection is allowed to the parties, though it is considered more respectable if the match The Santals.

[1] Dalton's Descriptive Ethnology of Bengal, p. 86.

[2] *Ibid.*

[3] Boolchand Kolita v. Janokee, 25 W. R., 386.

[4] Dalton's Descriptive Ethnology of Bengal, p. 91.

LECTURE VI. is settled by their parents or guardians. A price (generally five rupees) is paid for the bride; and the essential part of the nuptial ceremony consists in the *sindurdan*, or the painting of the bride's brow with vermilion, and the social meal which the bridegroom and the bride eat together; after which the bride ceases to belong to her father's clan, and becomes a member of her husband's family. The ceremony of messing together, you will observe, is not peculiar to the Santals, but resembles the Roman *confarreatio*, and a corresponding ceremony in the Hindu nuptials. The Santal always honors his wife; and polygamy, though not absolutely prohibited, is practised only under exceptional circumstances, such as barrenness of the first wife. Divorce is not common, and can only be allowed with the consent of the husband's clansmen.[1]

Tribes of Chota-Nagpore.

Among the Kisans,[2] the Bhuiyas,[3] and the Hos[4] of Chota-Nagpore, persons are not married until they attain maturity. Among some of these tribes, unmarried young men and women are allowed freely to mix with one another, and considerable freedom is allowed to the parties in the selection of their partners.

A price has generally to be paid for the bride. As with the Santals, eating the same meal together is the principal ceremony in marriage, so with the Hos, drinking beer together constitutes the chief nuptial rite. Among some of the Chota-Nagpore tribes, remarriage of widows is allowed, and the practice of taking to wife, in the *sagai* form, an elder brother's widow, is common.[5]

---

[1] See Dalton's Descriptive Ethnology of Bengal, pp. 215, 216; Hunter's Annals of Rural Bengal, pp. 205, 208.

[2] Dalton's Descriptive Ethnology of Bengal, p. 132.

[3] *Ibid*, p. 142. [4] *Ibid*, pp. 192, 193. [5] *Ibid*, p. 138.

The validity of the *sagai* marriage among one of these tribes, has been recognized in a reported case,[1] in which it has been further held that there is no distinction in point of heritable right between a son by a *sagai* and one by a *biahi* wife.

LECTURE VI.

The Kurmis in some places as in Singbhum, observe the singular but highly significant practice of making the married pair mark each other with blood drawn from their little fingers, as a sign that they have become one flesh. This, according to Dalton,[2] is probably the origin of the universal practice in India, of marking the bride with *sindur* or red lead. Among the Kurmis, widows are allowed to marry again.

Customs of the North-West and the Punjab.

Among the Jats in the North-Western Provinces, *Kurao Dhureecha*, or the marriage of a widow with the younger brother of her deceased husband, is common, and is recognized as lawful; and the children born of such marriage are considered legitimate, and are entitled to inherit their father's estate equally with other sons.[3]

In the Punjab, custom to a great extent takes the place of law; and, accordingly, by the Punjab Laws Amendment Act (XII of 1878), s. 1, it is expressly provided that custom, not being contrary to justice, equity, and good conscience, shall be the rule of decision in matters relating to marriage, betrothal, and the like. The compilation styled "Principles of Law," published in 1854 for the guidance of Judicial Officers in the Punjab, may be taken as furnishing some evidence of local usages; and Section VI of that compilation refers to some of the customs of the Punjab in

[1] Radaik Ghaserain *v.* Budaik Pershad Sing, Marsh., 641.
[2] Descriptive Ethnology of Bengal, pp. 220, 319.
[3] See Poorun Mull *v.* Toolsee Ram, 5 N. W. P. H. C. R. (1868), p. 350.

LECTURE VI. relation to marriage. Of these, I may notice one, namely, that marriage solemnized during the infancy of one of the parties, and not consummated, is, in some cases, deemed revocable, though the party revoking it, would be liabe to an action for damages; and the husband in such cases is not deemed entitled to the custody of the wife.[1]

Customs of the Bombay Presidency.

In the Presidency of Bombay, the customary law of marriage, especially among the inferior castes, differs considerably from the general Hindu law on the subject. The principal feature of the difference consists in these caste-customs freely allowing divorce and remarriage of widows and divorced wives. So well established is this custom of remarriage, that the prohibition against remarriage of widows in the *Kali* age, is held in the Western Presidency not to apply to Sudras.[2] The second marriage of a wife or widow is called *pat* by the Mahrattas, and *natra* in Guzerat.[3] Much valuable information regarding the customs of different castes in the Bombay Presidency is collected in Steele's Law and Custom of Hindoo Castes, which has always been accepted as an authority by the Courts.[4]

Parties to marriage.

The grounds of ineligibility for marriage according to these caste-customs, are generally speaking the same as those under the ordinary Hindu law. The parties must be of the same caste, of different *gotras*, and not related within the prohibited degrees. But the prohibited degrees are different from those prescribed by the ordinary law, and are somewhat different for different castes. Among several castes, a brother's children may marry a sister's children.[5] As to the

---

[1] See Jewun *v.* Sundhee, 5 Punjab Record, 9; cited in 2 Rattigan's Select Cases in Hindu Law, p. 385.

[2] Steele's Law and Custom of Hindoo Castes, p. 26.

[3] *Ibid.*

[4] See for instance Rahi *v.* Govind, I. L. R., 1 Bomb., 114.

[5] Steele's Law and Custom of Hindoo Castes, pp. 163, 346, 347.

validity of a girl's marriage without her parents' consent, there is some difference of opinion.[1] Generally, a girl is required to be married before *shanee* (puberty), but in some of the inferior castes a different rule obtains.[2] LECTURE VI.

Betrothment, called *mangni*, is with some castes irrevocable except for just cause; while according to others, it can be broken off by mutual consent.[3] It has been held, however, that specific performance of a contract of betrothal cannot be enforced;[4] and this is now the rule laid down by the Specific Relief Act.[5] Where the contract is broken off through the fault of either party, the other is entitled to a return of the jewels and other presents, as well as to compensation.[6] Betrothment.

Among the inferior castes, when the husband and the wife are found to belong to different castes, or to the same *gotra*, if the discovery is made before *shanee*, or even after *shanee* but before the birth of children, the husband may give the wife a *char chitti*, or deed of divorce, and she would then be competent to marry another in the *pat* form.[7] So, on the discovery of the husband's impotence before *shanee*, the wife, by the custom of certain castes, may, with the concurrence of the caste assembly, obtain a divorce, and contract *pat* marriage.[8] But the Courts have refused to recognize the authority of the caste assembly to grant divorce, and they have also refused to admit the validity of any custom Divorce—Remarriage.

---

1 Steele's Law and Custom of Hindoo Castes, pp. 163, 348, 349.

2 *Ibid*, pp. 162, 347.

3 *Ibid*, pp. 160, 343—346; 1 Morley's Digest, pp. 287, 288, pls. 3—7, 10.

4 Umedkika *v.* Nagindas Narotamdas, 7 Bom., O. C. J., 122.

5 Sec. 21, cl. (*b*) (illustration).

6 Steele, pp. 161, 344, 345, 361; Atmaram Kesoor *v.* Sheolal Mulookchund, 1 Borr., 358, cited in 1 Morley's Digest, p. 287, pl. 2.

7 Steele, p. 166.

8 *Ibid*, 167.

LECTURE VI. which allows divorce without the consent of the husband, on the ground of its being an immoral custom, and being opposed to the spirit of the Hindu law.[1] Where the divorce is obtained by mutual consent, the ceremony accompanying it consists in the husband breaking the wife's neck ornament, and giving her a *char chitti.*[2]

In addition to impotence, irregularity in marriage, and mutual consent, ill-treatment is a ground of divorce with certain castes.[3]

The ceremonies of *pat*, or remarriage, are different from those of marriage.[4] The remarriage of a wife is considered less honorable than that of a widow. Women, whether widows or wives, become lowered in social position by remarriage, and are excluded from preparing food at sacrifices, and from being present at marriages.[5] A woman by remarriage loses also all her rights over her first husband's property.[6] She looses likewise her right to the custody of her children (except infants) by the first husband.[7]

Children by *pat* are equally legitimate with those by marriage, and inherit equally with them.[8] But before the passing of Act XV of 1856, a wife by *lagna* (*i. e.*, one married when a maiden) had higher rights than one married by *pat.* Remarriage of widows being, however, now legalized

---

[1] Reg. *v.* Sambhu Raghu, I. L. R., 1 Bom., 347; Rahi *v.* Govind, *ibid*, 116; Narayan Bharthi *v.* Laving Bharthi, I. L. R., 2 Bom., 140; Reg. *v* Karsan Goja, 2 Bom., 117; Uji *v.* Hathi Lalu, 7 Bom., A. C. J., 133; Dyaram Doolubh *v.* Baee Umba, cited in 3 Morley's Digest, 181.

[2] Steele, pp. 168, 169.

[3] Kaseeram Kriparam *v.* Umbaram Hureechund, 1 Borr., 387, cited in 1 Morley's Digest, p. 289, pl. 14.

[4] Steele, pp. 364, 365.

[5] *Ibid*, p. 169.

[6] *Ibid*, p. 169.

[7] *Ibid*, pp. 169, 365.

[8] *Ibid*, pp. 179, 377. In 1 W. and B., 59—61, a different rule is apparently laid down, but the Bombay High Court, in Rahi *v.* Gobind (I. L. R., 1 Bomb., 115), accepted the rule given above as correct.

by that Act, a wife married when a widow has equal rights with a *lagna* wife.[1]

Customs of Southern India.

The difference between the customary law of marriage and the general Hindu law on the subject, is nowhere so considerable or so strongly marked as in Southern India; and the reason is obvious. The Hindu law was originally intended for the *Aryas*, or the people inhabiting Aryavarta, that is, the tract of country lying between the Eastern and the Western ocean, and the Himalaya and the Vindhya mountains. Within the region thus bounded, which is said to differ widely from the land of *Mlechchas*, the three twice-born classes are required by Manu invariably to dwell; and even the Sudra is not permitted to sojourn outside this region, except when distressed for subsistence.[2] Though this injunction of Manu has not been strictly observed, and Aryan Hindus of all castes have settled in the southern provinces, they form, according to most competent judges, only a small portion of the entire population of those provinces;[3] while the majority of the people are the descendants of the aboriginal tribes. This preponderance of the aboriginal element in the population has led to the preservation of a large body of primitive customs; and the so-called Hindu tribes of the Madras Presidency observe practices widely at variance with those of real Hindus.

"The Brahmins," says Ellis in one of his letters[4] to Sir T. Strange, "in introducing into this part of India their laws and religion, were obliged in many things to conform to the opinion of the aboriginal inhabitants, though in many instances immediately opposed to their prejudices; hence the Sudra high priests in most of the *Siva* Pagodas on this

---

[1] 1 W. and B., 89—98.

[2] Manu, II, 21—24.

[3] See Nelson's View of the Hindu Law, &c., Ch. IV.

[4] 2 Strange, 162.

LECTURE VI.

coast, the indiscriminate female intercourse and succession in the female line in Malabar, the primogeniture succession to landed estates among the *Velmawon* and other northern tribes, the exclusion of widows from succession even among the Brahmins, &c.; the truth being, that the law of the *Smritis*, unless under various modifications, has never been the law of the Tamil, and cognate nations,"

Speaking of these tribes, Mr. Justice Holloway is reported to have said,—[1] "I must be allowed to add that I feel the grotesque absurdity of applying to these Maravars the doctrine of Hindu Law. It would be just as reasonable to give them the benefit of the Feudal Law of real property. At this late day it is, however, impossible to act upon one's consciousness of the absurdity. I would not, however, be supposed to be unconscious of it." These words of that learned Judge have not, it seems, been altogether without effect. They have invited inquiry into the propriety of applying the Hindu law contained in the Sanskrit law-books to the so-called Hindus of the Madras Presidency. And it has since been expressly provided by the Madras Civil Courts Act, 1873, s. 16, that if there be any custom having the force of law and governing the parties, the same shall be the rule of decision in cases regarding marriage and certain other matters.

Prohibited degrees.

By the customary law of Southern India, the prohibition of intermarriage between collaterals is reduced within very narrow limits. The only collateral relations that are held prohibited to be taken in marriage by a man, are, his sister, father's sister, mother's sister, brother's daughter, mother's sister's daughter, and father's brother's daughter; but the marriage of a man with his sister's daughter, or

[1] In his judgment in Kattama Nachiar v. Dorasinga Tevar, 6 Mad., 341.

mother's brother's daughter, or father's sister's daughter, is usual in all classes, even among Brahmans.[1] This laxity in the law of prohibited degrees seems to have been in existence from very early times, and has been noticed by Hindu sages and commentators. Thus Baudhayana, quoted in the *Desadharma* Chapter of the Smriti Chandrika, says, marriage with one's maternal uncle's or paternal uncle's daughter is common in the South; and so Brihaspati.[2] This custom of the South is also noticed in the Vyavahara Mayukha.[3] Ellis is of opinion that intermarriage with the mother's brother's daughter, if she exist, is considered incumbent.[4] This is not quite correct; but marriage with such a relative is considered most desirable, as in that case the relations between the mother-in-law and daughter-in-law are thought likely to be of the most amicable kind.

Different forms of marriage.

Among the lower classes of Sudras, marriage with females who have lived in concubinage is allowed; and the law of legitimacy among some of these castes, resembles the Scotch law on the subject,—children begotten before marriage being legitimized on the marriage of the parents.[5]

Several of the castes openly practise polyandry. Thus, among the Tottiyars (a Telugu caste), it is customary with women after marriage to cohabit with their husband's brothers and near relatives. So the Kallars of the Madura District allow a woman to have simultaneously ten, eight, six or two husbands, who are all held to be the fathers jointly and severally of any children that may be born of her.[6]

---

[1] See Cunningham's Digest of Hindu Law, paras. 70—72, and note.

[2] See Nelson's View of the Hindu Law, &c., pp. 115, 116.

[3] Ch. I, Sec. I, 13.

[4] 2 Strange, 165.

[5] Strange's Manual of Hindu Law, Ch. II., paras. 40, 41.

[6] Nelson's View of the Hindu Law, &c., pp. 141, 142.

LECTURE VI.

"An extraordinary custom," says Nelson, "appears to prevail amongst the Vellalars of Caroor, of fathers getting adult women as wives for their infant sons, and themselves cohabiting with those women and begetting on their bodies children who are affiliated to the infant husbands. When the infant husbands grow up, they find wives for the male children affiliated to them, and cohabit with those wives, and so the custom goes on."[1]

Malabar law.

The Malabar law of marriage, which freely permits polyandry, is a most singular system. Excepting Brahmans and a few other castes, it obtains among the people of Malabar generally. In this system, "the females," says Mr. Strange, "before attaining maturity, go through a form of marriage, the bridegroom not necessarily taking the position of husband. After maturity they may consort with whom they please, and with as many as they please, provided that the connexion be with members of their own or some higher caste." In consequence of this promiscuous cohabitation, parentage is not generally ascertainable in the male line; and inheritence runs, therefore, in the female line. The children of a man are not his heirs; his sisters, sisters' children, and others related to him in the maternal line succeed to his estate.[2]

The origin of this practice of polyandry and of this rule of descent, termed *Marumakatayam*, or nepotism in the female line, is sought to be accounted for thus:—

It is alleged that Parasurama, the first king of Malabar, having introduced Brahmans into the district, and given them possessions therein, with a view to prevent division of their estates, ordained that they should vest in

[1] Nelson's View of the Hindu Law, &c., p. 144.

[2] See Strange's Manual of Hindu Law, Ch. XIII.

the eldest brothers, and that the eldest brothers alone should be permitted to marry. The younger brothers were allowed to consort with women of lower castes; but the offspring of these irregular unions, not being legitimate, could neither rank as Brahmans, nor be heirs to their fathers; and they could inherit only from their mothers. Gradually this system of irregular intercourse, with its peculiar rule of inheritance in the maternal line spread itself among the inferior castes, and in time became general among them.[1]

The truth, however, is, that the custom was never introduced by the Brahman settlers, but is the relic of a primitive practice.

Under a system so singular as this, the family group must necessarily be of a type different from the ordinary one. It is termed a *tarawad*, of which the remotest kindred is acknowledged to be a member, if living under the authority of the head of the family, and taking part in its religious observances. The eldest male member of whatsoever branch, is the head of the *tarawad*, and is termed the *Karnaven*, and the other members are called *Anandraven*. The *karnaven* has entire control over the affairs and the property of the family, and no member has the right to enforce partition of his share of the family property.[2]

The guardianship of children under the Malabar law belongs to their *karnaven*, and not to their father. In a reported case,[3] in which the Civil Judge had removed two children from the custody of their *karnaven*, and placed them under the guardianship of their father, on appeal, the High Court of Madras observed: "In the present case, by the principles of the law of Malabar, the mother herself

[1] See Strange's Manual of Hindu Law, Ch. XIII. [2] *Ibid.*

[3] Thathu Baputty *v.* Chakayath Chathu, 7 Mad., 179.

LECTURE VI. while alive and her children too were under the guardianship of the head of the family—the Karnaven. Their position was precisely analogous to that of the members of a Roman family under the *patria potestas.* The Karnaven is as much the guardian and representative, for all purposes of property, of every member within the tarawad, as the Roman father or grandfather.

"Moreover, the relation of husband and wife does not, in Malabar, disturb this condition. These children have no claim whatever upon the property of their father, but their rights are entirely in that of their Karnaven's family. There is no doubt at all that he was, during the mother's lifetime, and continues to be, after her death, the legitimate guardian of these children, and that the father has by positive law not the smallest right to their custody."

In a system of promiscuous intercourse like that in Malabar, the ordinary state of widowhood is necessarily unknown. Nor does the married state, or, more properly speaking, the state of alliance with males, effect any change in a female's relation to her family. Whether so allied or not, she continues alike a member of her family, and lives under the *tarawad* roof.[1]

Canarese law. The law of Canara, called the *Aliya Santana*[2] law, is similar to that of Malabar, with only this difference, that the principle that inheritance vests in the females in preference to the males, is more completely carried out in practice in Canara, where the management of property vests generally in females, than in Malabar, where the office of *karnaven* is commonly held by males.[3]

---

[1] Strange's Manual of Hindu Law, Ch. XIII.

[2] From Karnatic *Aliya*, 'son-in-law,' and Sanskrit *santana* 'offspring.'

[3] See Munda Chetti *v.* Timmaju Hensu, 1 Mad., 383; Strange's Manual of Hindu Law, 2nd ed., para. 404.

It has been held by the High Court of Madras, in the case of *Subbu Hegadi* v. *Tongu*,[1] that a female member of a family governed by the *Aliya Santana* law, while living with her husband apart from her family, is not entitled to maintenance out of the income of the family property. Touching the nature of the marriage relation under the *Aliya Santana* system, and the right of the wife to maintenance from her husband or his family, the High Court observed: "It remains to consider whether for any special reason arising out of the relation of husband and wife under the *Aliya Santana* system, a wife's residence with her husband should not be treated as a separation from her family. The relation is in truth not marriage, but a state of concubinage into which the woman enters of her own choice and is at liberty to change when and as often as she pleases. From its very nature then it might be inferred as probable that the woman remained with her family, and was visited by the man of her choice; but the case in this respect is not left to mere probability. Such has undoubtedly been the invariable habit under the Maroomakatayam law, and although women in Canara under the *Aliya Santana* system do, it seems, in some instances, live with their husbands, still there is no doubt that they do so of their free will, and that they may at any time rejoin their own families. We do not, therefore, see that residence with a husband can be regarded differently from any other separation by the voluntary act of the wife, and this conclusion is strengthened by the fact that Bhutala Pandiya is silent on the subject of residence after marriage.

---

[1] 4 Mad., 196.

LECTURE VI. "The ground of the husband's non-liability for maintenance, on which alone apparently the Principal Sadr Amin's decision rests, is, we think, altogether unsound. He may be right in saying that a wife cannot legally be maintained out of the funds belonging to the family of her husband for the very reason that living with the husband is not a necessary duty of the wife. It does not, however, follow, as the Civil Judge remarks in his judgment, that a husband is not bound to afford necessary maintenance to the woman from his self-acquired means so long as she continues to live with him as a wife. It will probably be found that the general law does impose such an obligation; but even supposing that it does not, still his non-liability to support her could not alter in any way the legal effect of the wife's residence with him or her right to maintenance out of the property of her family."

I ought to tell you that the work of Bhutala Pandiya, who is cited as an authority on the *Aliya Santana* law in the above extract and in other cases,[1] is now condered by some scholars to be a recent forgery; and it has, we are told by Dr. Burnell, been traced to two notorious forgers who lived not more than half a century ago.[2]

Divorce and remarriage. Among the lowest classes in the Southern Presidency, there is a custom which allows divorce,[3] and awards the husband damages in the nature of compensation for marriage expenses, where the wife separates from her husband of her own accord, or has been put away by him

---

[1] Munda Chetti *v.* Timmaju Hensu, 1 Mad., 380; Timmapa Heggade *v.* Mahalinga Heggade, 4 Mad., 28.

[2] Preface to the translation of Varada Raja's Vyavahara Nirnaya, p. xii, note; Nelson's View of the Hindu Law, &c., pp. 95—99.

[3] 1 Strange, 52.

for misconduct; and such custom has, to some extent, been recognized by the High Court of Madras in a case in which a husband sued his divorced wife and her father for promised compensation.[1]

Remarriage of widows and divorced wives is allowed by custom among the inferior castes in the Southern as well as in the Western Presidency;[2] but a widow is, by remarriage, deprived of her right to the property of her deceased husband.[3]

Forms of marriage according to sectarian customs.

The customs we have hitherto been considering are customs of families, tribes, and castes. The different forms of marriage according to the customs of different religious sects will be considered next.

Hinduism, as you are aware, has never been a homogeneous creed. It has always consisted of a great variety of sectarian creeds of varying degrees of orthodoxy, which its highly tolerant character has enabled it to hold together under a common name; while in a few instances, dissenting sects having denied the authority of the Vedas and the supremacy of the Brahmans, the fundamental doctrines of the Hindu faith, have been regarded as heretical, and excluded from the pale of Hinduism. The heretical and the less orthodox sects, though differing from the main body of Hindus in faith and ritual observances, have naturally found little reason to depart from the ordinary rules of Hindu law in the conduct of their civil affairs generally. But there are some civil matters in Hindu law that are intimately connected with religion, and marriage is pre-eminently one of them. It requires the consideration of caste distinctions in the selection of parties, and the performance of religious ceremonies

---

[1] Soobba Tevan v. Moothookoody, 6 Mad., 40.

[2] 1 Strange, 52.

[3] Murugayi v. Viramakali, I. L. R., 1 Mad., 226.

LECTURE VI. for the completion of the contract; and both these are points upon which the dissenting sects differ from the orthodox. In regard to marriage, therefore, the ordinary Hindu law does not, and cannot, form the common rule for all sects alike.

For our present purpose we may confine our attention to the Vaisnavas and Gosavis among admittedly Hindu sects, and the Buddhists, Jainas, Sikhs, and Brahmos among dissenters,—these being the sects whose rules relating to marriage differ in a marked degree from the ordinary Hindu law on the subject.

Vaishnavas.

Though, as one of the leading members of the Hindu pantheon, Vishnu is worshipped by all castes and sects of Hindus, his exclusive votaries, the Vaishnavas, form a distinct sect. This sect has two divisions. One of them is composed of persons who observe caste distinctions and all other Hindu practices and customs, and differ from the rest of the orthodox Hindu community only in worshipping Vishnu as their *Ishta Devata*, or chosen god: with this division we have at present nothing to do. The other division, composed of persons who are styled Vairagis, Jati Vaishnavas, or Vaishnavas simply, is more than a mere religious sect, being distinguished from the orthodox community by several social peculiarities. It is commonly regarded as a caste, but it wants one notable characteristic of caste,—namely, exclusiveness,—admitting as members Hindus of all castes from the highest to the lowest. In consequence of the absence of caste distinctions among them, and their belief in the inefficacy of ritual observances, choice in matrimony among the Vairagis is very little fettered, and their form of marriage is of the simplest and the least expensive kind. They also allow the marriage of widows.[1] There is very little in the shape of text or decision especially applicable to them; so that as regards marriage, they are entirely governed by custom. LECTURE VI.

Gosavis.

Among the Gosavis of the Bombay Presidency, a branch of the Saiva sect of the Dekhan, some lead a life of celibacy, while others marry. These latter are called Gharbaree Gosavis. The following are some of the principal peculiarities in their customs relating to marriage.[2]

A Gosavi can marry only a female Gosavi. If he marries any other woman, the marriage is not annulled, but the wife is not regarded as a Gosavini, or a member of the sect. A Gosavini must be married before she attains her fifteenth year.

Divorce is allowed on the ground of impotency. If a Gosavi separate from his wife, and give her a *char chitti,* or deed of divorce, they can never re-unite, and the wife may contract *pat* marriage with another man. If no such deed be given, she may be taken back by her husband, but without his permission she is not at liberty to contract a *pat* marriage with another man.

If the husband is absent and not heard of, the wife, being a grown-up woman, may form a left-handed or *pat* connection with another man. But the first husband, upon his arrival, is entitled to take her back, after reimbursing the second in the amount of his expenses.

The *pat* marriage, though allowed to divorced wives, is not allowed to widows.

---

[1] See Hunter's Statistical Account of Bengal, Vol. I, pp 65, 73; see also Wilson's Essays on the Religions of the Hindus, edited by Rost, Vol. I, pp. 152—171.

[2] See Mr. Warden's Report in Steele's Law and Custom of Hindoo Castes (Appx. B), pp. 444, 445; 1 W. and B., 257—259.

LECTURE VI. Concubinage is allowed among the Gosavis; but an illegitimate son, being the offspring of an adulterous intercourse, cannot inherit his father's estate.[1]

Buddhists. Of heretical sects, the Buddhists, the Jainas, and the Sikhs have, in some of the later enactments of the Legislature, been regarded as classes distinct from the Hindus.[2]

The Buddhists, from their denial of the authority of the Vedas and the supremacy of the Brahmans, have always been regarded as heretics; and though for a time successful in maintaining their ground against the Hindus, they were ultimately driven from India by the Brahmans, and they migrated to Ceylon on the south, and to Nepaul, Thibet, and China on the north.[3] At the present day the Buddhist population of British India is not large, and is composed chiefly of Chinese, Burmese, and Magh settlers.

The Buddhists have their written laws; but the laws of the Chinese Buddhists are not the same as those of the Buddhists of Burmah. Strictly speaking, therefore, the Buddhist law of marriage forms no part of the customary law of India; and I notice it here, only because in some cases it is evidently an adaptation of the Hindu law on the subjcet.

Though the religion of the Celestial Empire is of Indian origin, there is very little real or even pretended analogy between the jurisprudence of China and that of India. But the case is different with regard to the laws of Burmah. Indeed the apparent analogy between the laws of India and those of

---

[1] See Mr. Warden's Report in Steele's Law and Custom of Hindoo Castes, p. 440; and Narayan Bharthi *v.* Laving Bharthi, I. L. R., 2 Bom., 140.

[2] Act XXI of 1870, s. 2; Act III of 1872, s. 2.

[3] See Max Müller's Chips from a German Workshop, Vol. II, p. 345.

Burmah is even greater than the real. The Burmese have their Code of Manu in fourteen volumes or chapters, which in some places bears a striking resemblance to the Brahmanical code of that name. I may notice some of the chief peculiarities in the marriage-law as given in the twelfth volume (or chapter) of this Code. LECTURE VI.

"Amongst men there are only three ways of becoming man and wife, which are as follows:—1*st*, a man and woman given in marriage by their parents, who live and eat together; 2*nd*, a man and woman brought together by the intervention of a go-between, who live and eat together; 3*rd*, a man and woman who come together by mutual consent, who live and eat together."[1]

There are five kinds of wives who may be put away, namely, those who are barren; those who are mothers of daughters only; those who are diseased; those who do not conform to the rules of their class; and those who are disobedient. But a wife that is put away is entitled to her property.[2]

Upon separation between man and wife, their debts and assets are divided between them in definite shares, which are different in different cases; and the father gets the male children, and the mother the female children.[3]

Parental authority ranks very high; and accordingly if a daughter, living under the protection of her parents, without their consent runs off with a man and marries him, and gets children, nevertheless she must separate from her husband if her parents wish it.[4]

The Jainas differ much less from the Brahmanical Hindus than the Buddhists do. They recognize the divinity of Jainas.

[1] Richardson's Manu, p. 328.
[2] *Ibid*, p. 345.
[3] *Ibid*, p. 333 *et seq*.
[4] *Ibid*, p. 347.

LECTURE VI. some of the members of the orthodox pantheon, pay some deference to the authority of the Vedas, observe the institution of castes, and employ Brahmans as priests.[1] Accordingly, the Jainas have been generally regarded as a sect of heterodox Hindus, and it has been held by the High Courts of Bengal and Bombay, that the ordinary rules of Hindu law are to be deemed applicable to them, in the absence of evidence to show that they are governed by different rules.[2] The High Court of the North-West, in the case of *Sheo Singh Rai* v. *Dakho*[3] (which has been followed in a subsequent case[4]), appears to have taken a somewhat different view, holding that, in cases between Jainas, the customs of the sect are to be enquired into and given effect to. From this decision there has, I understand, been an appeal to the Privy Council, but the result of the appeal is not yet known.[5] The Jainas have their religious books, which occasionally contain rules of law; but the authenticity of these books is not deemed unquestionable.[6]

---

[1] Wilson's Essays on the Religions of the Hindus, edited by Rost, Vol. I, pp. 334, 335.

[2] See Maha Rajah Govindnath Ray *v.* Gulal Chand, 5 Sel. Rep. (New Series), p. 327, Remark by Sutherland; Lalla Mohabeer Persahad *v.* Mussamut Kundun Koowar, 8 W. R., 116; Bhagvandas Tejmal *v.* Rajmal, 10 Bom., 241.

[3] H. C. R., N. W. P., for 1874, p. 382.

[4] Hassan Ali *v.* Nagamal, I. L. R., 1 All., 289.

[5] The judgment of the Judicial Committee has since been reported. (See I. L. R. 1 All., 702). It affirms that of the High Court, but it contains certain observations, which show that though their Lordships hold that due weight ought to be given to any evidence of the customs of the Jainas that may be forthcoming, yet they do not dissent from the proposition that, in the absence of such evidence, the general Hindu law is applicable to that sect. See also the judgment of the Privy Council in Chotay Lall *v.* Chunno Lall (since reported), 3 Cal. L. R., 469.

[6] See Steele, pp. 22, 96; 5 Sel. Rep. (new ed.), 327, Remark by Sutherland.

Among the Jainas intermarriage between different castes or orders is not permitted.[1] The Jainas in the South of India observe all the Brahmanical *sanskars*, while those in Upper India generally observe only the initiation of the infant on the twelfth day after birth, and marriage.[2] Their marriage ceremony resembles that of the orthodox Hindus, and is generally performed with the intervention of a Brahman priest; but the Vedic *mantras* are omitted.[3] They permit polygamy, but do not allow divorce to the wife with right of remarriage. On the whole, the law of marriage among the Jainas does not, it seems, differ from the ordinary Hindu law except in minor details. LECTURE VI.

Sikhs.

The Sikhs are a far more heterodox sect than the Jainas. They eat objectionable flesh, ignore all caste distinctions, and admit proselytes even from Mahomedanism.[4] Though they have been sometimes regarded as a sect of Hindus,[5] the correctness of this view seems to be open to question.

They have no written laws, their social institutions being regulated by rules, which are rules of Hindu law modified by custom.[6]

Their forms of marriage are different from those of Hindus in general. They have an inferior form of marriage, called the *Anand* form, in which the ceremony consists in the recitation of a certain text called the *Anand* text, and which may be celebrated even with a concubine. But the issue by such marriage is entitled to inherit from the

---

1 See Wilson's Essays, Vol. I, pp. 344, 345.

2 *Ibid*, 322.

3 See Bhagvandas Tejmal *v.* Rajmal, 10 Bom., 256.

4 Wilson's Essays, Vol. II, pp. 143, 144.

5 See the evidence of Sir E. H. East before the House of Lords, referred to in Lopes *v.* Lopes, 5 Bom., O. C. J., 185.

6 1 Morley's Digest, Introd., p. ccci.

LECTURE VI. father.[1] Among the Sikhs, a woman has the same right to inherit the estate of her deceased husband, whether she was married by him when a maiden or espoused when a widow.[2]

Brahmos.

The last sect that I shall notice, namely the Brahmos, is quite of recent origin. The original sect, now called the Adi Brahmo Samaj, was founded by Ram Mohan Ray not more than fifty years ago; while the sect of Progressive Brahmos, a branch of the former, has come into existence within the last twenty years. The marriage law of both these sects is essentially the Hindu law on the subject, the only point of difference being in the ceremony of marriage. The former retain portions of the orthodox Hindu ceremony, while the latter omit it altogether, and substitute for it a form consisting of the exchange of mutual promises between the bridegroom and the bride, accompanied by certain prayers. The forms being of recent origin, doubts have been entertained as to how far the authority of custom can be invoked in their favor. The Progressive Brahmos, some years ago, consulted a learned lawyer, Mr. Cowie, then Advocate-General of Bengal, as to the validity of their form of marriage, and were told that it was not valid in law. They then petitioned the Legislature to enact a law for them, and this led to the passing of Act III of 1872, which I shall notice presently.

That Act prescribes a form of marriage for persons who do not profess the Christian, Jewish, Hindu, Mahomedan, Parsi, Buddhist, Sikh or Jaina religion; and as the Adi Brahmos do not admit that they are not Hindus by religion,

---

[1] Doe dem Juggomohun Mullick v. Saum Coomar Bebee, 2 Morley's Digest, 43.

[2] Doe dem Kissen Chunder Shaw v. Baidam Beebee, 2 Morley's Digest, 22.

the Act has no application to them. The Act, moreover, does not affect the validity of any mode of contracting marriage; and the Progressive Brahmos still celebrate their marriages in many instances according to their customary form. The validity of the forms of marriage among the Brahmos still remains, therefore, an important practical question. LECTURE VI.

This question, so far as it concerns the Adi Brahmos, who profess to be Hindus, has to be determined with reference to the Hindu law. I have in a former Lecture[1] already touched upon this question, and here I shall only quote the following remarks of Sir J. Stephen from his speech on the Native Marriage Bill:—[2] "I now come to the last point on which I shall have to address Your Lordship and the Council. It relates to that part of the saving section which applies to, and which is intended to save, such rights as may belong to what I may call the dissenting sects of Hindus, of which the Adi-Brahma-Samaja may be regarded as a specimen. The validity of the marriages of such bodies is obviously to be determined by the Hindu law, by which the members of the sect elect to abide. It would be presumptuous in me to express an opinion on the question, whether the Hindu law would treat such marriages as valid, and, if so, under what limitations. . . . . .
I apprehend, indeed, that there would not be much danger in affirming that the facility with which new sects form themselves, establish customs of their own adapted to the varying circumstances of the time and country, and yet continue in some sense or other to be, and to be considered, as Hindus, is one of the most characteristic

[1] See Lecture III.
[2] See Supplement to the *Gazette of India*, January 27, 1872, pp. 79, 80.

LECTURE VI. features of Hinduism. English law is the very antithesis to this. The first rule, as to the validity of a custom, is this—'It must have been used so long that the memory of man runneth not to the contrary.' Now, the memory of man runneth, according to English notions, to a particular point (I need not here enquire, precisely, what point) in the reign of Richard the First; that is, to the end of the twelfth century, or at present, for not much less than seven hundred years. No one, of course, would say that this rule ought to be applied to India. Its rational equivalent would be, that usage for a considerable period of time, usage of which the origin cannot be traced, is essential to the validity of a custom. I must say that even such a rule as this appears to me to be open to very great question, if it is to be applied to such a subject as the validity of particular forms of marriage. I hope that any Court of law in India would hesitate long, and look cautiously at the possible consequences of their decision, before they decided that a marriage was void, merely because it was celebrated according to the rites of a Hindu or other religious sect of recent origin. Surely it would be monstrous to deprive the Hindu religion, by judicial decisions, of what has hitherto been its most characteristic feature—its power of adapting itself to circumstances. It would, I should say, be a less evil to hold that the most irregular marriage was regular, than to bastardize, for instance, the whole Sikh community, on the ground that an English Court considered that the Sikhs were not orthodox Hindus."

Cases involving questions as to the validity of the form of marriage among the Progressive Brahmos, not being expressly provided for, must be determined according to justice, equity, and good conscience. Perhaps the best measure of justice, equity and good conscience, and one that is always resorted to by Indian Courts, is to be found in those parts of the decisions of English Courts which deal with broad general principles. And, as pointed out by Sir J. Stephen,[1] so far as the English cases[2] bearing on the point furnish argument by analogy, it is in favor of the view that the observance of ceremony is not essential to the validity of marriage as distinguished from its regularity. But there are other considerations which must not be lost sight of. The observance of ceremonious forms in marriage is required, not merely to give it a religious sanction but also to serve important civil purposes. The form must be a definite and well recognized one, to prevent all chance of confusion between marriage and concubinage; and it must also be such as to prevent the contracting of hasty and inconsiderate unions. If these conditions are fulfiled by any new form of marriage, and if the terms of the contract are unobjectionable, it would seem that the requirements of justice, equity, and good conscience would be satisfied. To quote again the words of Sir James Stephen:[3]—"If a considerable body of men, bound together by common opinions and known by a common name, appeared to be in the habit of celebrating marriages according to forms and on terms unobjectionable in themsevles, the Courts ought to recognize such marriages as valid, though, in any particular case, there might be circumstances which do not suggest themselves to my mind, and which would invalidate the marriage. The fixity of the sect, the propriety of its

LECTURE VI.

---

[1] See Supplement to the *Gazette of India*, January 27, 1872, pp. 70 73.

[2] See Dalrymple *v.* Dalrymple, 2 Haggard's Consistory Reports, p. 54; see also Reg. *v.* Millis, 10 Clark and Finnelly, 534.

[3] Supplement to the *Gazette of India*, January 27, 1872, pp. 77, 78.

LECTURE VI. forms, and the propriety of its terms, would all have to be considered by the Court."

Remarriage of widows—Act XV of 1856.

I shall now consider certain descriptions of marriage legalized by statute law.

Our Legislature has on principle been slow to interfere with the marriage laws of India; and in the first instance that I am going to give you,—namely, the legalizing of widow marriage, — its interference was not gratuitous, but was sought by the Hindus themselves. Pandit Iswar Chandra Vidyasagara, whose name will ever remain associated with the abolition of perpetual widowhood in India, pointed out in his celebrated tract, that the remarriage of widows was not unauthorized by the *sastras*; and his opinion was accepted by a considerable body of his educated countrymen. And it was to meet their wishes that the Legislature felt induced to pass Act XV of 1856, as we learn from the preamble to that Act.

The Act is a short one, consisting of seven sections:—Section 1 declares the marriage of Hindu widows legal, and the issue of such marriage legitimate, notwithstanding any law or custom to the contrary. The remaining six sections may be divided into two groups, whereof one, consisting of sections 6 and 7, lays down rules for the mode of contracting the marriage of a widow; and the other, consisting of sections 2, 3, 4 and 5, lays down rules touching the legal consequences of such marriage.

Section 6 enacts that the form of marriage of a Hindu widow shall be the same as the ordinary form of Hindu marriage.

Section 7 provides that if the widow remarrying is a minor, whose marriage has not been consummated, her guardians in marriage shall be in succession, her father, paternal grandfather, mother, elder brother, and other next male relative; and her marriage, without the consent such of legal guardian, shall, at any time before consummation, be liable to be declared void, upon the absence of such consent being proved. In the case of a widow who is of full age, or whose marriage has been consummated, her own consent shall be sufficient to render her remarriage valid. LECTURE VI.

Section 2, which is a very important section, provides that "all rights and interests which any widow may have in her deceased husband's property by way of maintenance or by inheritance to her husband or to his lineal successors, or by virtue of any will or testamentary disposition conferring upon her, without express permission to remarry, only a limited interest in such property, with no power of alienating the same, shall, upon her remarriage, cease and determine as if she had then died; and the next heirs of her deceased husband, or other persons entitled to the property on her death, shall, thereupon, succeed to the same."

Section 3 enacts that, on the remarriage of a widow, any member of the family of her deceased husband can, by petition to the proper Court, deprive her of the guardianship of her children by her late husband, except where she has been constituted their guardian by the will of their father.

Section 4, which is another important section, runs thus:—"Nothing in this Act contained shall be construed to render any widow, who, at the time of the death of any person leaving any property, is a childless widow, capable of inheriting the whole or any share of such property, if before the passing of this Act she would have been incapable of inheriting the same by reason of her being a childless widow."

Section 5 provides that a widow by her remarriage shall

LECTURE VI.

not forfeit any property or right, except as provided in the three preceding sections; and that a widow, who has remarried, shall have the same rights of inheritance as she would have had, had such marriage been her first marriage.

Remarks on its provisions.

Upon the provisions of the Act, I have a few observations to make.

You will observe that the Act does not give any rules for determining the eligibility of parties for marriage. It is clearly its intention that this matter should be governed by the ordinary rules of Hindu law. But these rules are not sufficient to meet every point which might arise in connection with the remarriage of widows. Thus, one of these rules of selection requires, that the parties to marriage should be of different *gotras*; but what is to be regarded as the *gotra* of a widow—the *gotra* of her father, in which she was born, or that of her deceased husband, to which she has been transferred by marriage? Vidyasagara maintains[1] that her father's *gotra* is to be deemed the *gotra* of a widow for the purposes of her remarriage; and, considering that her father or some other paternal relation is still her guardian in marriage, I think that view is in accordance with the intention of the Act. Again, the ordinary rules about prohibited degrees do not prohibit the marriage of a man with the mother of his wife, however repugnant to our feelings it may be. No express rule for the prohibition of such marriage is, however, necessary in the Hindu law, as it prohibits widow marriage altogether. But now that widow marriage has been legalized, the want of such prohibition may be deemed a defect in the law in theory, though, in practice, the universal feeling of repug-

[1] Marriage of Hindu Widows, pp. 165—172,

nance to such improper unions would be sufficient to supply the place of prohibitory rules. LECTURE VI.

Section 2, which is a very important one, may call for some explanation. In the first place, its language is not free from ambiguity, and a literal construction involves an anomaly. Thus, suppose that a Hindu dies, leaving a son and a widow. The son takes his estate, and the widow is entitled only to maintenance. Upon the death of the son, in the absence of any nearer heir, his mother would succeed to the property which he inherited from his father. If now the mother were to remarry, this section would clearly divest her of the property, and her son's next heir would take it. But suppose that the mother had remarried previous to her son's death: would she be entitled to succeed to the property in that case? This question arose before the High Court of Bengal in the case of *Akorah Sooth v. Boreani*,[1] Mr. Justice Kemp answered it in the affirmative, holding (upon a literal construction of the section) that, at the time of her remarriage, the widow had no rights in her deceased husband's property by inheritance to him or his lineal successor, which could cease and determine, and that, under the saving clause in section 5, she does not by remarriage forfeit any right, which she may subsequently acquire over it. But his colleague, Mr. Justice E. Jackson, differed from him, and in delivering judgment said, "But it is said that the widow had no such rights at the time of her remarriage, and such rights did not, therefore, cease and determine; that the law, in fact, alludes only to such property as the widow had inherited before her remarriage. I think that the words of the Act

[1] 2 B. L. R. (A. C.), 199; S. C., 10 W. R., 34, and 11 W. R., 82.

LECTURE VI. bear a more extended signification; and that "upon her remarriage" should not be read as at the date of such remarriage, but with reference to such remarriage. All right which the widow has in her deceased husband's property, by inheritance to him or to his lineal successor, ceases by reason of her remarriage, and in consequence of her remarriage, as if she had then died; and, thereupon, that is, when her right has ceased, the next heir shall inherit. The policy of the law appears to me to be one which is generally acknowledged in all society, and which is, perhaps, more especially required to be put in force in Hindu society, *viz.*, that the widow by remarriage shall not take her late husband's property away from his family, and into the hands of her new husband."

On appeal under section 15 of the Letters Patent, the decision of Mr. Justice Kemp was upheld; but Mr. Justice Louis Jackson observed,—"The words of section 2 are somewhat embarrassing, and the impression left on my mind is, that the Legislature had an intention which it has failed to carry out in words. I can hardly suppose that the Legislature intended a Hindu widow to be capable of inheriting the property of her son, she having previously remarried; when, if she had remarried while in the enjoyment of such property, she would have been, by such remarriage, entirely divested of that property. For although it is true that if the son had been living at the time of her remarriage, in certain circumstances, he would have had the option of depriving her of the succession, or confirming it on her; still it might, and probably would, in most instances, happen that at the time of remarriage the son was an infant. But it is not our province to set aside the clear meaning of the words of the Legislature merely for the purpose of getting rid of apparent inconsistencies."

In the second place you will observe, that it is only with reference to the property of her deceased husband, that remarriage deprives a widow of her rights; so that, if her son acquires any other property besides that inherited from his father, her right to such acquired property, as heir to her son, would not be affected by her remarriage. LECTURE VI.

In the third place, the widow's right as regards her share of her late husband's estate on partition among her sons,[1] not coming within the scope of section 2, would not, it seems, be affected by her remarriage; though I must tell you that it may, on the other hand, be contended that her right to such share is by way of maintenance.

Though remarriage under Act XV of 1856 would deprive a widow of her rights in her husband's estate, the question may arise, how far section 2 of the Act would affect the rights of a Hindu widow remarrying according to the custom of her caste, tribe, or sect, which sanctions such remarriage independently of Act XV. But the question is practically of little importance, as it is generally found that, wherever the remarriage of widows is allowed by custom, their rights to the estate of their deceased husbands are taken away by the same custom.[2]

A further question may arise touching the effect of remarriage upon a widow's right in her late husband's property. Suppose that a Hindu widow renounces her religion (a circumstance which by Act XXI of 1850, would not affect her rights), and suppose that she then remarries according to the law of the sect to which she becomes a

[1] Mitakshara, Ch. I, Sec. VII, 2; Dayabhaga, Ch. III, Sec. II, 29.

[2] See Steele, pp. 169, 176; W. and B., 96, 99; Parvati v. Bhikur, 4 Bom., A. C. J., 25; Murugay v. Viramakali, I. L. R., 1 Mad., 226.

LECTURE VI. convert, or according to Act III of 1872, if it applies to her. Would such remarriage divest her of her rights in the property inherited from her deceased husband? Clearly section 2 of Act XV of 1856 is inappliable to such a case; and accordingly it has been held[1] that her remarriage in such cases would not deprive her of the estate inherited from her deceased husband. But the correctness of this decision seems to be open to question. For though the enjoyment of the deceased husband's estate by the widow may not be conditional upon her continuing chaste,[2] it seems to follow from the spirit, if not from the letter, of the Hindu law,[3] that it is conditional upon her remaining a widow.

By the law of the Bengal school, the daughter's right of succession to her father's property being founded on her offering funeral oblations by means of her son,[4] a daughter who is a sonless widow is not entitled to inherit to her father.[5] But the remarriage of a widow being now legal, no daughter, though a childless widow at her father's death, can be said to have become a childless widow for ever. She may marry and have male issue; so that, unless she is passed the age of child-bearing, she would come under the description of a daughter likely to have male issue; and accordingly, it might be argued that she would be entitled to inherit. It is in anticipation of such an argument that section 4 of the Act provides that, if a woman is a childless widow, and incompetent to inherit by reason of her being so at the time when the succession opens,

---

[1] Gopal Singh v. Dhungazee, 3 W. R., 206.
[2] Kerry Kolitanee v. Monee Ram Kolita, 19 W. R., 367.
[3] Mitakshara, Ch., II, Sec. I. 18, *et seq*; Dayabhaga, Ch. XI, Sec. I.
[4] Dayabhaga, Ch. XI, Sec. II, 15.
[5] Dayabhaga, Ch. XI, Sec. II, 3.

the provisions of this Act shall not be construed to give her any heritable right. But a widowed daughter, by remarrying before her father's death, would, under the provisions of section 5 of the Act, be entitled to inherit her father's estate along with other married daughters. LECTURE VI.

The operation of section 4 may sometimes be attended with anomalous consequences. Thus, if a man dies leaving two daughters, the first, a sonless widow, and the second having, or being likely to have, male issue, the latter alone succeeds to his estate. Suppose that the former now remarries, and that both the sisters have sons: upon the death of the second daughter, who should succeed to her father's estate?—Her sons only, or the sons of both the sisters? The latter view seems to be correct, but it involves the anomaly that the sons of the first daughter, who are born subsequent to the death of the second daughter, would get no share of their maternal grandfather's estate.

No doubt, the anomaly here pointed out is not without a parallel in the Hindu law. The case of the sister's sons would furnish such a parallel. But I may add, that the anomaly noticed above is avoided in the ordinary Hindu law by recognizing the doctrine of survivorship among daughters, and postponing the succession of the daughter's sons till the death of the last of the daughters in whom the succession might have vested.[1]

Act III of 1872.

Act III of 1872, not being applicable to persons professing the Hindu religion, a detailed examination of its provisions does not come within the scope of a course of lectures on the Hindu law of marriage. But as persons

[1] See Aumirtolall Bose v. Rajoneekant Mitter, 23 W. R., 214.

LECTURE VI. who are Hindus by birth, and who are still governed by the Hindu law in some respects, may marry under that Act, I shall conclude this Lecture with a brief notice of its leading provisions.

"Marriages may be celebrated under this Act between persons neither of whom professes the Christian or the Jewish, or the Hindu, or the Mahomedan, or the Parsee, or the Buddhist, or the Sikh, or the Jaina religion, upon the following conditions:—

(1.) Neither party must, at the time of the marriage, have a husband or wife living:

(2.) The man must have completed his age of eighteen years, and the woman her age of fourteen years, according to the Gregorian calendar:

(3.) Each party must, if he or she has not completed the age of twenty-one years, have obtained the consent of his or her father or guardian to the marriage:

(4.) The parties must not be related to each other in any degree of consanguinity or affinity, which would, according to any law to which either of them is subject, render a marriage between them illegal.

1st Proviso.—No such law or custom, other than one relating to consanguinity or affinity, shall prevent them from marrying.

2nd Proviso.—No law or custom as to consanguinity shall prevent them from marrying, unless a relationship can be traced between the parties through some common ancestor, who stands to each of them in a nearer relationship than that of great-great-grandfather or great-great-grandmother, or unless one of the parties is the lineal ancestor, or the brother or sister of some lineal ancestor of the other." (Sec. 2.)

The requisite formalities are as follows:—Notice of an intended marriage is to be given to the Registrar of Marriage before whom it is to be solemnized. If no objection to the marriage is raised by any one within fourteen days after the receipt of such notice by the Registrar, he shall proceed to solemnize the marriage. A written declaration in a prescribed form, stating that the conditions mentioned above have been fulfilled, is to be signed by each party and by three witnesses in the presence of the Registrar. The marriage shall be solemnized in the presence of the Registrar and the three witnesses who signed the declaration, and may be in any form, provided that each party says to the other in the presence and hearing of the Registrar and the witnesses—"I, *A*, take thee, *B*, to be my lawful wife (or husband)."[1] The Registrar shall enter a certificate of the marriage having been solemnized, in a book kept for the purpose.

Neither of the parties married under this Act shall be at liberty to marry again during the lifetime of the other; and any violation of this rule shall make the offending party liable to punishment under the Indian Penal Code.

The Indian Divorce Act (IV of 1869) is declared to be applicable to marriages under this Act; and any such marriage may be declared null or dissolved for any cause mentioned in the Divorce Act, or on the ground that it contravenes any of the four conditions mentioned above.

[1] Secs. 4—11.

LECTURE VII.

WHAT CONSTITUTES STRIDHAN.

Questions for consideration—Great diversity of doctrine on the subject—Different descriptions of *stridhan* according to the sages—Manu—Narada—Vishnu—Katyayana—Apastamba—Vyasa—Devala—Yajnavalkya—Remarks on the preceding texts—Definition and classification of *stridhan* according to the commentators—Benares school—Mitakshara—Viramitrodaya—Bombay school—Vyavahara Mayukha—Dravida school—Parasara Madhavya—Smriti Chandrika—Mithila school—Vivada Chintamani—Bengal school—Dayabhaga—Dayatattwa—Dayakrama Sangraha—Does property inherited by a woman become her *stridhan?*—Bengal school—Other schools—*Thakoor Dayhee* v. *Rai Balack Ram*—*Bhugwandeen Doobey* v. *Myna Baee*—Decisions of Indian Courts—Bengal—*Chotay Lall* v. *Chunnoo Lall*—Madras—Bombay—Share on partition—Summary of the law—Gift—Purchase—Inheritance—Partition—Burden of proof where property is alleged to be *stridhan.*

HAVING given you in the preceding lectures an outline of the law concerning that relation which most materially determines the rights and *status* of the Hindu female, I now come to the second branch of my subject—the law relating to her *stridhan* or peculiar property.

This law will be considered with reference to the following three questions:—

Questions for consideration.

First—What constitutes *stridhan?*

Second—What are the rights of a woman over her *stridhan?*

Third—What is the order of succession to *stridhan?*

Great diversity of doctrine on the subject.

Upon each of these questions there exists great diversity of doctrine, in consequence of which the law of *stridhan* has become a rather complicated subject. It is a topic regarding which, Kamalakar says in the Vivada Tandava, " the lawyers fight tooth and nail." And Jimutavahana, in concluding his chapter on this branch of the law, complacently observes,—"Thus has been explained the most difficult subject of succession to a childless woman's *stridhan*."

LECTURE VII.

Different descriptions of *stridhan* according to the sages.

I begin with the first of the three questions stated above, namely, What constitutes *stridhan?* I shall first of all give you shortly the different definitions or rather descriptions of *stridhan* according to the sages, as these form the groundwork of the law on the subject, and the basis of the disquisitions of the commentators.

Manu.

Manu says: "What was given before the nuptial fire *(adhyagni)*, what was given on the bridal procession *(adhyá-váhanika)*, what was given in token of love *(pritidatta)*, and what was received from a brother, a mother, or a father, are considered as the six-fold separate property of a married woman."[1] And he further declares: "Such ornaments as women wear during the lives of their husbands, the heirs (of those husbands) shall not divide among themselves; they who divide it among themselves fall deep into sin."[2] The former of these texts, which professes to define *stridhan*, is evidently not in the nature of a logical definition; nor even does it contain an exhaustive enumeration of all the different sorts of *stridhan* noticed by other sages.

Narada.

According to Narada, "What was given before the nuptial fire, what was presented in the bridal procession, her husband's donation *(bhartridaya)*, and what has been given by her brother, mother, or father, is termed the six-fold property of a woman."[3] He further declares: "Property given to her by her husband, through pure affection, she may enjoy at her pleasure after his death, or may give it away, except land or houses."[4]

You will observe that Narada's description differs from

---

[1] IX, 194. [2] IX, 200. [3] XIII, 8.
[4] Colebrooke's Digest, Bk. V, 476.

LECTURE VII.

Manu's only in mentioning 'husband's donation' in the place of 'gift in token of love.' As this last sort, namely, gift in token of love, may be a gift by the husband or any other relation, Manu's definition is evidently more comprehensive than that given by Narada.

Vishnu.

Vishnu says: "That which has been given to a woman by her father, mother, sons or brothers, that which she has received before the sacrificial fire (at the marriage ceremony), that which she receives on supersession, that which has been given to her by her relations, her fee, and a gift subsequent, are called woman's property."[1] He further declares: "Those ornaments which the wives usually wear should not be divided by the heirs whilst the husbands (of such wives) are alive; if they divide them, they become outcastes."[2] The former of these texts enumerates nine sorts of *stridhan*, but these are not in every instance exclusive of one another; thus, a gift subsequent may also be a gift from the parents. Gifts from sons, gifts from kindred, gift on supersession (which has been already noticed in a former lecture[3]), and gift subsequent and woman's fee (which are defined by other sages as you will presently see) are the additional sorts mentioned by Vishnu, over and above those given in Manu's text; but a gift subsequent, as you will see from its definition, is in fact included in Manu's enumeration. The latter of the above two *sutras*,—namely, that relating to ornaments,—is in the original, word for word the same as the second of the two texts cited from Manu. The translation of Manu's text is given according to the gloss of Kulluka, while Vishnu's *sutra* has been rendered according to the gloss of Nanda Pandit. The

---

[1] XVII, 18 (1 W. & B., 342). [2] XVII, 22 (1 W. & B., 342).

[3] Lecture IV, *ante*, p. 163.

original would bear either interpretation. The *sutra* of Vishnu, as interpreted in the Vaijayanti, means, that if a father and his sons, or other coparceners divide, each woman of the family whose husband is alive retains her ornaments; but the ornaments of widows may be divided.[1]

Katyayana. Katyayana[2] mentions the same six sorts of *stridhan* as Manu, and he defines some of those six and also some of the additional sorts enumerated by Vishnu.

"Whatever is given to women," says he, "at the time of their marriage before the nuptial fire, *which is the witness of nuptials*, is denominated by sages *adhyagnika stridhan*."[3] You will observe that the gift here may be made by any one. The *adhyavahanika* is thus defined: "That again which a woman receives while she is led from her parental (abode to the house of her husband) is called *adhyavahanika stridhan*, or woman's property given at the bridal procession."[4] This is the meaning of the text according to its natural construction, and it is the meaning adopted by Vijnaneswara, Kulluka, Devanda Bhatta, Nilkantha, and Jagannatha.[5] But Jimutavahana and Srikrishna[6] give the text a different construction, according to which it should be rendered thus: "That again which a woman receives from the family of her parents while she is led (to the house of her husband) is called *adhyavahananika stri-*

---

[1] See 1 W. & B., 343 note. The text in the original runs thus:—

पत्यौ जीवति यः स्त्रीभिरलंकारो धृतो भवेत् ।
नतं भजेरन्दायादा भजमाना पतन्तिते ॥

[2] Colebrooke's Digest, Bk. V, 462. [3] *Ibid*, 464.

[4] See Mitakshara, Ch. II, Sec. XI, 5.

[5] See Mitakshara, Ch. II, Sec. XI, 5; note to Manu, IX, 194; Smriti Chandrika, Ch. IX, Sec. I, 2; Vyavahara Mayukha, Ch. IV, Sec. X, 3; Colebrooke's Digest, 465, commentary.

[6] Dayabhaga, Ch. IV, Sec. I, 5, 6; Dayakrama Sangraha, Ch. II, Sec. II, 8, 9.

LECTURE VII.

dhan." The difference between these two intrepretations is evidently not merely a verbal one, but affects the sense materially; for, according to the former, gifts to a woman at the bridal procession, by whomsoever made, whether relatives or strangers, come under the category of *stridhan;* while according to the latter, the definition would include only gifts to a woman from the family of her parents. The importance of this distinction will be seen presently. I may here notice, what appears to be rather curious, that Colebrooke, in his translation of Jagannatha's Digest, has translated this text according to Jimutavahana's construction, while in the Dayabhaga, he has rendered it in the other way. This has made paras. 5 and 6 of Sec. I, Chap. IV of his translation of the Dayabhaga appear somewhat incongruous.[1]

"Whatever has been given (to a woman) through affection by her mother-in-law or by her father-in-law, and what has been given to her as a token of respect, at the time of making obeisance at her feet (*padabandanika*), is denominated an affectionate gift (*pritidatta*) [or according to another reading, *lavanyarjita*, that is, acquisition through loveliness]."[2] Jagannatha interprets *padabandanika* to mean, 'what is given in return of her humble salutations.'[3]

"What is received by a woman after marriage from the kinsmen of her lord, or from those of her parents, is called a gift subsequent (*anwadheya*); but Bhrigu gives the name

---

[1] The verse in the original runs thus:—

यत् पुनर्लभते नारी नीयमाना हि पैतृकात् ।
अध्यावाहनिकं नाम तत् स्त्रीधनमुदाहृतं ॥

The Mitakshara reads पितुर्गृहात् for हि पैतृकात्.
This reading, of course, would remove all ambiguity.

[2] Colebrooke's Digest, Bk. V, 466; Mitakshara, Ch. II, Sec. XI, 5 note.

[3] Colebrooke's Digest, Bk. V, 466, commentary.

of 'subsequent gift' to anything received by her after the nuptial ceremony from her husband himself, or from her parents, through pure affection." LECTURE VII.

"The trifle which is received by a woman as the price or *reward* of household *labor*, of *using household* utensils, of *keeping* beasts of burden, of *watching* milch cattle, of *preserving* ornaments of dress, or of *superintending* servants, is called her perquisite (*sulka*)."[1]

"What a woman, either after marriage or before it, either in the mansion of her husband or in that of her father, receives from her lord or her parents, is called a gift from affectionate kindred (*saudayika*); and such a gift having by them been presented through kindness that the women possessing it may live well, is declared by law to be their absolute property."[2]

"But," says Katyayana, "whatever wealth she may gain by arts, *as by painting or spinning*, or may receive on account of friendship from any but her kindred, her lord alone has dominion over it. But the rest is declared to be woman's property (*stridhan*)."[3]

"Ornaments," says Apastamba, "are the exclusive pro- Apastamba.
perty of a wife, and so is wealth given to her by kinsmen or friends according to some legislators."[4]

Vyasa declares: "That which is given to bring the bride Vyasa.
to the family of her husband is her perquisite; which is

---

[1] Colebrooke's Digest, Bk V, 468. [2] *Ibid*, 475.

[3] Dayabhaga, Ch. IV, Sec. I, 19.

[4] Colebrooke's Digest, Bk. V, 472. This text appears to be the same as the 9th *sutra* of Kanda XIV, Patala VI, Prasna II (see 1 W. & B., 304); but the reading there is somewhat different. It runs thus :—"According to some, the share of the wife consists of her ornaments and the wealth (which she may have received) from her relations." The *sutra* occurs along with rules for partition.

LECTURE VII.

given as a bribe or the like, that she may cheerfully go to the mansion of her lord."[1]

"A portion amounting to two in the thousand out of the whole estate, should be given to a woman; that, and whatever wealth is bestowed on her by by her husband, she may use as she pleases."[2]

Devala.

According to Devala, "Food and vesture, ornaments, perquisites, and wealth received by a woman *from a kinsman,* are her own property; she may enjoy it herself, and her husband has no right to it, except in extreme distress."[3]

Yajnavalkya.

Yajnavalkya, whose text on the definition of *stridhan* has been the subject of much discussion, declares: "What was given (to a woman) by the father, the mother, the husband, or a brother, or received by her before the nuptial fire, or presented to her on her husband's marriage to another wife (*adhivedanika*), and the rest, is denominated *stridhan.* So, that which is given by kindred, as well as her fee and anything bestowed after marriage."[4] This version is according to the reading adopted in the Mitakshara and the commentaries which follow it.[5] But Jimutavahana[6] slightly

---

[1] Colebrooke's Digest, Bk. V, 471. [2] *Ibid*, 482. [3] *Ibid*, 478.

[4] II, 143, 144. The text in the original runs thus:—

पितृमातृपतिभ्रातृदत्तमध्यग्न्युपागतं ।

आधिवेदनिकाद्यं च स्त्रीधनं परिकीर्त्तितं ॥

बन्धुदत्तं तथा शुल्कमन्वाधेयकमेव च ।

Jimutavahana reads आधिवेदनिकं चैव (and also *adhivedanika*) for आधिवेदनिकाद्यं च (*adhivedanika* and the rest).

[5] See Mitakshara, Ch. II, Sec. XI, 1; Vyavahara Mayukha, Ch. IV, Sec. X, 2.

[6] Dayabhaga, Ch. IV, Sec. I, 13; see the edition of the Dayabhaga by Bharat Chandra Siromani. In Colebrooke's translation of the Dayabhaga, the same reading of the text is adopted as that given in the Mitakshara.

alters the reading by substituting the expletive *eva* for the suppletive term *adya* (and the rest), which changes the meaning very much; for this reading, by omitting the words 'and the rest,' would limit the application of the term *stridhan* to the descriptions of property specifically named.

Remarks on the preceding texts.

Though there are about eighty different sages or writers of institutes, the texts of the above-named eight sages are all that are referred to by commentators in their disquisitions on the definition of *stridhan*. And as according to the received opinion, the writings of these commentators are at the present day the real authorities on Hindu law,[1] we may spare ourselves the trouble of considering what other sages besides these eight may have said on the subject. But though the commentators have thus shortened his labor, the student of Hindu law has little reason to thank them after all. For, though they confine themselves to the consideration of a limited number of discordant authorities, they have introduced a new source of difficulty by their want of agreement among themselves in the reading and interpretation of the texts. There is hardly any text of importance on the subject, which has not received different constructions.

None of the foregoing texts gives any exact definition of *stridhan*. They enumerate and describe different kinds of *stridhan* without aiming at any logical classification. Nor is the number of kinds definitely settled, though it is sometimes said to be six. Thus Katyayana enumerates six kinds, but describes several additional sorts. But one thing is clear from an examination of the texts, namely, that the term

---

[1] See the remarks of the Judicial Committee in The Collector of Madura *v.* Muttu Ramalinga Satthupathy, 10 W. R. (P. C.), 21.

LECTURE VII.

stridhan is not used in its simple etymological sense, but has a technical meaning. If it were otherwise, and if by *stridhan* were meant any property belonging to a woman, the enumeration of particular descriptions of property as coming under that denomination would be useless. And the last text cited from Katyayana would go expressly to negative such a supposition. As for the suppletive term *adya*, 'and the rest' in the text of Yajnavalkya, apart from the authority of Vijnaneswara which I shall presently consider, there is nothing to show that it includes every description of property howsoever acquired. Indeed, according to the ordinary canons of interpretation, suppletory expressions can include such things only as are similar to those specifically mentioned, and nothing more besides.

It may, therefore, be deduced from the texts quoted above, that as a rule, it is only gifts obtained by a woman from her relations, and her ornaments and apparel, that constitute her *stridhan*; and that the only sorts of gifts from strangers which come under that denomination are, presents before the nuptial fire, and (according to some) presents made at the bridal procession. But neither gifts obtained from strangers at any other time, nor her acquisitions by labor and skill, would constitute her *stridhan*. These limitations may appear to you unreasonable; and judged according to our advanced notions about individual rights, so, no doubt, they really are. But you have seen that in the Hindu law the position of women is one of absolute dependence. Their time, therefore, is deemed to be absolutely at the disposal of their husbands; and consequently whatever is acquired by them at the expense of that time, is deemed to belong to their husbands. As for the distinction between gifts from relations and those from strangers, that appears to be based upon the idea that outside the circle of her near relations, the social existence of a married woman is completely merged in that of her husband, so that she cannot be the recipient of a gift from any one but her relations, without making her husband a participator in it. Nor is Hindu law singular in this respect. The restrictions upon the proprietary rights of married women were, until lately, far more stringent in the English law than they are with us.

Definition and classification of *stridhan* according to the commentators.

I shall now consider the definitions of *stridhan* deduced from the foregoing texts by the commentators of the different schools. At the present day, the commentators are the real authorities on the subject; and it is their definitions that Judges are bound to adopt, except where they have been modified by later, and practically more authoritative expositions of the law, I mean, judicial decisions.

Benares school —Mitakshara.

I begin with the Benares school. The highest authority in that school is the Mitakshara, which is also universally respected throughout India. That treatise is a continuous commentary on the institutes of Yajnavalkya; and the author accordingly adopts the text of that sage as the basis of his definition of *stridhan;* and he has the following commentary on the first *sloka* on the subject (II, 143):—

"That which was given by the father, by the mother, by the husband, or by a brother; and that which was presented by the maternal uncles and the rest, at the time of wedding before the nuptial fire; and a gift on a second marriage or gratuity on account of supersession, as will be subsequently explained in the text, 'To a woman whose husband marries a second wife, let him give, &c.;' [and, as indicated] by the word *adya* (and the rest), property obtained

LECTURE VII.

by inheritance, purchase, partition, acceptance, finding: all this is *stridhan* according to Manu and the rest."[1]

Vijnaneswara then remarks, "The term *stridhan* (woman's property) conforms in its import with its etymology, and is not technical: for, if the literal sense be admissible, a technical acceptation is improper."[2]

In order to obviate a possible objection,—namely, that Manu's enumeration of six kinds of *stridhan* would militate against the view that the term is used in its unlimited sense,—our author observes: "What again is said by Manu (in the verse) 'What was given before the nuptial fire, &c.' [here Manu's text is cited in full] about *stridhan* being of six sorts, is intended, not as a restriction of a greater number, but as a denial of a less."[3]

After giving Katyayana's definitions of gifts before the nuptial fire and the rest, the author next considers the first half of the next *sloka* of Yajnavalkya—"So, that which has been given by kindred, as well as her fee or gratuity, and anything bestowed after marriage,"—and explains 'kindred' as meaning 'relations of the mother and those of the father,' and the term 'gratuity' (*sulka*), as that for the receipt of which a girl is given in marriage.[4]

He then gives Katyayana's definition of a gift subsequent, which I have already given above along with Katyayana's other texts. And our author concludes his description of

---

[1] Mitakshara, Ch. II, Sec. XI, 2. The latter part of the above translation is somewhat different from Colebrooke's translation.

[2] *Ibid*, 3.

[3] *Ibid*, 4. The above translation differs slightly from that given by Colebrooke, which omits the words यत्पुनः 'what again' with which the verse begins. This omission, as pointed out by Messrs. West and Bühler (1 W. & B., Introduction, p. lxv), has rendered the sense liable to be misunderstood.

[4] *Ibid* 6.

LECTURE VII.

stridhan with an explanatory note that the words in the last hemistich, cited from Yajnavalkya, are connected with the words 'is denominated *stridhan*' which precede (in *sloka* 143, Chap. II).[1]

Nothing can be clearer or more simple than the above explanation of what constitutes *stridhan*. Leaving out of consideration the refutation of a possible adverse argument, and the descriptions of particular kinds of *stridhan* known by definite names, the author's explanation can be summed up in these few words, namely, that *stridhan*, conformably to its derivation, means property of any description belonging to a woman. And this unlimited sense is deduced from the suppletory term *adya* 'and the rest' in the text of Yajnavalkya. How far that word (*adya*), which is preceded and followed by the enumeration of particular sorts of property as coming under the denomination of *stridhan*, can correctly bear the signification attached to it, is certainly a matter of considerable doubt. I have already hinted at my reasons for entertaining this doubt, and I shall only add that the Madhaviya commentary, which is the work of a scholar of vast erudition, and is esteemed as a high authority in the South, gives to the words 'and the rest,' in Yajnavalkya's text, a limited signification, such as under the ordinary rules of interpretation they ought to bear. "By the words '*et cetera*,'" says Madhava, "property purchased with what is given during the procession, &c., is included."[2] And the

[1] Colebrooke's translation of this passage (Mitakshara, Ch. II, Sec. XI, 7) is slightly inaccurate. The last sentence in verse 7 in the original runs thus:—

स्त्रीधनं परिकीर्त्तित' इतिगतेन सम्बन्धः ।

"The relation (of the words in the last quotation) is with the words 'is denominated *stridhan*,' which precede."

[2] See Dayavibhaga (Burnell's translation), p. 41.

LECTURE VII.

highest Court of appeal for India has, upon a consideration of the general spirit of the Hindu law, been led to impose some limitation upon Vijnaneswara's meaning of the term *stridhan*, and to hold that property inherited by a widow from her husband does not become her *stridhan*.[1] The effect of this limitation, and the general question how far inherited property constitutes *stridhan*, will be considered in a subsequent part of the present lecture.

But it ought to be borne in mind that we are not now at liberty to put our own construction upon the Rishi texts. Whatever construction has been put upon them by authoritative commentaries like the Mitakshara, has become binding upon us. Vijnaneswara's opinion is as much an authority now, as the text he comments upon; and indeed, at the present day, the former is practically of greater importance than the latter. In the words of the Judicial Committee "the duty of an European Judge, who is under the obligation to administer Hindu law, is not so much to enquire whether a disputed doctrine is fairly deducible from the earliest authorities, as to ascertain whether it has been received by the particular school which governs the district with which he has to deal."[2]

Though the Mitakshara declares that every description of property belonging to a woman becomes her *stridhan*, it does not follow that her power of disposal is the same over every variety of it. Vijnaneswara admits with Narada the want of independence in women;[3] and, indeed, he is so far from allowing females to have absolute power over

---

[1] Bhugwandeen Doobey *v.* Myna Baee, 9 W. R. (P. C.), 23; Mussamut Thakoor Dayhee *v.* Rai Balack Ram, 10 W. R. (P. C.), 3.

[2] The Collector of Madura *v.* Muttu Ramalinga Satthupathy, 10 W. R. (P. C.), 21.

[3] Mitakshara, Ch. II, Sec. I, 21.

their property, that he does not allow such power even to male proprietors.[1] This point will be considered more fully in the next lecture. LECTURE VII.

If such a high authority as the Mitakshara stood in need of any support, it is amply supported on the point under consideration by the Viramitrodaya, a later commentary held in high esteem in the Benares school.[2]

Viramitrodaya.

The Viramitrodaya[3] contains a much fuller discussion on the point, and tries to answer almost every objection that may be urged against Vijnaneswara's definition of *stridhan*. After explaining that the enumeration of six sorts of *stridhan* by Manu and Narada is meant to be a denial of a smaller number, and not a restriction of a greater, the author observes, that the word *stridhan*, according to its etymology, means 'any property owned by a woman,' and that its meaning is not restricted by any technical definition; and he gives to the word *adya* the same general import that is given to it in the Mitakshara.

He then notices the following objection against his definition of *stridhan*:—If every kind of property owned by a woman is to be regarded as her *stridhan*, this interpretation would be opposed to the two texts of Katyayana, in one of which that sage observes,—"Whatever has been given to women under certain conditions, or with certain design, by their father, brother, or their husband, all that is declared not to be woman's property;"—and in the other he

---

[1] Mitakshara, Ch. I, Sec. I, 27.

[2] See Omrit Koomaree Dabee *v.* Lukhee Narain Chuckerbutty, 10 W. R. (F. B.), 86; Greedharee Lall Roy *v.* The Government of Bengal, 10 W. R. (P. C.), 34.

[3] See the edition by Jivananda Vidyasagara, pp. 688, 689; and 2 W. & B., p. 67, *et seq.*, where a translation of the chapter of the Viramitrodaya relating to *stridhan* is given.

LECTURE VII.

declares,—"But over that, which has been gained by mechanical arts, or which has been received out of affection from a stranger, the husband has dominion. But the rest is declared to be *stridhan*."[1]

And he answers the objection by maintaining, that Katyayana does not in these texts deny that such property (as conditional gifts, gains by mechanical arts, and the rest) is *stridhan*, but only denies that the woman who acquires it has the power of disposal over it; and in support of this view he refers to Katyayana's words, "the husband has dominion, &c." He further observes, that even if the former of the two verses of Katyayana indicate a denial that conditional gifts and gifts with a design (to defraud others) are woman's property, that would not militate against his view, as such gifts would be no gifts at all; for Manu says, "When the judge discovers a pledge or sale, gift or acceptance, made with a fraudulent design, or in whatever case he discovers a transaction to be conditional, let him annul that entirely."[2]

Thus you will observe that the Viramitrodaya, like the Mitakshara, maintains that whatever is owned by a woman is her *stridhan*, though it admits more clearly than the last named treatise, that the quality of being freely alienable by her without her husband's consent, which generally attaches to *stridhan*, may not attach to every kind of it.

Bombay school —Vyavahara Mayukha.

In the Bombay school, the leading authorities are the

[1] This is evidently the same text as that cited in Colebrooke's Digest, Bk. V, 470.

[2] VIII, 165. The translation given above, which is according to the interpretation of Mitramisra, differs from that by Sir W. Jones, who follows the gloss of Kulluka. The difference arises from the fact of different meanings being assigned to the word उपधि (*upadhi*), which Kulluka takes to mean 'fraud,' and Misra uses as meaning 'condition.'

Mitakshara and the Vyavahara Mayukha; and the question has sometimes been raised as to which of the two should prevail when they differ on any point. With the exception of Guzerat and the island of Bombay, where perhaps the Mayukha ranks as the foremost authority, in other parts of Western India, the first place is assigned to the Mitakshara, and only a subordinate, though an important one, to the Mayukha.[1] Upon the point under consideration, namely, the definition of *stridhan*, there is very little real difference between the two authorities.

The Mayukha, like the Mitakshara, interprets Manu's enumeration of six kinds of woman's property to mean only the denial of a smaller number, and refers to the word *adya* (and the rest) in Yajnavalkya's text in support of that interpretation;[2] though it does not, like the latter treatise, expressly declare that that word is meant to include all acquisitions whether by inheritance, partition, or the like. In treating of succession,[3] however, it draws a distinction between *paribha sikastridh an* or *stridhan* proper and what is acquired by the act of partition and the like; and this would show that the Mayukha assigns to the simple term *stridhan* the same unlimited signification that it has in the Mitakshara.

The different particular kinds of *stridhan* mentioned in the texts of Manu and Yajnavalkya, are defined as in the Mitakshara, with the exception of the *sulka* (perquisite), for which Katyayana's definition already cited above is adopted.

The two texts of Katyayana relating to conditional and fraudulent gifts, and gains by mechanical arts and gifts

---

[1] See Krishnaji Vyanktesh v. Pandurang, 12 Bom., 65.

[2] Vyavahara Mayukha, Ch. IV, Sec. X, 1, 2.

[3] *Ibid*, 26.

LECTURE VII.

from strangers, are explained in a way similar to that in the Viramitrodaya; and it is observed generally that a woman possesses absolute power of disposal only over some kinds of *stridhan*.

Dravida school—Parasara Madhavya.

The Southern school follows the Smriti Chandrika and the Parasara Madhavya, in addition to the Mitakshara, as its leading authorities. The Parasara Madhavya agrees with the Mitakshara in many respects, and it adopts the text of Yajnavalkya as the basis of its comments; but it gives to the suppletory term *adya*, as you have seen, a limited signification, as including property purchased with what is given during the bridal procession, &c.; and it admits upon the authority of Katyayana's texts, which are explained away in the Viramitrodaya, that gifts upon condition, or with a design, or from strangers, and gains by mechanical arts, do not constitute *stridhan*.[1] The Smriti Chandrika[2] agrees in substance with the Madhaviya commentary, with this difference only, that it does not assign any definite meaning to the notable word *adya* in Yajnavalkya's text. The Chandrika, like the Parasara Madhavya, gives no definition of *stridhan*, but it regards Manu's enumeration of six sorts as merely implying a denial of a less number. And it enumerates and defines the various sorts of *stridhan* according to the texts of Manu, Yajnavalkya, Vishnu, and Katyayana, which have been already cited. These several sorts are:—the *adhyagni*, or gift before the nuptial fire, and the *adhyavahanika*, or present at the bridal procession (both of which may be gifts from any person); the *pritidatta*, or gift through affection or as a token of respect obtained from kindred; gifts obtained

Smriti Chandrika.

---

[1] See Burnell's translation of the Dayavibhaga, pp. 40—42.

[2] Ch. IX, Sec. I.

from the husband, the parents, or a son, or from kindred; the *adhivedanika*, or present on supersession; and the *sulka*, or gratuity, and the *unwadheya*, or gift subsequent, as defined by Katyayana. But gains by mechanical arts, conditional gifts, and gifts from strangers are expressly excluded from the category of *stridhan*. LECTURE VII.

According to the Dravida school, therefore, the term *stridhan* has not that unlimited literal signification which it has under the Mitakshara, but is used in a limited and technical sense.

It is not very clear whether, according to the Smriti Chandrika, property inherited by a woman becomes her *stridhan;* but there is a passage in that work relating to the mother's succession, in which it is said, "whatever the mother takes, she takes for herself *like* the *stridhan* called *adhyagni* and the like;"[1] and from this passage it has been sometimes inferred that inherited property does not rank as *stridhan*.[2]

Mithila school—Vivada Chintamani.

I shall next consider the definition of *stridhan* according to the Mithila school. The leading authority for that school is the Vivada Chintamani. This work, too, does not give any definition of *stridhan;* but, like the Chandrika, it enumerates and defines the several descriptions of property which rank as *stridhan* according to it.[3]

These are, first of all, the six kinds as enumerated by Manu and defined by Katyayana in the texts already cited.

---

[1] Ch. XI, Sec. III, 8.

[2] This passage, which is given in Kristnasawmy Iyer's translation, is not, however, to be found in Bharat Chandra Siromani's edition of the Smriti Chandrika (chapter relating to inheritance), see p. 71.

[3] Tagore's translation, pp. 256—263.

LECTURE VII.

With reference to these it would be sufficient to remark, that, according to our author, the enumeration of six kinds means simply the denial of a less number; and the presents at the bridal procession are not merely what is received from kinsmen, but include all that is given to a woman by any person 'while she is proceeding the second time from the house of her father to that of her husband.'

The seventh variety of *stridhan* is the *adhivedanika*, or gift on supersession, as defined by Yajnavalkya.[1]

The eighth sort is *sulka*, or woman's perquisite,[2] and the ninth is the gift subsequent; and these are both defined according to the texts of Katyayana cited above. *Saudayika*, or gift of affectionate kinsmen, is explained as being a general name for several sorts of *stridhan*.

Ornaments constitute the tenth variety of *stridhan*. Regarding these, a text of Manu (IX, 200) is cited, and it is observed, that "any ornament which a woman wears with the consent of her husband shall be her peculiar property, even if it have been not given to her." And "food and vesture," mentioned in the text of Devala, and explained by our author to mean 'funds appropriated to a woman's support,' form the eleventh description of *stridhan*.

The author concludes his enumeration of the several kinds of *stridhan* by saying: "These are the several kinds of peculiar property of women." And the text of Yajnavalkya, which forms the basis of the unlimited interpretation of the term *stridhan* in the Mitakshara and the Viramitrodaya, is neither cited nor even referred to. Hence it may be inferred that, according to the Vivada Chintamani,

---

[1] II, 148.

[2] *Perquisite* is, in another place, defined as 'wealth given to a damsel on demanding her in marriage.' (Tagore's translation, p. 263.)

no other kind of property besides those enumerated above, comes under the denomination of *stridhan*. LECTURE VII.

As regards property inherited by a widow from her husband, the author's meaning is not very clear. He draws a distinction between moveables and immoveables, and holds that the widow's power of disposal over the former is absolute; but then he adds, that the texts of Katyayana, from which the distinction is deduced, do not refer to *stridhan*.[1]

Bengal school.

It remains now to consider the definition of *stridhan* according to the Bengal school. That school is represented by its founder Jimutavahana and his followers Raghunandana and Srikrishna.

Dayabhaga.

The Dayabhaga of Jimutavahana, which is the leading authority in that school, gives, like the Mitakshara, a general definition of *stridhan;* but, unlike the work of Vijnaneswara, from which it differs on many important points, it restricts the application of the term to certain descriptions of property belonging to a woman. Generally speaking, woman's property has two peculiarities attaching to it:—*first*, she has absolute power of disposal over it, notwithstanding her general want of independence; and, *secondly*, it follows a special order of succession. Now, the former of these peculiarities does not, according to certain texts of Katyayana cited above, attach to every sort of property belonging to a woman; and accordingly, to reconcile their unlimited literal interpretation of the term *stridhan* with these texts, the Viramitrodaya[2] and the Mayukha[3] expressly affirm that a woman's

---

[1] See Prosonno Coomar Tagore's translation, p. 262; see also Bhugwandeen Doobey *v.* Myna Baee, 9 W. R. (P. C.), 31.

[2] 2 W. and B., 69, 70. [3] Ch. IV, Sec. X, 7, 8.

LECTURE VII.

power of disposal is absolute, not with regard to every kind of her *stridhan*, but only with regard to certain kinds of it. Jimutavahana, however, on the contrary, maintains, that property belonging to a woman, in order that it may properly be called *stridhan*, must possess the quality of being alienable by her at pleasure.

After examining the various enumerations and definitions of different varieties of *stridhan* according to the different sages, the author of the Dayabhaga says: "Since various sorts of separate property of a woman have been thus propounded without any restriction of number, the number six [as specified by Manu and others] is not definitely meant. But the texts of the sages merely intend an explanation of woman's separate property. *That alone is her peculiar property which she has power to give, sell, or use independently of her husband's control.* Katyayana expresses this rather concisely: 'The wealth, which is earned by mechanical arts or which is received through affection from any other [but the kindred], is always subject to her husband's dominion. The rest is pronounced to be woman's property.'"[1]

As no general rule is anywhere laid down as to what property a woman can dispose of independently of her husband's control, the foregoing definition is open to the objection that it defines one unknown thing in terms of another.

From this definition it may be argued that a gift obtained from the husband, when consisting of immoveable property, does not constitute a woman's *peculium*; for a text of Narada, cited in the Dayabhaga,[2] declares: "What has been

---

[1] Dayabhaga, Ch. IV, Sec. I, 18, 19.

[2] Ch. IV, Sec. I, 23.

given by an affectionate husband to his wife, she may consume as she pleases when he is dead, or may give it away, excepting immoveable property."[1]

But on the other hand it may be said that such property does constitute a woman's *stridhan*, and that the absence of her power of alienation over it is noticed as an exception to the rule that a woman's *stridhan* is absolutely at her disposal. The point is not, however, free from doubt.

So completely does Jimutavahana reject Vijnaneswara's unlimited literal interpretation of the term *stridhan*, that he adopts a reading of Yajnavalkya's text[2] different from the ordinary one, substituting the expletive *eva* for the suppletory term *adya* (and the rest) which forms the basis of that interpretation.[3] The author further expressly declares that property inherited by a woman, whether it be from her husband, her father, her son, or other relation, does not constitute her *stridhan*, and does not, therefore, pass on her death to the heirs to her peculiar property.[4] And he explains the term *bhartridaya* in Narada's text, which might be supposed to signify the estate inherited from her husband, as meaning the husband's donation.[5] Of gifts from strangers, only those that are received before the nuptial fire constitute *stridhan*; and the term *adhyavahanika stridhan* (presents at the bridal procession) which, according to the usual interpretation of Katyayana's text, includes gifts from strangers, is, according

---

[1] This text is not to be found in Narada's Institutes, but is cited in other works also, such as the Vivada Chintamani. [2] II, 143.

[3] Dayabhaga, Ch. IV, Sec. I, 13. Colebrooke, in his translation of the Dayabhaga, gives Yajnavalkya's text with the same reading that occurs in the Mitakshara. This, however, is not the reading of the text according to the Dayabhaga. See Bharat Chandra Siromani's edition, 1863.

[4] Dayabhaga, Ch. IV, Sec. I, 11, 12; Ch. XI, Sec. I, 58; Sec. II, 30, 31.

[5] Dayabhaga, Ch. IV, Sec. I, 7, 8.

LECTURE VII.

to the Dayabhaga, limited to presents received from the parents and their kindred.[1]

The term *sulka*, or fee, is explained as having two meanings. It either means, according to the definition of Katyayana, "whatever has been received as a price of workmen (*karminam*)[2] on houses, furnitures and carriages, milking-vessels and ornaments," or it means, according to the text of Vyasa, "what is given to bring the bride to her husband's house."[3] The former of these meanings is thus explained: "What is given to a woman by artists constructing a house or executing other work, as a bribe to send her husband or other person [of her family] to labour on such particular work, is her fee. It is the price [of labour] since its purpose is to engage [a labourer]."[4]

Dayatattwa—Dayakrama Sangraha.

The Dayatattwa of Raghunandana and the Dayakrama Sangraha of Srikrishna substantially agree with the Dayabhaga, and so I need not give in detail the discussions contained in those works on the definition of *stridhan*.[5]

Does property inherited by a woman become her *stridhan*?

You will thus observe that the Dayabhaga excludes inherited property from the denomination of *stridhan* as expressly as the Mitakshara includes it under that denomination; while, of other commentaries, some follow the Mitakshara, and the rest seem to be in favor of the opposite doctrine. As the definition in the Mitakshara has to some extent been qualified and restricted by judicial decisions, I shall consider the question, how far property inherited

[1] Dayabhaga, Ch. IV, Sec. I, 5, 6, See *ante*, pp. 277, 278, remarks on Katyayana's texts.

[2] The usual reading is *karmanam*, 'of works.'

[3] Dayabhaga, Ch. IV, Sec. III, 19, 21.

[4] *Ibid* 20.

[5] See Dayatattwa, Golap Chandra Sarkar's translation, Ch. IX, p. 50 *et seq*; Dayakrama Sangraha, Ch. II, Sec. II.

by a woman constitutes her *stridhan*, with special reference to these decisions. LECTURE VII.

A woman may inherit the ordinary property of a male owner; and she may also inherit the *stridhan* of a female. These two cases are distinct, and should be separately considered. In the former case, the relations from whom a woman may inherit are, her husband, her father, her son, grandson or other male lineal descendant, and her brother and *sagotra* kinsmen of her husband (according to the Bombay school[1]); in the latter case, they are her mother, her mother's mother, and her daughter.

Bengal school.

As the decisions just referred to have been evidently influenced by, if not based upon, the law of the Bengal school, I shall, in the first place, shortly describe the process by which that law has been developed from the texts of the sages.

First take the case of the widow inheriting from her husband. Commentators of the different schools have taken no small pains to reconcile the conflicting texts of the sages upon the subject of the widow's succession; and considering the state of the authorities upon the subject, it is no wonder that they should have come to different conclusions. The Mitakshara recognizes the widow's right only when her husband was separated from his kinsmen; but it says nothing expressly as to the extent of her interest in the estate inherited by her, or the order of succession to it after her death.[2] The Dayabhaga, on the other hand, allows her to succeed to her husband's estate in all cases on failure of sons, grandsons, and great-grandsons; but, as if to counterbalance this

[1] See Vyavahara Mayukha, Ch. IV, Sec. VIII, 19; Lakshmi Bai *v.* Jayram Hari, 6 Bom., A. C. J., 152; Lallu-bhai *v.* Mankuvar Bai, I. L. R., 2 Bom., 388; Vinayak Anandrav *v.* Lakshmi Bai, 1 Bom., 126.

[2] Ch. II, Sec. 1.

LECTURE VII.

concession made in her favor, it limits her interest to mere enjoyment with moderation, and declares that, on her death, the estate should devolve, not on the heirs who inherit her *stridhan*, but on the next heirs of her husband. These restrictions are deduced from the following text of Katyayana (which is neither cited nor referred to in the Mitakshara):—"Let the childless widow, preserving unsullied the bed of her lord, and abiding with her venerable protector, enjoy with moderation [the property] until her death. After her let the heirs take it."[1]

This text is explained as referring to property inherited by a widow from her husband, and 'the heirs' spoken of here are said to mean the next heirs of her husband, and not the heirs to her peculiar property; "for," says Jimutavahana, "the right of those is relative to *stridhan;* and Katyayana has propounded by separate texts the heirs of *stridhan;* and his text declaratory of the succession to heritage would be tautology."[2]

Next take the case of the daughter succeeding to her father's estate. On her death, the estate "does not," says Jimutavahana,[3] "become the property of her husband or other heirs; for that [text, which is declaratory of the right of the husband and the rest,] is relative to a woman's peculiar property. Since it has been shown by a text before cited that, on the decease of the widow in whom the succession had vested, the legal heirs of the former owner, who would regularly inherit his property if there were no widow in whom the succession vested,—namely, the daughters and the rest,—succeed to the wealth; therefore

---

[1] Dayabhaga, Ch. XI, Sec. I, 56. [2] *Ibid*, 58.

[3] *Ibid*, Sec. II, 30, 31.

the same rule [concerning the succession of the former possessor's next heirs] is inferred *à fortiori* in the case of the daughter and grandson whose pretensions are inferior to the wife's.

"Or the word 'wife' [in the text above quoted], is employed with a general import: and it implies that the rule must be understood as applicable generally to the case of a woman's succession by inheritance."

From the above reasoning, which is quite general, you will observe that property inherited by a woman from a male relative does not become her *stridhan* in any case, according to the Dayabhaga.

Jagannatha, while agreeing with Jimutavahana in his conclusion, has some remarks upon his reasoning, which are worthy of notice. "As for the argument," says he, "that since this [reversion in favor of the heirs of the former owner] occurs in the succession of a wife, who is the first entitled to the estate of one who leaves no male issue by males, the same should be also established in other cases, when a daughter or the like has succeeded; that argument would be also intruded in other remote cases, such as the succession of a daughter's son or of a brother: and that is not founded on positive ordinances, but established by authors on the sole suggestion of their own understandings: it is not even noticed by Chandeswara and the rest."[1]

Let us next consider the second class of cases noticed above, namely, those in which the *stridhan* of one female is inherited by another. Touching this class of cases, the Dayabhaga says nothing explicitly; but the Dayakrama

[1] Colebrooke's Digest, Bk. V, 470, commentary.

LECTURE VII.

Sangraha expressly declares that *stridhan*, after it has once passed by inheritance, ceases to be *stridhan*. Speaking of the succession of daughters, Srikrishna observes:[1] "Here, however, on the death of a maiden daughter, or of one affianced, in whom the succession had vested, and who, having been subsequently married, is ascertained to have been barren; or on the death of a widow who has not given birth to a son;—the sucecssion to the property which had passed from the mother to her daughters would devolve next on the sisters having, and likely to have, male issue, and in their default, on the barren and widowed daughters; not on the husband of such daughter above-mentioned in whom the succession had vested: for the right of the husband is relative to the 'woman's separate property,' and wealth which has in this way passed from one to another can no longer be considered as the 'woman's separate property,'—This must be understood."

The doctrine that *stridhan* which has once passed by inheritance ceases to rank as such, is not easily deducible from Jimutavahana's definition of *stridhan*. That definition, as you have seen, restricts the term to property which a woman has power to dispose of independently of her husband's control. Now, there is no express provision in the law as to whether a woman has or has not such power over *stridhan* inherited by her; and in one case at least, namely, that of a widowed daughter inheriting her mother's *stridhan*, she must evidently hold it independently of her husband's control. The case of *stridhan* inherited by a female is one that is not sufficiently provided for by the original authorities on Hindu law, and the doctrine under

[1] Dayakrama Sangraha, Ch. II, Sec. III, 6.

notice rests almost entirely upon the authority of Srikrishna. But as his authority, when uncontradicted by any higher authority, is deemed of sufficient weight in the school to which he belongs, his doctrine has been adopted by Macnaghten,[1] and also, it would seem, by Strange,[2] and has been invariably followed by our Courts as the law of Bengal.[3] You will find the point fully considered in the recent case of *Bhoobun Mohun Banerjea* v. *Muddon Mohun Sing*, (1 Shome's Law Reporter, p. 3), in which the same doctrine has also been shown to be deducible from the Dayabhaga (Ch. XI, Sec. II, 30, 31).

Upon the point under consideration there is, therefore, no conflict of authority in the Bengal school; and the law of that school is sufficiently clear and precise in excluding from the category of *stridhan* all property inherited by a woman, whether as heir to the ordinary property of a male, or as heir to the *stridhan* of a female.

Other schools.

The law of the other schools is not equally clear. Though the Mitakshara, which is recognized as an authority more or less by all of them, gives a very simple definition of *stridhan*, including under it all property belonging to a woman, whether acquired by inheritance or by any other mode, yet the other authorities current in those schools (except the Viramitrodaya and the Mayukha) do not go quite so far. And Vijnaneswara's rule that inherited property ranks as *stridhan*, has been almost entirely ignored by our Courts in cases of property inherited from males.

Considering the high authority of the Mitakshara, and the

---

[1] Principles of Hindu Law, p. 38.

[2] Elements of Hindu Law, Vol. I, p. 31.

[3] See Prankissen Sing v. Mussamat Bhugwatee, 1 Sel. Rep., 4; Sreenath Gangooly v. Surbomongola Debia, 10 W. R., 488; Bhoobun Mohun Banerjea v. Muddon Mohun Sing, 1 Shome's Law Reporter, 3.

LECTURE VII.

clear language in which it declares that property inherited by a woman does constitute her *stridhan*, one cannot help feeling doubts as to the correctness of the decisions to the contrary.[1] But at the same time, considering the number of these decisions, and considering that some of them are decisions of the highest Court of appeal for India, it would perhaps be too late to expect any departure from the rules therein laid down. As, however, the point is not equally settled as regards every case of inherited property, it may not be deemed unprofitable to examine shortly the grounds of these decisions.

It should be borne in mind, that the question whether inherited property ranks as *stridhan* resolves itself into two others, namely, *first*, whether a woman has absolute power of disposal over property inherited by her; and, *secondly*, whether such property passes on her death to the heirs to her *stridhan*; and that a negative answer to the former of these two questions would not necessarily involve a negative answer either to the second or to the principal question; for, according to the doctrine of the Mitakshara as explained in the Viramitrodaya and the Mayukha, a woman's power of disposal is absolute only over some kinds of her *stridhan*.

Thakoor Dayhee v. Rai Balack Rai; Bhugwandeen Doobey v. Myna Baee.

To begin with the decisions of the Privy Council. The cases of *Mussamut Thakoor Dayhee* v. *Rai Balack Ram*[2] and *Bhugwandeen Doobey* v. *Myna Baee*[3] are the leading cases on the subject. In both these cases it has been laid down that, under the Mitakshara, property inherited by a widow from her husband is not alienable by her at her pleasure,

---

[1] See 1 W. & B., Introduction, lxiii; 2 *Ibid*, 103—112; and the judgment of West, J., in Vijiarangam *v* Lakshuman, 8 Bom., 244.

[2] 10 W. R. (P. C.), 3.

[3] 9 W. R. (P. C.), 23.

and that, on her death, it descends, not to her heirs, but to the next heirs of her husband.

The substance of the ruling of the Judicial Committee is stated in these words in their judgment in *Bhugwandeen Doobey* v. *Myna Baee*:—"Their Lordships, therefore, have come to the conclusion that, according to the law of the Benares school, notwithstanding the ambiguous passage in the Mitakshara, no part of her husband's estate, whether moveable or immoveable, to which a Hindu woman succeeds by inheritance, forms part of her *stridhan* or particular property: and that the text of Katyayana, which is general in its terms, and of which the authority is undoubted, must be taken to determine,—*first,* that her power of disposition over both is limited to certain purposes; and, *secondly,* that on her death both pass to the next heir of her husband."

Though this ruling of the Privy Council is not strictly in accordance with Vijnaneswara's doctrine, it is not likely that the Privy Council would ever feel induced to reconsider it; so that the case of property inherited by a widow from her husband must remain an exception to the general rule of the Mitakshara, that all property belonging to a woman (whether acquired by inheritance or otherwise) is her *stridhan,* and devolves on her death according to the special law of succession for *stridhan.* But the ruling ought not to be applied to other cases of inherited property. Those cases are left wholly untouched by the above decisions of the Judicial Committee, as an examination of the grounds of those decisions will show.

I may add, that though the decision of the Privy Council has introduced an exception to the simple rule of the Mitakshara, practically the consequences of the exception

LECTURE VII.

are not very different from those of the rule itself. As you have already seen, both the Mitakshara and the decisions of the Judicial Committee impose restraints on the widow's power of alienation; and, as you will see hereafter, the order of succession after the widow would very nearly be the same, whether the rule of the Mitakshara or the decision of the Privy Council be followed.

The correctness of the above-mentioned decisions of the Privy Council has been sometimes questioned by scholars and Judges.[1] But it is satisfactory to observe, that these decisions, as far as they go, are amply supported by a work of high authority in the Benares school. The Viramitrodaya, which is held in high repute in that school, refers to the text of Katyayana[2] relating to the widow's estate, and upon that text it has an elaborate commentary, of which the substance may be shortly stated thus:—

The provision that the widow is to enjoy her husband's estate with moderation, is made with a view to restrain wasteful expenditure for temporal purposes, and not with a view to qualify or limit her proprietary right. The word *heirs* in the text means 'heirs of her husband;' and were it not for the provision that the husband's heirs should take the estate on her death, the widow's heirs would have taken the estate inherited by her from her husband, according to the general rule, that property vested in any person descends to the heirs of that person and not to those of any former owner.[3]

---

[1] See 2 W. & B., 103—105; and judgment of West, J., in Vijiarangam v. Lakshuman, 8 Bom., O. C. J., 272.

[2] Cited in the Dayabhaga, Ch. XI, Sec I, 56; see *ante*, p. 298.

[3] See Viramitrodaya, Jivananda Vidyasagara's edition, pp. 629, 630.

Though, therefore, the Privy Council may not be right in not applying the name *stridhan* to the widow's estate, and though they may have imposed restrictions on her power of alienation to a much greater extent than the Viramitrodaya does, yet the rule of succession to such estate, as laid down by the Privy Council, is exactly in accordance with the doctrine of Mitramisra.

But the passage of the Viramitrodaya, of which the substance is given above, clearly shows that succession to the widow's estate forms an exception to the general rule, that the property of any person descends to the heirs of that person, and not to those of any former owner. So that the above decision of the Privy Council, which comes under the exception, can furnish no argument for dispensing with the rule, or for introducing a similar exception with regard to property inherited by a female from any relation other than her husband.

Another argument against the view that property inherited by a woman is not her *stridhan*, is deducible from the utter absence in the Mitakshara of any distinct provision concerning succession to such property. The Hindu law recognizes only two orders of succession, namely, that for property belonging to a male owner, and that applicable to *stridhan*. Now property inherited by a female is evidently not of the former description; and if, according to Vijnaneswara, it were likewise not of the latter kind, he would either have laid down a separate order of succession for it, or, like Jimutavahana and Srikrishna, have declared that such property, upon the death of the female owner, reverts to the next heirs of the last full owner. Vijnaneswara has, however, made no such provision; but, on the contrary, after declaring that the term *stridhan* is used in its unlimited

LECTURE VII.

literal sense, and that it includes inherited property, he says: "A woman's property has been thus described. The author next propounds the distribution of it." (Mitakshara, Ch. II, Sec. XI, 8.) The inference from this is obvious.

Moreover, there seems to be a very good reason why the Mitakshara and the Dayabhaga should differ from each other on the point under notice. According to the former, a woman is allowed to inherit the property of a sonless male relation, only when he was separated from, and not reunited with, his coparceners. In such cases there can be no prejudice to family interests in allowing the property inherited by a female heir to pass to her heirs after her death. But the Dayabhaga allows a woman to inherit the property of a male relation, whether he was separated from, or joint with, his coparceners; and consequently, in order to prevent any portion of the family property from passing out of the family, Jimutavahana is obliged to qualify the simple rule of inheritance that property vested in any person passes to the heirs of such person, by providing that a female heir takes the inheritance merely as a tenant for life, and that, after her, the estate passes, not to her heirs, but to the next heirs of the last male owner.

Decisions of Indian Courts—Bengal.

Of the decisions of Indian Courts, the earliest one that I shall notice is the case of *Mussumaut Gyan Koowur* v. *Dookhurn Singh.*[1] In that case, the question was, whether, according to the Mithila and Western schools of law, the daughter has the power of alienating the estate which she inherits from her father, and who, according to that law is entitled to it on her death; and it was held that she has not that

[1] 4 Sel. Rep., 330.

power, and that on her death the estate passes to her father's next heirs. The decision is based entirely upon the opinion of the Hindu law officers of the Court; and though that opinion professes to be based upon the Mitakshara, the Viramitrodaya, the Vivada Chintamani, and other works current in Behar and the North-West, the main argument adduced in its support is the well-known argument of Jimutavahana, that the restrictions on the widow's estate are *à fortiori* applicable to the case of the daughter, who claims the heritage after the widow, and whose right of inheritance is consequently inferior to that of the widow.[1] Now, though Jimutavahana's opinion is certainly binding upon the Bengal school, his argument in its support is not remarkable for its soundness: it finds no place in the Mitakshara, and it has failed to satisfy even the Bengal lawyer Jagannatha.[2] Further, the Viramitrodaya, as you have just seen, expressly declares the case of the widow to be an exception to the general rule, so that, according to that authority, it would be clearly wrong to extend the principle of that case to other cases by analogy.

The case, moreover, seems to have been one that was governed by the Mithila law, which differs from the law of Benares, and which uses the term *stridhan* in a technical or limited sense; so that the exposition of the law of Benares was not necessary for the decision of the case.

In the cases of *Sheo Sehai Singh* v. *Mussumat Omed Konwur*[3] and *Heera Lal Baboo* v. *Mussamut Dhuncoomary*,[4] the same rule is laid down; but no additional argument or authority is adduced in its support, except the opinion of

---

[1] See Dayabhaga, Ch. XI, Sec. II, 30.

[2] See Colebrooke's Digest, Bk. V, 470, commentary.

[3] 6 Sel. Rep., 301.

[4] S. D. A. R. for 1862, p. 190.

LECTURE VII.

Sir W. Macnaghten,[1] upon which the decision in the latter case is entirely based. But that learned author has not supported his opinion by referring to any authority; and the Mitakshara and the Viramitrodaya are, as I have tried to show, decidedly against that opinion.

The next case that I shall notice is that of *Punchanund Ojhah* v. *Lalshan Misser*,[2] which seems to have been a case under the Mithila law, and in which the question was whether property inherited by a mother from her son becomes her *stridhan*, and as such descends to her heirs. The High Court answered it in the negative, observing: "But we think the text clearly confines *stridhan* to be some sort of special separate property. The only words which in any way militate against this view, are the concluding words of the second Section of the Chapter; but we think that these are to be read in the same category with the last description of separate property given in the first Section. The words 'as also any other separate acquisition' correspond to the words 'also property which she may have acquired by inheritance, purchase, &c.' Now, the separate property of ladies of rank in this country very often devolves on their successors by inheritance, and ladies may, with the proceeds of their separate property, acquire other property. All such would be *stridhan*. It would be separate acquisition or acquisitions of separate property by inheritance, purchase, &c. But the property of her husband or her son, to which a woman may succeed as heir for her lifetime, is nowhere laid down in the text as thereby becoming *stridhan*. If the law of the Mitakshara on this point was so different from that prevalent in Bengal, as is contended, the commentators would have distinctly

[1] Principles of Hindu Law, 22.

[2] 3 W. R., 140.

laid down the discrepancy. As a general rule, the laws may be considered to correspond, although there are certain special points on which they differ. These points are well known; and if it is the case that, on a property devolving on a woman, the Mitakshara law at once changes the whole order of succession, surely there would have been some precedents to that effect in the law books. The rule laid down in Section III of the Chapter on *stridhan* in the Mitakshara, that the words 'woman's property' are not to be used in a technical sense, probably means that whatever estate really becomes the woman's property, so that she may act with it as she likes, may be considered *stridhan*, but not that any property, which at any time comes into a woman's hands, even the family property in which she is allowed only a life-interest, is also *stridhan*."

No doubt there is considerable force in much of these observations, so far as they apply to the law of Mithila. But the qualification sought to be attached to the definition of *stridhan* in the Mitakshara is opposed to the very spirit of that definition, which gives to the term an unlimited literal signification. You will also observe that unfettered alienability and descent according to a special order of succession, which are two distinct peculiarities of *stridhan*, are in this judgment considered as necessary concomitants; and it is supposed that where the former does not exist, the estate is only a life-estate of the female proprietor, and would, on her death, revert to the heirs of the former owner. But this is really applying analogies derived from the English law of real property to the Hindu law of inheritance, which, as the Privy Council have pointed out,[1] is

---

[1] See The Collector of Masulipatam *v.* Cavaly Venkata Narayanappah, 2 W. R. (P. C.), 63.

LECTURE VII.

"more likely to mislead than to direct the judgment aright."

In the cases of *Deo Pershad* v. *Lujoo Roy*[1] and *Dowlut Kooer* v. *Burma Deo Sahoy*,[2] the proposition is affirmed that, on the demise of the daughter, the estate inherited by her from her father goes, not to her heirs, but to those of her father. But the proposition is supported mainly by arguments derived from the case of the widow; and it does not appear from the report whether the first of these two cases was one under the Mitakshara law or the law of Mithila.

Chotay Lall v. Chunnoo Lall.

The case of *Chotay Lall* v. *Chunnoo Lall*[3] is the latest and the most important of the decisions of the Calcutta High Court. That also was a case of property inherited by a daughter from her father, and it was held that such property does not become the daughter's *stridhan*, and that it passes on her death, not to her heirs, but to those of her father. All the previous decisions are noticed in this case; but their correctness has not been examined at all; and the original authorities bearing on the point, and cited in the argument at the bar, have not been even referred to in the judgment. The ground of the decision is to be found in the following passage of the judgment: "Certainly, when we have the various decisions of the Sudder Court here upon the law which is applicable in this suit, and the decision of the High Court at Madras upon a similar law, in which no substantial difference can be pointed out with reference to this question, we ought not to unsettle the law, which appears to have been received on this side of India for the last fifty years, on account of the opinion of a Judge of the High Court at Bombay, however learned he may be. The consequences at the present time would be

[1] 20 W. R., 102. [2] 22 W. R., 54. [3] 22 W. R 496.

most serious. Courts ought always to bear in mind that it is no light matter to reverse a series of decisions, which must have been acted upon for many years, and have been regarded as declaring what was the law."

These observations, no doubt, embody a very sound and wholesome rule; but the rule is not without exceptions. Upon doubtful points, it would certainly be improper to depart from established precedents; but, where precedents are clearly shown to be erroneous, our Courts seldom deem it too late to corret the error.

That the decisions in the present instance are clearly opposed to the Mitakshara and the Viramitrodaya, the leading authorities in the Benares school, I have already tried to show; and in further support of that view, I may quote a passage from the judgment of Mr. Justice Pontifex, in the case under notice. That learned Judge says:[1] "Though I must confess that, speaking for myself, if the case had been untouched by authority, I should have felt compelled to give a plain meaning to the plain and unqualified words of the Mitakshara, rather than explain them away or in effect reject them by the application of principles of which after all we have only a hazy and doubtful knowledge."

Nor are the Courts in India wholly unanimous upon the present question. The majority of the Bombay decisions interpret the Mitakshara in a different way. Touching these adverse decisions Sir Richard Couch observes: "We may fairly say that a judgment of another High Court, in which no notice was taken of decisions of this Court upon the point, ought not to receive the same respect from us as it

---

[1] 22 W. R., 199.

would receive if the learned Judges had considered the decisions on this side of India." With all deference, one cannot help thinking that it were better if the learned Chief Justice had not allowed the reason herein stated to influence his estimate of the intrinsic value of the Bombay decisions, but had fully examined the grounds upon which they are based.

Some of the Bengal decisions noticed above refer to the law of Mithila. That law is not very clear. But it may be said that as that law does not, like the Mitakshara, use the term *stridhan* in its unlimited literal sense, and as inherited property is not mentioned among the several kinds of *stridhan* enumerated in the Vivada Chintamani such property does not under that law rank as *stridhan*.

It will be seen from the above, that the Bengal cases lay down broadly that property inherited by a woman from a male owner never ranks as her *stridhan*. This may be correct under the Mithila law. But how far such a rule is correct according to the law of the Benares school, as regards female heirs other than the widow, seems open to question.

[Since the above was written, the decision of the High Court in *Chotay Lall* v. *Chunno Lall* has been affirmed on appeal by the Privy Council (see 3 C. L. R., 465); so that it must now be taken to be the settled law of the Benares school, that property inherited by a daughter from her father does not rank as her *stridhan*, and that it descends not to her heirs, but to the next heir of her father. And what applies to the case of the daughter inheriting from the father would, by parity of reason, be held to apply to the case of a female inheriting from any other *male* relation.]

I shall next consider the Madras decisions. The Smriti Chandrika, one of the leading authorities in the Southern school, explains the well-known text of Katyayana on which Jimutavahana bases his restrictions on the widow's estate as applicable to the case of "undivided wealth which a widow may herself take on account of her subsistence, in consequence of her father-in-law and the like not being qualified to maintain her, or continuing engaged in other concerns," and not to the separate property of her husband which she takes by inheritance.[1] But it would be too late now to contend upon the strength of this authority alone, that the widow's estate under the Madras school is her *stridhan*. The case of *The Collector of Masulipatam* v. *Cavaly Venkata Narainapah*,[2] which is a Madras case, would perhaps be conclusive against such a contention.

LECTURE VII.

Madras.

The rule seems to be the same as regards property inherited by other female heirs. The High Court of Madras has held, in the case of *P. Bachiraju* v. *V. Venkatappadu*,[3] that the property which a mother inherits from her son does not become her *stridhan*. Though this decision is based upon the same restricted construction of the Mitakshara definition of *stridhan* that we have already noticed in the Bengal cases, and though it makes free use of the arguments and doctrines of the Dayabhaga in support of its conclusion, yet we cannot say that it is wholly opposed to the law of the Madras school. The Smriti Chandrika and the Madhaviya commentary, authorities peculiar to that school, do not, like the Mitakshara, use the term *stridhan* in its unlimited literal sense; and they do not mention inherited property as one of the different kinds of *stridhan*.

[1] Ch. XI, Sec. I, 32, 33. [2] 2 W. R. (P. C.), 61. [3] 2 Mad., 402.

LECTURE VII.

In *Sengamalathammal* v. *Valaynda Mudali*,[1] the High Court of Madras gave a further extension to the doctrine that inherited property is not *stridhan*, by holding that the mother's *stridhan* passing by inheritance to her daughter does not become the *stridhan* of the daughter. This decision also is based mainly upon the authorities of the Bengal school. So far as it combats the doctrine of Vijnaneswara, that inherited property is *stridhan*, its correctness has rightly been questioned by West and Bühler.[2] But so far as it is an exposition of the law of the Madras school, it is not easy to affirm that it is not correct.

Bombay.

The Bombay decisions need not detain us long. The Mitakshara and the Vyavahara Mayukha, the leading authorities in the Bombay Presidency, lay down the doctrine, that inherited property is *stridhan*; and the Bombay High Court has followed that doctrine in all cases except one, namely, the case of the widow succeeding to her husband. In that case the immoveable property inherited is held not to rank as *stridhan*, though over the moveable the widow's interest is regarded as absolute.[3] You will find almost all the Bombay cases[4] fully considered in the elaborate judgment of Mr. Justice West in *Vijiarangam* v. *Lakshuman*.[5]

Share on partition.

There is only one more question that remains to be considered, namely, whether the share which a woman obtains on partition becomes her *stridhan*.

The Mitakshara[6] and the Mayukha[7] answer this question

---

[1] 3 Mad., 312.

[2] 2 W. & B., 107—112.

[3] See Pranjivan Das Tulsi Das *v.* Devkuvar Bai, 1 Bom., 130.

[4] See Vinayak Anandrav *v.* Lakshmi Bai, 1 Bom., 117; Navalram Atmaram *v.* Nand Kishore Shivnarayan, *Ibid*, 209; Bhaskar Trimbak Acharya *v.* Mahadeb Ramji, 6 Bom., O. C. J., 1.

[5] 8 Bom., O. C. J., 244.

[6] Ch. II, Sec. XI, 2; see also Bhugwandeen Doobey *v.* Myna Baee, 11 Moo. I. A., 514.

[7] Ch. IV, Sec X, 26; see also 2 W. & B, 29, 30.

LECTURE VII.

clearly in the affirmative. Jagannatha gives conflicting answers to it, apparently assenting to both. In one place,[1] he says: "However, the share allotted to a wife and the rest, like that which is given to a son, may be disposed of at their pleasure. Hence, like female property, the gift, sale, or other alienation of that share is valid; for it is equally given her by her husband and the rest." And in another place[2] he observes: "Nor should it be objected, that since the share of a wife is in a manner *gratuitously* given, it ought to be held similar to female property. Being received in right of the relation of *a wife to her husband*, it is justly considered as similar to connected property, *or wealth devolving on heirs in right of affinity*."

This latter opinion is the one that has been generally accepted by the Bengal school. Sir Francis Macnaghten[3] observes on this point: "I believe it may now be laid down as the law, that mothers, who take a share upon partition, take an estate *for life* only,—and with respect to dominion over the property, stand upon the same footing with widows who succeed to their husband's rights. I am aware that a distinction has been made, and I admit that it is not without an *appearance* of reason, for it has been said that what is taken by a *mother* upon partition is more in the nature of a gift than that which is taken by a *widow* on the death of her husband. If *all* the sons agreed to divide, it might indeed be said to be in *the nature of a gift*, because they would all have concurred in the act by which their mother became entitled to a share of the estate; yet, if there be ten sons, any one of them may enforce a parti-

[1] Colebrooke's Digest, Bk. V, 88, commentary (Mad. edn., Vol. II, p. 253).
[2] *Ibid*, p. 251. [3] Considerations on Hindu Law, pp. 43, 44.

LECTURE VII.

tion; and although the other nine continue living in an undivided state, and although the tenth separated himself from them against their will, his separation alone will give the mother a right in severalty to one eleventh part of the estate. In such a case, what she takes can hardly be said to be in the nature of a *gift*—certainly it is not a gift from *her sons*; nine of them out of ten being desirous of withholding from her that which one enables her to take by compulsion from the rest;—but, whatever the reason may be, the law is conclusive upon the subject. She has a right on partition being made, although the greater number of her sons may have been unwilling to divide.

"The Supreme Court has not hitherto made any distinction between the interest taken by a mother upon partition and that taken by a widow upon the death of her husband."

The law according to the Mithila and the Dravida school is not very clear. The Vivada Chintamani gives an exhaustive enumeration of the different sorts of *stridhan*, and concludes the enumeration by saying, "these are the several kinds of the peculiar property of women;"[1] and as the share on partition is not one of these kinds, it may be inferred that it does not rank as *stridhan*.

In the Dravida school, while the Smriti Chandrika holds that the share which a woman obtains on partition is merely a provision for maintenance,[2] and the Parasara Madhavya maintains that it is the absolute assignment of a share of the estate,[3] neither commentary says anything as to whether it becomes *stridhan*. Apparently there is some

---

[1] Prosonno Coomar Tagore's translation, p. 263.

[2] Smriti Chandrika, Ch. IV, 11.

[3] Dayavibhaga (Burnell's translation), p. 15.

authority for holding that it ranks as *stridhan*;[1] but considering that the term *stridhan* is used in a limited sense in the Madras school, the correctness of this view seems open to question. LECTURE VII.

The difficulties besetting an enquiry into the question, what constitutes *stridhan*, arise from the fact that the majority of sages and commentators give neither an exact definition of *stridhan*, nor an exhaustive enumeration of the different descriptions of property that come under that denomination; and if the Mitakshara gives a simple and intelligible definition, that definition has been qualified and restricted in its application by our Courts, in consequence of its disagreement with the views of other authorities. Summary of the law.

As the foregoing account has been rather long, a brief summary of it may not be deemed unacceptable.

The modes in which a Hindu female may acquire property are gift, purchase (under which I include every mode of acquisition for valuable consideration), inheritance, and partition.

A gift may be received either from a relation or from a stranger. Gift.

In the former case, the property given always ranks as *stridhan* according to all the schools. To this rule, the case of immoveable property given by the husband perhaps forms an exception under the Bengal law. But it is doubtful whether it is really an exception.[2]

---

[1] See the Pandit's opinion cited by Sir T. Strange, and not disapproved by Colebrooke, 2 Strange's Hindu Law, 382, 383.

[2] See Dayabhaga, Ch. IV, Sec. I, 21; Vivada Chintamani, p. 261; Macnaghten's Precedents of Hindu Law, Ch. I, Sec. II, Case xiv; 2 Strange, 19. But see Dayabhaga, Ch. IV, Sec. I, 18; Colebrooke's Digest, Mad. edn., Vol. II, p. 626; and Venkata Rama Rau *v.* Venkata Surya Rau, I. L. R., 1 Mad., 286.

LECTURE VII.

In the latter case, except in the Benares and the Maharastra school, where all gifts constitute *stridhan*, the property given becomes *stridhan* only when received by a woman at the time of her marriage.[1]

A legacy is regarded in the light of a gift, and constitutes *stridhan* where a gift from the testator would have ranked as *stridhan*.[2]

Ornaments given by a man to his wife, or constantly worn by her with his permission, though belonging originally to him, become her *stridhan*.[3]

Gift to a widow in lieu of maintenance (which ought, properly speaking, to come under the head of purchase, being gift for valuable consideration) has been held to come within the definition of *stridhan*.[4]

Purchase.

Property acquired by purchase would include earnings or acquisitions by labor and skill, property bought for money, property acquired by exchange, and the like.

Wealth earned by a woman by the mechanical arts during coverture does not, except in the Benares and the Maharastra school, become her *stridhan*. But if earned during widowhood, or during maidenhood, it would be her *stridhan* under all the schools, as the text of Katyayana,

---

[1] The texts require the gift to be made before the nuptial fire; but it seems that the presence of fire is not absolutely necessary; and so nuptial presents received from strangers by a girl married in the Brahmic form in which no fire is kindled, would, nevertheless, become her *stridhan*.

[2] See Ram Dulal Sircar *v.* Sreemutty Joymoney Dabey, 2 Morley, 65; Judoo Nath Sircar *v.* Bussunt Coomar Roy Chowdhry, 19 W. R., 264.

[3] Gun Joshee Malkoondkar *v.* Sugoono Bai, 1 Morley's Dig., 595, Stridhana, pl. 3; 2 Strange's Hindu Law, 54—56; Smriti Chandrika, Ch. IX, Sec. II, 27, 28.

[4] Mussamut Durga Koonwar *v.* Mussamut Tejoo Koonwar, 5 W. R., Mis., 53; Nellaikumaru Chetti *v.* Marakathammal, I. L. R., 1 Mad., 166.

which places such wealth under the control of the husband, would be inapplicable to such cases. LECTURE VII.

Property purchased by a woman with funds absolutely belonging to her, or obtained in exchange for other property which is her *stridhan*, is her *stridhan* according to all the schools, it being evident that though such property is not expressly mentioned as one of the different sorts of *peculium*, it is really her original *stridhan* transformed into another shape.[1] So also property obtained by a compromise in consideration of her giving up any rights in relation to her *stridhan* would be her *peculium*. But property acquired with the accumulations of the income of her husband's estate would not constitute her *stridhan*, but would form part of the *corpus* of that estate.[2] A distinction, however, has been drawn between property acquired with *accumulations* of the income, and that acquired out of *current*, that is the year's, income; and it has been held [3] that over this latter description of property a widow has the same absolute right as over the income itself.

Where property had been inherited by a widow from her husband and afterwards confiscated by Government, such property, on being subsequently granted to the widow by a *sunnud* from Government, was held to rank as her *stridhan*.[4]

Inheritance.

As regards property acquired by inheritance, the decisions and the original authorities agree in laying down the rule

---

[1] See Luchmun Chunder Geer Gossain v. Kalli Churn Singh, 19 W. R., 292.

[2] See Chundrabulee Debia v. Mr. Brody, 9 W. R., 584; Mussamut Bhagbutti Daee v. Chowdry Bholanath Thakoor, 24 W. R., 168.

[3] Sreemutty Puddomonee Dossee v. Dwarkanath Biswas, 25 W. R., 335; see also Sreemutty Soorjoomoney Dossee v. Denobundoo Mullick, 9 Moo. I. A., 123; but see Gonda Kooer v. Kooer Oodey Singh, 14 B. L. R., 165.

[4] See Brij Indur Bahadur Singh v. Ranee Janki Koer, C. L. R., 318.

LECTURE VII.

that in Bengal it constitutes *stridhan* in no case, and that, according to the Bombay school, it becomes *stridhan* in all cases, except that of property inherited by a widow from her husband. The law of the other schools on this point, as expounded by a considerable body of decisions, seems to agree with that of Bengal, as regards property inherited from males; but as regards property inherited from a female, the law of those schools is not yet fully settled.

Partition.

The share which a woman obtains on partition is her *stridhan* according to the Benares and the Maharastra school, but it does not rank as *stridhan* according to the law of Bengal. The law of Mithila and that of Dravida are not very clear on the point, but there is reason for thinking that they do not differ from the law of Bengal.

Burden of proof where property is alleged to be *stridhan.*

As a consequence of the doctrine that only some particular descriptions of property belonging to a woman constitute her *stridhan,* it has been held that the burden of proving that any property belonging to a woman is her *peculium* lies on the party making such special allegation.[1]

[1] Sreemutty Chundermonee Dossee *v.* Joykissen Sircar, 1 W. R., 107.

LECTURE VIII.

RIGHTS OF A WOMAN OVER HER STRIDHAN

Proprietary rights of women under the Hindu law—Restrictions on a woman's rights over her *stridhan* depend on her *status* and on the nature of the property—Restrictions depending on the *status* of the woman—Maidenhood—Coverture—Husband's rights over wife's *stridhan*—Widowhood—Restrictions depending on the nature of the property—Gifts—from the husband—from strangers—Property acquired by personal exertion or by purchase—Property acquired by inheritance—Share on partition—*Stridhan* promised by the husband—Rights of an unchaste woman over her *stridhan*—*Stridhan* compared with woman's property under other systems—Roman law—*Dos*—French law—Married Woman's Property Acts—Sir H. Maine's remarks on *stridhan*.

Proprietary rights of women under the Hindu law.

ANCIENT law is remarkable for the stringency of its provisions against the proprietary rights of women, and primitive Hindu jurisprudence bears evident traces of this notable feature. Thus Baudhayana,[1] after declaring the perpetual tutelage of women, cites a passage from the Vedas to the effect that women are incompetent to inherit; and in the Institutes of Manu there occurs the well-known text, "Three persons,—a wife, a son, and a slave,—are declared by law to have *in general* no wealth exclusively their own; the wealth which they may earn is *regularly* acquired for the man to whom they belong."[2] But the effect of these texts has been counteracted by others of a contrary import, and there has been gradually developed the law of *stridhan*, which forms a singular chapter of ancient law.

Nowhere were the proprietary rights of women recognized so early as in India; and in very few ancient systems

[1] Prasna II, Kanda II, 27; 1 W. and B., 318. [2] VIII, 416.

LECTURE VIII.

of law have these rights been so largely conceded as in our own. In certain cases presently to be noticed, a woman's dominion over her *stridhan* is absolute.

The author of the Dayabhaga makes this absolute dominion follow from his definition of *stridhan;* for he applies the name *stridhan* only to such descriptions of property as are absolutely at the disposal of a woman.[1] This view is in accordance with the prevailing notion of the Bengal school regarding property,—namely, that power of alienation is a necessary concomitant of ownership. But this is not the doctrine of the other schools, according to which even male proprietors are not always held to possess absolute power of disposal over their property; and accordingly some of these schools use the term *stridhan* in an unlimited sense, applying it to all descriptions of property belonging to a woman, whatever the extent of her power of disposal over such property may be. In the present lecture I propose to consider the extent of a woman's rights over her *stridhan* in the more general sense of the term,—that is, over property belonging to her, whether technically called by that name or not.

Over certain descriptions of her property a woman possesses absolute power of disposal. Katyayana declares:[2] "What a woman, either after marriage or before it, either in the mansion of her husband or of her father, receives from her lord or her parents, is called a gift from affectionate kindred (*saudayika*); and such a gift having by them been presented through kindness, that the women possessing it may live well, is declared by law to be their absolute property. The absolute exclusive dominion of women over such a gift is perpetually celebrated; and they have power to

[1] Dayabhaga, Ch. IV, Sec. I, 18.

[2] Colebrooke's Digest, Bk. V, 475.

sell or give it away as they please, even though it consist of lands and houses. Neither the husband, nor the son, nor the father, nor the brother, has power to use or to aliene the legal property of a woman."

To this rule Katyayana attaches the following exception:—

"What a woman has received as a gift from her husband she may dispose of at pleasure after his death *if it be moveable;* but as long as he lives, let her preserve it with frugality, or she may commit it to his family." [1]

And Narada declares:—

"Property given to her by her husband through pure affection she may enjoy at her pleasure after his death, or may give it away, except land or houses." [2]

So that a woman has independent and absolute ownership over her *saudayika stridhan* (gifts from affectionate relations) with the exception of gifts from her husband; and over these last, if not consisting of immoveable property, her power of disposal becomes absolute after his death This is the law according to all the schools. Though the Mitakshara contains no express provision on the subject, the Viramitrodaya, a work of recognized authority in the Benares school, and the leading commentaries of the other schools, are clear on this point.[3]

Restrictions on a woman's rights over her *stridhan* depend on her *status* and on the nature of the property.

It will be seen from the above, that the restrictions on a woman's rights over her *stridhan* depend upon her *status* in relation to marriage, as well as on the nature of the property.

Over certain descriptions of property a woman has at

---

[1] Colebrooke's Digest, Bk. V, 477. [2] *Ibid*, 476.

[3] See Viramitrodaya, 2 W. and B., 74; Vivada Chintamani, pp. 260, 261; Vyavahara Mayukha, Ch. IV, Sec. X, 8, 9; Smriti Chandrika, Ch. IX, Sec. II, 3, 10, 12; Dayabhaga, Ch. IV, Sec. I, 21—23; see also Gosain Chand Koberaj *v.* Mussamat Kishen Munee, 6 Sel. Rep., 77.

LECTURE VIII.

all times absolute power of disposal, and over certain other descriptions she never has such power; while regarding a third class of property her power of disposal is restrained during coverture only. Her husband again has, under certain circumstances, a qualified right to use all her *stridhan*, of whatever description. These different cases re-require detailed consideration. I shall, for convenience of treatment, consider separately the two classes of restrictions, namely, those depending on a woman's *status*, and those attaching to the nature of the property

Restrictions depending on the *status* of the woman.

First, take the restrictions depending upon the *status* of the woman. Though the condition of a Hindu female is one of perpetual tutelage, her father protecting her during maidenhood, her husband during coverture, and her sons during widowhood,[1] yet this want of independence does not disqualify her to exercise independent control over her own property.

Maidenhood.

During maidenhood, excepting the disqualification by reason of nonage, a Hindu female labors under no other incapacity as regards her power over her *stridhan;* and except in the capacity of guardian, her father and her other relations have no control over it. Jagannatha notices an argument to the contrary thus: "Who has a right to that which is acquired by a woman before marriage? A daughter may be also comprehended in a text formerly cited (Bk. III, Chap. I, v. 52, 1),[2] because the masculine gender is not there used in a determinate sense, or because the particle 'and' connects the terms with that which is unexpressed; or lastly, because the term '*son*' is illustrative of a general

---

[1] Manu, IX, 3; Colebrooke's Digest, Bk. IV, 4, 5, 6.

[2] This is the text of Manu (VIII, 416) which declares that three persons—a wife, a son, and a slave—can have no property exclusively their own.

meaning: her father has, therefore, property in the wealth acquired by her, as he has a claim to the son produced by her before marriage. Such is the method founded on the opinion of ancient authors. It should be thoroughly examined by the wise."[1] But the point is almost concluded by authority. Manu, upon whose text the argument is based, has himself declared: "Such kinsmen as, *by any pretence*, appropriate the fortunes of women during their lives, a just king must punish with the severity due to thieves."[2] And the leading commentaries of some of the schools expressly declare that the father and other kinsmen have no right over a woman's *stridhan*.[3]

LECTURE VIII.

Coverture—Husband's rights over wife's *stridhan*.

During coverture, a woman's rights over her *stridhan* are subject to certain restrictions. You have seen that a text of Manu[4] declares, that the wife can have no wealth exclusively her own, and that her acquisitions belong to her husband. Apastamba says nearly the same thing, though his doctrine is perhaps more equitable; for he seems to recognize the right of the wife over the property of the husband, as well as the right of the latter over the property of the former.[5] These restrictions have, however, been considerably removed by other texts; and by the law as expounded by the commentators of the different schools, the unqualified dominion of the husband is limited to only some descriptions of the wife's property, while as regards the rest he is allowed only a qualified right of use under certain circumstances specifically defined.

---

[1] Colebrooke's Digest, Bk. V, 477, commentary. [2] VIII, 29.

[3] Mitakshara, Ch. II, Sec. XI, 33; Vyavahara Mayukha, Ch. IV, Sec. X, 10; Smriti Chandrika, Ch. IX, Sec. II, 27; see also Dantuluri Rayapparaz *v.* Mallapudi Rayudu, 2 Mad., 360. [4] VIII, 416.

[5] Prasna II, Patala VI, Kanda XIV, vv. 16—18; 1 W. and B., 308.

LECTURE VIII.

On this subject Yajnavalkya says: "A husband is not liable to make good the property of his wife taken by him in a famine, or for the performance of a duty, or during illness, or while under restraint."[1]

So Devala: "Food and vesture, ornaments, perquisites, and wealth received by a woman *from a kinsman*, are her own property: she may enjoy it herself, and her husband has no right to it except in extreme distress.

"If he give it away on a false consideration, or consume it, he must repay the value to the woman with interest. And he may use the property of his wife to relieve a distressed son."[2]

And Katyayana declares: "Neither the husband, nor the son, nor the father, nor the brother, has power to use or to aliene the legal property of a woman. And if any of them shall consume such property against her own consent, he shall be compelled to pay its *value with* interest to her, and shall also pay a fine *to the king*. But if he consume it with her assent, after an amicable transaction, he shall pay the principal only, when he has wealth enough to restore it. Whatever she has put amicably into the hands of her husband afflicted by disease, suffering from distress, or sorely pressed by creditors, he should repay that by his own freewill."

"Yet more; if he have taken a second wife, and no longer give his first wife the honour due to her, the king shall compel him, even by violence, to restore her property, though it was put amicably into his hands."[3]

Vijnaneswara, in commenting on the above text of Yajnavalkya, explains 'duty' to mean "indispensable religious

---

[1] II, 147.

[2] Colebrooke's Digest, Bk. V, 478.

[3] Colebrooke's Digest, Bk. V, 475, 4—7, 481.

duty," and 'restraint' to mean "confinement in prison, or under corporeal penalties;" and he observes: "But if he seize it in any other manner [or under other circumstances] he must make it good."[1] The provision in the same text that the "husband is not liable to make good the property of his wife," is explained in the Viramitrodaya as referring only to the case in which he is unable to repay it on account of poverty and the like reasons. "But," says Mitramisra, "if he is able (to repay it), he must necessarily do so, even in case the property had been taken in times of famine or similar (misfortunes)."[2] LECTURE VIII.

In the Vivada Chintamani, the concluding portion of the first hemistich of Yajnavalkya's text is interpreted somewhat differently, thus: "or during illness which prevents the husband from following his avocations."[3]

The word 'distress' in the above text of Devala is explained in the Viramitrodaya[4] to mean "pain caused by the want of food and the like," and it is said that the word *cha* (and) is used to indicate "that the husband has a right to give away or to consume the wife's separate property, without her permission, in other difficulties which are caused by the want of money." In the Smriti Chandrika[5] it is said,—"The distress referred to must be of such a character as it is impossible to get rid of except with the use of *stridhan*."

---

[1] Mitakshara, Ch. II, Sec. XI, 32. [2] 2 W. and B., 78.

[3] Tagore's translation, p. 264; see also Viramitrodaya, 2 W. and B., 78. The text in the original runs thus:—

दुर्भिक्षे धर्मकार्ये च व्याधौ सम्प्रतिरोधके ।
गृहीतं स्त्रीधनं भर्त्ता न स्त्रियै दातुमर्हति ॥

The Vivada Chintamani takes सम्प्रतिरोधके as qualifying व्याधौ

[4] 2 W. and B., 77. [5] Ch. IX, Sec. II, 18.

LECTURE VIII.

The term 'son' in the same text is explained in both the above-named commentaries[1] to denote any member of the family. The maintenance of dependent members of the family, though not always a legal duty, is enjoined as a moral duty in all cases; and this liberal interpretation of Devala's text is, therefore, in harmony with the general spirit of the Hindu law.

Here a point of difference between the Dayabhaga and the Mitakshara ought to be noticed. Vijnaneswara, after explaining the term *stridhan* to mean woman's property generally, and after giving the order of succession to it, cites the above text of Yajnavalkya with the following remarks:[2] "It has been declared, that the property of a woman leaving no issue goes to her husband. The author now shows that, in certain circumstances, a husband is allowed to take his wife's goods in her lifetime, and although she have issue." From this it would seem that, according to Vijnaneswara, the husband's right to take the wife's property is equally limited with regard to every description of that property. But Jimutavahana, following a text of Katyayana, observes, with reference to property obtained by the wife by gift from strangers or earned by her by mechanical arts, that it is always subject to her husband's dominion, and that he has a right to take it even though no distress exist.[3]

But as Katyayana is an authority according to all the schools, and as the Viramitrodaya[4] takes the same view of his text as the Dayabhaga, it may be doubted whether there is any difference between the Bengal and Benares schools on this point.

[1] Smriti Chandrika, Ch. IX, Sec. II, 18; and 2 W. and B., 77.
[2] Mitakshara, Ch. II, Sec. XI. 31. [3] Dayabhaga, Ch. IV, Sec. I, 20.
[4] 2 W. and B., 69, 70.

Subject to the differences of interpretation noticed above, the foregoing texts of Yajnavalkya, Devala, and Katyayana have been adopted by all the schools as the law on the subject.[1] You will therefore observe that the husband can use the wife's *stridhan* strictly so called (that is, her *saudayika stridhan*, her ornaments and the like) without her consent, and, as a matter of right, only in cases of distress; and in such cases repayment is optional with him if he is poor. If he uses it in any other case without her consent, he is guilty of a wrong, and is bound to restore it with interest; and if he uses it with her consent, he is bound to make good the principal only, when he is able to do so. But even in this latter case, he is compellable to restore her property, if he neglects her for the sake of another wife. But property acquired by the wife by gift from strangers, or by the mechanical arts, is always subject to her husband's dominion. LECTURE VIII.

It is said in the Smriti Chandrika[2] and the Viramitrodaya,[3] that the husband has no independent power over any sort of *stridhan* belonging to the wife. "It also appears," says Devanda Bhatta, "from repayment of the principal being enjoined even where *stridhan* is used with permission, that the husband and the like are wanting not only in independent power, but also in ownership over *stridhan*. It must hence be understood that, in a husband's property, the wife, by reason of her marriage, possesses always ownership, though not of an independent character; but that the

[1] Mitakshara, Ch. II, Sec. XI, 31, 32; Viramitrodaya, 2 W. and B., 78; Vivada Chintamani, 264; Vyavahara Mayukha, Ch. IV, Sec. X, 10, 11; Smriti Chandrika, Ch. IX, Sec. II, 10—23; Dayabhaga, Ch. IV, Sec. I, 24. 25.

[2] Ch. IX, Sec. II, 13.

[3] 2 W. and B., 75.

LECTURE VIII.

husband does not possess even such ownership in his wife's property."[1]

According to this authority, therefore, the effect of marriage on the proprietary rights of the parties is more advantageous to the wife than to the husband

Property earned by the mechanical arts, or received as a gift from strangers, is said to be subject to the husband's dominion.[2] The meaning of this rule seems to be this, that though these sorts of property belong to the wife and not to the husband, and are enjoyable by her, they cannot be alienated by her without the consent of her husband; and they can be used by him at pleasure.

The right to use a woman's *stridhan* is personal in her husband.[3] Accordingly it has been held that though the husband might have applied such property to the payment of a debt to procure his discharge from arrest in execution of a decree, his creditor has no right to seize it.[4]

So also, though the husband may use the wife's *stridhan* in order to relieve from distress any member of his family, such member has no right to use it for such purpose.

The question whether a woman has absolute power of alienation over her *stridhan* was considered by the High Court of Madras in *Doe dem Kullammal* v. *Kuppu Pillai*,[5] and the Court answered it in the affirmative. And though in a subsequent case[6] the Court remarked that, considering the perpetual dependence of women, it could not, "without the greatest consideration, conclude that a woman can, with-

---

[1] Smriti Chandrika, Ch. IX, Sec. II, 14.

[2] Colebrooke's Digest, Bk. V, 470; Dayabhaga, Ch. IV, Sec. I, 19.

[3] Smriti Chandrika, Ch. IX, Sec. II, 17.

[4] 1 Strange, 27, 28; 2 *Ibid*, 23, 24.

[5] 1 Mad., 85.

[6] Dantuluri Rayapparaz *v.* Mallapudi Rayudu, 2 Mad., 360.

out the consent of her husband, during coverture, absolutely alienate even her own landed property;" yet, considering that the authorities are clear on the point, and that the text of Katyayana cited above[1] expressly gives to women the power of alienating immoveable property, there seems to be very little room for any doubt on the subject, as regards the *saudayika stridhan.*

In a still later case,[2] the Madras High Court has held, that the proposition that what is acquired by a woman during coverture belongs to her husband, has no foundation in Hindu law, and that the contrary of that proposition is unquestionably true.

Nor can the husband bind the wife by his dealings with her property. Thus, in a recent case[3] before the Privy Council, it was held that a husband could not affect his wife's rights over her property by any engagements he might enter into with reference to it.

In cases of dispute with the husband's creditors, the burden lies upon the wife to prove that any particular property is her *stridhan* and does not belong to her husband.

Widowhood.

During widowhood, a woman's rights over her *stridhan* are larger than what they are during coverture. Her kinsmen, as you have seen, have never any right to use her *stridhan;* and her husband, the only person who can use it in certain cases, and has control over certain descriptions of it, being dead, her right to use and enjoy it becomes unlimited. As regards her power of alienation, moveable property

---

[1] See *ante*, pp. 322, 323.

[2] Ramasami Padeiyatchi *v.* Virasami Padeiyatchi, 3 Mad., 278.

[3] Mohima Chunder Roy *v.* Durga Monee, 23 W. R., 184.

[4] George Lamb *v.* Musst. Govind Money, S. D. A. R (Beng), 1852, p. 125; Brojo Mohun Mytee *v.* Musst. Radha Koomaree, W. R. (1864) 60.

LECTURE VIII.

given by her husband, which she is required to enjoy frugally during his lifetime, becomes absolutely alienable by her after his death.[1]

Property acquired by a woman during widowhood, by her skill and labor, or by gift from strangers, would become her *stridhan*, according to all the schools. For though such property, if it is acquired during coverture, would come under the control of her husband, yet, if it is acquired when his control is no longer possible, it must belong to her absolutely.[2] On this point Jagannatha observes:[3] "What is acquired by the wife during the state of deprivation of her husband is also her peculiar property. How can it be so, since it is exclusive of the six sorts? The answer is, authors do not acknowledge the restrictive enumeration of six kinds; and even though it were admitted, the difficulty would be removed by affirming *that* this maxim *is true* of a woman who is herself sole mistress *of the wealth acquired.*"

Restrictions depending on the nature of the property.

I shall next consider the restrictions on a woman's power over her *stridhan*, as depending upon the nature of the property.

Gifts.

First, take the case of property obtained by gift. Gifts of affectionate kindred, which are known by the name of *saudayika stridhan*, constitute a woman's absolute property, which she has at all times independent power to alienate, and over which her husband has only

---

[1] Viramitrodaya, 2 W. and B., 74; Vivada Chintamani, 261, 262; Vyavahara Mayukha, Ch. IV, Sec. X, 8, 9; Smriti Chandrika, Ch. IX, Sec. II, 10, 11, 12; Dayabhaga, Ch. IV, Sec. I, 23.

[2] See Macnaghten's Precedents of Hindu Law, Ch. VIII, Case xxxiii; Brij Indar Bahadur Singh *v.* Ranee Janki Koer, 1 C. L. R., 325, 326; see also Vencata Rama Rau *v.* Venkata Suriya Rau, I. L. R., 1 Mad., 281.

[3] Colebrooke's Digest, Bk. V, 477, commentary.

a qualified right, — namely the right of use in times of distress.[1]

from the husband;

Over property obtained by a woman by gift from her husband, her power is not absolute. During coverture she has no right to alienate such property; and even after the death of her husband, her right becomes absolute over only so much of such property as consists of moveables.[2]

The above is the general rule as regards gifts from the husband. But where the husband gives any property to the wife with express power of alienation, she would acquire absolute power of disposal over it, whether it is moveable or immoveable; and there is nothing in the Hindu law to prevent her from exercising such power.

If immoveable property obtained by gift from the husband is held by the wife subject to his control during coverture, and is never alienable by her, the question arises, who has control over it after his death, and how far would her unauthorized alienation of it be valid? There is nothing expressly said in the Hindu law in answer to this question. But it would follow by parity of reason, that the heirs to such property have the same sort of control over it that the reversioners have over the widow's estate; and that any unauthorized alienation by the widow, in the one case, as in the other, would be valid only for her life.[3] The heirs in this case are the heirs to her *stridhan*, and not the reversionary heirs of her husband, as the husband's donation is regarded as *stridhan* even in the

---

[1] See the references in note 1, page 329, and Macnaghten's Precedents of Hindu Law, Ch. VIII, Cases vi and vii; Gosain Chand Koberaj *v.* Mussamat Kishen Munee, 6 Sel. Rep., 77.

[2] See the references given in note 1, page 332; and see also Kotarbasapa *v.* Chanverova, 10 Bom., 403.

[3] Gangadaraiya *v.* Parameswaramma, 5 Mad., 111.

LECTURE VIII.

technical and restricted sense of the term, though the woman's ownership over it is of a qualified nature. But the point is not absolutely free from doubt.[1]

from strangers.

Over property obtained by a woman by gift from strangers, her ownership is of a qualified nature. The Mitakshara says nothing expressly on the point; but the Viramitrodaya and the Mayukha cite the following text of Manu (IX, 199)—"A woman should never expend money belonging to her family, which is common to (her and) many, nor even her own (separate property), without the consent of her lord"—to show that women are in general not free to alienate even their own separate property; and they declare that she is competent to dispose of only some descriptions of her property, amongst which they name the *saudayika*.[2] The mention, however, of the "consent of her lord" in the above text implies that the restriction holds good only during coverture.

So long as the husband is alive, according to the Viramitrodaya,[3] "the husband, and not the wife, is at liberty to dispose of such property."

According to the Smriti Chandrika and the Dayabhaga, gifts from strangers do not rank as *stridhan*, and are always subject to the husband's dominion.[4] But during maidenhood and widowhood, such dominion not being possible, and no other relation having control over a woman's property, a woman's ownership over gifts received from strangers would be absolute.

---

[1] See *ante*, p. 317.

[2] Viramitrodaya, 2 W. and B, 73, 74; Vyavahara Mayukha, Ch. IV, Sec. X, 7, 8.

[3] 2 W. and B., 70.

[4] Smriti Chandrika, Ch. IX, Sec. I, 16; Dayabhaga, Ch. IV, Sec. I, 20; see also Ramdulol Sircar *v.* Sreemutty Joymoney Dabey, 2 Morley's Digest, 65.

LECTURE VIII.

Property acquired by personal exertions or by purchase.

What has been said about gifts from strangers applies equally to wealth earned by mechanical skill or acquired by purchase, for the restrictions upon a woman's ownership in both are contained in one and the same text of Katyayana.[1] But if property is acquired by a widow by her own personal exertions, she has absolute power of disposal over it.[2]

The restrictions on alienation relating to acquisitions by labor or skill do not, however, apply to property acquired by means of other property over which a woman has absolute power of disposal. It has been held by the Judicial Committee, in the case of *Luchmun Chunder Geer Gossain* v. *Kallichurn Singh*,[3] that if immoveable property is purchased by a married woman by means of money which constitutes her *stridhan*, she is competent to transfer it by sale.

Where a widow by adverse possession acquires title to any property, it would follow that her power of disposal over such property would be absolute.

Property acquired by inheritance.

With regard to property acquired by inheritance, the law is not very clear in all cases. According to the Bengal school, property inherited by a woman never ranks as her *stridhan*. Whether it is inherited from her husband, or her father, or any other male relation, her interest in it is of a qualified nature in every case. This general rule is deduced by Jimutavahana[4] from Katyayana's text relating to the widow, by a process of reasoning which may be stated thus: The restraint on alienation in Katyayana's

---

[1] Dayabhaga, Ch. IV, Sec. I, 19.

[2] Macnaghten's Precedents of Hindu Law, Ch. VIII, Case xxxiii. See also Venkata Rama Rau *v.* Venkata Suriya Rau, I. L. R., 1 Mad., 285.

[3] 19 W. R., 292.

[4] Dayabhaga, Ch. XI, Sec. II, 30, 31.

LECTURE VIII.

text[1] relating to the widow is *à fortiori* applicable to the daughter and the rest, because their claims are certainly inferior to the widow's: or the word 'wife' in the same text is employed with a general import, and it implies that the rule must be understood as applicable generally to the case of a woman's succession by inheritance.

In the recent case of *Bhoobun Mohun Banerjee* v. *Muddun Mohun Sing*[2] the same rule has been held applicable to the case of *stridhan* passing by inheritance to a female heir. That rule, it is true, occurs in a chapter of the Dayabhaga relating to succession to the property of a male owner, but the reasoning on which its extended application is based will be found in the following passage of the judgment of Mr. Justice Romesh Chunder Mitter: "The chapter in question, it is true, mainly deals with rules of succession to properties left by a deceased male owner, but the paragraph referred to above appears to me to lay down a rule applicable generally to succession by women, whether to the properties of a man or to *stridhan* of a woman. If it were not so, there would be no provision in the Dayabhaga relating to succession to property inherited by a woman from a female ancestress who held it as *stridhan*. I do not think that this is probable. Having regard to this circumstance, and having regard to the language of the paragraph in question, which is very general, it seems to me that the rule there laid down is also applicable to *stridhan* property inherited by a woman.

"Further it seems to me also clear that the rule referred to in the aforesaid paragraph is that laid down in para. 56 of Sec. I, Chap. XI. It has been said that the whole of the

---

[1] Cited in the Dayabhaga, Ch. XI, Sec. I, 56.

[2] 1 Shome's Law Reporter, 3.

latter rule is not intended to be extended to a woman's succession by inheritance generally, but that part of it which provides that, after the death of a female heiress, the heirs of the last owner take the inheritance.

"If we adopt this limited construction we must then come to the conclusion that, according to the Dayabhaga, there is no restriction to the powers of alienation of women succeeding by inheritance to the properties of a deceased male owner except in the case of a widow. It is too late now to contend for such a construction of the law as this. Repeated decisions have settled the question beyond the possibility of a doubt. It seems to me, therefore, clear that, by the paragraph in question, what is rendered applicable 'generally to the case of a woman's succession by inheritance' is the whole of the rule laid down in para. 56 of Sec. I of Chap. XI of the Dayabhaga."

The Mitakshara, while it includes property inherited by a woman under the denomination of *stridhan*, is silent as regards her power of alienation over it. There is a suggestion in Mr. Justice West's judgment in *Vijiarangam's* case, that, according to the Mitakshara, a woman's power of alienation over property inherited by her is subject to restrictions analogous to those imposed upon the power of a male owner as regards his ancestral property That learned Judge observes:[1] "Vijnaneswara, like all the Hindu lawyers, denounces the appropriation of a woman's property by her husband except in cases of great pressure, and by the other kinsmen under any circumstances. But he lays down no rule as to the extent of the woman's own power over the property. The natural conclusion would seem to be, that he considered this already sufficiently pro-

[1] 8 Bom., O. C. J., 264, 265.

vided for as to his immediate subject, inheritance, by other lawyers, and by the analogies to be drawn from his rules as to the estate of a male proprietor. Now, in Chap. I, Sec. I, pl. 27, 28, it is laid down that a man is 'subject to the control of his sons and the rest (of those interested) in regard to the immoveable estate, whether acquired by himself or inherited,' though he may make a gift or sale of it for the relief of family necessities or for pious purposes. It is clear, therefore, that a right of absolute disposal did not enter into Vijnaneswara's conception of the essentials of ownership. He admits (Mitakshara, Chap. II, Sec. I, pl. 25) the genuineness and the authority of the text of Narada, which, with so many others, proclaims the dependence of women, which he says does not disqualify them for proprietorship."

This view of the law derives some support from the Viramitrodaya, which, upon the authority of Manu (IX, 199) declares a woman's incompetency to alienate her property without her husband's assent, unless such property be of some particular descriptions, such as the *saudayika stridhan*.[1] But this rule can operate only during coverture.

As regards the widow, it has been held by the Privy Council that, under the Mitakshara as well as under the Dayabhaga, her ownership over the estate inherited from her husband is of a qualified nature, and that the restrictions on her power of alienation are inseparable from her estate.[2] The rights of other female heirs over property inherited from male relations are also subject to the same

---

[1] 2 W. and B., 73, 74.

[2] See The Collector of Masulipatam *v.* Cavaly Venkata Narainapah, 2 W. R. (P. C.), 61; Mussamut Thakoor Dayhee *v.* Rai Balack Ram, 10 W. R. (P. C.), 3; Bhugwandeen Doobay *v.* Myna Baee, 9 W. R. (P. C.), 23.

restrictions.[1] And considering the general policy of the Mitakshara law, it may, I think, be safely affirmed, that the restraints on a woman's power of alienation over inherited property under that law, are as much binding when such property is inherited from a female relation as when it is inherited from a male, and are as much binding during widowhood as they are during coverture.

The law of Mithila does not differ from that of Benares on this point, except in one respect, namely, that a distinction is drawn between moveable and immoveable property, and the widow is declared to have absolute power over moveable property inherited from her husband.[2] The Vivada Chintamani expressly declares that the mother has no power of alienation over immoveable property inherited from the son.[3]

The law of Southern India is in this respect similar to that of Benares. The Smriti Chandrika lays down the rule that a woman's power is not independent over other sorts of property besides the *saudayika* and moveables received from the husband.[4] And the Madras High Court in one case[5] has directly decided that the mother inheriting from her son takes like the widow a qualified estate without power of alienation.

---

[1] The cases bearing upon this point have been considered in the judgments of the High Court in Chotay Lall *v.* Chunnoo Lall (22 W. R., 496). Since the above was written, the Privy Council has held in the case of Chotay Lall *v.* Chunnoo Lall (affirming the judgment of the High Court) that the estate which the daughter inherits from her father under the Mitakshara, is a restricted and a qualified one like that of the widow; see 3 C. L. R., 465.

[2] Vivada Chintamani, Tagore's translation, p. 262.

[3] *Ibid*, 263.

[4] Ch. IX, Sec. II, 12.

[5] P. Bachiraju *v.* Venkatappadu, 2 Mad., 402.

LECTURE VIII.

In Bombay the rights of a woman over her inherited property have been recognized to a much larger extent than in the other Presidencies. She has been held to possess absolute power of alienation over moveable property inherited from her husband,[1] and over all property, both moveable and immoveable, inherited from her father or her brother.[2] The case of *Pranjivandas Tulsidas* v. *Devakuvarbai* may be taken as the leading case on the point. In that case, Sir M. Sausse, C. J., observed:

"On the whole, I think the spirit and practice of Hindu law, as recognised in Western India, will be best construed by treating the widow as having uncontrolled power over the moveable estate, but as having nothing more than a life-use in the immoveable estate. . . . . The widow, then, not having an absolute estate in the immoveable property, it remains to determine who are entitled to the absolute interest subject to the estate taken by her. In this case there are daughters. Now, according to all the authorities, the daughters take next after the widow. What then is the nature of the estate they take? Here again there are differences of opinion, but, dealing with the question according to the three books I have mentioned, it appears to me that the daughters take an absolute estate. We find quoted in the Mayukha a passage from Manu,—'The son of a man is even as himself, and the daughter is equal to the son; how then can any other inherit his property but a daughter, who is as it were himself.' With reference to this point also I consulted the Shastris both here and at Puna, and enquired whether daughters could

---

[1] Bechar Bhagvan v. Bai Lakshmi, 1 Bom., 56; Pranjivandas Tulsidas v. Devakuvarbai, 1 Bom., 130.

[2] Vinayak Anandrav v. Lakshmi Bai, 1 Bom., 117.

LECTURE VIII.

alienate any, and what, portion of the property inherited from a father who died separate. The answer was, that daughters so obtaining property could alienate it at their will and pleasure, and in this the Shastris of both places agreed, both also referring to the above text in the Mayukha as their authority for that position. On reviewing all accessible authorities, I have come to the conclusion that daughters take the immoveable property absolutely from their father after their mother's death."[1]

The rule laid down in *Devakuvarbai's* case was extended to the case of sisters inheriting from their brothers in *Vinayak Anandrav* v. *Lakshmi Bai*,[2] on the authority of Nanda Pandita, who says: "The daughters of the father and other ancestors must be admitted, like the daughters of the man himself, and for the same reason."[3]

But considering the general spirit of the Hindu law as laid down in the Mitakshara and the Mayukha, and bearing in mind the remarks of Mr. Justice West in *Vijiarangam's* case (8 Bom., O. C. J., 264, 265), already quoted, the correctness of the rule that female heirs have absolute power of alienation over property inherited by them, seems to be open to question.

Share on partition.

The Hindu law is not very clear regarding the rights of a woman over the share obtained by her on partition. Jagannatha, as you have already seen,[4] gives two opposite views of the law, apparently assenting to both. The argument in favor of the view that a woman has absolute right over such share, is based upon the ground that it may be regarded as a gift from the sons. But on the

[1] 1 Bom., 133, 134.

[2] 1 Bom., 117.

[3] See Colebrook's note to Mitakshara, Ch. II, Sec. V, 5.

[4] Lecture VII, *ante*, p. 315.

LECTURE VIII.

other hand it is said, that "being received in right of the relation of a wife to her husband, it is justly considered as similar to connected property, or *wealth devolving on heirs in right of affinity* ;"[1] so that a woman can have no greater rights over it than over the property of her husband which devolves on her by inheritance. The latter seems to be the more correct view; for, as has been pointed out by Sir Francis Macnaghten,[2] the share on partition can hardly be regarded as a gift from the sons, when a woman has a right to obtain such share even against the wish of her sons, whenever there is a partition among them.

Stridhan promised by the husband.

Not only is a woman entitled to enjoy what is given by her husband, but she is also entitled to claim from his heirs property promised to her by her husband. On this subject Katyayana declares:

"What has been promised to a woman by her husband, as her exclusive property, must be delivered by her sons, provided she remain with the family of her husband, but not if she live in the family of her father."[3]

So Devala: "Property promised by a husband to his wife must be paid by his sons just as his debts."[4]

The author of the Viramitrodaya, in commenting on this text of Devala, observes: "Since the expression 'just as his debts' is used, the word 'sons' includes 'grandsons' and 'great grandsons.'"

Rights of an unchaste woman over her *stridhan*.

A woman is declared to be liable to forfeit her *stridhan* for any violation of the duties of obedience and fidelity to her lord.

---

[1] Colebrooke's Digest, Bk. V, 87, commentary (Mad. ed., Vol. II, p. 251).

[2] Considerations on Hindu Law, 43.

[3] Colebrooke's Digest, Bk. V, 483; Vivada Chintamani (Tagore's translation), p. 265; Smriti Chandrika, Ch. IX, Sec. II, 25.

[4] Viramitrodaya, 2 W. and B., 79.

Thus Katyayana declares: "But a wife who does malicious acts injurious to her husband, who has no sense of shame, who destroys his effects, or who takes delight in being faithless to his bed, is held unworthy of separate property."[1]

This text of Katyayana has been cited in almost all the leading commentaries of the different schools.

According to the Viramitrodaya "the words 'is unworthy' mean that the separate property which she may have received shall be forcibly taken from her."[2]

The author of the Vivada Chintamani takes the same view, observing with reference to this text,—"This shows that the kindred should demand the peculiar property from such a woman."[3] The Mayukha[4] seems to interpret the text as meaning this, that a wicked wife should not receive any *stridhan*.

But the Smriti Chandrika[5] gives the text a different interpretation, which greatly softens the rigour of the rule. It explains the word 'unworthy' to mean 'unworthy to alienate at will;' so that, according to this authority, an unchaste or a disobedient wife does not forfeit her *stridhan* altogether, but forfeits only the right to alienate it at pleasure.

Of the Bengal authorities, Raghunandana[6] and Jagannatha[7] cite the text of Katyayana; and the latter quotes apparently with approbation the explanation given of it

---

[1] Colebrooke's Digest, Bk. V, 484.
[2] 2 W. and B., 76.
[3] Tagore's translation, p. 266.
[4] Ch. IV, Sec. X, 12.
[5] Ch. IX, Sec. II, 24.
[6] Dayatattwa (Golap Chandra Sastri's translation), Ch. IX, 6.
[7] Colebrooke's Digest, Bk. V, 484.

LECTURE VIII.

in the Vivada Chintamani, but the former gives no opinion on the point.

You will observe that the rule laid down by Katyayana is too vague to admit of its being enforced as a strict rule of law in every case. A woman is declared to be unworthy of *stridhan* not only if she is unchaste, but also if she is malicious or shameless or prodigal. This, though a very wholesome moral injunction, would hardly be fair as a rule of law. Jagannatha accordingly puts a narrow construction upon the text to remove its vagueness. He explains the words "acts injurious to her husband" to mean, "the administering of poison or the like," and the words "destroys his effects" to mean "incurs expenses for immoral purposes."

The rule, if meant to be a rule of forfeiture, would be open to objection also on another ground. It does not definitely state who the persons are that would become entitled to take a woman's *stridhan* in the event of her becoming liable to forfeit it.

Accordingly the rule has never been enforced by our Courts. In a case cited in Macnaghten's Precedents of Hindu Law,[1] an adulteress was declared entitled to her parents' gift of jewels. And in the recent case of *Musammat Ganga Jati* v. *Ghasita*,[2] a Full Bench of the Allahabad High Court has put a very limited construction upon the text of Katyayana. Mr. Justice Pearson says: "As to the text which says that 'a woman, who acts maliciously, and is shameless, and a destroyer of property, and addicted to immorality, is unworthy of wealth,' I have had occasion in another case to observe that it cannot, without violence, be construed to mean that she is to be deprived of property which has come into her possession, and there is reason to believe that the text

[1] Ch. III, Case vii.

[2] I. L. R., 1 All., 46.

refers only to property received by her from her husband." And Oldfield, J., speaking of the same text, observes, that it "refers to a particular kind of property, that which the wife has given to her husband for his use, or which she is entitled to receive from him on his taking another wife."

LECTURE VIII.

It may not be uninteresting to compare *stridhan* with woman's property under other systems of law.

Stridhan compared with woman's property under other systems.

Roman law.

Under the Roman law, in early times, when marriage was entered into with the *conventio in manum*, the wife came entirely under the *manus* or authority of the husband, and all her property became his. At a later period, when the *conventio* was abandoned, the wife's property remained her own, and was disposable by her without the consent of her husband.[1]

Dos.

With regard to the *dos*, or dowry, the law was different. The *dos* was, as Sir H. Maine says,[2] "a contribution by the wife's family, or by the wife herself, intended to assist the husband in bearing the expenses of the conjugal household." The *dos* of the wife belonged to the husband, and originally his rights over it were unrestricted. But gradually restrictions were imposed upon these rights, and at last the husband could neither mortgage nor sell the immoveable property forming part of the *dos*, even with the consent of the wife.[3]

All the property of the wife not included in the dowry was called her *parapherna*, and was her absolute property, over which her husband had no control.[4]

You will observe, therefore, that, in marriage with the *conventio in manum*, the wife could have no property

[1] See Mackenzie's Roman Law, p. 106.
[2] Early History of Institutions, p. 319.
[3] Institutes, Lib. II, Tit. VIII note, by Sandars.
[4] See Mackenzie's Roman Law, p. 107.

LECTURE VIII.

resembling the *stridhan*. The *dos* may, in many respects, be said to resemble the *adhyagni stridhan* (called also *yautuka*[1]), but it differs from the *yautuka stridhan* in this, that it was more completely under the dominion of the husband as regards its profits. It is only the *parapherna* that may properly be compared with *stridhan* strictly and technically so called.

French law.

By the Code Napoleon, the parties to a marriage are declared competent to enter into any special agreement (provided it is not contrary to good morals) respecting their property, or into a general agreement that they intend to be married either under the *law of community* or under the *law of dowry*. In the absence of any agreement, general or special, to the contrary, their proprietary rights are regulated by the law of community. By the law of community, all moveables belonging to the married parties on the day of marriage, or acquired subsequently during the marriage, as well as immoveables acquired during marriage (otherwise than by title of succession or by gift in favor of only one of the parties) belong jointly to both; but the husband alone administers such property, and he alone has the right of alienating it, though the consent of wife is necessary in certain cases. Property subject to the law of dowry resembles the *dos* of the Roman law. The husband alone has the management of it during the marriage; but the immoveables forming part of such property cannot be alienated either by the husband or by the wife or by both conjointly, except where the alienation thereof is necessary in order to relieve either party from prison, or to provide sustenance for the family, or to serve some other like purpose.[2]

---

[1] See Dayabhaga. Ch. IV, Sec. II, 14.

[2] Code Napoleon, arts. 1387—1581.

Independently of express contract, the French Code, therefore, does not allow a woman much independent power over her property during coverture. You will observe, however, that, like the Hindu law, it excludes from the husband's dominion property obtained by the wife by gift, and that it goes a little further than that law, as it applies the same rule to all gifts whether from relations or from strangers. LECTURE VIII.

By the English law as it stood previous to the passing of the Married Woman's Property Act, generally speaking, all the property of the wife became vested in the husband, who acquired absolute power of disposal over the chattels, and a limited power over the real estate; and the only property over which she possessed independent and absolute power were her *paraphernalia*, consisting of her bed, apparel, and personal ornaments suited to her degree, and property settled on her to her separate use.[1] English law.

But the Married Woman's Property Act (33 & 34 Vict., Cap. 93) and the coresponding Indian Act (Act III, 1874) provide that the wages and earnings of any married woman, acquired or gained by her in any employment, occupation, or trade, and also any money or other property acquired by her through the exercise of literary, artistic, or scientific skill, shall be deemed to be her separate property, over which she has absolute right. These provisions are no doubt more equitable than the provisions of the Hindu law, which, while they make large concessions in favor of the proprietary rights of women, do not allow them any independent right over their acquisitions by labor and skill during coverture. Married Woman's Property Acts.

---

[1] See Stephen's Commentaries, Bk. III, Ch. II.

LECTURE VIII.

Sir H. Maine's remarks on *stridhan.*

Before concluding this lecture, I may call your attention to the following observations of an eminent jurist,[1] on the nature and origin of *stridhan* :—

"The settled property of a married woman, incapable of alienation by her husband, is well known to the Hindoos under the name of *Stridhan*. It is certainly a remarkable fact that the institution seems to have been developed among the Hindoos at a period relatively much earlier than among the Romans. But instead of being matured and improved, as it was in the Western society, there is reason to think that in the East, under various influences, which may partly be traced, it has gradually been reduced to dimensions and importance far inferior to those which at one time belonged to it.

"The definition of Stridhan or 'woman's property,' given in one of the oldest and most authoritative of the Hindoo juridical treatises, the Mitakshara, is as follows: 'That which is given (to the wife) by the father, the mother, the husband, or a brother, at the time of the wedding, before the nuptial fire.' Up to this point the doctrine has the concurrence of all the schools of Hindoo law, but the compiler of the Mitakshara adds a proposition not found elsewhere: 'also property which she may have acquired by inheritance, purchase, partition, seizure, or finding, is denominated by Manu and the others "woman's property."' (Mitakshara, xi, 2.) These words, attributed, you see, to the mythical legislator, Manu, have excited the most vehement controversies among later Brahminical commentators, and have caused considerable perplexity to Anglo-Indian Judges, bound as they are to elicit consistent doctrine from the Hindoo legal texts. 'All the property which a woman

[1] Maine's Early History of Institutions, pp. 321-324.

may have acquired by inheritance, purchase, partition, seizure, or finding,' is a comprehensive description of all the forms of property as defined by the modes of acquisition, and, if all this be Stridhan, it follows that the ancient Hindoo law secured to married women, in theory at all events, an even greater degree of proprietary independence than that given to them by the modern English Married Woman's Property Act. No doubt there is much difficulty in understanding this. . . . .
I think, however, that if we extend our examination to other bodies of Aryan custom, we may partly understand the amplitude which the Mitakshara, one of the most archaic of Hindoo compendia, assigns to the Stridhan. A full enquiry would take me much beyond the limits which I have proposed to myself in this Lecture, but its results would shortly be these. Among the Aryan communities, as a whole, we find the earliest traces of the separate property of women in the widely diffused ancient institution known as the Bride-Price. Part of this price, which was paid by the bridegroom either at the wedding or the day after it, went to the bride's father as compensation for the patriarchal or family authority which was transferred to the husband, but another part went to the bride herself, and was very generally enjoyed by her separately, and kept apart from her husband's property. It further appears that, under a certain number of Aryan customs, the proprietary rights of other kinds, which women slowly acquired, were assimilated to their rights in their portion of the Bride-Price, probably as being the only exsisting type of woman's property."

LECTURE IX.

SUCCESSION TO STRIDHAN ACCORDING TO THE BENARES SCHOOL.

Nature of the Hindu law of succession—Order of succession to *stridhan* different from that in the case of a man's property—Order of succession to *stridhan* different in the different schools—Order of succession to *stridhan* according to the Benares school—Daughters—Competition between daughters married and unmarried—provided and unprovided—Unchastity no disqualification for inheriting *stridhan*—Insanity and other grounds of exclusion from inheritance how far applicable to succession to *stridhan*—Succession by survivorship among daughters—Daughter's daughters—Daughter's sons—Daughter's adopted son—Sons—Adopted son—Grandsons—Order of succession to the *stridhan* of a woman dying without issue—When the woman was married in one of the first four forms—Husband—His *sapindas*—The order in which they inherit—When the woman was married in one of the disapproved forms—The mother, the father, and their *sapindas*—Their order of succession—*Sulka* or woman's fee—Heirs to the property of a maiden—Order of succession according to the Viramitrodaya.

Nature of the Hindu law of succession.

I NOW come to the last head of our subject,—namely succession to *stridhan*. In the Hindu law, the order of succession is partly given by direct enumeration of heirs, and is partly left to be deduced from certain general rules. Most of the Rishis, such as Apastamba,[1] Baudhayana,[2] Gautama,[3] Vasistha,[4] and Manu,[5] specifically mention only the several kinds of sons among a man's heirs, and leave the order of succession after sons to be determined by the general rule that the inheritance belongs to the nearest person allied by funeral oblation (*sapinda* and *sakulya*), or by libation of water (*samanodaka*).

---

[1] Prasna II. Patala VI, Kanda 14; 1 W. and B., 307.

[2] Prasna I, Adhyaya V, 2, 3; 1 W. and B., 313.

[3] Adhyaya XXVIII. 18; 1 W. and B., 323.

[4] Ch. XVII, 29; 1 W. and B, 334.

[5] IX, 185—187.

In the institutes of Vishnu[1] and Yajnavalkya[2] a more full enumeration of heirs is given, but even that is far from being complete.

Whether we take the case of succession to ordinary property, or that of succession to *stridhan*, the enumeration of heirs, so far as it is given, is in neither case the same according to every sage; nor are the general rules referred to above sufficiently definite and clear in their terms to admit of their ready application in practice; and it is owing to these circumstances that the Hindu law of inheritance becomes such a difficult subject.

Hindu commentators have, it is true, tried to reconcile discrepant texts, and to work out an order of succession by the application of the rules referred to above; but they have left the work only half done. The only treatise which gives a tolerably complete table of succession, is the comparatively recent work of Srikrishna Tarkalankar, I mean his Dayakrama Sangraha.

Order of succession to *stridhan* different from that in the case of a man's property.

The law of succession applicable to *stridhan* differs from the law of succession applicable to the property of a male; and Hindu commentators have sometimes assigned a most fanciful reason for this difference. Thus Vijnaneswara says:[3] "The woman's property goes to her daughters, because portions of her abound in her female children; and the father's estate goes to his sons, because portions of him abound in his male children."

The true reason is perhaps to be found in the natural desire to make a sort of equitable distribution of the effects of the parents among children male and female. For a variety of reasons, some of which are not peculiar to the

[1] XVII, 4—12; 1 W. and B., 341, 342.

[2] II, 135, 136.

[3] Mitakshara, Ch. I, Sec. III, 10.

LECTURE IX. Hindu law, the sons exclusively take the property of their father; and as a sort of compensation for this, as it were, the daughters are allowed preference in the order of succession to their mother's estate.

Succession to *stridhan* different in the different schools.

The different schools of Hindu law differ from one another on the subject of succession to *stridhan* perhaps more widely than they do on any other subject; and it would therefore be necessary to consider the law of succession to *stridhan* separately for each school.

Order of succession to *stridhan* according to the Benares school—Mitakshara.

I begin with the law of the Benares school as expounded in the Mitakshara. That treatise lays down a very simple order of succession to *stridhan*, which is based upon the text of Yajnavalkya, explained now and then by verses of Manu, Gautama, and Narada.

Daughters.

From the text of Yajnavalkya,—"The daughters share the residue of their mother's property after payment of her debts; and the male issue succeed in their default,"[1]—the rule is deduced that, on the death of a woman, her daughters take her property in the first instance.[2]

Competition between daughters married and unmarried, provided and unprovided.

In the case of competition between married and maiden daughters, the latter succeed in the first instance, and it is only on failure of them that the married daughters take the inheritance. Among these last again, in the case of competion between daughters who are provided and those who are unprovided, the latter take the estate first; and it is only in their default that the daughters who are provided succeed. This rule is deduced from the following text of Gautama,[3]—"A woman's property goes to her daughters unmarried or unprovided." And the word 'un-

---

[1] II, 117 [2] Mitakshara, Ch. II, Sec. XI, 13.
[3] XXVIII, 21; see 1 W. and B., 320.

provided' is interpreted by Vijnaneswara to mean 'indigent' or 'childless.'[1] LECTURE IX.

The above rule may require some explanation. In the first place, the question may arise whether a betrothed daughter is to be deemed 'unmarried' within the meaning of the rule. The word used in Gautama's text is the word '*apratta.*' This word, according to Jimutavahana, means unbetrothed; so that, under the Bengal law, so far as this text applies, the unbetrothed daughter alone succeeds in the first instance.[2] But Vijnaneswara takes it to mean unmarried; and as he makes no distinction between betrothed and unbetrothed daughters, they may, I apprehend, be taken to be equally entitled to their mother's *stridhan* under the law of Benares.

In the second place, though the rule that unprovided daughters have precedence over those that are provided may be a very reasonable and equitable one, yet its practical application is not always easy. The word 'unprovided,' as you have seen, means either poor or childless. Now as regards the relative claims of rich daughters having children and childless poor daughters, there is little difficulty, the former not being 'unprovided' in any sense of the word, and the latter being 'unprovided' in every sense. But as regards the relative claims of childless rich daughters and poor daughters having children, the law is not equally clear. But I think Vijnaneswara's meaning is, that the rich daughters, whether they have children or not, should all be excluded by the indigent daughters, whether they are childless or have children. And I presume that the childless daughters would be preferred to

[1] Mitakshara, Ch. II, Sec. XI, 13.

[2] Dayabhaga, Ch. IV, Sec. II, 13, 23, 25; see also Sreenath Gangooly *v.* Surbo Mongola Debia, 10 W. R., 488.

LECTURE IX. those having issue only when the competitors are not poor, and their means and circumstances are equal. In the case of daughters who are poor in different degrees, no hard and fast rule can be laid down; but a Court of Justice should look to the circumstances of each case, and order distribution accordingly.

In the case of *Baku Bai* v. *Manchha Bai*,[1] the Bombay High Court said,—"As amongst daughters, succession to their father's estate must be regulated by their comparative endowment and non-endowment;" and they remanded the suit to the Court below to try whether the pecuniary circumstances of the two daughters, who were the parties to the appeal, were so far different as to give one of them a prior right of inheritance under the Hindu law as compared with the other, on the ground that she was an unprovided (*nirdhan*) daughter. Though this was a case of succession to the father's estate, yet as that case is governed by the same text of Gautama,[2] the rule laid down by the Bombay High Court in their remand order would equally hold good in the case of succession to *stridhan*.

I may add that, according to Apararka and the author of the Kalpataru, cited in the Viramitrodaya,[3] the word 'unprovided' in Gautama's text means also 'unlucky' or 'widowed.'

The High Court of Bengal, in the case of *Binode Koomaree Debee* v. *Purdhan Gopal Sahee*,[4] observed: "By the law of Benares preference is given to the maiden daughter; failing her, the succession devolves on the married daughters who are indigent, to the exclusion of wealthy daughters, who succeed in default of indigent daughters. But no preference is given to a daughter who has or is likely to

---

[1] 2 Bom., 5.
[2] Mitakshara, Ch. II, Sec. II, 4.
[3] See 2 W. and B., 83.
[4] 2 W. R., 176.

have male issue over a daughter who is barren or a childless widow."

We might go further and say, that barren and childless widowed daughters are actually preferred to those who have or are likely to have issue, when the means and circumstances of the competitors are equal. This preference of the childless daughter over one having issue, and the preference of daughters in general over sons in the line of succession, would show that the law of succession to *stridhan*, according to the Benares school at least, is based, not upon the doctrine of spiritual benefit, but upon the equitable principle of giving to the female children (and in the first instance to such of them as are most in need) an exclusive right to their mother's estate, as a compensation for their being excluded by the male children from inheriting their father's estate. Even in the Bengal school, where the doctrine of spiritual benefit is carried to its utmost extent, Jagannatha in one place observes,[1] that "the advantages afforded are not principally considered in treating of separate property held by women."

Unchastity no disqualification for inheriting *stridhan*.

The considerations just adverted to have some bearing upon the question, whether unchastity bars a woman's right to inherit *stridhan*. That question was raised before the Allahabad High Court in the case of *Musammat Ganga Jati* v. *Ghasita*,[2] and it was held that unchastity will not disqualify a woman from inheriting the *stridhan* of her female relations. In that case, Oldfield, J., observed:[3] "It was argued before us that the right of succession to *stridhan*, equally with the succession to other property, is inseparable from the capacity to confer benefits on the ancestors, and that this capacity is

[1] Colebrooke's Digest, Bk. V, 498, commentary.

[2] I. L. R., 1 All., 46.

[3] *Ibid*, 49, 50.

LECTURE IX. lost by reason of unchastity. It may be that the right of succession to *stridhan* is intimately connected with such a principle by the law current in Bengal, as would appear from the Dayabhaga, Dayakrama Sangraha, Vyavastha Darpana; but it is also certain that, even by that law, the right of succession to this kind of property does not rest exclusively on such a principle. This appears from the permitted succession of barren and widowed daughters, notwithstanding they confer no direct benefits through the medium of sons; and the note to ccccxcviii, Colebrooke's Digest, vol. 2, page 612, gives the general opinion that the advantages afforded are not principally considered in treating of separate property held by women. Under the law of the Mitakshara this is still more the case, and throughout that work, and the commentators, no allusion is made to the principle of succession to *stridhan* resting on a capacity to benefit the ancestors by offering funeral oblations. In Macnaghten's Hindu Law it is stated—'this description of property is not governed by the ordinary rules of inheritance: it is peculiar and distinct, and the succession to it varies according to circumstances.' In fact a woman succeeds to *stridhan* rather by reason of consanguinity, and in order to afford her some provision. This is shown to be so from the fact that those persons who are worst provided for, or least capable of providing for themselves, are the first in the order of heirs. The argument must therefore, I think, be dismissed, which rests the exclusion from inheritance on the incapacity to confer benefits on the deceased. Nor does the fact that the unchaste widow is excluded from inheriting her husband's separate estate afford any argument in the case before us, as the widow's exclusion rests on express texts and with reference to grounds inapplicable to the case of a woman's succession to the *stridhan* of her female relations; and the same may be said of the rule which imposes chastity as a condition on the claim of dependent female members of a family to be supported from the estate in the hands of the male members."

Touching the argument based upon the text of Narada (Mitakshara, Ch. II, Sec. X, 3) that a person addicted to vice does not inherit, Turner, Offg. C. J., said:[1] "No doubt this rule is cited and treated as well established by the author of the Mitakshara, but for many years it has not been enforced in our Courts."

Insanity and other grounds of exclusion from inheritance how far applicable to succession to *stridhan*.

Though unchastity is no bar to a woman's right to inherit *stridhan*, the question may arise how far insanity, blindness, and the other grounds of exclusion from inheritance would hold good in the case of succession to *stridhan*. After citing the following text of Yajnavalkya,[2]—"An impotent person, an outcast and his issue, one lame, a madman, an idiot, a blind man, and a person afflicted with an incurable disease, as well as others (similarly disqualified) must be maintained; excluding them, however, from participation;"—and a text of Manu,[3]—"Impotent persons and outcasts are excluded from a share of the heritage; and so are persons born blind and deaf, as well as madmen, idiots, the dumb, and those who have lost a sense (or a limb);"—Vijnaneswara adds the following among other comments: "The masculine gender is not here used restrictively in speaking of an outcast and the rest. It must be therefore understood that the wife, the daughter, the mother or any other female being disqualified for any of the defects which have been specified, is likewise excluded from participation."[4]

[1] I. L. R., 1 All., 47, 48. [2] II, 140. [3] IX, 201.
[4] Mitakshara, Ch II, Sec. X, 8.

LECTURE IX. From this it is clear that, according to Vijnaneswara, the grounds of disqualification specified above bar the right of a female heir just as much as that of a male. The question whether the disabilities which exclude male heirs would affect the heritable rights of females, was raised before the High Court of Bombay in a case[1] in which dumbness was the disqualification alleged; and upon the authority of the above passage of the Mitakshara, the Court felt bound to answer it in the affirmative. But the point remains to be settled whether the above rule of exclusion is applicable to the case of succession to *stridhan.* The passage of the Mitakshara quoted above has immediate reference only to the case of succession to the property of a male; and it may be said that, as exclusion on some of the grounds therein referred to, such as blindness and lameness, is obviously a hardship, the rule laid down in the above passage ought not to be extended to the case of succession to *stridhan,* in the absence of any express provision showing that it is applicable to such a case. But on the other hand, it should be borne in mind that the rule of exclusion from inheritance as laid down by the sages and explained by commentators, is quite general in its terms, and that the hardship attending its operation is not altogether unmitigated. On this point Sir T. Strange has well observed,[2]—"At first sight, it appears harsh to divest of their heritable rights, not only idiots and madmen, but the deaf, the dumb, and the blind, the lame and the impotent; and certainly, disqualification, in this respect, is extended, by the law in question, beyond what takes place in our own, or other codes; but when it is considered, how unfitted

[1] Vallabhram Shivanarayan *v.* Bai Hariganga, 4 Bom., A. C. J., 135.

[2] 1 Strange, 152.

these in general are for the ordinary intercourse of the world, and that they are, by the same law, anxiously secured in a maintenance for life, chargeable upon those who replace them as heirs, the severity of the enactment is not only in some degree abated, but it even admits of comparison with our own institutions." Lecture IX.

Where several daughters jointly inherit their mother's *stridhan*, it has been held by the High Court of Madras that, upon the death of any one of them, her share would pass to the surviving co-heirs.[1] Though this rule may be in accordance with the law of the Dravida school, its correctness under the Mitakshara law is open to question. Succession by survivorship is recognized by Vijnaneswara only in the case of joint male coparceners. Moreover, the property which a daughter inherits from her mother becomes her *stridhan* according to the Mitakshara, as you have seen in a former lecture. It is therefore difficult to see how, in the absence of any express provision to the contrary, such inherited property of the daughter can pass on her death to any person other than the heir to her *stridhan*. Succession by survivorship among daughters.

On failure of daughters, the succession devolves on daughter's daughters.[2] Daughter's daughters.

This preference of the female issue of daughters over their male issue is probably based upon the same equitable considerations as those upon which the daughters of the deceased are preferred to her sons. Manu recognizes the claims of daughter's daughters when he says,[3]—"Even to the daughters of those daughters something should be given as may be fit from the assets of their maternal grandmother on the score of natural affection." The state of society which

[1] Sengamalathammal *v.* Valaynda Mudali, 3 Mad., 317.
[2] Mitakshara, Ch. II, Sec. XI, 15. [3] IX, 193.

LECTURE IX. could tolerate the succession of daughter's daughters must have been considerably in advance of that primitive state in which females had been declared altogether incompetent to inherit. But the succession of the daughter's daughter, it must be owned, has been deduced by Vijnaneswara from a forced construction of the text on which it is meant to be based. That text runs thus:—

"The property of a childless woman married in one of the four forms of marriage denominated the *Brahma*, &c., belongs to her husband; if she have issue, it goes to daughters; and in the other forms of marriage, it goes to her father."[1]

"In this place, by the term 'daughters,'" says Vijnaneswara,[2] "grand-daughters are signified; for the immediate female descendants are expressly mentioned in a preceding passage,—'the daughters share the residue of their mother's property, after payment of her debts.'"[3] As it is not for us to go behind an authoritative commentary like the Mitakshara, I need not pause to consider the correctness of Vijnaneswara's interpretation; but I shall only add that his rule has not been accepted by the Bengal lawyers, according to whom the daughter's daughter has no place in the order of succession.

If there be several grand-daughters, children of different mothers, they take *per stirpes* through their mothers, and not *per capita*.[4] This rule is deduced by Vijnaneswara from the text of Gautama,[5]—"or the partition may be according to the mothers."

If there be daughters as well as daughter's daughters, these latter, according to Manu,[6] are entitled to something

---

[1] Yajnavalkya, II, 145.
[2] Mitakshara, Ch. II, Sec. XI, 12.
[3] Yajnavalkya, II, 117.
[4] Mitakshara, Ch. II, Sec. XI, 16.
[5] XXVIII, 14.
[6] IX, 193.

out of affection; but this rule seems to be a mere moral injunction. LECTURE IX.

Daughter's sons.

In default of daughter's daughters, daughter's sons succeed.

Yajnavalkya's text containing no provision regarding the rights of daughter's sons, Vijnaneswara deduces the above rule from the following text of Narada:—"Let daughters divide their mother's wealth, or on failure of daughters, their male issue."[1]

There is no express provision in the Mitakshara as to whether the daughters' sons take their grandmother's *stridhan per stirpes* or *per capita*. But as the above text of Gautama is quite general in its terms, and is in fact cited in the Smriti Chandrika[2] as authority for the proposition that daughters' sons take as daughters' daughters, the correct rule seems to be that they take *per stirpes*.

Daughter's adopted son.

The question may arise, whether a daughter's adopted son can inherit the *stridhan* of his maternal grandmother by adoption; and if so, what would be the extent of his share when there are also legitimate sons of daughters. Some of the reasons presently to be noticed as supporting the right of a woman's adopted son to inherit her *stridhan*, are no doubt applicable to the present case, and may be urged in favour of the daughter's adopted son. But considering that the law of succession to *stridhan* is based mainly upon grounds of natural love and affection, and upon a principle of equitable distribution, and considering that the daughter's son excludes the son of the deceased herself, it would, I think, be unreasonable to hold, in the absence of any express authority to that effect, that

[1] XIII, 2; Mitakshara, Ch. II, Sec. XI, 18. [2] Ch. IX, Sec. III, 25.

LECTURE IX. an adopted son of a daughter is entitled to succeed in the same way as her legitimate son. But I must say this with some diffidence, as there is no authority one way or the other bearing upon the point. As my answer to the first part of the above question is in the negative, it becomes unnecessary to consider the latter part of it.

Sons. On failure of grandsons by daughters, sons take the property.[1]

This rule is easily deduced from the text of Yajnavalkya[2] already cited: "The daughters share the residue of their mother's property after payment of her debts; and the [male] issue succeed in their default." But it is not equally easy to reconcile this rule, and the text upon which it is based, with the texts of other sages on the same subject. And hence, the question as to the relative positions of the son and the daughter in the order of succession to *stridhan*, has been one on which not only do the different schools, and notably those of Benares and Bengal, differ most widely, but the two leading authorities of the Benares school itself, I mean the Mitakshara and the Viramitrodaya, present most marked points of difference. The principal text upon the interpretation of which the difference between the Dayabhaga and the Mitakshara on the present subject may be said to be based, is the following text of Manu:[3]—

"When the mother is dead, let all the uterine brothers and the uterine sisters equally divide the maternal estate." A literal translation of the text without any transposition

---

[1] Mitakshara, Ch. II, Sec. XI, 19. [2] II, 117.

[3] IX, 192. The text in the original runs thus:—

जनन्यां संस्थितायान्तु समं सर्वे सहोदराः ।
भजेरन् मातृकं रिक्थं भगिन्यश्च सनाभयः ॥

of words would stand thus:—"When the mother is dead, let all the uterine brothers equally divide the maternal estate, and so let the uterine sisters do." The language of this text is no doubt ambiguous, and it has accordingly been explained in different ways by different commentators, each supporting his view by reference to certain grammatical rules of construction. Vijnaneswara's interpretation of the text, which agrees with the latter rendering, and is in accordance with his doctrine that the daughters are the first to inherit their mother's *stridhan*, is here subjoined in full in his own words:[1]—

"'All the uterine brothers should divide the maternal estate equally; and so should sisters by the same mother.' Such is the construction: and the meaning is, 'not that brothers and sisters share together,' for reciprocation is not indicated, since the abridged form of the conjunctive compound has not been employed: but the conjunctive particle (*cha*) is here very properly used with reference to the person making the partition; as in the example, Devadatta practises agriculture, and so does Yajnadatta.

"'Equally' is specified to forbid the allotment of deductions [to the eldest and so forth]."

Jimutavahana,[2] on the contrary, adopts the former rendering as correct, and he supports his view by citing other texts declaratory of the joint succession of sons and daughters, amongst which he considers the following text of Devala[3] to be conclusive in his favor:—"A woman's property is common to her sons and unmarried daughters,

---

[1] Mitakshara, Ch. II, Sec. XI, 20, 21. See note to the same by Colebrooke for an explanation of the rules of grammar referred to in the above passage.

[2] Dayabhaga, Ch. IV, Sec. II, 1—8.

[3] *Ibid*, Ch. IV, Sec. II, 6.

LECTURE IX. when she is dead; but, if she leave no issue, her husband shall take it, her mother, her brother, or her father."

As regards the law of the Benares school however, it is needless to consider whether Jimutavahana's interpretation is the correct one. Vijnaneswara is the authoritative expounder of that law; and whether his doctrine be a correct deduction from the Rishi texts or not, it must be accepted as correct by the followers of that school.

Adopted son. Is a woman's adopted son entitled to inherit her *stridhan*; and if so, can he take the estate jointly with a son of the body, and what would be the extent of his share in that case? There is no express provision in the Hindu law, as far as I have been able to ascertain, bearing directly on these questions. On the one hand it may be said that it is the 'male issue' (*anwaya*), by which term must be understood male issue of the body, that succeed according to Yajnavalkya's text; that though the adopted son is declared to have the same rights as the son of the body, for certain purposes,[1] yet, succession to the adoptive mother's *stridhan* is nowhere specified as one of those purposes; and that, as a rule, adoption is more an act of the husband than of the wife, so that the adopted son is more a son of the former than of the latter. But on the other hand it should be borne in mind that the Dattaka Mimansa, the highest authority in the Benares school in matters of adoption, lays down the doctrine that by the husband's "mere act of adoption, the filiation of the adopted, as son of the wife, is complete in the same manner as her property in any other thing accepted by the husband;"[2] so that an adopted son is in law as much a son of the adopter's wife as of the adop-

[1] See Dattaka Mimansa, Sec. VI; and Sutherland's Synopsis, Head Fourth.

[2] Dattaka Mimansa, Sec. I, 22.

ter himself. Moreover the ancestors of the adoptive mother are declared by the same authority to be the maternal ancestors of the adopted son.[1] The point is not wholly untouched by direct authority. On the one hand, there is a case decided by the Bombay Sudder Court, in which a son adopted by a widow with her husband's permission was held not entitled to inherit her property.[2] But on the other hand the case of *Teencowree Chatterjea* v. *Dinonath Banerjee*,[3] decided by the Bengal High Court, distinctly lays down the opposite rule. In that case, though the reported judgment shows a slight misapprehension touching the competency of the adopted son to perform the adoptive maternal grandfather's *sraddha*, the point under consideration is decided in favor of the adopted son by a process of reasoning which, as far as it goes, is not open to any objection. The Court there observed: "On the first point we think there is no doubt that an adopted son has all the rights and privileges of a son born. He is the son of the father and of the mother, and succeeds to the paternal property, and also to the *stridhan* of his adoptive mother, in the absence of daughters, as a son born would do. In support of his argument, the pleader for the plaintiff quoted the texts noted in the margin,[4] showing the *status* of an adopted son, and urged that he had in all respects equal

---

[1] Dattaka Mimansa, Sec. VI, 50; See also Sham Kuar *v.* Gya Din, I. L. R., 1 All., 255; 1 W. and B., 207.

[2] 2 Bom. S. A. R., 178, cited in Norton's Leading Cases on Hindu Law, Part I, p. 101. See also Sree Narain Rai *v.* Bhya Jha, 2 Sel. Rep., 34 (new ed.) (Bengal). This last case was, however, one under the peculiar law and usage of Mithila.

[3] 3 W. R., 49.

[4] These references are:—Sutherland's Dattaka Chandrika Synopsis, p. 219; Dayakrama Sangraha, Sec. V; Dayabhaga; Macnaghten's Hindu Law, Vol. I, 39, 40.

LECTURE IX. rights with the son born. Against this argument the learned counsel quoted the case reported at page 128, Select Reports, Volume III, Gunga Mya, appellant, in which it was ruled that a son adopted by a woman, on whom her father's estate had devolved, would not be entitled to such estate on his adopting mother's death, but such estate would go to her father's heirs. We are not now disposed to differ from or call in question the correctness of that opinion, though in fact it was a mere *obiter*, for the question of the *status* of an adopted son was not then before the Court, but it arose from a supposed case put by the second Judge. We think it inapplicable to the present case. The question put to the pundit related to property which had descended to a woman from her father, not as *stridhan*, but in the ordinary course of inheritance; and it may be, as explained to us by Baboo Kishen Kishore, that the reason why the adopted son is excluded from the succession in such cases, is, that he is adopted into his adoptive father's family, and not into his mother's family, and cannot perform the *shrad* of his maternal grandfather, though he can perform that of his adoptive mother. . . . .

"It has also been asked by the learned counsel for the respondent, whether a son, adopted by one wife, would be looked upon as the son of a co-wife and succeed to her property. Though this question does not arise, we may point out that the Hindu law of inheritance provides even for this case, and mentions the son of a contemporary wife among the heirs of a woman entitled to succeed to her *stridhan*."

If a legitimate son is born subsequent to the adoption of a son, then, following the rule in the case of succession to the father's estate, it may be said that they would both be entitled to their mother's *stridhan*, the adopted son taking a third part of the share of a son of the body.[1] But I ought to tell you that the point is not touched by any authority in shape of text or of precedent, and that there are also arguments against the recognition of the adopted son's right in such cases.

The rule about shares is based upon a text of Vasistha,[2] which declares, "When a son has been adopted, if a legitimate son be afterwards born, the given son shares a fourth part."

The meaning of this text is by no means clear, and it is not therefore easy to say what would be the correct rule deducible from it. The text may have any one of four different meanings:—

I.—It may mean that the adopted son is to take an absolute fourth part of the estate. This would, however, be obviously unjust, as the legitimate sons, if numerous, would in that case each receive a share less than that of the adopted son. This meaning has not accordingly been accepted by any authority.

II.—It may mean that the adopted son should take a fourth part of what he would have taken had he been a legitimate son. Thus, supposing there to be only one legitimate son, the adopted son would take one-fourth of one-half, or an eighth. This construction would reduce the share of the adopted son very much. But this is supposed to be the meaning of the text according to Nanda Pandit.[3]

---

[1] Mitakshara, Ch. I. Sec. XI, 24; Dattaka Mimansa, V, 40, X, 1; Sutherland's Note XXII; see also Ayyavu Muppanar *v.* Niladatchi Ammal, 1 Mad., 45; 1 W. and B., 43; Macnaghten's Principles of Hindu Law, 70.

[2] XV, 8.

[3] See Dattaka Mimansa. Sec. V, 40; Sutherland's Note XXII; and also Canungoe Raghubanund Das *v.* Sadhuchurn Das (3 C. L. R., 510), in which a similar interpretation seems to have been adopted.

LECTURE IX.

III.—It may mean that the share of the adopted son is to be one-fourth of that of a legitimate son. Thus, supposing there to be an adopted son and only one legitimate son, their shares would be one-fifth and four-fifths respectively. This meaning has been adopted in Madras and Bombay.[1]

IV.—Or it may mean that the share of the adopted son should be one-third of that of a legitimate son. According to this meaning, when there is only one legitimate son, the adopted son would really take one-fourth of the estate, as provided by the text, and the legitimate son, the remaining three-fourths; and this probably is the case contemplated by the text. This interpretation is the one that has been adopted by Macnaghten[2] as the correct interpretation of the text according to the Benares school.

A further question remains to be considered. An adopted son may become affiliated to a woman either by being taken in adoption by her husband in association with her; or by being taken by the husband alone, the child nevertheless becoming a child of the wife according to the reason stated in the Dattaka Mimansa in the passage[3] quoted above; or by being taken by the husband in association with another wife, the child still becoming affiliated to the unassociated wife by the text of Manu,[4]—"If among several wives of the same husband one bring forth a male child, Manu has declared them all by means of that son to be mothers of male issue." In the first two cases, the adopted son would of course be regarded as a son of the

---

[1] See Ayyavu Muppanar v. Niladatchi Ammal, 1 Mad., 45; 1 W. and B., 43.

[2] Macnaghten's Principles of Hindu Law, p. 70.

[3] Sec. I, 22.

[4] IX, 183.

woman. But in the last case the question arises whether the adopted son is to be regarded as a son of the woman herself, or merely as the son of a co-wife. LECTURE IX.

The observations of the High Court in their judgment in the case of *Teencowree Chatterjee* v. *Dinonath Banerjee*,[1] which I have quoted above, would go to show that a son adopted by the husband of a woman in association with another wife, should be regarded not as her son, but only as the son of a rival wife, for purposes of succession to *stridhan*.

Suppose that a woman adopts a son in conjunction with her husband, becomes a widow, remarries, and then dies; will the adopted son be still entitled to inherit her *stridhan?* The point is not provided for in the Widow Marriage Act, and the Hindu law does not, I think, contemplate such a case at all. Of course there would be no difficulty if the son were a ligitimate son of the woman by her former husband. But seeing that the husband's adopted son becomes a son of the wife merely by reason of her relation to the husband, and seeing that such relation is wholly severed by the widow's remarriage, it is not easy to see how an adopted son of her former husband can still have the right to inherit her *stridhan*. But perhaps it would not be safe to hazard any opinion upon such a point.

From the use of the word 'uterine' in the text of Manu (IX, 192) quoted above, it follows that children of rival wives are excluded from participation in their step-mother's *stridhan*. To this rule Vijnaneswara notices an exception (which he deduces from another text of Manu),[2] namely, that the daughter of a rival wife of a superior class is entitled to

---

[1] 3 W. R., 49.

[2] IX, 198.

LECTURE IX. take the property of a childless woman.[1] But as marriage in a different caste or class is prohibited in the present age, this exception must be taken to have become obsolete now.

Grandsons. In default of sons, grandsons inherit their paternal grandmother's *stridhan*. This rule is based by Vijnaneswara upon the following process of reasoning :—" On failure of sons," says he,[2] " grandsons inherit their paternal grandmother's wealth. For Gautama[3] says,—' They who share the inheritance must pay the debts :' and the grandsons are bound to discharge the debts of their paternal grandmother, for the text expresses, ' Debts must be paid by sons and son's sons.'[4]

Grandsons by different sons inherit *per stirpes* and not *per capita.* There is no express provision in the Mitakshara on this point, but the Smriti Chandrika[5] lays down the rule just stated.

Touching the question, whether a son's adopted son is entitled to inherit his adoptive paternal grandmother's *stridhan,* and if so, what is the extent of his share when there are grandsons by birth as well, there is no provision to be found in the Mitakshara. But considering that the adopted son is regarded as having all the rights of a son born as regards succession in the adopter's family,[6] there seems to be no reason why he should not succeed to the *stridhan* of his paternal grandmother by adoption. The extent of his share in this case will, by analogy, be the same as that in the case of his succeeding to his paternal grandfather's estate. Now, with reference to this last mentioned case, there is a passage in the Dattaka Chandrika (perhaps inadvertently

---

[1] Mitakshara, Ch. II, Sec. XI, 22, 23. [2] *Ibid*, 24.
[3] XII, 32. [4] Yajnavalkya, II, 50. [5] Ch. IX, Sec. III, 25.
[6] Sutherland's Synopsis, Head Fourth ; Mitakshara, Ch. I, Sec. XI, 30, 31.

omitted in Sutherland's translation) which runs thus:[1]— LECTURE IX.
"And in the event of the existence of another son of the proprietor, the grandson by adoption, whose father is dead, is entitled to the share proper for a *dattaka*." That is, if the proprietor has a son, and an adopted son of a deceased son, the latter would not take his adoptive father's share, but would get only the share which his adoptive father would have taken had he been an adopted son of the proprietor. This rule, though laid down in a treatise which is chiefly followed in Bengal, has been applied to cases governed by the Mitakshara law.[2]

Order of succession to the *stridhan* of a woman dying without issue.

If a woman die "without issue," that is (as explained by Vijnaneswara),[3] leaving no daughter, nor daughter's daughter, nor daughter's son, nor son, nor son's son, her kinsmen, namely her husband and the rest, take her property. This rule is deduced from the text of Yajnavalkya,[4]— "Her kinsmen take it (her property) if she die without issue."

At this point, that is on failure of heirs down to a woman's son's son, the order of succession ceases to be uniform, and begins to vary with the form of her marriage; there being one order of succession to her *stridhan* if her marriage took place in one of the four superior forms, namely, the *Brahma*, the *Daiva*, the *Arsha*, and the *Prajapatya*; and a different order, if her marriage took place in one of the inferior or remaining four forms. In the former case, the heirs are the husband and his kinsmen; and in the latter,

---

[1] See Bharat Chandra Siromani's edition, p. 30. The passage ought to have occurred in Sutherland's translation, Sec. V, 24. See also Vyavastha Darpana, p. 974, note.

[2] See Canungoe Raghubanund Das *v* Sadhuchurn Das, 3 C. L. R., 534.

[3] Mitakshara, Ch. II, Sec. XI, 9.

[4] II, 144.

LECTURE IX. they are the parents and their kinsmen. This rule is based upon the following text of Yajnavalkya:[1]—

"The property of a childless woman, married in one of the four forms denominated *Brahma*, &c., goes to her husband; but if she leave progeny, it will go to her (daughter's) daughters: and in other forms of marriage (as the *Asura*, &c.,) it goes to her father (and mother on failure of her own issue)."

To this text, Vijnaneswara adds the following commentary:[2]—

"Of a woman dying without issue, as before stated, and who had become a wife by any of the four modes of marriage denominated *Brahma*, *Daiva*, *Arsha*, and *Prajapatya*, the property, as before described, belongs in the first place to her husband. On failure of him, it goes to his nearest *sapindas*. But, in the other forms of marriage called *Asura*, *Gandharba*, *Rakshasa*, and *Paisacha*, the property of a childless woman goes to her parents, that is, to her father and mother. The succession devolves first (and the reason has been before explained) on the mother, who is virtually exhibited (first) in the elliptical phrase *pitrigami*, implying 'goes *(gachhati)* to both parents *(pitarau)*, that is, to the mother and to the father.' On failure of them, their next of kin take the succession."

Neither the text nor the commentary gives the order of succession in detail.

In the one class of cases (namely, those in which the marriage was in one of the approved forms) the husband is the first heir, and on failure of him, his nearest *sapindas* come next; and in the other class of cases, the mother

---

[1] II, 145.

[2] Mitakshara, Ch. II, Sec. XI, 11.

comes first, then the father, and then their next of kin. But who are successively the next of kin in either case, or, in other words, what is the order of nearness among kindred, the author of the Mitakshara does not at all explain.

One thing, however, seems clear, namely, that the word *sapinda* in the foregoing passage is used in the sense assigned to it in the Acharadhyaya of the Mitakshara.[1] It means a *sagotra sapinda* or any ancestor within the seventh degree as well as any male descendant within the seventh degree of any such ancestor; and also a *bhinnagotra sapinda* or *bandhu*.

When the woman was married in one of the first four forms—The husband—His sapindas—The order in which they inherit.

First take the case in which the proprietress was married in one of the first four forms. The heirs are the husband and his *sapindas* in order of proximity.

In the absence of any provision in the Mitakshara for determining this order of proximity among the husband's *sapindas*, we turn to the Viramitrodaya, a work of high authority in the Benares school. But that work does not help us much. The order of succession as given there is different from that in the Mitakshara, as far as there are express provisions in both; and where the express enumeration of heirs in the latter treatise stops, the Viramitrodaya does not carry it much further. Nor does it simply follow out Vijnaneswara's general rule by specifying the order of proximity among the husband's *sapindas*, but it gives the order in a different way upon the authority of a text of Brihaspati not referred to in the Mitakshara. That text runs thus:—

"The mother's sister, the maternal uncle's wife, the paternal uncle's wife, the father's sister, the mother-in-law, and the wife of an elder brother, are pronounced to be similar to mothers. If they leave no legitimate offspring

---

[1] See *ante*, p. 62.

LECTURE IX. of the body, no stepson, nor a daughter's son, nor their son, then the sister's son and the rest shall take their property."[1]

You will observe that the order of succession here indicated differs from that according to Vijnaneswara, in omitting to assign any place to the husband or the parents, and in giving promiscuously the *sapindas* of the husband and those of the parents, without noticing the distinction in the devolution of property depending upon the form of marriage of the proprietress.

After citing the above text of Brihaspati, and enumerating the heirs down to the son and son's son, Mitramisra observes:[2] "On failure of these (the inheritance devolves) on the stepson, his sons and grandsons, because, under such circumstances, these offer the funeral oblations, and pay the debts, and because it has been ordained in this manner in the above text of Manu (IX, 183).

"Then, on failure of these, though *sapindas*, such as a father-in-law, may be living, the sister's son and the rest have a right to inherit, according to the scale of their nearness mentioned in the text of Brihaspati, the property of their mother's sister and the rest, by virtue of that special text (of Brihaspati) which cannot have any other application."

This order of succession is no doubt in accordance with the text of Brihaspati. And there is this additional argument in its favor, that it is the same as that given in the Vyavahara Mayukha (Ch. IV, Sec. X, 30) and the Smriti Chandrika (Ch. IX, Sec. III, 36). But being in conflict with that indicated by Vijnaneswara, it cannot be accepted as law in the Benares school, which recognizes the authority of the

---

[1] See 2 W. and B., 99.

[2] *Ibid*, 100 and 101.

Viramitrodaya only when it is not contradicted by the superior authority of the Mitakshara. LECTURE IX.

It would be useless to refer to the Bengal authorities for elucidation of the point. It is true that they carry the enumeration of heirs much further than the Mitakshara. But considering that the founder of the Bengal school controverts almost every doctrine of the Mitakshara on the present subject,[1] he would not, I think, be a safe guide for clearing anything that is obscure in that work.

According to Kamalakar,[2] the 'nearness' of *sapindas* in the above rule of Vijnaneswara is to be determined by the rule given in the Mitakshara for the devolution of the property of a male owner dying without male issue. So that the heirs of a woman after her husband would be her husband's widow, his daughter, his daughter's son, that is, her rival wife, step-daughter, step-daughter's son; then the husband's mother, next his father, and so on.[3] And as the son and the grandson of the husband, that is, the stepson and the step-grandson of the woman, are undoubtedly the nearest *sapindas* of the husband, these two ought, consistently with the above view, to come next after the husband, and before the heirs just named.

"This opinion," observe Messrs. West and Bühler,[4] "seems to be based on the consideration that, as the *sapindas* inherit only through the husband, they virtually succeed to property

---

[1] See Dayabhaga, Ch. IV, Secs. II and III.

[2] See Vivadatandava, chapter on the Distribution of *Stridhan*.

This is what Kamalakar says on this point in one place :—

"In default of the husband, the daughter, sons, and daughter's sons of the rival wife, and in their default, the mother-in-law, the father-in-law, the husband's brother, his sons, and other next of kin of the husband (succeed) according to the text, 'The wife, and the daughters also &c.' This is the opinion of Vijnaneswara and Apararka."

[3] See Mitakshara, Ch. II, Secs. I—VI.

[4] 1 W. and B., 213.

LECTURE IX. coming from him, and that consequently they must inherit in the order prescribed for the succession to a male's estate."

"Against this," continue the same learned authors, "it may be urged, that the word 'pratyasanna,' 'nearest,' if employed in regard to persons generally, has the sense of 'nearest by relationship;' and that the list of heirs to a man without male descendants, is not made solely with regard to nearness by relationship, since, for instance, it places the daughter's son before the parents and the brothers, though he is further removed than the former, and not nearer related than the latter.

"It is, therefore, perhaps more advisable to take the word 'pratyasanna' in its first sense, and to assume that Vijnaneswara really intends 'nearness by relationship' to be the principle regulating the succession of *sapindas*.

"If this interpretation is accepted, the heirs of childless widows in the first instance would be those kinsmen related to the husband in the first degree, *i. e.*, rival wives of the deceased, their offspring, and the husband's parents, all inheriting together; next, the kinsmen related to the husband in the second degree, as the husband's brothers, deceased's stepchildren's children, &c., and so on, to the sixth degree inclusive."

In this conflict of authority, it is not easy to say which view is correct. But Kamalakara's opinion is entitled to be followed as authority in the Benares school,[1] when it is not in conflict with that of any higher authority; and in the present instance, the rule based upon his opinion has the further recommendation of being simple, as it makes the order of succession to *stridhan* correspond, after a certain point, to that applicable to a man's property. It may

[1] See 1 Morley. Introduction, ccxxi.

also be urged that if this were not Vijnaneswara's meaning, and if he had not referred to this known order of succession after the husband, he would in all probability have expressed himself more explicitly.

LECTURE IX.

Accepting then Kamalakara's interpretation of Vijnaneswara's rule, the successive heirs after the husband would be, the stepson, the step-grandson, the rival wife, the step-daughter, her son, the husband's mother, his father, his brothers, their sons, and the husband's other *gotraja sapindas* and *bandhus* in the order in which they inherit his property.[1]

When the woman was married in one of the disapproved forms,—The mother, the father, and their *sapindas* —Their order of succession.

Next take the case in which the marriage of the proprietress took place according to one of the four disapproved forms, namely the *Asura, Gandharba, Rakshasa,* and *Paisacha.* The heirs to her *stridhan* are in succession her mother, her father, and their nearest kinsmen.

Following the above mode of determining nearness among kinsmen, the successive heirs after the father would be, the brother, his son, the stepmother, the sister, her son, the father's mother, the father's father, the paternal uncle, his son, and the father's *gotraja sapindas* and *bandhus* in the same order in which they would succeed to his property.

The questions relating to the succession of the *samanodakas,* or distant *gotrajas,* will be considered in the next lecture, under the head of succession according to the Maharashtra school.

Sulka, or woman's fee.

The above order of succession is not applicable to a woman's fee or gratuity, (*sulka*), that is, (as defined by Vijnaneswara,[2]) the wealth 'for the receipt of which the woman was

---

[1] See Mitakshara, Ch. II, Secs. V and VI; Omrit Koomaree Dabee *v.* Lukhee Narain Chuckerbutty, 10 W. R. (F. B.), 76; Gridhari Lall Roy *v.* The Government of Bengal, 10 W. R. (P. C.), 31.

[2] Mitakshara, Ch. II, Sec. XI, 6.

LECTURE IX.

given in marriage.' "For that goes," says Vijnaneswara, "to brothers of the whole blood conformably with the text of Gautama: 'The sister's fee belongs to the uterine brothers; after [the death of] the mother.'"[1] The foregoing version of Gautama's text, which places the brothers after the mother, is, we are told by Colebrooke,[2] according to the interpretation given by the Subodhini and certain other authorities. But the text would also bear another interpretation, according to which it would be rendered thus:—

"The sister's fee belongs to the uterine brothers; after (them) it goes to the mother."[3] This is the sense in which the text is understood concurrently in the Viramitrodya,[4] the Smriti Chandrika,[5] and the Dayabhaga;[6] and even in the Mitakshara, it would appear from the context, that it is understood in the same sense; for the uterine brothers are mentioned as the first among the heirs.

Heirs to the property of a maiden.

It remains only to say a few words about the devolution of the property of a maiden. If she die after betrothal, the bridegroom is to get back the gifts presented by him, after paying the charges on both sides.[7] To the other property of an affianced girl, and to all the property of an unbetrothed maiden, the heirs are her uterine brothers, her mother, her father in succession.[8] This rule is based upon a text quoted from Baudhayana.

Order of succession according to the Viramitrodaya.

I shall conclude this lecture with a brief summary of the order of succession according to the Viramitrodaya.

---

[1] Mitakshara, Ch. II, Sec. XI, 14; Gautama, XXVIII, 23.

[2] Mitakshara, Ch. II, Sec. XI, 14, note.

[3] The text in the original runs thus:—

भगिनी शुल्कं सोदर्याणामूर्ध्वं मातुः ।

[4] 2 W. and B., 98.

[5] Ch. IX, Sec. III, 32, 33.

[6] Ch. IV, Sec. III, 27, 28.

[7] Mitakshara, Ch. II, Sec. XI, 29.

[8] Mitakshara, Ch. II, Sec. XI, 30.

That work is only a second rate authority in the Benares school, being entitled to be followed where the Mitakshara is silent or ambiguous, but not where it contains any express provision to the contrary. On the present subject, as the two works differ, the provisions of the Viramitrodaya are of very little practical value. LECTURE IX.

Touching the relative claims of sons and daughters to the estate of their deceased mother, Mitramisra adopts a sort of middle course between the Mitakshara and the Dayabhaga. While the former gives the daughters preference over the sons in all cases, and the latter limits such preference to the case of nuptial gifts (*yautuka stridhan*) and gifts received from the father, and allows equal participation among sons and maiden daughters in all other cases, the Viramitrodaya, upon the authority of Manu (IX, 195, 131) and Gautama (XXVIII, 21), admits the exclusive right of daughters over all kinds of *stridhan*, except the gift subsequent (*anwadheya*) and the affectionate gift of the husband (*pritidatta*), which are declared to be subject to equal division among sons and daughters; and it declares that the *yautuka* goes to the unmarried daughters alone.[1] This result is arrived at after a lengthy discussion, much of which is practically unprofitable. I shall have to say more on this point in the next lecture, when considering the devolution of *stridhan* according to the Mayukha and the Smriti Chandrika.

The text of Yajnavalkya, which declares that the order of succession to a childless woman's estate depends upon the form of the woman's marriage, is interpreted in the Viramitrodaya in a sense slightly different from that adopted in the Mitakshara; and this difference of interpretation is the result of Mitramisra's attempt

[1] See 2 W. and B., 89.

LECTURE IX. to reconcile the text of Yajnavalkya with that of Manu (IX, 196, 197). According to Mitramisra, the property of a childless woman married in any of the first five (not four) forms of marriage, namely the *Brahma*, the *Daiva*, the *Arsha*, the *Prajapatya*, and the *Gandharba*, goes to her husband and his relations, and the succession of the parents and their relations is limited to the case in which the woman was married in one of the remaining three forms.[1]

The order of succession among the relations of the husband and among those of the parents is not very definitely stated; and, as far as it goes, it is based mainly upon the text of Brahaspati cited above.

[1] See W. and B., 95.

LECTURE X.

SUCCESSION TO STRIDHAN ACCORDING TO THE MAHARASHTRA, DRAVIDA, AND MITHILA SCHOOLS.

The Maharashtra school—Comparative weight of authority of the Mitakshara and the Mayukha—Succession of children—Four different cases of this—*First*, as regards the *anwadheya* and the husband's gifts—*Second*, as regards the *yautuka*—*Third*, as regards other kinds of *stridhan* technically so called—*Fourth*, as regards woman's property other than *stridhan* technically so called—Heirs to a childless woman—As regards her *stridhan* proper—Husband and parents—Other relations—On some unsettled questions concerning them—Are the husband's *samanodakas* entitled to inherit a woman's property—Whether paternal kinsmen succeed on failure of husband's relations—Order of succession to woman's property other than *stridhan* proper—Wealth given by kindred—*Sulka*—Succession to the property of a maiden—Devolution of *stridhan* according to the Dravida school—Parasara Madhavya—Smriti Chandrika—Succession of children—Succession to the *stridhan* of a childless woman—The *sulka*—Succession to the property of dancing-women—Succession to *stridhan* according to the Mithila school—Succession of descendants—Other heirs—Woman's fee—Succession to a maiden's property—*Kritrima son.*

I HAVE in the preceding lecture given you the order of succession to *stridhan* according to the Benares school; and I shall here give you the order according to each of the three cognate schools—the Maharastra, the Dravida, and the Mithila, reserving the consideration of the law of the Bengal school on the present subject for the next lecture.

The Maharashtra school—Comparative weight of authority of the Mitakshara and the Mayukha.

I begin with the Maharashtra school. Here, in addition to the Mitakshara, the Vyavahara Mayukha of Nilkantha is recognized as a work of authority. As the Mayukha, as you will presently see, does not agree with the Mitakshara on the law of succession to *stridhan*, the first question that arises is, which of the two works should be followed when they differ. This question was raised before the High Court of Bombay in the case of *Krishnaji*

LECTURE X. *Vyanktesh* v. *Pandurang*,[1] and the Court in delivering judgment observed:—"The present case turns on the comparative authority on questions of inheritance in the Southern Maratha Country of the Mitakshara and Vyavahara Mayukha. Their relative weight has been estimated in Vol. I, West and Bühler, Introduction i., ii., so far as an opinion could be gathered from the numerous responses with which the editors of that work had to deal, as delivered officially by the Shastris of the Courts, and from the oral statements of persons learned in the Hindu law of this Presidency. . . . . . The first place is, on such authority, assigned to the Mitakshara, only a subordinate, though still an important one, to the Mayukha. . . . . . In cases of direct conflict between the two authorities, there can be no doubt, after these expressions of opinions, that preference should, in general, be given to the Mitakshara doctrine, although where the Mayukha's gloss may not seem easily reconcilable with the text, its construction is to be received, if not absolutely contradictory to the 'supreme authority.'

"It is true that that doctrine has, in some instances, been broken in upon in Guzerat, by an adoption of the different views propounded in the Mayukha; and, in the island of Bombay, where a large and intelligent part of the population has been furnished by Guzerat, the Mayukha may perhaps rank as the foremost authority. This is the utmost that can be deduced from the language attributed to the Chief Justice in the report of *Vijiarangam's case*."

Though, therefore, the law on the subject of succession to *stridhan* as laid by Vijnaneswara is the law for the Bombay school in the majority of cases, yet, as the Mayukha may serve

---

[1] 12 Bom., 65.

to supplement the rules of the Mitakshara where they are incomplete, and as it has independent authority in Guzerat and the island of Bombay, I shall briefly state the substance of its provisions on the same subject. LECTURE X.

Succession of children.

Nilkantha, like Mitramisra, maintains, that Vijnaneswara's rule, that the maiden and the married daughters in succession inherit their mother's *stridhan* to the exclusion of her sons, is subject to certain exceptions. These, according to him, are two in number, namely, one, in the case of the gift subsequent *(anwadheya)* and the affectionate gifts received from the husband *(pritidatta)*, which go to the sons and daughters jointly; and another (not noticed in the Viramitrodaya), in the case of woman's property of any description other than those specified in the texts of sages, that is, property obtained by partition and the like, which goes to the sons alone.[1] And the nuptial gift *(yautuka)*, which goes to the maiden daughter alone, perhaps also forms a distinct class.

Four different cases of this.

With regard to the succession of lineal descendants according to the Mayukha, the different kinds of *stridhan* may, therefore, be classed as follows :—

I.—The *anwadheya stridhan*, or gift received after marriage from the husband's family; and the *pritidatta stridhan*, or property given by the husband through affection.

II.—The *yautuka*, or nuptial gifts.

III.—The other descriptions of *stridhan* (besides those mentioned above under classes I and II), which are specifically enumerated in the texts of the sages (the *sulka*, or perquisite, excepted),—namely, wealth given by relations other than the husband, and wealth received on supersession *(adhivedanika)*.

---

[1] See Vyavahara Mayukha, Ch. IV, Sec. X, 13—18, 24—26.

IV.—Property acquired by a woman by partition and the like, that is woman's property of all descriptions other than those that are technically called *stridhan,* and are specifically named in the texts of the sages.

First, as regards the *anwadheya stridhan* and the husband's gifts.

With regard to class I, Nilkantha cites[1] the following text of Manu —" What she received after marriage from the family of her husband, and what her affectionate lord may have given her, shall be inherited, even if she die in his lifetime, by her children ;" [2]—and from this text, he deduces the rule, that *stridhan* coming under this class is inherited by the sons who share it with unmarried daughters, and, in default of these last, with married daughters.[3] On failure of sons as well as daughters, if there be son's sons as well as daughter's children, the latter would, it seems, be entitled to inherit in preference to the former.[4] But the order of succession among grandchildren is not clearly stated. On failure of daughter's children, son's sons become heirs.

Second, as regards the *yautuka.*

The rule of succession applicable to class II, (*yautuka* property), is deduced from a text of Manu,[5] which says that " property given to the mother on her marriage is inherited by the unmarried daughters ;" and *yautuka* is explained to mean property received by a woman " at the time of marriage or other (ceremony) whilst seated together with her hnsband," the word being derived from *yuta,* 'joined together.'[6]

The heirs to the *yautuka* property of a woman in default of maiden daughters, are not clearly mentioned in the Mayukha. It may, therefore, be contended that Vijnanes-

[1] Vyavahara Mayukha, Ch. IV, Sec. X, 13.
[2] Manu, IX, 195.
[3] Vyavahara Mayukha, Ch. IV, Sec. X, 15.
[4] *Ibid*, 20. [5] IX, 131.
[6] Vyavahara Mayukha, Ch. IV, Sec. X, 17.

wara's general rule should be followed, and that the married daughters and their issue should successively be the next heirs.

Third, as regards other kinds of *stridhan* technically so called.

In regard to class III, Nilkantha admits the correctness of Vijnaneswara's rules;[1] so that the order of succession to such property according to the Mayukha is the same as the order laid down in the Mitakshara.

Fourth, as regards woman's property other than *stridhan* technically so called.

Stridhan coming under class IV comprehends all those descriptions of woman's property which Vijnaneswara[2] includes under the suppletory term *adya* (and the rest) in Yajnavalkya's text.[3] Such property goes to the sons and other heirs even though there be daughters. This rule of succession is deduced from the following text of Yajnavalkya,[4]—

"Let sons divide equally both the effects and the debts, after (the demise of) their two parents,"—which, according to Nilkantha, relates to what is acquired by the act of partition and the like.[5]

Heirs to a childless woman.

For the purposes of succession, a childless woman's property is divided by Nilkantha into two sorts—first, the *paribhasika stridhan*, or that which is technically called *stridhan*, comprising the above mentioned classes I to III; and, secondly, the *aparibhasika stridhan*, or that which does not come under the first mentioned description, and which forms class IV in the above classification.

As regards her *stridhan* proper—Husband and parents.

For the first of these two descriptions of woman's property, Nilkantha, like Vijnaneswara, gives a two-fold order of succession depending upon the form of the woman's marriage,[6] and he bases his rule upon the same text of Yajnavalkya[7] that is followed in the Mitakshara on this subject. But

---

[1] Vyavahara Mayukha, Ch. IV, Sec. X, 18.

[2] Mitakshara, Ch. II, Sec. XI, 1, 2. [3] II, 143. [4] II, 117.

[5] Vyavahara Mayukha, Ch. IV, Sec. X, 26. [6] *Ibid*, 28, 29. [7] II, 145.

LECTURE X. the Mayukha, like the Viramitrodaya,[1] differs from the Mitakshara in construing this text, and holds that the husband and his kinsmen are the heirs when the marriage of the woman took place in the *Brahma* form, or in any of the other four unblamed forms, that is, the *Daiva*, the *Arsha*, the *Prajapatya*, and the *Gandharba*; and that the parents and their kinsmen succeed if the marriage took place in any of the remaining forms,—the *Asura*, the *Rakshasa*, and the *Paisacha*.

Other relations.

On failure of the husband of a deceased woman, if she was married according to an approved form, or of the parents, if she was married in an unapproved form, the heirs to her *stridhan* are successively—her sister's son, her husband's sister's son, her husband's brother's son, her brother's son, her son-in-law, and her husband's younger brother, according to the following text of Brihaspati:—"The mother's sister, the maternal uncle's wife, the paternal uncle's wife, the father's sister, the mother-in-law, and the wife of an elder brother, are pronounced similar to mothers. If they leave no son born in lawful wedlock, nor daughter's son, nor his son, then the sister's son and the rest shall take their property."[2] Herein also, you will observe, the Mayukha agrees with the Viramitrodaya.

Nothing is expressly said in the Mayukha as to whether these heirs succeed in the order in which Brihaspati's text suggests their enumeration. Jimutavahana[3] and Srikrishna,[4] it is true, declare that Brihaspati's text only shews that the persons therein mentioned are heirs, but that the text does not indicate their order of suc-

---

[1] See 2 W. and B., 95. [2] Vyavahara Mayukha, Ch. IV, Sec. X, 30.
[3] Dayabhaga, Ch. IV, Sec. III, 36.
[4] Dayakrama Sangraha, Ch. II, Sec. VI, 2.

cession; but in the absence of any similar declaration by Nilkantha, it is not easy to come to any other conclusion than this, that, according to the Mayukha, the text of Brihaspati indicates the order in which the heirs therein referred to are entitled to succeed.

After these, the next heirs are the nearest kinsmen of the woman in her husband's family, if she was married in an approved form; and her nearest kinsmen in her father's family in other cases.[1] But in what way this nearness is to be determined, has not been clearly explained by Nilkantha. The following rather obscure passage[2] contains all that our author has said on the subject:—

"In the one case, if there be no husband, then the nearest to her in his (*tat*) own family takes it; and in the other case, if her father do not exist, the nearest to her in her father's family succeeds, (for the law that) 'To the nearest *sapinda*, the inheritance next belongs,' as declared by Manu,[3] denotes, that the right of inheriting her wealth is derived even from nearness of kin to the deceased (female) under discussion—and though the Mitakshara holds, 'that on failure of the husband it goes to his (*tat*) nearest kinsmen (*sapinda*) allied by funeral oblations,' and, 'on failure of the father, then to his (*tat*) nearest *sapindas*;' yet from the context it may be demonstrated, that her nearest relations are his nearest relations, and (the pronoun *tat* being used in the common gender) it allows of our expounding the passage 'those nearest to him, through her, in his own family;' for the expressions are of similar import."

Therefore, the remarks I have made in the last lecture in connection with the succession of the husband's and the

---

[1] Vyavahara Mayukha, Ch. IV, Sec. X, 28. [2] *Ibid.* [3] IX, 187.

LECTURE X. father's kinsmen under the Mitakshara, are generally applicable to their succession under the Mayukha, with only this difference, that, among the husband's and the father's kinsmen, those enumerated in the above text of Brihaspati take the places assigned to them in that text. Touching the succession of distant kinsmen, Messrs. West and Bühler observe,—"The *sapindas* have been divided into *sagotra* or *gotrajas*, *i. e.*, those belonging to the same family as the husband, bearing the same name; and *bhinnagotras*, *i. e.*, those belonging to a different family; and the former, as a body, have been placed before the latter. The opinion that the *sagotras* inherit before the *bhinnagotras*, seems to have been held by most of the Shastris also who wrote the following Vyavasthas, and is shared by the Law Officer who assisted in the compilation of the Digest. It is based on the principle which prevails in the case of a male's property, namely, that no property should be allowed to pass out of the family through inheritance, as long as a single member of the family survives."[1]

I ought to add that, as the High Court of Bombay has held in the case of *Lakshmi bai* v. *Jayram Hari*,[2] that the wives of all *gotraja sapindas* and *samanodakas* have rights of inheritance co-extensive with those of their husbands, these female relations of a woman's husband are entitled to inherit her *stridhan*, and have their places in the order of succession just after their respective husbands.[3] But in some cases, as in that of the daughter-in-law, their position in the order of succession would evidently be somewhat different.

---

[1] 1 W. and B., 215.
[2] 6 Bom., A. C. J., 152; see also Lallubhai *v.* Mankuvarbai, I. L. R. 2 Bom., 388.
[3] See 1 W. and B., 219, 228, 231.

The text of Yajnavalkya[1]—"The property of a childless woman married in the form denominated *Brahma*, or in any of the other four unblamed modes of marriage, goes to her husband; but if she leave progeny, it will go to her daughters; and in other forms of marriage (as the *Asura*, &c.), it goes to her father, and mother, on failure of her own issue"—contains no mention of the kinsmen, either of the husband or of the father, as being among the heirs to a woman's *stridhan;* and it is only the exposition of that text by Vijnaneswara and Nilkantha that forms the basis of the law on the subject of succession of remote heirs. And as these commentators do not enumerate any more distant heirs than the *sapindas* of the husband, or the next of kin of the father, the question might arise whether relations of the husband, not within the third degree (that is, not coming strictly within the denomination of *sapindas*),[2] can be regarded as heirs. Looking into the other commentaries, we find that the enumeration in the Dayabhaga does not extend beyond the *sapindas;*[3] but Srikrishna, in his commentary on the Dayabhaga and also in his Dayakrama Sangraha,[4] enumerates the husband's *sakulyas* and *samanodakas* as well; and Jagannatha also in his Digest[5] recognizes the rights of these remote kinsmen. The word *sapinda*, moreover, is used in the Mitakshara and the Mayukha to mean any relation within the seventh degree of descent from any common ancestor, not more remote than the seventh,—that is a *sapinda* in the more limited sense, as well as a *sakulya*.[6] The opinion of the Bombay Shastris is in favor

LECTURE X.

On some unsettled questions concerning them—Are the husband's *samanodakas* entitled to inherit a woman's property?

---

[1] II, 145. [2] See Manu, IX, 186. [3] See Ch. IV, Sec. III.

[4] Ch. II, Sec. VI. [5] Bk. V, 513, commentry, Vol. II, p. 624 (Mad. ed.)

[6] See Mitakshara Acharadhyaya (Sans.), leaf 6; Mitakshara (Colebrooke's translation), Ch. II, Sec. V, 6; Vyavahara Mayukha, Ch. IV, Sec. VIII, 18; Manu, V, 60.

LECTURE X. of this interpretation;[1] and Steele, in his Law and Custom of Hindoo Castes,[2] takes the same view. Therefore the husband's kinsmen within the seventh degree of descent from any of his ancestors within the seventh degree, are heirs to a woman's property according to the Mitakshara and the Mayukha.

The only point which remains unsettled is, whether the *samanodakas* of a woman's husband are also her heirs. We have only the authority of Srikrishna and Jagannatha, both Bengal lawyers, in favor of the rights of the *samanodakas.* Of European writers, Sir W. Macnaghten enumerates them as heirs;[3] and his authority would have been entitled to great weight, but for the fact that he seems to disregard the differences in the law of succession to *stridhan* according to the different schools, and to accept the law laid down by the Bengal lawyers as of universal application.[4] The learned editors of the Digest of Hindu Law according to the Bombay school, merely state that the *samanodakas* are not named as heirs to a woman's property, but they give no opinion on the point.[5] The reasoning upon which Jagannatha bases his conclusion that the husband's *samanodakas* are entitled to inherit, is founded upon a text of the Vishnu Purana, which says, that in default of *sapindas,* the *samanodakas* perform the *sraddha.* Upon this text he observes:[6]— "In like manner women also requiring obsequies, the right of performing for them ceremonies relative to another world, should follow the same order." And hence, by the

[1] See 1 W. and B., 234–238.
[2] P. 68.
[3] Principles of Hindu Law, p. 39.
[4] *Ibid*, 40, note.
[5] See 1 W. and B., 239.
[6] Colebrooke's Digest, Bk. V, 514, commentary.

application of the principle of spiritual benefit, the *samanodakas* are shewn to be heirs. But the Dharmasindhu, a work of authority in the Western Presidency, greatly weakens the basis of this argument; for it gives a different enumeration of persons competent to perform the *sraddha* of a married woman, an enumeration in which the husband's *samanodakas* find no place.[1] In this state of the authorities, the point cannot be regarded as a settled one. But I may observe that, considering how carefully the Hindu law tries to prevent escheat to the Crown by introducing the disciple, the preceptor, and, sometimes, even utter strangers into the line of heirs, it would not be in any way contrary to the spirit of that law to allow the husband's *samanodakas* to inherit the *stridhan* of a woman, though the Mitakshara and the Mayukha be silent on the point.

According to some authorities,[2] the daughter's grandson and the husband's sister are heirs to a woman's property by the law of the Western Presidency, they being regarded as the husband's *sapindas* belonging to a different family. But their precise position in the order of succession is not clearly stated.

Whether paternal kinsmen succeed on failure of husband's relations.

Another important question ought to be next considered, namely, whether, on failure of all relations on the husband's side, a woman's relations on the father's side are entitled to inherit her property, if she had been married in one of the approved forms. The Mitakshara says nothing on this point. The Mayukha, upon the authority of Brihaspati's text, names some of the father's *sapindas* as heirs to a

---

[1] See Dharmasindhu, III, cited in 1 W. and B., 244, note.

[2] See 1 W. and B., 239, 240.

LECTURE X. woman, but it places them before the *sapindas* of the husband. But we learn from West and Bühler[1] that the Shastris of Bombay unanimously declare that the father's *sapindas* are heirs to a woman in default of her husband's kinsmen. Messrs. West and Bühler suggest certain arguments in support of this opinion. One of these arguments is based upon the doctrine that the right of guardianship over a female reverts to her paternal relations upon the extinction of her husband's family, as is shown by a text quoted in the Mitakshara,[2]—"On failure of relations on both sides (the husband's and the parent's) the king becomes the supporter and master of a female;" and another argument is deduced from the doctrine that the right of performing the obsequies of a married woman belongs to her father's *sapindas*, in default of certain persons amongst whom are some of the *sapindas* of the husband.[3] The learned compilers of the Digest go on to observe:[4]—"As now the widow's kinsmen would, but for her marriage, undoubtedly have the right to inherit her estate on account of their blood-relationship, it seems not unreasonable to suppose that this right revives on failure of the persons who barred it.

"The objection which might be raised against this view, that the silence of the Mitakshara and of the Mayukha regarding the rights of the widow's blood-relations is equivalent to a denial of these rights, cannot be sustained, since the lists of heirs given in the two law books are not exhaustive. For neither the persons connected by spirit-

---

[1] 1 W. and B., 243.

[2] Acharadhyaya, leaf 12, p. 1.

[3] See the Dharmasindhu, III, Uttarardha, leaf 6, page 1, cited in 1 W. and B., 244, note.

[4] 1 W. and B., pp. 244, 245.

ual ties with the widow, *i. e.*, the husband's *acharya* and pupil, nor the Brahminical community in the case of a Brahman widow, nor the king in the case of other castes, are mentioned as heirs, though their eventual rights to the inheritance would not be disputed by any Hindu lawyer.

"If, therefore, the right of the widow's own blood-relations revives on failure of the husband's *sapindas*, it seems natural to allow them to succeed in the same order as they would have done before her marriage, and to place the mother first, next the father, after him the brothers and the rest of the *sapindas*, according to the nearness of their relationship."

As this view is in accordance with the general spirit of the Hindu law which, as I have said above, anxiously tries to prevent escheat to the Crown, I may venture to think that it would be accepted as correct by the Courts, should the question come to be discussed before them. But I ought to add that it is not clear whether the paternal kinsmen should come after the husband's *sapindas* or after his *samanodakas*.

How the nearness of relationship, mentioned in the foregoing passage, is to be determined, or, in other words, in what order the paternal kinsmen should succeed, has not been explained. The order of succession for paternal kinsmen when they inherit on failure of the husband's relations, ought to be the same as that in the case where they take the estate in the first instance, that is, where the woman had been married according to one of the inferior forms of marrige; and so the remarks I made in the last lecture[1] with reference to this latter case are equally applicable to the former.

[1] See *ante*, p. 377.

LECTURE X.

A sister's daughter has been held entitled to inherit a woman's *stridhan* as a *sapinda* relation on the father's side.[1]

Order of succession to woman's property other than *stridhan* proper.

With regard to the *aparibhasika stridhan*, that is, property acquired by a woman by the act of partition and the like, the order of succession, according to Nilkantha, is the same as that for a separated male's property, the successive heirs being her son, son's son, &c.[2]

Wealth given by kindred.

In respect of property given by the kindred (*bandhu*) at an *Asura* marriage or the like, Nilkantha cites[3] a text of Katyayana, which runs thus:—"That which was given to her by her kindred, goes on failure of kindred to her son."

Sulka.

The Mayukha[4] like the Mitakshara, declares, upon the authority of Gautama's text, that the sister's perquisite (*sulka*) belongs to the uterine brothers after the death of the mother.

Succession to the property of a maiden.

Touching the devolution of the property of a maiden, the Mayukha cites[5] the same text of Baudhayana that is quoted in the Mitakshara, and follows the same rule that is laid down by Vijnaneswara.

Devolution of *stridhan* according to the Dravida school.

I now proceed to consider the devolution of *stridhan* according to the Dravida school. Here, among the other authorities commonly followed besides the Mitakshara, the most important are the Parasara Madhavya and the Smriti Chandrika.[6] But the question as to the comparative weight of the authority of these works has not been judicially determined.

---

[1] See 1 W. and B., 254.

[2] Vyavahara Mayukha, Ch. IV, Sec. X, 26; see also 1 W. and B., 215; Vijiarangam *v.* Lakshuman, 8 Bom., O. C. J., 260.

[3] Vyavahara Mayukha, Ch. IV, Sec. X, 31.

[4] Ch. IV, Sec. X, 32.

[5] Ch. IV, Sec. X, 34.

[6] But see the remarks of Nelson in his View of the Hindu Law, &c., pp. 111—114.

LECTURE X.

The Parasara Madhavya.

On the subject of succession to *stridhan*, the Madhaviya commentary generally follows the Mitakshara, differing from it only in the enumeration of heirs after the husband and the parents.[1]

Smriti Chandrika.

The Smriti Chandrika is a much fuller treatise, and differs from the Mitakshara oftener than the Parasara Madhavya does. The order of succession to *stridhan*, as laid down in the Smriti Chandrika, does not differ much from that given in the Viramitrodaya and the Vyavahara Mayukha.

Succession of children.

Devandabhatta, like Mitramisra and Nilkantha, divides *stridhan* into the following classes, with reference to the relative rights of sons and daughters to inherit it:[2]—

I.—The gift subsequent *(anwadheya)*, and the affectionate gift by the husband *(pritidatta)*.

II.—The *yautuka*.

III.—All other kinds of *stridhan*.

But as he holds that the term *stridhan* is used in a technical and not in an unlimited literal sense, he does not recognize the fourth class of *stridhan* according to Nilkantha (the *aparibhasika stridhan*, or woman's property other than her *stridhan* proper).

This classification is made with a view to reconcile certain apparently discrepant Rishi texts. While Yajnavalkya[3] and Gautama[4] declare that the daughters inherit their mothers' property, and the Mitakshara (which is based upon Yajnavalkya), deduces from these texts the general rule that the daughters in the first instance inherit

---

[1] Dayavibhaga (Burnell's translation), p. 43—46.

[2] See Smriti Chandrika, Ch. IX, Sec. III, 6, 12, 16.

[3] II, 117, cited in the Mitakshara, Ch. II, Sec. XI, 12.

[4] XXVIII, 21, cited in the Mitakshara, Ch. II, Sec. XI, 13.

LECTURE X. all their mother's *stridhan*, Manu[1] lays down the rule that all the uterine brothers and all the uterine sisters equally divide their maternal estate. This text of Manu has been a source of some embarrassment to Vijnaneswara, who tries to explain it as meaning that the sons as a class divide the mother's estate equally, and so do the daughters, each class taking the estate in its turn.[2] But this explanation has been rejected by all subsequent commentators of repute, such as Jimutavahana, Devandabhatta, Nilkantha, and Mitramisra. And indeed Vijnaneswara's view seems irreconcilable with the following text of Brihaspati cited in the Smriti Chandrika :[3]—

"A woman's property goes to her children [male], and the daughter also is a sharer with them, provided she be unaffianced; but, if married, she receives a mere token of respect."

It is, therefore, inferred by the authors of the Smriti Chandrika, the Mayukha, and the Viramitrodaya, that the said texts of Yajnavalkya, Gautama, Manu, and Brihaspati do not indiscriminately relate to all kinds of *stridhan* alike, but that each text relates only to some particular kinds of it. And this inference is supported by Manu himself, who declares—

"What she received after marriage from the family of her husband, and what her affectionate lord may have given her, shall be inherited, even if she die in his lifetime, by her children." (IX, 195.)

"Property given to the mother on her marriage is inherited by her unmarried daughter; and the son of a daughter, appointed in the manner just mentioned, shall

---

[1] IX, 192. [2] Mitakshara, Ch. II, Sec. XI, 20, 21. [3] Ch. IX, Sec. III, 7.

inherit the whole estate of her father, who leaves no son by himself begotten." (IX, 131.) LECTURE X.

From these texts the rule is deduced, that the joint succession of sons and daughters relates to the *anwadheya stridhan* and the affectionate gifts of the husband; that the exclusive right of maiden daughters relates to the mother's *yautuka;* and that to other kinds of *stridhan,* the daughters succeed to the exclusion of sons, according to the texts of Yajnavalkya and Gautama. It is only by this limited interpretation that the texts of the two last named sages can be reconciled with those of the other sages quoted above; and this, accordingly, is the interpretation adopted in the Smriti Chandrika.[1]

To the *anwadheya* and the husband's gift, the widowed daughter is not, according to Devandabhatta, entitled to succeed. This rule is deduced from the text of Katyayana:— "Sisters having husbands shall share with kinsmen."[2]

Touching the rights of children, the Smriti Chandrika[3] lays down the important doctrine that "survival is the only circumstance recognized by law as creating a right to inherit the property of a deceased woman;" so that, unlike the case of the paternal estate, to which sons become entitled by birth, and of which they can enforce partition in some cases even during the father's lifetime, the maternal estate can become subject to the rights of the sons only on the mother's demise.

In the case of the *yautuka stridhan,* sons succeed on failure of maiden daughters.[4]

The text of Gautama,[5]—" A woman's property goes to her

---

[1] Ch. IX, Sec. III, 1—16. [2] Smriti Chandrika, Ch. IX, Sec. III, 9.
[3] Ch. IX, Sec. III, 5.
[4] Smriti Chandrika, Ch. IX, Sec. III, 26. [5] XXVIII, 21.

LECTURE X. daughters unmarried and unprovided," has a construction put upon it, which is different from that adopted in the Mitakshara. Upon this text Devandabhatta says:[1] "The meaning is, that such kinds of *stridhan* as are denominated '*adhyagni*' and the like belong to daughters unmarried, and married but unprovided. The wealth is to be divided among such daughters alone. The term 'unprovided,' used in the above text of Gautama, is to be interpreted according to Apararka as implying an issueless, unendowed (that is, destitute of wealth), unfortunate *(durbhaga)*, or a widowed daughter. The construction which Vijnaneswara has put upon the passage is to be rejected as founded on assumptions unwarranted." So that *stridhan* coming under class III is taken by maiden daughters jointly with unprovided married daughters. In other respects, succession to this class of *stridhan* under the Smriti Chandrika follows the rules of Vijnaneswara, and the successive heirs after daughters are daughter's daughters, daughter's sons, sons, and son's sons.[2]

Grandchildren, whether son's sons or daughter's issue, take *per stirpes* and not *per capita.*[3]

In the case of the *anwadheya* and the husband's gift *(pritidatta stridhan)*, sons, and daughters who are not widows, succeed simultaneously; and it would, therefore, follow that in the absence of either class of children the other would inherit the whole estate. But where there is failure of both sons and daughters, the question arises, who are the next heirs? Should the children of sons and daughters inherit simultaneously in the same way as the

---

[1] Smriti Chandrika, Ch. IX, Sec. III, 17.

[2] *Ibid*, 20—24. [3] *Ibid*, 25.

sons and daughters of the deceased do, or should the children of either alone succeed? and in either case, should the grandsons succeed jointly with or to the exclusion of grand-daughters? Nothing is said in the Smriti Chandrika in answer to these questions. The law of the Bengal school, which allows the joint succession of sons and maiden daughters over all kinds of *stridhan* except the *yautuka* and the father's gifts, makes the son's son succeed in default of children of the deceased, and admits the daughter's sons only in default of the son's sons.[1] But as the Dayabbaga is not accepted as authority in the Dravida school when it is in conflict with the Mitakshara, and as in the absence of any express provision to the contrary in the Parasara Madhavya and the Smriti Chandrika, works peculiar to that school, the commentary of Vijnaneswara is generally followed, it may, I think, be fairly contended that, in default of children of the deceased, her daughter's daughters, her daughter's sons, and her son's sons would be the successive heirs to her *anwadheya* and husband's gift (*pritidatta stridhan*).

The question, who should succeed to the *yautuka* in default of sons, is left equally unsettled in the Smriti Chandrika.

So much for the succession of children and grandchildren.

Succession to the *stridhan* of a childless woman.

The order of succession to the property of a woman who leaves no progeny, that is, neither children nor grandchildren, is here, as in the other schools, regulated by the form of her marriage; and it is deduced in the Smriti Chandrika from the following texts of Manu, Yajnavalkya, Yama, and Katyayana.

---

[1] See Dayabhaga, Ch. IV, Sec. II, 11.

LECTURE X. Manu:—"It is ordained that the property of a woman married by the ceremonies called *Brahma, Daiva, Arsha, Gandharba* or *Prajapatya,* shall go to her husband, if she die without issue." (IX, 196.)

Yajnavalkha:—"The property of a childless woman married in the form denominated *Brahma,* or even in any of the four unblamed modes of marriage, goes to her hnsband." (II, 145.)

Yama:[1]—"Wealth which is given at the marriage called '*Asura*' or the like, is to be taken by the father alone, where the woman dies without issue."

Katyayana:[2]—"What was given by kinsmen goes, in default of the kinsmen, to her husband."

"What is received from parents by a woman married in the form called '*Asura*' and the like, goes, in default of her isssue, to her mother and father."

From these texts the rule is deduced that the property of a childless woman goes to her husband if she had been married in one of the first five forms; in other cases, it reverts to her father or other kinsmen from whom she had received it; and it is only in default of such kinsmen that the husband inherits in such cases.[3]

The *sulka*. But the *sulka,* or wealth received as "the price of household utensils, of beasts of burthen, of milch cattle, or ornaments of dress or for works,"[4] is declared,[5] on the basis of the text of Gautama,[6] to devolve first on the uterine brothers, and, on their default, on the mother.

The sister's son, the husband's sister's son, the husband's brother's son, the brother's son, the son-in-law, and the

---

[1] Cited in the Smriti Chandrika, Ch. IX, Sec. III, 31.

[2] See Smriti Chandrika, Ch. IX, Sec. III, 30.

[3] *Ibid*, Sec. III, 29—32. [4] *Ibid*, Sec. I, 5. [5] *Ibid*, Sec. III, 32.

[6] XXVIII, 23.

husband's younger brother, are declared to be successive heirs in the order in which they are enumerated, upon the authority of the following text of Brihaspati:[1]—

"The sister of a mother, the wife of a maternal or of a paternal uncle, the sister of a father, the mother of a wife, and the wife of an elder brother are declared equal to a mother. If they leave no male issue of their body, nor the son of a daughter, nor a daughter, the sister's son and the rest shall inherit their property."

But the exact position of this group of heirs is not given in the Smriti Chandrika. If Brihaspati's text is followed without qualification, this group would come after children and grandchildren, and before the husband and the parents. This, however, would conflict with the rule laid down in the texts of Manu, Yajnavalkya, and other sages quoted above. The Mayukha[2] expressly places this group after the husband or the parents according to the form of the woman's marriage. And the same may be taken to be the position of the group according to the intention of Devandabhatta; for he mentions this group after stating that the husband or the paternal kinsmen succeed to the *stridhan* of a childless woman, according as her marriage was in an approved or in a disapproved form.

The issue of a rival wife are declared competent to inherit, if the deceased leaves "no progeny, husband, or the like."[3] But their exact position in the order of succession is not given in the Smriti Chandrika, though from the context it would seem that by the words '*the like,*' the author means the heirs referred to in the text of Brihaspati. Nor is there anything to shew in what order the issue of a

---

[1] See Smriti Chandrika, Ch. IX, Sec III, 36, 37.

[2] Ch. IV, Sec. X, 30.

[3] Smriti Chandrika, Ch. IX, Sec. III, 38.

LECTURE X. rival wife inherit. But in the absence of any express provision, I think it may be taken, according to the general spirit of the Hindu law on the subject,[1] that the daughters come first and then the sons.

The law relating to the rights of the issue of rival wives of different classes or castes I need not consider, as by the prohibition of marriage in a different caste in the present age, that law is become mere matter of speculative curiosity.

The enumeration of heirs in the Smriti Chandrika stops at this point, and neither the husband's *sapindas* nor those of the father are even referred to. In the absence of any provision to the contrary in the Parasara Madhavya and the Smriti Chandrika, the remarks I have made regarding the succession of distant heirs according to the Mayukha (with which the Chandrika agrees in so many respects) may be taken as applicable to the school of law we are now considering.

It is only in one respect that those remarks are inapplicable to the Dravida school, namely, that the widows of the *sapindas* are not recognized here as heirs. In the case of *Bandam Settah* v. *Bandam Maha Lakshmy*,[2] the High Court of Madras held that a daughter-in-law could not be the heiress of her mother-in-law.

The mode of devolution of a maiden's property according to the Chandrika[3] is the same as that according to the Mitakshara.

Succession to the property of dancing-women.

In connection with the law of succession to *stridhan* according to the Dravida school, I ought to consider the law of succession to the property of that unfortunate class

---

[1] See Mitakshara, Ch. II, Sec. XI, 22; and Smriti Chandrika, Ch. IX, Sec. III, 39. [2] 4 Mad., 180. [3] Ch. IX, Sec. III, 34, 35.

of females, the dancing-girls attached to the numerous pagodas in the South. LECTURE X.

You must not imagine that the Hindu law which visits unchastity in a woman with the direst penalties, and which declares the disloyal wife to be unworthy of *stridhan*,[1] could have ever cared to lay down any order of succession to the property of such women. The Anglo-Indian Courts being now and then called upon to decide contested questions of inheritance to such property, have been obliged to lay down some rules; and these constitute the whole law on the subject.

The earliest reported case on the point is that of *Taramunnee Dassee* v. *Motee Buneanee*,[2] a Bengal case. In that case a woman, who had lapsed into prostitution, having died leaving two prostitute daughters born after her degradation, and another daughter born in lawful wedlock, the last-named daughter, as guardian on behalf of her minor sons, sued the other daughters to recover her maternal estate. The Sudder Court put the following question to the Pandit :—

"If a Hindu woman, who is an outcast in consequence of living by prostitution, die, and leave three daughters, one a married woman, and mother of several children, and respectable; the other two, prostitutes, who lived with the outcast mother, and had all things in common with her: which will inherit the mother's property?" The Pandit replied :—"The two prostitute daughters alone inherit whatever the mother may have left; because the relation of the married and respectable daughter to the outcast mother

---

[1] See Viramitrodaya, 2 W. and B., 76; Smriti Chandrika, Ch. IX, Sec. II, 24.

[2] 7 Sel. Rep., 273.

LECTURE X. has been severed." Upon receipt of this reply, the Court affirmed the judgment of the Principal Sudder Ameen who had dismissed the plaintiff's claim. The opinion given by the Pandit in this case was recognized as correct by the High Court of Madras in *Myna Bai* v. *Uttaram*, in which the Court observed:[1]— "The Doctrine of Mr. Justice Strange in section 363 of his Manual is fully borne out by a dictum in the case quoted.[2] It was a suit by the daughter, born in wedlock of a mother, who afterwards lapsed into prostitution, to recover from the daughters born in prostitution the property of the mother. The Court held the plaintiff's title not made out, because the conduct of the mother had entirely severed her from her natural family, so that the plaintiff, the daughter born in wedlock, could not succeed to her. There is also the dictum that the prostitute daughters are entitled to succeed, but the plaintiff's case failing this was not actually necessary to the decision. In Madras too it has never been doubted that the children of the prostitute succeed to the property of their mother. We have been unable to find the least authority either in the books or in practice, for an opinion of Mr. Justice Strange, that the children must be adopted children. The decisions upon the question are not numerous, as indeed they seldom are, upon points so well established as to leave to the reckless litigants of this country no hope of benefit from contesting them. The newspaper report of a case in the High Court of Bombay contains the opinion of the Judges, in a case which did not call for it, that the Courts in future ought not to under-

---

[1] 2 Mad., 202.

[2] Taramunnee Dassea *v.* Motee Buneanee, 7 Sel. Rep., 273.

take the settlement of questions of inheritance between persons of the prostitute class and their offspring, whether natural or adopted. The Court, however, admitted that their own precedents were in favor of doing so. The case was there one of an adopted daughter, and of course there would be much reason for contending that there was an intention to bring up the child, when so adopted, to prostitution. Even, therefore, if the case could be considered an authority, it would be none upon the present question.

"Our reasoning, therefore, is, that there is no authority against the existence of heritable blood between the woman and her illegitimate offspring."

In the case of *Kamakshi* v. *Nagarathnam*,[1] the question was raised whether on the death of one of two sisters, to whom the office of dancing-girl to a pagoda had passed by right of succession from their mother, the share of the deceased sister devolved on her daughter (the plaintiff) or the office with its emoluments passed in their entirety to the surviving sister (the first defendant). The Court in its judgment said:—

"There is no doubt that in Madras the issue of a dancing-woman are her legal heirs, and the Hindu law of inheritance appears not to warrant any distinction between the descent of her property and the descent of paternal property, except that daughters are placed before sons in the order of succession as in the case of the succession to *stridhanum*, and this without any qualification. Now as the property in dispute was not *stridhanum* of the plaintiff's mother and her sister, the 1st defendant (and for this position the recent decision of this Court in *Sengamathammal* v. *Valayuda*

---

[1] 5 Mad., 161.

LECTURE X. *Mudali*, 3 Madras H. C. Reports, 312, is a direct authority), the general rule must, we think, be considered to be that the children of dancing-women take by descent the estate of coparceners in their mother's property; their daughters as a class first, and on failure of daughters their sons as a class. There would not be a doubt about this being the nature of the estate in the case of sons succeeding, and in reason and principle we can see nothing on which to found any distinction as to the estate of inheritance which daughters take. The ordinary law of inheritance must, it appears to us, govern in both cases alike.

" The objection on the part of the appellant that the 1st defendant and her sister took a joint estate with rights of survivorship, was sought to be supported by an argument of analogy drawn from the rules of inheritance in the cases of several widows being heirs and of the succession of several daughters to the *stridhanum* of their mother. We are not prepared to lay down that in the latter case the right of survivorship to the exclusion of the children of a deceased sister exists, but assuming that it does, the argument appears to us to be of no force. There is obviously no analogy between the present case and that of widows inheriting the estate of their husband; and as to the law of succession to *stridhanum* we think it a sufficient answer that it is a peculiar law, and its positive restriction to maternal property acquired in a particular manner precludes its being extended by analogy to a widely different kind of maternal property, the descent of which may be regulated by the ordinary law of inheritance."

From these cases it would appear that the rights of children of dancing-women to inherit their maternal property has been recognized by our Courts. The law on the subject has been summed up by Strange in his Manual of Hindu Law,[1] thus:—

I.—"The property of a dancing-girl will pass to her female issue first, and then to her male, as in the case of other females."

II.—"On failure of issue, the property of a dancing-girl will go to the pagoda to which she is attached."

III.—"With prostitutes, the tie of kindred being broken, none of their relatives who remain undegraded in caste, whether offspring or other, inherit from them." "Their issue after their degradation succeed."

In Cunningham's Digest of Hindu Law[2] the broad rule is laid down that "the succession to dancing-women is the ordinary succession of Hindu heirs to family property, except that daughters are placed before sons in the order of succession." It is true that this is opposed to the second of the above rules quoted from Strange, which is based upon the opinion of the Sudder Pandits; but it is supported by the ruling of the Madras High Court in the case of *Kamakshi* v. *Nagarathnam* just referred to. Moreover, the correctness of the rule laid down by Strange seems open to question. There is nothing in the Hindu law in its support, the only escheat which that law allows, being one in favor of the Crown; and the rule can therefore be maintained only on the ground of its being based upon usage.

Succession to *stridhan* according to the Mithila school.

The consideration of the law of succession to *stridhan* according to the Mithila school need not detain us long. The Vivada Chintamani, one of the leading authorities in that school, lays down a very simple order of succession to woman's property; not indeed simpler than that given in

---

[1] P. 89, Sec. 361, 363. [2] P. 112.

LECTURE X. the Mitakshara, but certainly more simple than the order given in the Mayukha or the Chandrika.

Succession of descendants.

The text of Manu,[1]—"On the death of the mother, let all the uterine brothers and (if unmarried) the uterine sisters divide the maternal estate, &c., in equal shares,"—and that of Brihaspati,[2]—"A woman's property goes to her children, and the daughter is a sharer with them, provided she be unaffianced; but, if she be married, she shall not receive the maternal wealth,"—which allow the joint succession of sons and daughters, and which, according to the Mayukha and the Chandrika, are limited in their application to the *anwadheya* and the *pritidatta stridhan*, are held by Vachaspati Misra[3] to be applicable to *stridhan* of every description except the nuptial gifts, furniture, and the like; and it is to these last that the texts of Manu,[4] Yajnavalkya,[5] and Gautama,[6] declaring the exclusive succession of daughters, are said to refer.

In the former case, that is the case of joint succession, the word 'sisters' in Manu's text is explained by the light of that of Brihaspati's text to mean only the unmarried daughters; and married daughters are declared entitled to something only, so that their feelings may not be wounded.[7]

Other heirs.

In default of descendants down to the daughter's sons, the property of a woman, if married in one of the five approved forms of marriage, namely, the *Brahma*, *Daiva*, *Arsha*, *Prajapatya* and *Gandharba*, goes to her husband; and if married in any of the other forms, it goes to her

---

[1] IX, 192.

[2] See Smriti Chandrika, Ch. IX, Sec. III, 7; Vyavahara Mayukha, Ch. IV, Sec. X, 15, where the text is quoted as a text of Manu.

[3] Tagore's translation of the Vivada Chintamani, pp. 266—269.

[4] IX, 131.

[5] II, 117.

[6] XXVIII, 21.

[7] Vivada Chintamani, Tagore's translation, p. 267.

mother, and then to her father.[1] This rule is deduced from the text of Manu.[2] LECTURE X.

Here the enumeration of heirs in the Vivada Chintamani stops. But the Madana Parijata[3] mentions the co-wife's daughter and her daughter's son, and the Vivada Ratnakara[4] mentions the group of heirs given in Brihaspati's text, namely, the sister's son, the husband's sister's son, &c., as entitled to inherit. As the Vivada Ratnakara is a high authority in the Mithila school, the heirs after the husband or the parents would be those mentioned by Brihaspati. After them the order of succession would, I presume, be the same as that according to the Dravida school.

Woman's fee.

A woman's fee, that is property received by her at the time of marriage if it was celebrated in any of the three disapproved forms, is declared to belong to her uterine brothers, her mother, and her father in succession.[5]

Succession to a maiden's property.

The order of succession to a maiden's property, according to the Mithila school, is the same as that according to the Mitakshara, being in fact based upon the same text of Baudhayana:[6]—

"The wealth of a deceased damsel, let the uterine brothers themselves take; on failure of them, it shall belong to the mother, or, if she be dead, to the father."

Kritrima son.

A son adopted by a woman in the *kritrima* form is, under the Mithila law, entitled to inherit her *stridhan*.[7]

---

[1] Tagore's translation, 269. [2] IX, 196, 197.

[3] Tagore's translation of the Vivada Chintamani, Table of Succession to the peculiar property of women, para. v. [4] *Ibid*, para, vi.

[5] Vivada Chintamani, Tagore's translation, p. 270. [6] *Ibid.*

[7] See Macnagten's Principles of Hindu Law, 76; 2 Strange, 204; Sreenarain Rai *v.* Bhya Jha, 2 Sel. Rep., 34; The Collector of Tirhoot *v.* Huro Pershad, 7 W. R., 500; Mussamut Shibo *v.* Joogun Singh, 8 W. R., 155.

LECTURE XI.

SUCCESSION TO STRIDHAN ACCORDING TO THE BENGAL SCHOOL.

Succession to *stridhan* according to the Bengal school—Succession of children and their descendants—*Ayautuka stridhan*—Sons and daughters—Barren and widowed daughters—*Yautuka stridhan*—Property given by the father—Adopted son—Daughter's adopted son—Grandsons, whether by sons or daughters, take *per stirpes*—Succession of the group of heirs consisting of the husband, the brother, and the parents—Heirs after the husband, the brother, and the parents—The group of heirs according to Brihaspati's text—The *sapindas*, *sakulyas*, and *samonadakas*—Paternal kinsmen—The Crown—Heirs to immoveable property given by the husband—Heirs to the property of a maiden.

Succession to *sridhan* according to the Bengal school.

It remains now to consider the law of succession to *stridhan* according to the Bengal school. That law differs from the law of the other schools in many respects; and its expounders refer to the doctrine of spiritual benefit much more frequently than the commentators whose works we have hitherto considered.

Happily the leading authorities of the Bengal school, the Dayabhaga of Jimutavahana, the Dayatattwa of Raghunandana, the Dayakrama Sangraha of Srikrishna, and the Vivadavangarnava of Jagannatha, are almost entirely at one on the subject under discussion; and I shall not, therefore, have to consider separately the opinions of these writers.

You must have noticed already, that the order of succession to *stridhan* is according to no school the same in all cases. It varies with the nature of the *stridhan*, and also with the form of the marriage of the deceased proprietress. Thus, according to the Mitakshara, the orders of succession vary according as the marriage of the late proprietress took place in an approved or a disapproved form; and, also, according as the property is her *sulka* or is one of the other descriptions of *stridhan*. This treatise gives the law on the subject in its simplest form, there being a uniform order of succession for children applicable to every kind of *stridhan*. The Smriti Chandrika, however, with reference to the relative rights of sons and daughters, divides *stridhan* into three classes, the *yautuka*, the *anwadheya*, and the *pritidatta*, and all other kinds besides these; while the Mayukha adds a fourth class, the *aparibhasika stridhan*, or woman's property of every description other than what is technically called *stridhan*. In the Vivada Chintamani, the classification is a very simple one, there being only two classes, the *yautuka*, and *stridhan* other than the *yautuka*.

Succession of children and their descendants.

The Bengal lawyers divide *stridhan* into the following three classes with reference to the relative rights of sons and daughters :—

I.—The *yautuka*.

II.—Property given by the father.

III.—All other descriptions of *stridhan*.

Ayautuka stridhan.

With reference to class III, which is the main class, Jimutavahana cites the following texts :[1]—

Manu :—"When the mother is dead, let all the uterine brothers and the uterine sisters equally divide the maternal estate." (IX, 192.)

This text, as I have already said, is explained in the Dayabhaga as declaring the joint succession of sons and daughters.

---

[1] Dayabhaga, Ch. IV, Sec. II, 1—6.

LECTURE XI.

Brihaspati:—"A woman's property goes to her children; and the daughter is a sharer with them, provided she be unaffianced; but, if married, she shall not receive the maternal wealth."

Devala:—"A woman's property is common to her sons and unmarried daughters, when she is dead; but, if she leave no issue, her husband shall take it, her mother, her brother, or her father."

Sons and daughters.

And from these texts the rule is deduced[1] that "the son and maiden daughter have a like right to succession. On failure of either of them, the goods belong to the other. On failure of both of them, the succession devolves, with equal rights, on the married daughter who has a son, and on her who may have male issue. For, by means of their sons, they may present oblations at solemn obsequies."

Here 'maiden daughter' means one not only unmarried but also unbetrothed; and it has been held by the High Court of Bengal in the case of *Sreenath Gangooly* v. *Surbomongola Debia*,[2] that a betrothed daughter has no right to inherit the mother's *stridhan* jointly with a son. The Court in their judgment in that case said:—"The question then arises whether under the Hindoo law the plaintiff, as a betrothed daughter, was entitled to a share in this property with her brothers. On turning to the Dayabhaga, Chapter IV, Section 2, on the succession of a woman's children to her separate property in the third *sloke*, the law is thus laid down—'A woman's property goes to her children, and the daughter is a sharer with them, provided she be unaffianced; but if married she shall not receive the maternal wealth.' In the next paragraph, the commentator interprets the meaning of the above sentence by saying,—

[1] Dayabhaga, Ch. IV, Sec. II, 9.

[2] 10 W. R., 488.

'Here the word 'children' intends sons, and they share their mother's goods with unbetrothed daughters.'

"The Principal Sudder Ameen has decided that the betrothed or unbetrothed daughter inherits her mother's property with sons. We think that the quotations which we have above made from the Dayabhaga distinctly show that, under the Hindu law, the unbetrothed daughter alone inherits with sons. Taking, therefore, the evidence as showing that the plaintiff was a betrothed daughter, we are of opinion that she is not entitled to inherit.

"In paragraph 4 and paragraph 6 of the same Section, the law is laid down on this point by other commentators, but it is not equally distinct. The words are, that 'the brothers are entitled to succeed with unmarried daughters.' It may be a question whether 'unmarried' is used as distinguished from 'unbetrothed.' The sanskrit word which is used on both these occasions is the word '*Coomaree*' which is the word used generally for an unbetrothed daughter; and that the word 'unmarried' does here mean 'unbetrothed' is clear from what precedes it, which we have already quoted."

Jagannatha, however, seems to be of a different opinion; and he notices an adverse argument thus:[1]—"But as a son, who would be debarred by the existence of his own father, has an equal claim to the patrimony with his paternal uncle, who had an equal right with his father, so likewise, in the present instance a betrothed daughter, who would have been debarred by a daughter not betrothed, has an equal title with a son who had an equal title with the daughter who was not betrothed."

---

[1] Colebrooke's Digest, Bk. V, 490, commentary.

LECTURE XI. After giving the rule stated above, the author of the Dayabhaga continues:[1]—"Hence the daughter's son is entitled to the property on failure of the daughters above described: for the text of Manu[2] expresses, 'Even the son of a daughter delivers him in the next world like the son of a son.' Neither a barren nor a widowed daughter inherits; for these present not oblations at solemn obsequies, either in person or by means of their offspring."

"But," adds he,[3] "if there be a son's son and a daughter's son claiming the succession, the son's son has the exclusive title; for, it is reasonable, since the married daughter is debarred from the inheritance by the son, that the son of the debarred daughter shall be excluded by the son of the person who bars her claim."

Barren and widowed daughters.

After the daughter's son, Jimutavahana admits the barren and the widowed daughters, though they are unfit to confer spiritual benefit, on the ground that "they also are her offspring," and that "the right of others to inherit is declared to be on failure of issue,"[4]—that is, in other words, on the ground of natural love and affection.

Thus Jimutavahana so far allows the doctrine of spiritual benefit to be subordinated to other considerations. But his followers, Raghunandana and Srikrishna, who are more rigid and systematic in following out that doctrine, interpose other heirs between the daughter's sons and the barren and widowed daughters, on the ground of their competency to confer spiritual benefit. Both these commentators place the son's grandson in the male line immediately after the daughter's son; and Srikrishna adds a further group of heirs, namely, the son, grandson, and

---

[1] Ch. IV, Sec. II, 10. [2] IX, 139. [3] Ch. IV, Sec. II, 11. [4] *Ibid*, 12.

great grandson (in the male line) of a rival wife, after the great grandson of the deceased, and before her barren and widowed daughters.[1] There is, therefore, a clear conflict of authority on this point, and the ordinary explanation that the enumeration of heirs in the Dayabhaga is not meant to be exhaustive, will be of little avail here, as the barren and widowed daughters are placed immediately after the daughter's sons in plain and unambiguous language.[2] In this conflict of authority, the order according to Srikrishna is the one that has been generally accepted.[3] But it may be urged that Jimutavahana's rule is more authoritative, and, in the present instance, also more equitable than that of his followers.

Yautuka stridhan.

With regard to class I, or *yautuka stridhan*, Jimutavahana cites the following text of Manu:—"Property given to the mother on her marriage (*yautuka*) is the share of her unmarried daughters." (IX, 131.)

The term *yautuka* is thus explained.[4] "Here *yautuka* signifies property given at a marriage: the word *yuta*, derived from the verb *yu*, to mix, imports 'mingling;' and mingling is the union of man and woman as one person, and that is accomplished by marriage. For a passage of scripture expresses,—'Her bones become identified with his bones, flesh with flesh, skin with skin.' Therefore what has been received at the time of the marriage is denominated *yautuka*.

---

[1] See Dayatattwa, Golap Chandra Sarkar's translation, Ch. X, 8; Srikrishna's commentary on the Dayabhaga, Ch. IV, Sec. III; Dayakrama Sangraha, Ch. II, Sec. IV, 9. [2] Dayabhaga, Ch. IV, Sec. II, 12.

[3] See Macnagten's Principles of Hindu Law, 39, 40; Shama Churn's Vyavastha Darpana, 716—719; see also 1 Strange, 251.

[4] Dayabhaga, Ch. IV, Sec. II, 14, 15. The word may be read as *yautuka* or *yautaka*, see the Viramitrodaya, 2 W. and B., 82.

LECTURE XI.

"Accordingly (since the term signifies wealth received at the time of the marriage), Vasistha says,—'Let the females share the nuptial presents (*parinayya*) of their mother.' For *parinayya* signifies wealth received at a marriage (*parinayana*)."

Touching the meaning of the term *yautuka*, the following observations of Mr. Justice Ainslie, in his judgment in *Bistoo Pershad Burral* v. *Radha Soonder Nath*[1] may, I think, be usefully consulted. Speaking of certain items of property in dispute in that case, the learned Judge observed:—"The Munsif has found distinctly that these articles were given *before* the bride was taken from her father's house. He seems indeed to treat these as gifts in the bridal procession, but the Judge, who has adopted the facts as found by the Munsif, has more correctly described them as gifts to the bride at her marriage, which was not concluded at the time of presentation, as the *basee bibaho* is, we understand, a part of the marriage ceremonies among persons of the class of the parties to this suit. It has been contended that the gifts which rank as '*yautuka*' are those given before the nuptial fire only, that is, while the fire is maintained; but in the Dayakrama Sangraha, page 34, it is said, the expression, 'before the nuptial fire' occurring in the text (of Katyayana) before cited, and that 'at the time of the nuptials' in the text of Vyasa, are both illustrative. The text of Katayayana is—'What is given to women *at the time of their marriage* near the nuptial fire, is celebrated by the wise as the women's peculiar property bestowed before the nuptial fire.' So that the restriction contended for cannot be maintained. 'Given before the nuptial fire' is

[1] 16 W. R., 115.

only a term to signify all gifts during the continuance of the marriage ceremonies." LECTURE XI.

This view is in accordance with the opinion of Raghunandana, who says in the Dayatattwa (Golap Chandra Sastri's translation, Ch. X, 15):—"The time of marriage means time previous and posterior to the actual time of marriage. This is described in the treatise on marriage to begin from the *sraddha* for prosperity, and to end with the ceremony of prostrating before the husband."

From the foregoing text of Manu (IX, 131), it is inferred that the texts of Gautama[1] and Yajnavalkya,[2] from which the Mitakshara deduces the exclusive succession of daughters to their mother's *stridhan*, relate only to the *yautuka*, or property received by a woman at the time of her marriage.[3]

The relative rights of different classes of daughters are here, as in the other schools, based upon the text of Gautama referred to above; but the construction put upon that text by Jimutavahana and his followers[4] is altogether different from that according to the lawyers of the other schools. The text in accordance with Jimutavahana's interpretation has been thus rendered by Colebrooke:[5]—"A woman's separate property goes to her daughters unaffianced, and to those not actually married,"—the word '*apratta*' being taken in the sense of 'unaffianced,' and the word '*apratisthita*' in the sense of 'not actually married.' The order in which daughters succeed to the *yautuka*, therefore, stands thus:[6]—First, unaffianced daughters;

---

[1] XXVIII, 21. [2] II, 117. [3] Dayabhaga, Ch. IV, Sec. II, 13.

[4] See Dayabhaga, Ch. IV, Sec. II, 23; Dayatattwa, Ch. X, 13; Dayakrama Sangraha, Ch. II, Sec. III, 4, 5.

[5] Dayabhaga, Ch. IV, Sec. II, 13. The text in the original runs thus:
स्त्रीधनंदुहितॄणामप्रत्तानामप्रतिष्ठितानां च ।

[6] *Ibid*, 23.

LECTURE XI. then, affianced daughters; next, married daughters. "For," says Jimutavahana,[1] "the right of the female issue generally is suggested by the term 'daughters' (in Gautama's text), and the special mention of 'unaffianced' and 'unmarried' which follows, is pertinent as declaratory of the order of succession (and not as a limitation of the preceding general term)."

Among married daughters again, Srikrishna makes a distinction, giving precedence to the daughters who have, or are likely to have, male issue, and allowing barren and widowed daughters to inherit equally in their default.[2]

Touching the rights of barren and widowed daughters generally, Jagannatha[3] makes the following remarks, which, though not very lucid in themselves, may serve to illustrate the nature of the reasoning employed by the Bengal lawyers in treating of this subject:—"But others hold, that these female heirs succeed merely as daughters; they were before debarred by persons who confer benefits on the female ancestors, but have now gained the opportunity of asserting their claim. Is not this inaccurate, since the son of a daughter confers no benefit on his maternal grandmother? If it be said, benefiting her husband and the rest, he immediately confers benefits on her; it is answered, a married daughter would not in that case succeed in preference to the son's son. To the question thus proposed the answer is, since a married daughter may confer benefits on the husband of her mother by means of her son, she, who thus affords some advantage,

---

[1] Dayabhaga, Ch. IV, Sec. II, 23.

[2] See Summary of the Order of Succession by Srikrishna in his note to the Dayabhaga, Ch. IV, Sec. III, and also the Dayakrama Sangraha, Ch. II, Sec. III, 5, 7.

[3] Colebrooke's Digest, Bk. V, 498, commentary, Vol. II, pp. 611, 612 (Mad. ed.)

being at the same time 'daughter' and 'issue of the body' of her mother, cannot be debarred by those who confer greater benefits; for the advantages afforded are not principally considered in treating of separate property held by women. But barren and widowed daughters, conferring not the least benefit, ought to inherit after the great-grandson in the male line, but before the husband, because they are daughters, and sprang from the body of their mother. Then, should not these two inherit before the grandsons of a son, whether in the male or female line of descent from him? It may be answered, what should prevent their succession to this property any more than to the estate of one who leaves no male issue? LECTURE XI.

"But others again affirm, since there is no proof that the funeral cake offered at the double set of oblations shall be chiefly considered in the succession to separate property held by women, therefore the barren and the widowed daughters who offer the anniversary cake may inherit before a daughter's son."

And in another place[1] he says,—"The succession of a daughter to the separate property of her mother is expressly ordained by law, not deduced from reasoning. Were it inferred from argument, she would have no right if a son existed."

The last sentence in the former of the above two quotations may require a word of explanation. 'The double set of oblations' means the *parvana sraddha*, at which two sets of oblations are offered, one to the paternal, and one to the maternal, ancestors; while the anniversary *sraddha* is the *ekoddishta sraddha*, or *sraddha* in honor of a single ancestor. The same passage shows that, in the opinion of some

[1] Colebrooke's Digest, Bk. V, 495, commentary.

LECTURE XI. lawyers at least, the spiritual benefit which is taken into consideration in determining the right to inherit *stridhan*, is of a nature different from that which is taken into account in laying down the order of succession to the property of a male owner.

On failure of all daughters, the right of inheritance devolves on the son.[1] This rule is deduced by Jimutavahana from the text of Narada,[2] upon which Vijnaneswara[3] bases his doctrine, that after daughters their sons, and not the sons of the deceased proprietress, are entitled to the heritage.

In default of the son, the daughter's son inherits wealth received at the time of marriage; "for," says Srikrishna,[4] "it is reasonable that since the daughter's claim is preferred to that of the son, the son of the debarred son should be excluded by the son of the person who bars his claim."

In default of the daughter's son, the son's son succeeds, and failing him the son's grandson in the male line.[5]

Failing the great grandson, the succession devolves on the son of a rival wife.[6]

In default of the son of the rival wife, a woman's *yautuka* goes to the grandson, and failing him, to the great-grandson of the rival wife; for, says Srikrishna, "they

---

[1] Dayabhaga, Ch. IV, Sec. II, 25; Dayakrama Sangraha, Ch. II, Sec. III, 8.

[2] XIII, 2, cited in the Dayabhaga, Ch. IV, Sec. II, 13. The text runs thus:—"Let the daughters take the mother's wealth: on failure of daughters (*tat*), her (or their) issue." The pronoun *tat* which is uninflected, and may be taken in either number, is taken by Jimutavahana to stand for 'mother,' and by Vijnaneswara to stand for 'daughters.' See Dayabhaga, Ch. IV, Sec. II, 17—20.

[3] Mitakshara, Ch. II, Sec. XI, 18.

[4] Dayakrama Sangraha, Ch. II, Sec. III, 9.

[5] *Ibid*, 10. [6] *Ibid*, 11.

both present oblations to her husband in which she also participates."[1]

Property given by the father.

The order of succession relating to *stridhan* falling under class II, or property given by the father, is not clearly settled. It is deduced from the following text of Manu:[2]—

"The wealth of a woman, which has been in any manner given to her by her father, let the Brahmani damsel take; or let it belong to her offspring." Upon this text, Jimutavahana has the following commentary:[3]—"Since the text specifies 'given by her father,' the meaning must be, that property, which was given to her by her father, even at any other time besides that of the nuptials, shall belong exclusively to her daughter: and the term *Brahmani* is merely illustrative [indicating that a daughter of the same tribe with the giver inherits]. Or, lest the term should be impertinent, the text may signify that the *Brahmani* damsel, being daughter of a contemporary wife, shall take the property of the *Cshatriya* and of other wives dying childless, which had been given to them by their fathers."

In regard to this class of *stridhan*, the authorities differ on two points:—

In the first place, it is not clear whether this class comprehends property given by the father *even at the time of marriage*; or whether it includes only property given by him at any time *other than the time of marriage*, nuptial presents by the father coming under the head of *yautuka*. The former view is maintained by Srikrishna in the Dayakrama Sangraha.[4] But the latter seems to be in accordance with the opinion of Jimutavahana, as

[1] Dayakrama Sangraha, Ch. II, Sec. III, 13.

[2] IX, 198, cited in the Dayabhaga, Ch. IV, Sec. II, 16.

[3] Dayabhaga, Ch. IV, Sec. II, 16.

[4] Ch. II, Sec. V, 1.

LECTURE XI. may be gathered from the above extract; and it is the view that is maintained by Srikrishna himself in his commentary on the Dayabhaga, and is accepted as correct by Macnaghten[1] and Shamacharan,[2] and perhaps also by Strange.[3]

In the second place, the order of succession to this class of *stridhan* as laid down by Srikrishna in the Dayakrama Sangraha,[4] is different from that given in the commentary on the Dayabhaga by Srikrishna himself. The order given in the Dayakrama Sangraha is the same as that for the *yautuka;* and it seems to be in accordance with the opinion of Jimutavahana and of Raghunandana.[5] But the order given in Srikrishna's commentary is the one that has been generally accepted as correct;[6] and according to it the successive heirs are,—the maiden daughter, the son (and then, as in the case of the *ayautuka*), the daughters having and likely to have male issue, the son's son,[7] the daughter's son, the son's grandson in the male line, the son of a rival wife, her grandson, and her great-grandson in the male line, and the barren and the sonless widowed daughters.

Adopted son.

Has a son by adoption the same rights as a son of the body? This question I have already considered in a previous lecture[8] with reference to the Mitakshara law, and I have only to add, that the remarks I have made there are equally applicable to the law of the Bengal school. There is only this difference which ought to be noted, that in the event of the co-existence of an adopted

---

[1] Principles of Hindu Law, 39, 40. [2] Vyavastha Darpana, 718, 719.

[3] 1 Strange, 251. [4] Ch. II, Sec. V. [5] Dayatattwa, Ch. X, 16.

[6] See Macnaghten's Principles of Hindu Law, 39, 40; 1 Strange, 251; and Vyavastha Darpana, 718, 719.

[7] See Dayabh. Siromani's ed., 1863, p. 178. Colebrooke's translation is here slightly different. [8] Lecture IX, *ante*, pp. 364—369.

son and a son of the body, the share of the former will be here a half (and not a third) of the share of a legitimate son.[1]

LECTURE XI.

So in the case of grandsons by adoption (in the male line), the remarks I have made before[2] are equally applicable to the Bengal law, subject to the difference in the rule about shares, noticed above.

Daughter's adopted son.

The question whether the adopted son of a daughter is entitled to succeed in the same way as the son of her body, has also been considered already in a former lecture,[3] with reference to Mitakshara law, and the conclusion arrived at there, seems to be equally true for the Bengal school. It is true that one of the strongest arguments against the rights of the daughter's adopted son under the Benares law is based upon the fact that, according to that law, he would, if admitted as an heir, exclude the son of the deceased herself; and that this argument does not hold good under the Bengal law. But in the Bengal law, a new argument against the daughter's adopted son's claim is furnished by the fact that a very inferior position is assigned to the barren daughter owing to her inability to confer spiritual benefit through a son, which would not have been the case had her adopted son been regarded as holding the same position as her legitimate son in relation to her mother.

Grandsons whether by sons or by daughters take *per stirpes.*

The question whether the son's sons and the daughter's sons inherit *stridhan per stirpes* or *per capita* has not been considered by the Bengal lawyers. In the absence of any express provision to the contrary in their writings, the rule laid down in the Mayukha[4] and the

[1] See Dayabhaga, Ch. X, 9; Dayakrama Sangraha, Ch. VII, 23; Dattaka Chandrika, Sec. V, 15, 16; Vyavastha Darpana, pp. 909, 910; see also Sutherland's Note, XXII. [2] See Lecture IX, *ante*, pp. 370, 371.
[3] See Lecture IX, *ante*, p. 361. [4] Ch. IV, Sec. X, 21.

LECTURE XI. Smriti Chandrika[1] that grandsons by daughters as well as grandsons by sons inherit their grandmother's property *per stirpes*, may be taken to be the correct rule also for the Bengal school.

Upon the question—"Why do not a son, a son's son, and the son of a grandson, jointly inherit the estate of a married woman, as they do the property left by a man?"—Jagannatha observes:[2]—"To this some reply, Jimutavahana does not deduce the rule of succession to the estate of a woman from a text relative to the inheritance of property left by a man; but on some occasions he cites a text concerning this subject in a form of illustration to confirm the rule *otherwise deduced:* thus the same reasoning not being equally applicable to the property of a man, and to that of a woman, it is improper to deduce rules concerning the estate of a woman from texts relative to property left by a man."

The daughter's daughter is no heir to *stridhan* under the Bengal law.

So much for the succession of children (a term which also means the sons of a rival wife and their male issue).

Succession of the group of heirs consisting of the husband, the brother, and the parents.

If a woman dies leaving no progeny, that is, none of the heirs enumerated above, the next group of heirs consists of her parents, her brother, and her husband; but the order in which they inherit is not the same for every description of *stridhan*. The different orders of their succession to her property are deduced by the Bengal lawyers from the following texts:—

Manu:[3]—"It is ordained that the property of a woman

---

[1] Ch. IX, Sec. III, 25.

[2] Colebrooke's Digest, Bk. V, 498, commentary, Vol. II, 612 (Mad. ed.)

[3] Cited in the Dayabhaga, Ch. IV, Sec. II, 27; Ch. IV, Sec. III, 3; Dayatattwa, Ch. X, 20; Dayakrama Sangraha, Ch. II, Sec. III, 14, 19.

married by the ceremonies called *Brahma, Daiva, Arsha,* Gandharba, and *Prajapatya,* shall go to her husband, if she die without issue. But her wealth, given to her on her marriage in the form called *Asura,* or either of the other two (*Racshasa* and *Paisacha*), is ordained on her death without issue to become the property of her mother and of her father." (IX, 196, 197.)

LECTURE XI.

Yajnavalkya:[1]—"That which has been given to her by her kindred, as well as her fee or gratuity, and anything bestowed after marriage, her kinsmen take, if she die without issue."

"The separate property of a childless woman married in the form denominated *Brahma,* or in any of the four (unblamed forms of marriage,) goes to her husband." (II, 144, 145.)

Katyayana:[2]— "Immoveable property which has been given by parents to their daughter, goes always to her brother, if she die without issue."

"That which has been given to her by her kindred, goes on failure of kindred to her husband."

Devala:[3]— "A woman's property when she is dead becomes the common inheritance of the sons and the daughters: in default of children, let the husband, mother, brother or father take."

Gautama:[4]— "The sister's fee (*sulka*) belongs to the uterine brothers; after them it goes to the mother, and next to the father. Some say before her." (XXVIII, 22, 23.)

---

[1] Cited in the Dayabhaga, Ch. IV, Sec. III, 10, 2; Ch. IV, Sec. II, 24; Dayakrama Sangraha, Ch. II, Sec. III, 15.

[2] Cited in the Dayabhaga, Ch. IV, Sec. III, 12, 29; Dayatattwa, Ch. X; 11, Dayakrama Sangraha, Ch. II, Sec. III, 16, 21.

[3] Cited in the Dayatattwa, Ch. X, 26; the Dayakrama Sangraha, Ch. II, Sec. IV, 3. [4] Cited in the Dayabhaga, Ch. IV, Sec. III, 27.

LECTURE XI.

Unlike the commentators of the other schools, who hold that the text of Manu and the second of the two verses of Yajnavalkya quoted above apply to all kinds of *stridhan* except the *sulka,* Jimutavahana maintains that these passages relate only to property obtained by a woman at the time of her marriage. To the foregoing text of Manu, he subjoins the following commentary:[1]—"It is not right to interpret the text as signifying, that any property of whatever amount, which belongs to a woman married by any of those ceremonies termed *Brahma,* &c., whether received by her before or after her nuptials, devolves wholly on her husband by her demise. For the terms employed in the text signifying 'at marriages in the form denominated *Brahma,* &c.,' indicate time, &c."

"Therefore the observation of Viswarupa, that the text relates to woman's property received at the time of the nuptials, should be respected."

The first of the two verses quoted from Yajnavalkya is taken to relate only to the three kinds of *stridhan* mentioned there,[2] and Jimutavahana has the following comments upon

---

[1] Dayabhaga, Ch. IV, Sec. III, 4, 5.

[2] See Dayabhaga, Ch. IV, Sec. III, 10. The above interpretation of Yajnavalkya's text is different from that adopted in the Mitakshara. In the original, this text and the couplets immediately preceding and following it run thus:—

पितृ मातृ पति भ्रातृदत्तमध्यग्न्युपागतं ।
आधिवेदनिकाद्यं च स्त्रीधनं परिकीर्त्तितम् ॥
बन्धुदत्तं तथा शुल्कमन्वाधेयकमेव च ।
अतीतायामप्रजसि बान्धवास्तदवाप्नुयुः ॥
अप्रज स्त्रीधनं भर्त्तुर्ब्राह्मादि षु चतुर्ष्वपि ।
दुहितॄणां प्रसूता चेच्छेषेषु पितृगामि तत् ॥

According to Vijnaneswara, the first three lines form one sentence; the fourth line is a complete sentence by itself; and the last two lines are explanations of the fourth. See Mitakshara, Ch. II, Sec. XI, 1—10.

it :—"Given by her kindred. Presented to her by her father or mother [during her maidenhood]. Hence (since the words 'given by kindred' intend given by the father and mother) their sons, who are her brothers, are the kinsmen here signified."[1] And the first of the foregoing two verses of Katyayana is referred to[2] as authority in support of this interpretation.

To understand the above comments, it should be remembered that the word for 'kindred' in Yajnavalkya's text in the original is *bandhu*, and that for 'kinsmen' is *bandhava*, which, taken literally, would mean the offspring of a *bandhu*.

So that, with reference to the relative rights of the husband, the brother, and the parents, under the Dayabhaga, *stridhan* may be divided into the following classes :—

I.—Property obtained at the time of marriage, under which class are—

(*a.*) Property obtained at marriage in one of the five approved forms ; and

(*b.*) Property obtained at marriage in one of the three disapproved forms.

II.—The three kinds of *stridhan* mentioned in Yajnavalkya's text, namely—

(*a.*) Property given by kindred, that is by the parents during maidenhood.

(*b.*) The *sulka*, or perquisite.

(*c.*) The gift subsequent (*anwadheya*), or what is obtained after marriage.

You will observe that this classification is not exhaustive. Though class I includes *all* property that is acquired *at the time of* marriage, and class II, all that is acquired *after* marriage and *some* property acquired *before*

---

[1] Dayabhaga, Ch. IV, Sec. III, 11. [2] *Ibid*, 12.

LECTURE XI. marriage, yet there are *other* descriptions of property acquired *before* marriage, such as that obtained by gift from relations other than the parents, which are *stridhan* according to the Dayabhaga, but which find no place in the above classification. It is not easy to say under which of the above heads such property would come. Possibly it may come under class II (*a*), according to an extended interpretation of the word kindred (*bandhu*).

In regard to class I (*a*), the husband is the first heir in the group we are now considering. But it is not clear who should succeed in default of the husband. There is a passage in the Dayabhaga (Ch. IV, Sec. III, 31), in which it is said that on failure of heirs down to the husband, the succession devolves on the group of heirs in Brihaspati's text; and from this it might be inferred that that group comes after the husband. But that is contrary to the opinions of Raghunandana and Srikrishna. Raghunandana,[1] upon the authority of the text of Devala, cited above, intimates that after the husband, the mother, the brother, and the father, successively take the inheritance. And Srikrishna, in the Dayakrama Sangraha,[2] places the brother after the husband, upon the authority of the first verse of Yajnavalkya quoted above; and he places the mother and the father in succession after the brother according to a text of Katyayana;[3] and the same is the order laid down by him in his commentary on the Dayabhaga. As this last named order has been generally accepted,[4] it may be taken as the correct law for the Bengal school.

---

[1] Dayatattwa, Ch. X, 26. [2] Ch. II, Sec. III, 15.

[3] See Dayakrama Sangraha, Ch. II, Sec. III, 16, 17; and commentary on the Dayabhaga.

[4] See Macnaghten's Principles of Hindu Law, 39, 40; 1 Strange, 251; Vyavastha Darpana, 718, 719.

As regards class I (*b*), the mother and the father are the first and the second in the group of heirs under notice.[1] Failing the father, the brother succeeds, and in default of the brother, the succession devolves on the husband according to Srikrishna.[2] LECTURE XI.

The three descriptions of property under class II require some explanation. Jimutavahana has explained them very fully. I have already given you his account of class II (*a*). Class II (*b*), the *sulka*, is described thus:[3]—

"What is given to a woman by artists constructing a house or executing other work, as a bribe to send her husband or other person [of her family] to labour on such particular work, is her fee. It is the price [of labour]; since its purpose is to engage [a labourer].

"Or a fee is that which is described by Vyasa: 'What [is given] to bring the bride to her husband's house, is denominated her fee.' That is, what is given by way of bribe or the like to induce her to go to the house of her husband."

Class II (*c*) is thus defined:[4]—

"What has been received by a woman from the family of her husband, and at a time posterior to her marriage, is called a gift subsequent; and so is that which is similarly received from the family of her kindred:"

"From the family of her husband. From her father-in-law and the rest. From the family of her kindred. From that of her father and mother."

The husband's family is explained to mean the father-in-law and the rest. This explanation was the subject of

[1] Dayabhaga, Ch. IV, Sec. III, 6.

[2] See Dayakrama Sangraha, Ch. II, Sec. III, 19-22; and commentary on the Dayabhaga.

[3] Dayabhaga, Ch. IV, Sec. III, 20, 21.

[4] *Ibid*, 16, 17.

LECTURE XI. some discussion before the High Court of Bengal in the case of *Hurry Mohun Shaha* v. *Sonatun Shaha*,[1] but the Court held that the term 'family of her husband' was wide enough to include the husband's father's sister's son.

According to Jimutavahana,[2] the heirs to class II are successively the whole brother, the mother, the father, and the husband. His followers, however, do not seem to agree with him. Thus Raghunandana[3] seems to place the husband first, except as regards class II (*a*); and Srikrishna places him first as regards class II (*c*)[4] and also as regards class II (*a*).[5]

The order given in the Dayabhaga is, however, the one that has been accepted by our Courts as applicable to all the three descriptions of property coming under class II. There is a very lucid exposition of the law of the Dayabhaga on this point by Mr. Justice Dwarkanath Mitter in his judgment in *Judoo Nath Sircar* v. *Busunta Coomar Roy Chowdhry*.[6] The question in that case was, whether the husband or the mother is entitled to succeed to the property obtained by a woman before her marriage from her father by a testamentary gift. Justice Mitter, in answering this question, observed :—

"It is admitted on both sides that the case before us is governed by the Hindu law current in the Bengal school, and as the Dayabhaga is the highest of all the authorities

---

[1] I. L. R., 1 Cal., 275.

[2] Dayabhaga, Ch. IV, Sec. III, 10-29.

[3] Dayatattwa, Ch. X, 10, 11, 26.

[4] Dayakrama Sangraha, Ch. II, Sec. IV, 11; commentary on the Dayabhaga.

[5] Dayakrama Sangraha, Ch. II, Sec. V, 3, 4; and commentary on the Dayabhaga. Justice Dwarkanath Mitter, in his judgment in Judoo Nath Sircar v. Busunta Coomar Roy Chowdhry, has tried to reconcile to some extent this discrepancy between the Dayakrama Sangraha and the Dayabhaga: see 19 W. R., 266, 267.

[6] 19 W. R., 264.

recognized in that school, it is to the Dayabhaga that we will first direct our attention. LECTURE XI.

"Now, Clause 29, Section 3, Chapter IV of that treatise (Colebrooke's translation, page 95), appears to us to be conclusive on the point. That clause is as follows:—

"'Therefore the property goes first to the whole brothers; and if there be none, to the mother; if she be dead, to the father; but on failure of all these, it devolves on the husband. Thus Katyayana says:—"That which has been given to her by her kindred goes on failure of kindred to her husband.'"

"It has been argued that the passage above quoted refers to that kind of *stridhan* only which is called *sulka* (fee or perquisite). But this argument is evidently founded on a mistake. The very text of Katyayana, cited by the author in the passage in question, shows that it also refers to property given to a woman by her kindred, that is to say, by her father and mother; and if this is not sufficient to remove all doubts on the point, we have only to examine a few of the preceding clauses.

"In Clause 10 of the same section and chapter the author introduces the subject by saying that 'property received by a woman after her marriage from the family of her father, of her mother, or of her husband, goes to her brothers (not to her husband),' and in support of this position he cites a text of Yajnavalkya, which declares:— 'That which has been given to her by her kindred as well as her fee or gratuity (*sulka*), and anything bestowed after marriage, her kinsmen take, if she die without issue.' It should be borne in mind that this text of Yajnavalkya refers to three different kinds of *stridhan*—namely, *first*, property given to a woman by her kindred; *second*, her

LECTURE XI. (*sulka*) fee or gratuity; and *third*, property bestowed on her after her marriage. . . . .

"In Clauses 22, 23, 24, 25, 26, and 27 he discusses the opinions of several authors about the order of succession to be followed in regard to such property, and in verse 28 he concludes the discussion by saying that 'in the first place it goes to brothers of the whole blood, then to the mother, and on her default, to the father.'

"It is clear, therefore, that the proposition laid down in Clause 29 is nothing but the final *resumé* of the various matters discussed in the preceding clauses, commencing from Clause 10; and its applicability to all the three kinds of *stridhan* mentioned in the text of Yajnavalkya, referred to in the last mentioned clause, is, consequently, beyond all dispute. It would be absurd to contend that the author of the Dayabhaga has laid down in the case of property given by a woman's kindred a rule of succession different from that laid down by him in the case of *sulka* property, when it is beyond all question that both those kinds of property are governed by the same text of Yajnavalkya, which is cited by him at the very threshold of the discussion."

This decision was followed in the case of *Hurry Mohun Shaha* v. *Sonatun Shaha*,[1] in which the property in dispute fell under the description of gift subsequent, being a gift received after marriage from the husband's father's sister's son; and it was held in accordance with the rule laid down in the Dayabhaga (notwithstanding the opinions of Raghunandana and Srikrishna to the contrary), that the husband was not the heir to such property until after the brother, the mother, and the father.

---

[1] I. L. R., 1 Cal., 275.

LECTURE XI.

Heirs after the husband, the brother, and the parents, the group of heirs according to Brihaspati's text.

After the point at which we have arrived, the further order of succession to *stridhan* is uniform, being the same for all descriptions of *stridhan*. After the husband, the brothers, and the parents, the next group of heirs is that indicated in the following text of Brihaspati:[1]—

"The mother's sister, the maternal uncle's wife,[2] the paternal uncle's wife,[3] the father's sister, the mother-in-law, and the wife of an elder brother, are pronounced similar to mothers. If they leave no issue of their bodies, nor son [of a rival wife,] nor daughter's son, nor son of those persons, the sister's son and the rest shall take their property."

But the Bengal lawyers, while adopting this text as indicative of the group of heirs that comes next, do not, like Devandabhatta,[4] accept it as declaratory of the order in which those heirs succeed one after another. Thus Jimutavahana observes:[5]—

"For want, then, of sons and other linear heirs as here specified, and in default of brothers or other preferable claimants, including the husband, the inheritance passes to the sister's son and the rest, although kinsmen, as the father-in-law, the husband's elder brother, or the like, be living. For the text bears no other import; and the chief purpose of indicating, under the head of inheritance, the competency to present funeral oblations, as is done by describing the women as similar to mothers, and certain

[1] Cited in the Dayabhaga, Ch. IV, Sec. III, 31.

[2] In Colebrooke's translation 'the maternal uncle' occurs in the place of 'the maternal uncle's wife.' This is evidently a mistake. See the edition of the Dayabhaga by Bharat Chandra Siromani, published in 1863.

[3] This is altogether omitted in Colebrooke's translation. But this must be a mistake, as will be seen by referring to paragraph 36 of Sec. III, Ch. IV, of the Dayabhaga. See also the edition of the Dayabhaga by Bharat Chandra Siromani.

[4] Smriti Chandrika, Ch. IX, Sec. III, 36, 37.

[5] Dayabhaga, Ch. IV, Sec. III, 35, 36.

LECTURE XI. persons as standing in the relation to them of sons, is to suggest the right of succession to their property.

"Hence, since the text enumerates 'sister's son,' &c., if the order of succession consequently be, first the sister's son, then the husband's sister's son, next the child of the husband's younger brother, afterwards the child of the husband's elder brother, then the son of the brother, after him the son-in-law, and, subsequently, the younger brother-in-law, the right would devolve last of all on the younger brother of the husband, contrary to the opinion and practice of venerable persons. Therefore, the text is propounded, not as declaratory of the order of inheritance, but as expressive of the strength of the fact, [namely, of the benefits conferred]."

The order of succession as deduced from the above text by the application of the doctrine of spiritual benefit, is thus stated by Jimutavahana :[1]—

"This then is the order of succession, according to the various degree [of benefit to the owner of the property] from the oblation of food at obsequies. In the first place, the husband's younger brother is entitled to the woman's property; for he is a kinsman (*sapinda*) and presents oblations to her, to her husband, and to three persons to whom oblations were to be offered by her husband. After him, the son either of her husband's elder or of his younger brother, is heir to the separate property of his uncle's wife; for he is a kinsman, and presents oblations to her, to her husband, and to two persons to whom oblations were to be offered by her husband. On failure of such,

[1] Dayabhaga, Ch. IV, Sec. III, 37. For an account of the doctrine of spiritual benefit, see the Dayabhaga, Ch. XI, Sec. I, 37—40; Sec. VI, 5, 6, and 13; and the judgment of Mr. Justice Mitter, in Gooroo Gobind Shaha v. Anund Lall Ghose, 13 W. R. (F. B.), 57.

the sister's son, though he be not a kinsman (*sapinda*), inherits the separate property left by his mother's sister, because he presents oblations to her, and to three persons (her father and the rest) to whom oblations would have been offered by her son. In default of him, the son of her husband's sister (for it is reasonable, since the husband has a weaker claim than the son, that persons claiming under them should have similar relative precedence) is heir to the property of his uncle's wife; because he presents oblations to three persons to whom they were to be offered by her husband, and also presents oblations to her and to her husband. On failure of him, the brother's son is the successor to his aunt's property, for he presents oblations to the father, to her grandfather, and to herself. If there be no nephew, the husband of his daughter is heir to his mother-in-law's property, since he presents oblations to his mother-in-law and father-in-law."

Raghunandana,[1] Srikrishna,[2] and Jagannatha[3] agree with the author of Dayabhaga in laying down the same order of succession for these six heirs; and they refer to the same doctrine of spiritual benefit as the basis of their conclusion.

The *sapindas*.

On failure of these six heirs, the succession devolves on the father-in-law, the husband's elder brother, and the rest, according to their nearness of *sapinda* kinship.[4]

Here the enumeration of heirs stops in the Dayabhaga and the Dayatattwa.

After the husband's elder brother, the other *sapindas*

---

[1] Dayatattwa, Ch. X, 27—36.

[2] Dayakrama Sangraha, Ch. II, Sec. VI, 1—9.

[3] Colebrooke's Digest, Bk. V, 513, commentary, Vol. II, 623, 624.

[4] Dayabhaga, Ch. IV, Sec. III, 39; Dayatattwa, Ch. X, 38; Dayakrama Sangraha, Ch. II, Sec. VI, 10.

LECTURE XI. succeed in the following order, as pointed out by Jagannatha:[1]—First the father-in-law's great-grandson in the male line succeeds (for his grandson, that is the husband's brother's son, who is a nearer *sapinda*, has already a place assigned to him among the six heirs in Brihaspati's list); after him, the husband's paternal grandfather and his issue; and next, the husband's paternal great-grandfather and his offspring.

Sakulyas and *samanodakas*. "Failing the *sapindas*," says Srikrishna,[2] "the *sakulays*, and after them the *samanodakas*, and next the *samanapravaras* (persons descended from the same patriarch in the male line), succeed *in the same order as in the case of the property of males*."[3] After these, according to Srikrishna, the learned Brahman co-villagers take the property of a Brahmani woman, and the king takes the property of a woman of any other class.[4]

Whether the *samanapravaras* mentioned above are the *samanapravaras* of the husband or those of the father, Srikrishna does not explain. According to the received opinion, based upon a text of Brihaspati cited in the Udvahatattwa, as a woman is, by marriage, transferred from her father's *gotra* to that of her husband, the husband's *samanapravaras* become the *samanapravaras* of the wife. There is, however, a text of Katyayana, also cited in the Udvahatattwa, which declares that a woman remains in her father's *gotra* until her *sapindikarana*; and this text might perhaps support the view that the *samanapravaras* in question are those of her father.[5]

---

[1] Colebrooke's Digest, Bk. V, 513, commentary, Vol. II, 624.

[2] Dayakrama Sangraha, Ch. II, Sec. VI, 11; and commentary on the Dayabhaga, Ch. IV, Sec. III.

[3] The words in *italics* are omitted in Wynch's translation of the Dayakrama Sangraha. See Vyavastha Darpana, p. 727, note.

[4] Dayakrama Sangraha, Ch. II, Sec. VI, 12, 13.

[5] See Udvahatattwa, Institutes of Raghunandana, Vol. II, p. 72. These texts are also cited in Vidyasagar's Tract on Widow Marriage, 165—172.

Paternal kinsmen.

Srikrishna's authority is not clear on the point as to whether kinsmen of a woman on the father's side, other than those already definitely named, can be her heirs. But Jagannatha[1] expressly recognizes their right of succession. After naming the *samanadakas* of the woman's husband, he adds,—"After these, her kindred on her father's side, as far as the tenth person; after them, the family of her mother; and lastly, the king takes the estate, except the property of a *Brahmani* woman. This brief exposition may suffice.

"The ground of this order of succession is the performance of obsequies; for it is shown, in the case of property left by a man, that heirs succeed in right of benefits conferred."—And in support of this rule he cites the following text of the Vishnupurana:[2]—

"By the *sapindas* and *samanadakas* of the father and mother, by intimate companions, or by the king, who takes an escheat, the first rites must be performed; but the last rites shall only be celebrated by sons and the rest."

Considering how anxiously the Hindu law tries to prevent escheat to the Crown, and bearing in mind the other reasons stated in the last lecture, I think it may be safely affirmed, on the authority of Jagannatha, that on failure of other heirs, a woman's kinsmen on the father's and the mother's side succeed to her *stridhan* according to the Bengal school. One of the strongest arguments in support of this view is the fact that it is deducible from the doctrine of spiritual benefit, which is so emphatically and so repeatedly declared by the founder

---

[1] Colebrooke's Digest, Bk. V, 513, commentary, Vol. II, 624.

[2] *Ibid*, Bk. V, 514.

LECTURE XI. of the Bengal school to be applicable to the devolution of *stridhan*.

The Crown. The limitation imposed on the general rights of the Crown, in the case of the property of a Brahmani woman dying without heirs, must be taken to be practically inoperative now, according to the ruling of the Privy Council in the case of *The Collector of Masulipatam* v. *Cavaly Vencata Narainapah*,[1] in which the corresponding restriction in the case of the property of a Brahmin has been held to be no bar to the right of the Crown to take heirless property by escheat.

Heirs to immoveable property given by the husband. The rules given above do not, according to Jagannatha, govern the devolution of immoveable property obtained by a woman by gift from her husband. Such property according to him passes to the heirs of her husband;[2] and in support of this view he refers to the following text of Katyayana:[3]—

"What a woman has received as a gift from her husband, she may dispose of at pleasure after his death, if it be moveable; but as long as he lives, let her preserve it with frugality, or she may commit it to his family.

"The childless widow, preserving inviolate the bed of her lord, and strictly obedient to her spiritual parents, may frugally enjoy the estate until she die; after her, the legal heirs shall take it."

The same view has been expressed by Kindersley, J., in an *obiter dictum* in his judgment in *Venkata Rama Rau* v. *Venkata Suriya Rau*.[4] But the opposite view has also

---

[1] 2 W. R., 59 (P. C.).

[2] Colebrooke's Digest, Bk. V, 515, commentary, Vol. II, p. 626.

[3] *Ibid*, Bk. V, 477.

[4] I. L. R., 1 Mad., 286.

been maintained,[1] though its correctness under the Bengal law is not free from doubt. LECTURE XI.

Heirs to the property of a maiden.

The order of succession to the property of a maiden, according to the Bengal law, is the same as that according to the other schools. It is based upon the text of Baudhayana, which is followed by almost all the commentators, and which runs thus:[2]—

"The wealth of a deceased damsel, let the uterine brethren themselves take. On failure of them, it shall belong to the mother; or, if she be dead, to the father."

On failure of the heirs mentioned in this text, the next heirs would, I presume, be the paternal kinsmen in order of proximity.

If any property left by a maiden was received as a gift from the bridegroom to whom she was betrothed, the bridegroom is entitled to take back such property.[3]

---

1 Macnaghten's Precedents of Hindu Law, Ch. I, Sec. II, Case XIV.

2 Dayabhaga, Ch. IV, Sec. III, 7; Dayatattwa, Ch. X, 21.

3 Dayakrama Sangraha, Ch. II, Sec. I.

LECTURE XII.

SUCCESSION TO WOMAN'S PROPERTY OTHER THAN HER STRIDHAN.

Succession to woman's property other than her *stridhan*—*First*, succession to inherited property—According to the Benares school—According to the Maharashtra school—The Mayukha—According to the Bengal school—According to the Dravida and Mithila schools—*Secondly*, succession to property acquired otherwise than by inheritance and not coming under the technical definition of *stridhan*—According to the Mitakshara—According to the Mayukha—According to the Bengal, the Dravida, and the Mithila schools—Share on partition—Property acquired by gift from strangers or by labor and skill—during widowhood and maidenhood—during coverture.

Succession to woman's property other than her *stridhan*.

IN the last three lectures I have treated of succession to *stridhan* according to the different schools. As there are certain descriptions of woman's property (among which the most important is that obtained by inheritance) which do not always rank as *stridhan*, it remains now to say a few words regarding the devolution of such property. I shall consider, *first*, property acquired by inheritance; and, *secondly*, other descriptions of woman's property which do not rank as *stridhan*.

First, succession to inherited property.

As regards property acquired by inheritance, there are two classes of cases; one, where the property is inherited by a woman from a male, and another, where it is inherited by her from a female.

According to the Benares school.

According to the Mitakshara, such property would, in either case, rank as *stridhan*, and descend as such. To this simple rule of Vijnaneswara, an important exception has been attached by the decision of the Privy Council in the cases of *Bhugwandeen Doobey* v. *Myna Baee*[1] and *Mussamut Thakoor Dayee* v. *Rai Balack Ram*,[2] in which

[1] 9 W. R. (P. C.), 23.

[2] 10 W. R. (P. C.), 3.

it has been held that property inherited by a widow from her husband passes on her death, not to her heirs, but to the next heir of her husband. This is the ruling of the highest Court of Appeal for India; and it is, moreover, in accordance with the Viramitrodaya,[1] which declares succession to the widow's estate to be an exception to the general rule, that property passes on the demise of the owner to the heirs of such owner, and not to the heir of any previous owner. Vijnaneswara's rule must, therefore, be taken subject to this exception.

LECTURE XII.

Following what is considered to be the spirit of the above ruling, the Indian Courts by their decisions have introduced other exceptions, which really tend to substitute for Vijnaneswara's rule the opposite doctrine maintained by the Bengal school, that property inherited by a female does not become her *stridhan* in any case, and that it passes on her death to the next heir of the person from whom she inherited it. These decisions I have already examined in a former lecture.[2] And I think it would not be incorrect to affirm that, except in cases in which the point is absolutely concluded by authority, property inherited by a female should, according to the Benares law, descend to the heirs to her *stridhan*.[3]

According to the Maharashtra school.

In the Maharashtra school, except in certain places, such as Guzerat and the Island of Bombay, which follow the

[1] Pp. 629, 630, edition by Jivananda Vidyasagara.

[2] Lecture VII, *ante*, pp. 302—314.

[3] Since the above was written, the Privy Council has held in the case of Chotay Lall *v.* Chunnoo Lall (3 C. L. R., 465) that, under the Mitakshara law, property inherited by a daughter from her father passes on her death to her father's heirs. The same principle would evidently apply to the case of any other female heir inheriting to a male. So that it must now be taken to be the settled law of the Benares school, that property inherited by a woman from a *male* relation passes on her death to his heirs.

LECTURE XII.

Mayukha,[1] the law is the same as in the Benares school. And the decisions of the Bombay Courts are more in accordance with the doctrine of the Mitakshara than the decisions of the Courts on this side of India.

The Mayukha.

The Mayukha agrees with the Mitakshara in including inherited property under the denomination of *stridhan*, but differs from it in regarding such property (along with certain other descriptions of woman's property) as a peculiar class of *stridhan*, and in prescribing for it an order of succession different from that laid down for *stridhan* strictly and technically so called.[2] The passage of the Mayukha[3] bearing upon this point has been rendered by Borradaile thus:—

"However, the text of Yajnavalkya—'Let sons divide equally both the effects and the debts, after [the demise of] their two parents'—relates to [what is] acquired by the act of partition and the like, with the exception of that declared in the above texts [as woman's property]. From this it is clear that, if there be daughters, the sons or other heirs even succeed to the mother's estate, distinct from that part before described [as woman's property]."

This passage is thus explained by Mr. Justice West in his judgment in *Vijiarangam's* case:[4]—

"Inherited property, Nilkantha says, though it is *stridhan*, not being one of those kinds of *stridhan* for which express texts prescribe exceptional modes of descent, goes, on the woman's death, to her sons and the rest, as if she were a male, and this too notwithstanding her having left daughters (Vyavahara Mayukha, Ch. IV, Sec. X, pl. 26). The passage

[1] See Krishnaji Vyanktesh *v.* Pandurung, 12 Bom., 65.

[2] Vyavahara Mayukha, Ch. IV, Sec. X, 25, 26.

[3] *Ibid*, 26.

[4] 8 Bom., O. C. J., 260.

which sets forth this doctrine being somewhat obscure in Mr. Borradaile's translation, it may be as well to say that its true purport is this: 'It is clear that although there be daughters, the sons or other heirs still succeed to the mother's estate, so far as it is distinct from the part already described (as subject to peculiar devolution under texts applicable to particular species of *stridhan*).'"

Though the rule deduced by Mr. Justice West from the foregoing passage of the Mayukha,—namely, that property inherited by a woman descends to her sons or other relations who would have been her heirs if she had been a separated male proprietor,—is simple enough, its practical application is not altogether free from difficulty. According to this rule, the heirs to a woman's inherited property are successively, the son, the grandson, the great-grandson, the husband (who comes in place of the widow), the daughter, the daughter's son, the father (who, according to Nilkantha,[1] comes before the mother), the mother, the brother, the brother's son, the *gotrajas*, and the *bandhus*.

Down to the brother's son, the above order is quite clear and explicit. But then the question arises whether the *gotrajas* are the *gotrajas* of the woman's father, or those of her husband.

Vijnaneswara's opinion seems to be this, that though the father's *gotrajas* are the *gotrajas* of a maiden, the husband's *gotrajas* would be the *gotrajas* of a married woman. For he distinguishes the *gotrajas* from the *bhinnagotras*, and in one place, uses the term *samanagotra* as synonymous with the term *gotraja* (Mitakshara, Ch. II, Sec. V, 3, 5). So that, as pointed out by Messrs. West and Bühler,[2] *gotraja*

---

[1] Vyavahara Mayukha, Ch. IV, Sec. VIII, 14. [2] 1 W. and B., 147.

LECTURE XII.

in the Mitakshara means a person of the same *gotra*. And as a woman is, by marriage, transferred from her father's *gotra* to that of her husband,[1] it follows that a married woman can have no other *gotraja* relations besides those of her husband.

Nilkantha, however, appears to take a different view. He uses the term *gotraja* in the sense of 'born in the family;' and it is by taking the term in this sense, that he admits the sister as an heir among the *gotrajas*;[2] so that, according to him, the *gotrajas* of the father would be the *gotrajas* of the daughter, whether married or unmarried. This interpretation of the Mayukha derives some support from the following observations of Mr. Justice West in *Vijiarangam's* case:[3]—

"According to this law of *stridhan*, the property inherited by Yesu would, in the absence of descendants, go to her parents, just as if she had been their only son, and failing them, to the paternal grandmother and the *sapindas* of the father, the *gotrajas* taking precedence of the *bhinnagotras*. Nilkantha's view of what constitutes a *gotraja-sapinda* is shown by the Vyavahara Mayukha, Ch. IV, Sec. VIII, 19. He regards this relationship as constituted by birth in the family, and for this reason assigns to a man's sister the first place amongst his *sapindas*."

But the point is not very clear, and the remarks of Mr. Justice West himself in a recent case[4] have thrown considerable doubt upon it.

---

[1] See the texts of Brihaspati and Laghu Harita cited in the Udvahatattwa, Raghunandana's Institutes, Vol. II, 72.

[2] Vyavahara Mayukha, Ch. IV, Sec. VIII, 19.

[3] 8 Bom., O. C. J., 260, 261.

[4] Lallubhai Bapubhai *v.* Mankuvarbai, I. L. R., 2 Bom., 446.

"Nilkantha," observes that learned Judge, "while he admits the paternal grandmother, makes no provision for the paternal great-grandmother, by his subsequent arrangements: if they are to be considered as in any way exhaustive, he rather implicitly excludes her. Yet, being able to provide for the paternal grandmother apart from all *gotraja* connexion by means of Manu's text in her favour, he has chosen to rank her amongst the *gotraja-sapindas.* She does not, like the great-grandmother in the Mitakshara, rest on this connexion, and this alone, for her place in the line of inheritance; but being designated a *gotraja-sapinda,* and being so only in virtue of her marriage, it follows of necessity that Nilkantha thought that marriage as well as birth created the *gotraja* relationship. This might lead to absurd results, as women, inheriting in two families, while men inherited only in one, might gradually absorb all the property; but, as we have seen, the blood *gotraship* of women cannot safely be extended beyond the sister."

After the *gotrajas* come the *bandhus,* who, according to the explanation given in the Mayukha,[1] are certain blood relations of the deceased female proprietress. Among these come, first, her own *bandhus* in the following order,—her father's sister's son, her mother's sister's son, and her mother's brother's son; then, her father's *bandhus,* in the same order; and lastly, her mother's *bandhus,* in the same order. Whether in the case of succession to woman's property, according to the Mayukha, this enumeration of *bandhus* is to be deemed exhaustive or not, has not yet been decided.

[1] Ch. IV, Sec. VIII, 22.

LECTURE XII.

According to the Bengal school.

According to the Bengal school, property inherited by a female, whether as heir to the ordinary property of a male relation, or as heir to the *stridhan* of a female, does not rank as her *stridhan* in any case, but passes on her death to the next heir of the person from whom she inherited it.

In the case of property inherited from a male relation, this rule is clearly laid down by the founder of the Bengal school, as a deduction from Katyayana's text relative to the widow's estate.

"But, if a maiden daughter," says Jimutavahana,[1] "in whom the succession has vested, and who has been afterwards married, die [without bearing issue], the estate, which was her's, becomes the property of those persons, a married daughter or others, who would regularly succeed if there were no such [unmarried daughter] in whom the inheritance vested, and in like manner succeed on her demise after it has so vested in her. It does not become the property of her husband or other heirs; for that [text which is declaratory of the right of the husband and the rest] is relative to a woman's peculiar property. Since it has been shown by a text before cited, that, on the decease of the widow in whom the succession had vested, the legal heirs of the former owner, who would regularly inherit his property if there were no widow in whom the succession vested,—namely, the daughters and the rest—succeed to the wealth; therefore, the same rule [concerning the succession of the former possessor's next heirs] is inferred, *à fortiori*, in the case of the daughter and grandson whose pretensions are inferior to the wife's.

[1] See Dayabhaga, Ch. XI, Sec. II, 30, 31.

"Or the word 'wife' [in the text above quoted, Sec. I, 56] is employed with a general import, and it implies that the rule must be understood as applicable generally to the case of a woman's succession by inheritance."

The case in which property is inherited by a female as heir to the *stridhan* of another female, is not so clearly provided for by the Bengal commentators. But the rule laid down above, that the property would pass to the next heir of the original owner of such *stridhan*, is deducible from the following passage of the Dayakrama Sangraha:[1]—

"Here, however, on the death of a maiden daughter, or of one affianced, in whom the succession had vested, and who having been subsequently married, is ascertained to have been barren, or on the death of a widow who has not given birth to a son, the succession to the property which had passed from the mother to her daughters, would devolve next on the sisters having, and likely to have, male issue, and in their default, on the barren and widowed daughters;—not on the husband of such daughter above-mentioned in whom the succession had vested: for the right of the husband is relative to the 'woman's separate property,' and wealth which has in this way passed from one to another, can no longer be considered as the 'woman's separate property:'—This must be understood."

The same rule may also be deduced from the Dayabhaga independently of the authority of Srikrishna, as you will observe in the following passage of the judgment of

[1] Ch. II, Sec. III, 6.

LECTURE XII.

Mr. Justice Romesh Chunder Mitter in the case of *Bhooban Mohan Banerjee* v. *Muddun Mohun Sing:*[1]—

"It seems to me that the same rule is laid down in the Dayabhaga, Chap. XI, Sec. II, para. 30. The chapter in question, it is true, mainly deals with rules of succession to properties left by a deceased male owner; but the paragraph referred to above appears to me to lay down a rule applicable generally to succession by women, whether to the properties of a man or to *stridhan* of a woman. If it were not so, there would be no provision in Dayabhaga relating to succession to property inherited by a woman from a female ancestress who held it as *stridhan.* I do not think that this is probable. Having regard to this circumstance, and having regard to the language of the paragraph in question, which is very general, it seems to me that the rule there laid down is also applicable to *stridhan* property inherited by a woman."

The above rule of succession seems to have been recognized by the Sudder Court of Bengal so far back as the year 1793, in the case of *Pran Kishen Singh* v. *Mussammaut Bhagwutee.*[2] I ought to tell you, however, that there are certain remarks of Jagannatha[3] which throw some doubt upon the correctness of the above rule. "A daughter," says he, "may at pleasure give away to any person whomsoever the exclusive property of her mother, which has devolved on her; after her death, the daughter's son-in-law and the rest shall obtain that *which has not been aliened.* It should not be argued, that a daughter is only permitted to enjoy for life the peculiar property of a woman *which she has inherited,* like

---

[1] 1 Joygobind Shome's Law Reporter, p. 5. [2] 1 Sel. Rep., 4.
[3] Colebrooke's Digest, Bk. V, 515, commentary, Vol. II, p. 628.

the estate left by a man, *to which she has succeeded.* That has not been asserted by Jimutavahana, and no reasoning supports it." LECTURE XII.

The law on the present subject is not at all clearly laid down by the commentators of the Dravida and Mithila schools. One thing, however, may be taken as settled by repeated decisions,[1]—namely, that property inherited by a woman from a male relation does not rank as her *stridhan* according to those schools. According to the Dravida and Mithila schools.

It seems that there are only three possible modes as regards the devolution of a woman's inherited property:—

First,—It may pass to the next heir of the previous owner from whom the last proprietress inherited it, as is the rule in the Bengal school; or

Secondly,—It may descend to those relations of the last proprietress who would have been her heirs if she were a separated male owner, as is the rule according to the Mayukha;[2] or

Thirdly,—It may follow the order of succession applicable to *stridhan,* as is the rule according to the Mitakshara.

As regards property inherited from a male relation, the first of the above three rules seems to be the correct one.[3]

In the case in which the property inherited by a female was the *stridhan* of her predecessor, it is by no means clear which of the rules ought to be followed. Macnaghten says:[4]—"*Stridhan,* which has once devolved according to the law of succession which governs the descent of this

[1] *Doe dem* Ramasami Mudaliar *v.* Vallata, 2 Strange's Notes of Cases, 211; P. Bachiraju *v.* V. Venkatappadu, 2 Mad., 402; Mussammaut Gyaukoowar *v.* Dookhurn Singh, 4 Sel. Rep., 330; Sheo Sehai Singh *v.* Mussummat Omed Konwar, 6 Sel. Rep., 301; Punchanund Ojhah *v.* Lalshan Misser, 3 W. R., 140.

[2] Vyavahara Mayukha, Ch. IV, Sec. X, 26.

[3] See the cases cited in note 1 above.

[4] Principles of Hindu Law, 38.

LECTURE XII.

peculiar species of property, ceases to be ranked as such, and is ever afterward governed by the ordinary rules of inheritance: for instance, property given to a woman on her marriage is *stridhan*, and passes to her daughter at her death; but at the daughter's death it passes to the heir of the daughter like other property; and the brother of her mother would be heir in preference to her own daughter, such daughter being a widow without issue."

But as pointed out by Mr. Justice Romesh Chunder Mitter in his judgment in the case of *Bhoobun Mohun Banerjee* v. *Muddon Mohun Sing*,[1] the rule of succession indicated in this passage seems to be based upon a misconception of the provisions of the Hindu law on the subject. It is not true that there is an ordinary rule of succession applicable to woman's property generally, and a special rule of succession applicable to her *stridhan*. The only rules of succession to woman's property that are recognized in the Hindu law, are the special rules relating to *stridhan*. What is meant in the above passage by the 'ordinary rules of inheritance' must, therefore, be the law of succession to the property of a male owner. But that law is evidently intended to apply only to the property of a male owner. Thus, Vijnaneswara, after giving that law, commences his exposition of the law relating to woman's property in these words:[2] "After briefly propounding the division of wealth left by the husband and wife ('Let sons divide equally both the effects and the debts after the demise of their two parents'), the partition of a *man's* goods has been described at large. The author, now intending to explain fully the distribution of a *woman's* property, begins by setting forth the

[1] Joygobind Shome's Law Reporters, Vol. I, p. 5.

[2] Mitakshara, Ch. II, Sec. XI, 1.

nature of it." It is only in the limited class of cases under the Mayukha, noticed above, that a woman's property devolves according to the law of succession applicable to the property of a male.

It may be urged that the first of the above three rules is applicable to the case of property inherited from a female in the same way as to the case of property inherited from a male owner. This view derives some support from the decision of the Madras High Court in the case of *Sengamalathammal* v. *Valayuda Mudali;*[1] and it has the further recommendation that it reduces to a uniform rule the law of succession to a woman's inherited property in all cases.

But on the other hand, it may fairly be contended that as the decision in the Madras case just referred to is opposed to the doctrine of Vijnaneswara, and is based mainly upon the Bengal commentaries, it ought not to be accepted as a correct exposition of the law of the Dravida and Mithila schools. It is the Mitakshara, and not the Dayabhaga, that is followed in those schools in the absence of express provision in their special text-books. Now, under the Mitakshara, a woman's inherited property ranks as *stridhan;* and though in the case of property inherited from a male relation the doctrine of Vijnaneswara has been dissented from, its correctness has never (except in the above-mentioned Madras case) been questioned as regards property inherited from a female. On the contrary, there is a suggestion by the Madras High Court itself in the case of *P. Bachiraja* v. *Venkatappada* (2 Mad., 405), that property inherited by a woman from her mother would rank as *stridhan.* Considering all these circumstances, it may be doubted whether the case of *Sengamalathammal*

---

[1] 3 Mad., 312.

LECTURE XII.

should be taken as settling the point; or whether it should be held that, according to the law of Mithila and Dravida, property inherited by one female from another should devolve like the *stridhan* of the former.

Secondly, succession to property acquired otherwise than by inheritance, and not coming under the technical definition of *stridhan*.

So much for the order of succession to property inherited by a woman. Next take the case of property acquired by females otherwise than by inheritance, and not coming within the technical meaning of *stridhan*.

According to the Mitakshara.

Under the Mitakshara, which does not limit the signification of the term *stridhan* in any way, but takes it to mean woman's property of every sort, property of the description we are now considering would devolve according to the law of succession for *stridhan*.

According to the Mayukha.

The Vyavahara Mayukha,[1] as you have seen, draws a distinction between *stridhan* in the literal sense of the term and that technically so called, and provides that woman's property other than what is technically called *stridhan*, follows the same order of succession that is prescribed for the estate of a separated male owner.

According to the Bengal, the Dravida, and the Mithila schools.

The law of the Bengal, the Dravida, and the Mithila schools is not very clear upon the point under consideration. Besides inherited property, the other descriptions of woman's property not coming under the denomination of *stridhan* acccording to these schools, are property obtained on partition of the husband's estate, property obtained by gift from strangers, and wealth earned by labor and skill.

Share on partition.

With regard to the first,—that is, the share obtained by a woman on partition,—there is some authority for holding that, by the law of Bengal, it would, on the woman's death,

---

[1] Ch. IV, Sec. X, 26.

devolve, like the widow's estate, on the heir of her husband.[1] And the same is, I presume, the law of Mithila.[2] The law according to the Dravida school is more uncertain; and this uncertainty is partly due to the conflict between the Smriti Chandrika and the Parasara Madhavya, the authorities peculiar to that school, the former holding that the share on partition is merely a provision for maintenance,[3] and the latter, that it is the absolute assignment of a share.[4] The opinion of the Pandit given in the case of *Tommee Reddy* v. *Narasimma Reddy*,[5] and apparently approved by Colebrooke, would go to support the view that such share constitutes *stridhan*, and devolves as such. But the correctness of this opinion is open to question, as there seems to be no reason why the share of the husband's estate which a woman obtains on partition, should follow a rule of descent different from that applicable to the case in which she takes the whole estate by inheritance.

LECTURE XII.

The other two descriptions of woman's property, namely, gifts from strangers and earnings by labor and skill, are excluded from the category of *stridhan* by the following text of Katyayana quoted in the Smriti Chandrika[6] and the Bengal commentaries:[7]—

Property acquired by gift from strangers or by labor and skill

"The wealth which is earned by mechanical arts, or which is received through affection from a stranger, is subject to her husband's dominion. The rest is pronounced to be woman's property."

---

[1] See Macnaghten's Considerations on Hindu Law, pp. 43, 45.

[2] See Vivada Chintamani (Tagore's translation), pp. 261, 262.

[3] Smriti Chandrika, Ch. IV, 11.

[4] Dayavibhaga (Burnell's translation), p. 15.

[5] 2 Strange, 382—384.

[6] Ch. IX, Sec. I, 16.

[7] Dayabhaga, Ch. IV, Sec. I, 19; Dayatattwa, Ch. IX, 1; Dayakrama Sangraha, Ch II, Sec. II, 25.

LECTURE XII.

during widowhood and maidenhood;

This text is evidently not applicable to acquisitions made during widowhood, which would, therefore, rank as *stridhan*, and devolve as such.[1] It is equally inapplicable to acquisitions made during maidenhood, if the girl dies before marriage. The text of Baudhayana, which is cited by commentators[2] as the basis of the law of succession to the property of a maiden, in speaking of such property, uses the term *riktha* (property generally), and not the ambiguous word *stridhan;* and Srikrishna, in the Dayakrama Sangraha,[3] gives the order of succession to the property of a maiden before discussing the definition of *stridhan*. So that the wealth of a maiden, even though obtained by gift from strangers or earned by mechanical arts, would devolve in the same way as other property that may be technically called her *stridhan*.

during coverture.

The above text of Katyayana no doubt applies to acquisitions made during coverture. But even here, if the woman dies after her husband, it is not easy to understand how any one except the heirs to her *peculium* can succeed to such property; for, upon the death of her husband, his control would cease, and the property would become hers absolutely. It is only in the case in which the woman dies before her husband, that the question involves some difficulty. In such cases, on the one hand, it may be urged that as the husband had complete dominion over such property during the lifetime of the wife, and held it jointly with her, upon her

---

[1] See the observations of the Judicial Committee in Brij Indur Bahadur Singh *v.* Ranee Janki Koer, 1 Calc. L. R., 325, 326; and those of Kindersley, J., in Venkata Rama Rau *v.* Venkata Suriya Rau, I. L. R., 1 Mad., 286.

[2] See Dayabhaga, Ch. IV, Sec. III, 7; Smriti Chandrika, Ch. IX, Sec. III, 35; Vivada Chintamani (Tagore's translation), p. 270.

[3] Ch. II, Sec. I.

death, he would become solely entitled to it according to the principle of survivorship, a principle of succession not unknown to the Hindu law.[1] But on the other hand, it may be contended that the above text of Katyayana excludes the acquisitions in question from the category of *stridhan*, only so far as to declare that they are not freely alienable by a woman like other sorts of her *stridhan;* but it does not exclude them from that category so as to render the law of succession to *stridhan* inapplicable to them. On this point Jagannatha says:[2] "But, according to Jimutavahana, Raghunandana, and the rest, the wife is sole owner of wealth acquired by her even during coverture; yet she has not independent power over it so long as her husband lives: for the negative in the text of Manu[3] (Book III, Ch. I, v. 52, 1) conveys the sense of imperfection. Consequently, they have no wealth exclusively their own; and the imperfection of their property consists in the want of uncontrolled power. It must be therefore understood, that the legal heirs of a woman's peculiar property succeed also to this wealth." There is no other express provision on this point in any of the commentaries specially followed in the Bengal, Mithila, and Dravida schools. In this state of the authorities, in which no conclusive argument can be adduced on either side, we may, I think, safely follow the opinion of Jagannatha, which is, moreover, in harmony with the doctrine of Vijnaneswara.

[1] See Kattama Nauchear *v.* The Rajah of Shivagungah, 2 W. R. (P. C.), 39.

[2] Colebrooke's Digest, Bk. V, 515, commentary, Vol. II, p. 628.

[3] VIII, 416.

INDEX.